$\mathcal{A}$ $\mathcal{B}$it $\mathcal{M}$ore $\mathcal{L}$ike $\mathcal{W}$ork
or
Life After D'Oyly Carte

A memoir of the years 1982–2020

David Mackie

Grosvenor House
Publishing Limited

This book is published by
Grosvenor House Publishing Ltd
Link House
140 The Broadway, Tolworth, Surrey, KT6 7HT.
www.grosvenorhousepublishing.co.uk

A CIP record for this book
is available from the British Library

ISBN 978-1-83975-494-4

"A thing of shreds and patches...
My catalogue is long..."
W.S. Gilbert – *The Mikado*

Acknowledgements

I am indebted to a number of friends and colleagues who have suggested that I continue the account of my working life after *Nothing Like Work or Right in the D'Oyly Carte* or who have contributed to this sequel by answering a number of questions or assisting in other ways. I would particularly like to thank Christine Airey, Elisabeth Bradley, Jane and Philip Button, Donna Chapman, Louise Denny, Ann Dick, Jon Ellison, the late Ian Gray, Clive and Jeanette Harré, Glen Hayes, Paul Huggins, the late Nathan Hull, Tim Hurst-Brown, Ginny Jenkins, Sandy Leiper, Morven A. Lyle, John MacLeod, Ralph MacPhail, Jr., Sylvia and Stuart MacWhirter, Nina McKechnie, Stewart and Kate McMillan, Patricia Meadmore, Ralph Meanley, John Megoran, Kareth Paterson, Lorraine and Brian Patient, Angie Penn, Charles and Jean Roberts, Paul Seeley, Lorraine Shore, the late Billy Skelly, Billy Strachan, Stephen Turnbull, Mark Underwood, Pam White, Linda Wood, Vivian Woodrow and Renee (Mrs Percy) Young. Finally, my thanks to all at Grosvenor House Publishing for seeing this second volume into print. Any errors and shortcomings are, as before, entirely my own.

Errata – *Nothing Like Work or Right in the D'Oyly Carte*

Errata slips were often inserted into theatre programmes, usually to inform patrons of cast changes. Some parts of *Nothing Like Work or Right in the D'Oyly Carte* were written from memory, and memory can play tricks after forty years. I have become aware of one or two errors in the book, and in the absence of errata slips I beg the reader's indulgence as I enumerate them along with others that have been pointed out to me. I include the relevant page numbers in *Nothing Like Work*.

1. pp. 2, 53, 109, 124, 132, 146. For O'Keefe read O'Keeffe.

2. p. 62. Harold Oakley was indeed interested in Gilbert and Sullivan, but he was rather deaf, and for this reason he didn't often join in conversations with Hazel and me. As someone who is also hard of hearing I should have been more aware of that. See also p. 217.

3. p. 113. The hotel in San Diego was the El Cortez (spelling as in the El Cortez in San Francisco: see p. 105). I took the San Diego spelling (El Cortes [sic]) from a list of hotels provided by the D'Oyly Carte office, but I have since found some headed notepaper from the San Diego hotel confirming the correct spelling.

4. pp. 176-177. For Alistair read Alastair.

5. p. 231. The three-piece suite was given to me after D'Oyly Carte's closure in 1982. When I bought the flat in 1980 my upstairs neighbours were Bob and Elsie Miller. They later moved to another address in Eastbourne, and Dorothy Walden moved in: she gave me the photograph of the *Admiral Graf Spee* on April 28, 1983. Bob Miller died in June 1983.

6. pp. 238-39. I have not been able to confirm the exact date of Victor Borge's appearance at the Grand Theatre, Leeds, but former chorister Jane Guy remembers the occasion; as Jane was with D'Oyly Carte for just one season (1976-77) it would seem that this performance must have been during the week of November 29-December 3, 1976.

7. p. 272. Sandy Oliver's first-floor flat in London was owned by Val Crossley: the actress Beryl Cooke lived in the ground-floor flat.

Mea culpa.

Prelude

The D'Oyly Carte Opera Company, of which I was successively répétiteur (1975-76) and chorus master and associate conductor (1976-82), celebrated its centenary in 1975 by taking *Trial by Jury* (1875) as the start of the enterprise although the Company as such wasn't formed until 1879 (that centenary was celebrated in Melbourne during the Company's tour of Australasia in 1979). *Trial by Jury* was the second collaboration of W.S. Gilbert and Arthur Sullivan, but it was the first with the involvement of the impresario Richard D'Oyly Carte, hence the celebrations in 1975. Having survived for one hundred years there were numerous toasts at the time to the next hundred years, and I fully expected that I might have a job for the rest of my working life. But this was not to be. Despite the optimism times were changing rapidly, and the Company lasted for just seven more years. I have written of those years in *Nothing Like Work or Right in the D'Oyly Carte*; in a short postscript I also outlined the work that I subsequently managed to do, ending with the words "but all of that, as they say, is another story". What follows is that other story.

Chapter 1 – The Eastbourne years

I – 1982

The D'Oyly Carte Opera Company gave its last performances (a matinée in the afternoon and a concert in the evening) on Saturday February 27, 1982 at the Royal Adelphi Theatre in London's Strand; as of Monday March 1 I was now unemployed. As associate conductor I had been entrusted with the matinée (*HMS Pinafore*) which was the last complete performance of an opera given by the original D'Oyly Carte Opera Company (it was later revived), and I was now a foot-note to history: very interesting, but no great help in my current situation. With the demise of the Company we all had to think about the future. Would money magically appear from somewhere to put D'Oyly Carte back on its feet? Many of us hoped that it would; in the meantime all we could do was to go back to our respective homes and wait for our phones to ring.

As recently as 1980, still with no thought that D'Oyly Carte might close, I had purchased a flat in Eastbourne: 23a Old Orchard Road, the first floor of a large semi-detached house. As the Company was on the road for forty-eight weeks of the year you were not able to be at home very often, and so it didn't really matter where you lived. But I didn't want to buy property in London for two very good reasons: you would get more for your money outside the city, and I didn't like the idea of leaving a flat in London empty for long periods. Having property in a quiet seaside town was "all very well in

1

its way" when fully employed by D'Oyly Carte, but I now had no job, and I wasn't going to find very much musical work in Eastbourne.

Almost the first thing that I did was to sign on at the local DHSS office: I was to do this at fortnightly intervals. The staff seemed to think that you would take any job that came along (perhaps even filling up shelves in a supermarket), but most of us were looking for work in the theatre (or in my case any other musical work), and that was never going to come via the DHSS: if D'Oyly Carte didn't start up again fairly soon I would have to look for work through the normal theatrical channels. Some of my D'Oyly Carte colleagues went into musicals in the West End, and some managed to get into other opera companies; I hoped that I might find similar work somewhere. One thing that sustained many of us, at least in the early days, was G&S and the D'Oyly Carte connection.

The only other thing that happened during that first week was a return visit, on March 6, to Colonel Kenneth Osborne's home near Henley-on-Thames where some of the D'Oyly Carte principals and I had performed at a sponsorship event in 1976. This time, knowing of our plight, I think Colonel Osborne had asked us to perform at what was simply a private party, and we were grateful for his gesture. I drove up to London from Eastbourne to meet the other members of the group - Vivian Tierney, Lorraine Daniels, Meston Reid and John Ayldon - at Sadler's Wells; we then drove down to Oxfordshire. The following two weeks were without any work, and after signing on for the second time I decided to go back to Greenock for a short break. This was a journey of roughly one thousand miles, there and back, but I had received enough redundancy money from D'Oyly Carte to tide me over for a year, and I felt that I could afford it. I did try to go back to Scotland fairly regularly to see my mother who was now on her own (my father having died in 1980), but as time went on and I began to get more work I was only able to do this two or three times a year. Shortly after I got back I had to play at the YMCA in London on March 24, the first concert (discounting Colonel Osborne's party) for almost a month since the closure of D'Oyly Carte.

Of all my former colleagues the only one who was now within striking distance was Geoffrey Shovelton who lived at Little London, near Heathfield, some twelve miles north of Eastbourne. This was particularly fortuitous as Geoffrey and I had become good friends during our time in D'Oyly Carte; we would remain so until his untimely death in 2016. With time on our hands we saw each other regularly in those early days; we often got quite depressed about the situation: the end of D'Oyly Carte and no immediate prospects. We were both writing to companies and individuals in the hope of finding work although Geoffrey already had other sources of occasional employment. But he also had another problem which I wasn't aware of at first: his marriage was breaking up, and this was an added strain on him. My own relationship with former D'Oyly Carte chorister Caroline Hudson (known professionally as Madeleine Hudson) had also broken up, and that was something else we had in common. If I had been married when D'Oyly Carte closed, and perhaps with children as well, I would probably have had to take any job that I could find in order to support my family. But with no such responsibilities I only had to worry about supporting myself.

As well as bemoaning our situation Geoffrey and I were wondering if we could create work for ourselves and other former members of the Company: it would all depend on our availability and what jobs, if any, we were able to find. We also made a number of tape recordings for our own use, mainly of items from the operatic repertoire with which Geoffrey was very familiar: he had been with Scottish Opera before joining D'Oyly Carte. I was more familiar with the operetta repertoire. This was all very good experience for me, and it would come in useful later. Geoffrey was also a keen photographer; he took some publicity shots of me, one of which I used for many years.

Perhaps the only good thing about being unemployed was that I was able to undertake something I had had at the back of my mind for some time, namely to attempt to reconstruct Sullivan's lost cello concerto. Briefly, this work had been composed in 1866 and had had several performances during the composer's lifetime, but it had never been published. The manuscript score, soloist's copy and a set of band parts were available for hire from the music publishers Chappell & Co., and the last known performance had been a BBC Third Programme broadcast in 1953: the soloist was William Pleeth, and the conductor was the young Charles Mackerras who had recently completed his ballet *Pineapple Poll* (1951), the music being an arrangement of themes from the Gilbert and Sullivan operas (known as the Savoy Operas). After the broadcast performance of the concerto the music was returned to Chappell where it lay until 1964 when it was destroyed in a fire along with a vast amount of other music. As far as is known, no recording of the broadcast was made, and as (at that time) little was known of Sullivan's considerable output beyond his work with Gilbert it was thought that the concerto had vanished forever.

In 1975 Reginald Allen, the American trustee on the board of the D'Oyly Carte Opera Trust, published *The Life and Work of Sir Arthur Sullivan*, compiled from the vast Gilbert and Sullivan collection at the Pierpont Morgan Library in New York (the collection had actually been started by Reginald Allen many years before, and he later gifted it to the Morgan Library). From this book, which I acquired in 1976, I learned that the collection included a copy of the soloist's part of the cello concerto: this had been made for a performance in 1887, and it had not been returned with the score and band parts that were destroyed in Chappell's fire. I wondered if it might be possible to attempt a reconstruction from this surviving part, but I was about to become chorus master and associate conductor of D'Oyly Carte, and I had to put this idea to the back of my mind. My colleague Paul Seeley (who took over my position as répétiteur) acquired a copy of the manuscript from the Pierpont Morgan Library, and sometimes, during the performances in our long London seasons at Sadler's Wells, I would borrow it, go to one of the rehearsal room pianos and play over the music: perhaps one day I might be able to do something with it. (Paul eventually produced an accompaniment to the slow movement.) With the closure of D'Oyly Carte I now had the time. I acquired my own copy from the Pierpont Morgan Library, the postmark on the envelope being 13 April 1982; I then set about trying to reconstruct the work.

All that I had of the original was the solo part and some melodic indications as to what was happening in the orchestra when the soloist wasn't playing, a sort of Ariadne thread running through the entire work which ensured that whatever I came up with there would at least be some genuine Sullivan in every bar. It was rather like a typical exam question where you were given a short melody with the instruction "Harmonise this chorale in the style of J.S. Bach". Here, I had a very long melodic thread (actually three separate movements amounting in all to 679 bars) that had to be harmonised in the style of Arthur Sullivan; as I had been immersed in Sullivan's music for the last ten years, first of all studying his songs at Birmingham University (1972-75) and then working exclusively with the Savoy Operas in D'Oyly Carte (1975-82), I thought that I should be able to produce something that hopefully sounded like Sullivan. I started by writing out all 679 bars of the melodic line with two empty staves below each bar for the underlying harmony: in effect, for a piano accompaniment. If I managed to finish the reconstruction in short score I would then have to orchestrate the entire work.

I had recently acquired a second-hand upright piano, a Squire & Longson, and I sat at it for hours on end playing the single cello line over and over again in the hope that it would suggest some suitable harmony; perhaps even some orchestral ideas. It was something of a novelty to have so much time on my hands after seven years of full employment with D'Oyly Carte, and it was almost like being a full-time student again. I had also found a small brown R&L bust of Sullivan in another second-hand shop in Eastbourne (serendipity?), and I placed it on the piano to give me some inspiration. To attempt a full reconstruction of the concerto from one line was quite a formidable undertaking, particularly as I had never heard the original. I wasn't sitting at the piano for eight hours every day, of course, as I played at concerts occasionally (more often as time went on), saw Geoffrey Shovelton regularly and would sometimes go out if the weather was fine. But without having so much free time I don't think I would have been able to finish the reconstruction.

On April 5 I drove up to Manchester, stopping overnight with Harold and Hazel Oakley in Appleby Magna which is midway between Birmingham and Nottingham. When I was with D'Oyly Carte I had found digs with them in their lovely old Georgian rectory, and I had stayed with them many times on our visits to the Midlands. I got to know them very well. This was my first visit since D'Oyly Carte had closed in February; it was the first of many stop-overs in the coming years. Next day I gave a talk to the Manchester Gilbert and Sullivan Society on the closure of D'Oyly Carte and on some aspects of Sullivan's music, following on from articles I had written for *The Savoyard*, the D'Oyly Carte Opera Trust's house magazine (the penultimate edition of which had just appeared in March); I was then given overnight accommodation before continuing northwards for another short stay in Greenock with my mother. On these home visits I would often see fellow-Greenockian Gordon MacKenzie, latterly D'Oyly Carte's business manager; on one occasion I accompanied his daughter Michelle when she sang at a church concert. Back in Eastbourne I signed on again; later that month there was a concert performance of *The Mikado* at the recently refurbished Leas Cliff Hall in Folkestone, the first time I had played there.

The following day I had to go up to London to meet the composer and conductor Cyril Ornadel at the Apollo Victoria Theatre. A colleague had suggested that I write to him in the hope that he might be able to offer me some work. Perhaps not such a well-known name now, he was a major figure in London's West End in his day, conducting many musicals including *My Fair Lady*; he was also the musical director of the London Palladium and the composer of the musical *Pickwick* which included "If I ruled the world", a big hit for Harry Secombe. The one thing I remember about meeting him was that he said he couldn't offer me any work as I wasn't a member of the Musicians' Union (MU). Following on from this I *did* join, but to no avail as regards work as he still didn't offer me anything. I didn't need to be a member of the MU while I was with D'Oyly Carte, but I had joined the Incorporated Society of Musicians (ISM). Although not a union it was a professional body that covered me for any eventuality that might occur in the course of my work, and I felt that it suited me much better. Thinking that I might get some work doing walk-on parts I even applied to join the actors' union Equity. As I had been fully employed by D'Oyly Carte for seven years I thought that they might accept me, but perhaps not surprisingly my application was rejected. However, as I continued to work with orchestral musicians it was probably useful that I became a member of the MU: whether I would have joined without Cyril Ornadel's prompting is a moot point. I was a member for many years, but I finally left while remaining with the ISM.

When I was a student at Birmingham University in the 1970s I was introduced to the world of clerihews. The clerihew is a literary form consisting of a single verse of poetry; it was invented by Edmund Clerihew Bentley, the author (as E.C. Bentley) of a famous detective story *Trent's Last Case*. (The author's unusual middle name, from which the form took its name, was his mother's maiden name.) Clerihews are always biographical, encapsulating some aspect of the subject in a simple four-line AABB stanza, but unlike the limerick (an AABBA stanza) the metre can be irregular with the lines being of indeterminate length, the first line often consisting solely of the subject's name. Several books of these, including all of Bentley's, have been published; I often compose them myself, particularly if I'm sending someone a birthday card.

Geoffrey Shovelton was aware of my addiction to clerihews, and as a talented cartoonist he suggested that if I wrote some G&S ones he would illustrate them (Bentley's first clerihews were illustrated by G.K. Chesterton); we might then have them printed as greetings cards which could be sold through the various Gilbert and Sullivan Societies such as London and Manchester where we were both well-known personally: Geoffrey had already produced greetings cards and Christmas cards with G&S themes. To save any potential embarrassment the subjects would not be individuals (e.g. D'Oyly Carte principals) but characters from the operas. Two of my efforts were:

O Sergeant in blue,   Who's playing that mellow
You   Cello?
Have a tough job tonight,   It's Lady Jane
Some pirates to fight.   and Again! (*Patience*)
(*The Pirates of Penzance*)

These are not really clerihews by strict definition, merely approximations based on the ideas of a human subject, an AABB rhyme scheme and, particularly, the idea of an irregular metre. I don't recall that we ever made any money out of the venture, but it was something else to keep us occupied when there was no work, and they were fun to do. A number of them were produced, and some may still be around in G&S collections. Less than a year earlier, around September 1981, I had entered a *Sunday Times* clerihew competition with several efforts that are perhaps closer to Bentley's originals. Despite the brevity of the clerihew it is a deceptively subtle and elusive style to imitate, and I didn't win a prize. Among my entries were:

Richard D'Oyly Carte		Field-Marshall Montgomery
Fostered Gilbert and Sullivan's Art.		Abhorred the taste of Pommery.
But it was really just a ploy		He said one shouldn't oughter
To help him build the Savoy.	and	Drink anything but water.

As the months rolled on into summer there was still no sign of regular work. My life became a routine of signing on, seeing Geoffrey, and sometimes seeing other friends in London. I also started to explore Eastbourne and the surrounding countryside. Among many interesting places to visit was the iconic Bodiam Castle (often used as a location for films set in the Middle Ages); the countryside, very different to what I had been used to in Scotland, was always a delight to drive through. The routine was broken up from time to time by one event or another, one of these, on July 5, being a visit to the London Arts Club where we sometimes sang for our supper when I was with D'Oyly Carte. Like the visit to Colonel Osborne's house in March I think this too was just a friendly gesture from the Arts Club. It was also good to catch up with former members of the Company.

In Eastbourne itself I often walked past a handsome double fronted house (Kent Lodge, in a road called Trinity Trees) that I much admired. To my astonishment I found out that it was the home of the notorious Dr John Bodkin Adams who had been accused of murdering one of his patients, a wealthy widow who had made a number of bequests to him (including a Rolls-Royce), by administering overdoses of morphia and heroin; it was thought that he had despatched several other

9

(mainly elderly) patients, who had also made bequests to him, in this way: "to ease their passing", as he said. I was at school when the trial took place in 1957, but I remember it well as the death penalty was still in force then, and it was assumed that he would hang if found guilty. However, he was acquitted thanks to a brilliant defence by Geoffrey (later Sir Geoffrey) Lawrence, and he lived out the rest of his days in Eastbourne: he even continued to treat a number of patients who still believed in his innocence. The case was a major sensation in its day, and it must have been a terrible shock for quiet, genteel Eastbourne, but it seems largely forgotten now (a forerunner of the Dr Harold Shipman case many years later). I had almost forgotten it myself, partly because I didn't know much about Eastbourne until we played there with D'Oyly Carte. Despite walking past Kent Lodge numerous times I never saw anyone go in or out. Dr Adams died in 1983.

With the closure of D'Oyly Carte approaching in February, Geoffrey Shovelton and some other colleagues had already discussed the idea of forming a small group. They all knew the G&S repertoire inside out, and they could put on a concert at the drop of a hat, but it would be a good opportunity to broaden their repertoire to include other Victorian material. This eventually crystallised into London Airs, a pun on Londoners. The group consisted of soprano Vivian Tierney, mezzo-soprano Lorraine Daniels, tenor Geoffrey Shovelton and baritone Clive Harré, with me as the musical director/pianist; Clive's wife Jeanette (who had formerly been head of wardrobe at the London Opera Centre) provided splendid Victorian evening wear for us. We then placed an advertisement in the final edition of *The Savoyard* in September (I also contributed an article to this edition on the possible source of one of Gilbert's lyrics in *The Grand Duke*). But it took a long time to get it all going, including getting the costumes ready, and it wasn't until halfway through July that we were able to assemble in London for a photo session for our publicity. Geoffrey, with his artistic skills, was always happy to provide the artwork for our programmes and publicity material (he had designed a cover for the programme of D'Oyly Carte's very last performance on February 27); the advertisement in *The Savoyard* was a reproduction of one of his cartoons of the group. Later, during July and August, I made a number of arrangements for London Airs – *A Medley of British Folk Songs*, *A Medley of Drinking Songs* and *A Medley of American Songs* - which were for use in our mixed programmes, but the following year I added *A Medley of G&S Finales* for a programme that we called *A Savoy Assortment*.

The next major event was a series of G&S concerts at Pencarrow House in Cornwall. It was good to be in harness again for a full week: this was my longest period of continuous work since February. Pencarrow was the home of the Molesworth-St Aubyn family, the estate having been in their hands since Elizabethan times. The current owner was Sir John Molesworth-St Aubyn, 14th Baronet, but we dealt mainly with his son Arscott and daughter-in-law Iona. A previous owner, Sir William Molesworth (MP for Southwark from 1845), also had a home in London where he and his wife Andalusia entertained in style. Lady Andalusia continued to do this long after her husband's death in 1855, and Arthur Sullivan was among her many friends in her later years. Sullivan's mother died in 1882 as he was about to start work on *Iolanthe*, and Lady Andalusia invited him to come down to Pencarrow to continue working on the opera away from the pressures of London. He was there from July 27 until August 7, and our concerts were to celebrate both the centenary of his visit and the centenary of *Iolanthe* itself whose première took place on November 25, 1882: this was the first G&S première in Richard D'Oyly Carte's new Savoy Theatre.

G&S concert at Pencarrow House. Lorraine Daniels
and Kenneth Sandford.

Pencarrow House was already open to the public, but it was
hoped that a series of concerts would attract more visitors.
Peter Riley, latterly D'Oyly Carte's deputy general manager,
had been asked to provide a team of singers, and a number of
the recent D'Oyly Carte principals - Vivian Tierney, Lorraine
Daniels, Kenneth Sandford, John Ayldon, Meston Reid and
James Conroy-Ward – took part. I was the musical director,
and a chorus was provided by Duchy Opera, a local amateur
group. Peter also came down to help with the staging of the
concerts which, weather permitting, were to be held outside.
Peter and I stayed with the family, and we got to know them
well (dining there one night I had an artichoke for the first
time, and I had to be shown how to deal with it): the others
were accommodated elsewhere. I drove down to Pencarrow
on July 25, and I had a rehearsal with the chorus that evening.
We did four concerts in all, giving one programme on July 27
and 29 and a different one on July 28 and 30. We were also
blessed with exceptionally good weather, and the concerts

went ahead as planned: they took place in an open area in front of the house, and they attracted a very good turnout with over two thousand people attending. Arscott and Iona had a daughter Emma, and to thank the family for their hospitality I wrote a short piece called *Emma's Waltz*, based on the notes E and A, after the manner of a Victorian albumleaf.

It was a very enjoyable week, but as with so many other 'gigs' that I was to do it was a one-off. If I could get a sufficient number of these I might have a chance of surviving without a permanent job, but it would take some time to build up enough contacts for this to be feasible. There was some difficulty in obtaining our fees and expenses (not, I hasten to add, from the Molesworth–St Aubyn family but from the treasurer of Duchy Opera as it was they who had engaged us), and we still hadn't received any payment by the middle of September: this was my first encounter with a problem that was to surface from time to time. It had also been good to see some of my former colleagues, and there was much anxious enquiry as to how everyone was getting on.

Next, it was back to the routine in Eastbourne which included signing on and seeing Geoffrey Shovelton. During the summer months numerous army bands played in the famous bandstand on the sea-front. These concerts attracted good audiences (not just Eastbourne inhabitants but many visitors as it was still a popular holiday resort), and I would often go down and listen to the music while getting some good sea air. I also started to do a bit of baking. When D'Oyly Carte closed in February I treated myself to the three-volume *Delia Smith's Cookery Course* which I thought might come in handy. I tried out various recipes, and I was soon able to produce a reasonable Victoria sponge; this was useful as a cost-saving exercise. I also continued to scour the town for cutlery, crockery and other household items.

My upstairs neighbour Elsie Miller (see Errata) helped to organise the local Meals on Wheels; knowing of my situation, and that I had a car, she asked me if I would help out with this which I was happy to do. It was voluntary work, but drivers were allowed to claim for petrol. I did the first one on a Tuesday, but as every second Tuesday was a signing on day I changed to doing it on Thursdays: I kept it going for some time, and occasionally I did other days as well. I was certainly finding things to fill in the time, but there was still no regular work, and, no word of D'Oyly Carte reforming. But any such hope that we might have had initially had been slowly fading away like a ship disappearing over the horizon, and by this time I think we knew that it just wasn't going to happen. I had also realised by then that sooner or later I would have to move into London, and the estate agents from whom I had purchased the flat came round to value it in August. I hadn't even begun to think about how I was going to find a flat in London, but eventually this happened in an unexpected way.

I attended the Golden Jubilee dinner of the Manchester Gilbert and Sullivan Society (at which the toast, The Immortal Memory of Gilbert and Sullivan, was given by Geoffrey Shovelton) at Hartley Hall on September 4, and I was in Manchester again on the 26th for a concert with the ex-D'Oyly Carte group, now comprising both former principals and former choristers, with myself and Paul Seeley as accompanists on two pianos. These concerts were still being arranged by Gordon MacKenzie, but the group could no longer be called D'Oyly Carte in Concert. The programme here was called *An Evening of Gilbert and Sullivan*; sometimes it would be *Gilbert and Sullivan in Concert*. Later, the group was organised jointly by Gordon MacKenzie and the Birmingham-based Second City Management, but this was not the happiest of collaborations. It was eventually run by its own members as G&S A La Carte Ltd, performing as The Magic of D'Oyly Carte: by that time the group had negotiated with the D'Oyly Carte Opera Trust, and it was able to use the name again until such time as the D'Oyly Carte Opera Company might reform. For the moment, Gordon was now able to use other ex-D'Oyly Carte members who had left the Company before I joined in 1975.

October was a good month for these concerts: there was one in Bournemouth, one in Northampton and a whole week at the New Theatre, Hull from the 18th to the 23rd. I particularly remember that week for two reasons. I had digs on the coast at Withernsea, and after a week of exposure to the North Sea I found that the chromium on my Renault 16's bumper was showing signs of rusting (bumpers of that type are now a thing of the past). But I also had money stolen from my dressing-room in the theatre having foolishly left my jacket and wallet there while we were onstage: another lesson painfully learned. However, despite the financial loss October had been a good month, and there was more to come - at least up to the end of the year. I could only hope that this would continue, but I would still have to leave Eastbourne to find more regular work.

Our first London Airs concert was to have been in Hornchurch in Essex, but through one of Geoffrey Shovelton's connections a date came in earlier, and so the first one was in Oswaldtwistle (pronounced Ozzel Twizzel), a small town in Lancashire, on Sunday October 24. Next day I started rehearsals in London for a week of performances at the Sunderland Empire presented by the theatre's managing director Russell E. Hills in association with Tom Round and Donald Adams (two former principals who had formed their own group Gilbert & Sullivan for All when they left D'Oyly Carte) and given under the title *Gilbert & Sullivan Afloat*.

These were not concerts, as in the week at Hull, but full performances of *HMS Pinafore* and *The Gondoliers* which I conducted. John Cartier, who was in D'Oyly Carte in the 1960s, took the comedy baritone roles (Sir Joseph Porter (*Pinafore*) and the Duke of Plaza-Toro (*Gondoliers*)): John had appeared frequently with Gilbert & Sullivan for All. The cast also included several of my former colleagues. Now that D'Oyly Carte had closed, Tom and Donald were hoping to fill a niche by setting up a company based in the North-East; *Gilbert & Sullivan Afloat* was a trial run for this venture although in the end nothing came of the plan. But it was good to be conducting again for a week. We performed *Pinafore* for three days (November 1-3) followed by *Gondoliers* (November 4-6).

After this there was a veritable flurry of G&S concerts. It started with a week in Richmond (Surrey), and this was followed by dates in Bristol, Blackpool, Colne, Leeds, Oxford, Birmingham and Manchester, all of which took us into December. After the Leeds concert I decided to drive back to Eastbourne to save spending money on a B&B. It wasn't too bad for the first part of the journey, but by the time I got to within striking distance of Eastbourne I was so tired that it is a wonder that I was spared to write this memoir. Luckily, there was very little traffic around at that time of the morning. But this was just another facet of working free-lance with little or no financial security: trying to save as much of one's fee as possible was not only understandable but very necessary, and my redundancy money from D'Oyly Carte was slowly going down.

With the recent increase in the amount of work it was now more like the old days, but would this last? It certainly seemed promising enough; there was still much demand for G&S whatever other work any of us might manage to find. We were not constrained by having to work only for one company as we did with D'Oyly Carte, doing eight shows every week, and we could perform wherever and whenever we wished as free-lance artists: the $64,000 question was simply "Will there be *enough* work?" Just at that moment it looked as if there might be. On December 11 I played for Geoffrey Shovelton at a concert in Manchester, and we then had three days of concerts in Buxton from December 16-18. These were appropriately called *Christmas with Gilbert and Sullivan in Concert*, and they were the last concerts this year. We were to have been in Edinburgh from December 27-30, but for some reason this was cancelled. It was disappointing, but we hoped that this was just a temporary blip. I was to find out that it would be a fairly normal part of a free-lance artist's working life, but we had ended the year on a comparatively promising note. What would 1983 bring?

II – 1983

After the encouraging build-up towards the end of 1982 it all went very quiet at the beginning of the year, but I was to find that this too was quite normal, no matter how busy I had been during any particular year. This was the first time I had experienced a drop in work (and income), and it was somewhat depressing. There were a few concerts scattered throughout the month (in London, Brighton, Farnham and Nottingham), but that wasn't going to sustain me for very long.

Although I had steadfastly refused to go back to school teaching I thought that I might try to supplement my meagre income by taking a few piano pupils, and I put an advertisement in the local paper. I did get a few replies, but I found, as before, that teaching (even one-to-one) was just not for me. One of my pupils was an elderly lady who had had a few lessons as a child and who wanted to take it up again so that she could play one of her favourite pieces which she brought to her first lesson - Rachmaninov's second piano concerto! Her technique was, understandably, very limited, and I told her that she couldn't possibly cope with it and would have to go back to basics, but she insisted that she was paying for the lessons, and that was the piece she wanted to play. Not a very happy situation.

Another pupil, a teenage boy, was the son of someone who was also in the music business (I think he was in the pop world) and who wanted his son to be able to play. The boy wasn't interested, and that wasn't much of a success either.

I soon realised that I was quite right in not wanting to take up any form of teaching: you really have to want to teach, and actually welcome these challenges, to make a success of it rather than attempt to do it merely to earn some money. The best thing about that particular pupil was that the father sometimes asked me to go to their house in the country for lessons instead of having the boy come in to Eastbourne. It was a lovely, centuries-old, timber-framed house (obviously much more money in pop music), and just going there was a treat, but eventually the boy decided that he had had enough, and the lessons stopped. I continued with the few other pupils that I had, but I was happy to give it all up when I eventually moved into London. I never heard a performance of Rachmaninov 2 from my senior citizen.

There was even less work in February which again was worrying. However, this gave me more time to spend on the reconstruction of Sullivan's cello concerto. But I was also involved in something else. A fellow-student at Birmingham University, Martin Delgado, was the son of the author Alan Delgado. One of Alan's books was called *The Annual Outing and Other Excursions*, and it told the story of how Victorian and Edwardian employers would organise a day at the seaside, or perhaps an outing to one of the famous exhibitions, for their employees. He had thought of devising an entertainment, based on the book, to be called *Have a Nice Day!*, and Martin, knowing of my interest in Victorian music, had suggested to his father that I might like to collaborate with him on the project. I first met Alan on August 25, 1981 at the start of D'Oyly Carte's last year, and I saw him again from time to time.

Alan's idea was to use a number of Victorian and Edwardian music hall songs that he had collected from various sources and which were appropriate for the particular scenes that he had in mind (one scene was to be called *At the Seaside*), but he also wrote lyrics which I had to set to suitable music. I wouldn't call myself a composer although I have made many arrangements, but it isn't too difficult to provide music that is essentially pastiche. The first song that I completed, for a scene depicting the photographer recording the great day out, was *Watch the Birdie!* Alan's lyrics for this were surprisingly *risqué* at times. I finished that one in November 1982. Then, during this quiet time at the beginning of 1983, I finished two other songs: *My Exhibition Lodging House* (which I adapted from an existing song relating to the 1851 Exhibition, the music based on the old Scottish country dance tune *Kate Dalrymple*) and *Let Every Prospect Please* (words by Alan) which was to be the opening chorus. Between these, on February 18, Alan came down to Eastbourne for a meeting about the project.

Sadly, despite producing a draft of the show, Alan died in September of that year, but I continued to tinker with it from time to time. Alan had found another song about the Great Exhibition of 1851 called *The Meeting of the Nations*; looking at it again in 1986 I decided to make a setting myself. And that, finally, was the end of *Have a Nice Day!* I was given permission by Alan's widow to use the existing material if I could put it all together, but like so many other projects it has remained incomplete. In his youth Alan Delgado had known the Victorian composer Sir Frederic Cowen (1852-1935), and he kindly gave me a postcard that Sir Frederic had written to him on his 21st birthday in 1930, an interesting link with a man, well-known in his day, who was one of Arthur Sullivan's contemporaries.

Around this time I was asked to make arrangements of two well-known twentieth century American songs - Burton Lane and Ralph Freed's *How About You?* and Rodgers and Hart's *Manhattan* – to which new words had been added by Brian Jones who had been the last editor of *The Savoyard*. *How About You?* became *Welcome to New York!* and *Manhattan* became *Future Expansion Megatrends*. I have long forgotten what the publicity was for, but they were to be recorded by our London Airs group, and so I arranged them for the standard SATB. I completed the arrangements during the first week of April. This was another one-off engagement.

There were a few concerts during February and March: one was at the Hippodrome Theatre in Birmingham, and another, the second London Airs concert, was at the Queen's Theatre in Hornchurch. Both of these were new venues for me. But another new contact was made around this time. Geoffrey Shovelton's cousin, Irene Sheridan, who lived in Bolton, was keen to organise concerts for him now that D'Oyly Carte had closed; these would also involve me and another singer. Geoffrey enjoyed working with Vivian Tierney: as tenor and soprano (traditional hero and heroine) they not only had a wide range of solo items to choose from but a wealth of duet material from the G&S repertoire, opera, operetta and ballads. They formed a duo called Two of Hearts, and we did a number of concerts together.

The first of them was in Bolton on Saturday April 23; Irene's hospitality was always a welcome part of these week-ends. We stayed overnight, but we had to leave early on Sunday as we had another concert in Watford, and on the Monday we had to record my song arrangements with London Airs. This was another facet of the free-lance world that was new to me: sometimes there would be no work for quite a while, and then there would be several jobs close together (the phenomenon is usually referred to as 'feast or famine'), often on consecutive days and invariably in venues very far apart. But that was something else you had to get used to: when work came along you took it, and you were thankful to have it.

I had now managed to complete my reconstruction of Sullivan's cello concerto which was finished on March 1. I started the orchestration on March 23 and finished it on April 20. I then wrote to Sir Charles Mackerras who had conducted the work in 1953. He was in Australia at the time, but he wrote back to say that he was very interested to hear that I had completed a reconstruction, and, that he would like to see it on his return to England. He also said that as he had conducted the concerto he had often been asked if he would attempt a reconstruction himself, but with a busy international career he had never found time. I sat back to await developments.

It was now over a year since D'Oyly Carte had closed, and I still had no permanent job. But the idea of being a free-lance musician was becoming more of an attractive proposition despite patches of little or no work. There had been a number of concerts, and we had now formed London Airs. But I couldn't just rely on occasional concerts: I had to have more regular work, whatever it was, and it was only in London that I was going to find it. Also, I had to have a London phone number: there were already enough musicians in London looking for work, and no prospective employer was going to ring anyone outside the metropolis. There was, of course, the double problem of finding a buyer for my flat and finding a property in London. So far, despite one or two enquiries, there had been little movement in the former. I had had no difficulty in finding the flat myself as first-floor flats were always available (with so many elderly people in, or retiring to, Eastbourne ground-floor flats sold more quickly), but it wasn't so easy trying to sell it. The latter problem, however, was soon to be solved.

I am an inveterate hoarder, mainly of books, music, memorabilia and miscellaneous papers: this is very useful if you are writing an account of your life, but it takes up a great deal of room, and it has to be sorted out from time to time. I was going through a box of papers one day to see if I could discard anything, and I came across a wedding invitation dating back to my years in Glasgow in the late 1960s and early 1970s. At that time I had digs in a large house along with several other people: I shared a double bed-sit with an old school friend Norman Adam, and on the top floor there was a small self-contained flat occupied by two girls, Virginia 'Ginny' Wood and Jill Hickson, who were both English. Ginny was getting married to Ross Jenkins, a Scot, and in due course Norman and I received wedding invitations from the bride's parents. If I had been asked, years later, where these had come from I could only have said "somewhere in England". As usual, I didn't discard my invitation after the wedding but filed it away – luckily, as it turned out.

Coming across it again after all these years I was amazed to find that it had in fact come from Eastbourne. I checked in the local phone book and found that a Mr James Wood was still listed at that address - surely the same couple. I rang the number and discovered that they were indeed Ginny's parents James and Norah; I was then invited round for a meal. I had only met them briefly at the wedding, but they remembered me as I had shared digs with Ginny. I discovered that James Wood and I had something in common: he too had worked in the theatre, on the lighting side. But I was also interested to catch up with Ross and Ginny and their children Katy and Stuart as I hadn't been in touch with them for some time. I knew that they had been living in Bristol, but I now discovered that they had just moved into London and had bought an old semi-detached house in Hackney where property was then comparatively cheap. The house had been converted into bed-sits, and they were in the process of turning it back to single occupancy (Ross was a 'do-it-yourself' fanatic). To help with the cost of this they intended to have a spare room in the basement which they would rent out to a student lodger, and it didn't take me long to wonder if I might become that lodger. I had explained my current situation to James and Norah Wood, and the idea was passed on to Ross and Ginny who said that they would be happy to have me with them when the room was ready. I could stay until my flat in Eastbourne was sold, and I could then start to look for one in London. My problem had been solved at a stroke although I didn't move into London immediately.

The year continued in much the same way: signing on every two weeks, doing my Meals on Wheels, seeing Geoffrey Shovelton regularly and playing occasionally for the ex-D'Oyly Carte group - and with the formation of London Airs there was now the prospect of even more concerts. We still performed G&S, which we all much enjoyed, but we also devised other programmes: one was called *An Evening of Gilbert & Sullivan and Victorian Songs*. It was good to be performing new material such as "When other lips" from Balfe's *The Bohemian Girl* and the duet "The moon has raised her lamp above" from Benedict's *The Lily of Killarney*. Along with Wallace's *Maritana* these operas had been known collectively as *The Irish Ring*, and they were once enormously popular. Now they were remembered only by a handful of individual numbers.

London Airs – first birthday celebration at the Abbey Community Centre, London. L-r: David Mackie, Vivian Tierney, Lorraine Daniels, Geoffrey Shovelton, Clive Harré.

There was a London Airs concert at the Planet Theatre, Slough on May 15, and there were more concerts with the larger group including return visits to Birmingham and Manchester. Geoffrey and I did a concert at a school in Uckfield, similar to several concerts we had done in D'Oyly Carte's last year, and I also played for some of my former colleagues at Luton

Hoo. This latter performance was not a full concert but simply two 'spots' during a function, the sort of 'gig' that was to become more familiar to me as a free-lance performer. Some years later I played for my colleagues at a similar function at Brocket Hall, a stately home that was also used as a location for filming. On that occasion we were just part of the entertainment, the star performer being Bob Monkhouse. Patricia Leonard, our former principal contralto in D'Oyly Carte, was with us, and she got Bob Monkhouse's autograph for her young son. Some artists found these jobs irksome as there was usually much sitting around waiting to perform (which was often later than billed), but I was quite happy to take any work that was offered, particularly if it was in a venue like Brocket Hall that I wouldn't otherwise have had a chance to see.

A further development in the progress of Sullivan's cello concerto came when I received an unexpected communication from the publishers Joseph Weinberger. They had been informed by Sir Charles Mackerras that I had completed a reconstruction, and they said that they would like to see it. I went up to London on May 17 and played the reconstruction to them; I also met Gerald Kingsley with whom I would deal regularly as the project progressed. Weinberger said that they would be interested in publishing the reconstruction, but they stipulated that Sir Charles should be involved: he was an international figure, and he had conducted the original work. Any changes he wished to make would have to be incorporated, and the concerto would be published as a joint reconstruction. I didn't feel that I could refuse this offer. It was good to be working with someone of Sir Charles's reputation, and to have something published, even as a joint reconstruction, was a positive step forward.

Concerts continued throughout the year. There was a further visit to St Michael's Church in Bray where we had given a number of concerts during my time with D'Oyly Carte, and we went to the army base at Aldershot where we had also previously performed (as before, this was organised by Father Paul Lenihan, the Roman Catholic chaplain). I now had a number of contacts, but concerts weren't happening every day, and I couldn't rely solely on these to keep the wolf from the door. I was in the early stages of paying off a mortgage, and there was always the possibility that my home might be repossessed if I couldn't keep up the payments. Luckily, this never happened. My building society, Nationwide, was extremely helpful regarding my position, and my local branch was always pleased to get interim reports on how my new 'career' was progressing. However, every penny that I earned was immediately gobbled up to help stave off the possibility of repossession. But another two doors were about to open, the first of these again in connection with G&S.

An agency in New York - Byers, Schwalbe & assoc. [sic] Inc. - had heard of D'Oyly Carte's closure, and they thought that it might be possible for a small group, perhaps four or five singers and a pianist, to undertake concert tours of the United States and Canada. The D'Oyly Carte Opera Trust considered the idea, and it was agreed that the tours could go ahead although at first they were reluctant to let the D'Oyly Carte name be used. After various suggestions had been put forward the group was eventually called The Best of Gilbert and Sullivan, but sponsors, if they wished, could also add Stars from the D'Oyly Carte Opera Company. This often came out differently on each programme. The agency had wanted John Reed, D'Oyly Carte's comedy baritone for many years, to be one of the artists, but John had left the Company in 1979 and was now busy with other engagements. The agency then insisted that if John wasn't available the group would have to include Kenneth Sandford who had become the senior male principal after John's departure: he would often get a round of applause on his first entrance as had happened with John. I was asked to be the musical director, and I was more than happy to accept the offer. It was the start of a sixteen-year series of concerts throughout North America.

The group was initially soprano Vivian Tierney, mezzo-soprano Lorraine Daniels (covering alto roles where appropriate), baritone Kenneth Sandford, tenor Geoffrey Shovelton and baritone Alistair Donkin. John Reed's successor in the comedy baritone roles had been James Conroy-Ward, but John had been a hard act to follow, and Alistair Donkin had made quite a name for himself as James's understudy due to his frequent appearances on James's many absences. On August 4 we had a meeting in London with Douglas 'Doug' Schwalbe who was to be in charge of this enterprise: I was not to meet his partner Monty Byers until 1989. This was perhaps the most promising development yet in my new free-lance career: the first tour was to take place the following year.

In the meantime the concerts continued with various groups, and these covered much of the country from Inverness to Brighton with dates also in Carlisle, Bolton, Bradford, Ashton-under-Lyne, Wolverhampton, Warwick, Northampton, Dartford and Westcliff-on-Sea although, to paraphrase Eric Morecambe's immortal words, not necessarily in that order. It could take a long time to get back to Eastbourne after some of these concerts; equally so for Geoffrey Shovelton living just north of Eastbourne. But it was always better to be working, even with the constant travelling which also ate into the fees. If we were in the Midlands I could sometimes combine business with pleasure by staying with Harold and Hazel Oakley at the old rectory in Appleby Magna. London Airs paid a return visit to Hornchurch in November; we had a new programme of Victorian items for which I made arrangements of Stephen Foster's *Beautiful Dreamer* and J.L. Molloy's *Love's Old Sweet Song*. As well as singing in this concert Vivian Tierney read *The Way of Wooing*, one of Gilbert's *Bab Ballads*. But shortly before this the second door opened, and I found myself with work of quite a different kind with Charles Haley Productions.

My introduction to this came about through D'Oyly Carte's charismatic principal bass-baritone John Ayldon who had already worked for them: they were looking for a musical director for a pantomime, and John kindly gave them my name. (This form of introduction was something I also came to appreciate: word of mouth is often the open door to many a job.) When I first heard of Charles Haley Productions I not unnaturally assumed that it was run by a Mr Charles Haley, but it was in fact a name derived from the surnames of Phillip [sic] Charles and his wife Jennifer Haley. Phillip was the son of Hugh Charles (1907-1995) who was perhaps best-known for co-writing with Ross Parker (1914-1974) the songs *We'll Meet Again* and *There'll Always Be an England*. Hugh and the band leader and impresario Jack Hylton (1892-1965) had once co-owned a revue company called the Fol-de-Rols, but Hugh had eventually bought out Jack and was now sole owner. Phillip, a pianist, had often played in the Fol-de-Rols shows.

I went up to London on October 18 to meet Phillip and Jennifer and to hear about my duties as musical director. They put on several pantomimes in London and around the country; ours was to be a touring one taking in three venues - Dunfermline, Barnstaple and Ealing (we referred to this as 'the Bermuda Triangle'). Jennifer organised the dancing troupes for the London shows, but the touring ones had to have a different set of girls from a dancing school in each venue: there simply wasn't enough money to pay for a professional line-up. Whatever aspirations I might have had in using my D'Oyly Carte experience to gain entry into the operatic world I seemed to be veering towards quite another, and decidedly lighter, area of performance although I was quite happy with this and found that it suited me very well. I had had experience of playing for shows since my school-days, and I was always happier as an accompanist or being 'in the pit', whatever the musical content.

On November 23 I met Sir Charles Mackerras at his London home. We sat at his piano and went through my reconstruction of Sullivan's cello concerto. Afterwards he said that he thought it was too heavily scored as he recalled it being much lighter; he had previously said that he thought the accompaniment in the outer sections of the slow movement had been *pizzicato* and that the original scoring had lacked trumpets and timpani. He suggested that I take it away and 'thin it out a bit' which I did, but rather than just alter what I had written I made a second full score incorporating some of his suggestions such as marking the string parts *pizzicato* in the slow movement. In the end we retained both trumpets and timpani. This took me from November 27 until February 2, 1984 in between other concerts and the pantomime. Just before starting work on the second orchestration I reached my fortieth birthday on November 25. It used to be said that life begins at forty, and despite a slow start after the closure of D'Oyly Carte, when I was often at a low ebb as this milestone approached, I now had some reason to hope that there might be some truth in the idea and that some sort of new life was indeed about to begin.

And so to my first pantomime *Cinderella*. I had to see Phillip Charles again to sort out various details including my salary; I also had to collect the musical arrangements before we had a run-through with everyone in London. These arrangements had been done by Phillip although the musical side of the pantomimes was now in the hands of a London musician David Harrison whose own arrangements were more complicated: in later shows I often had to simplify these as they were beyond the capabilities of most of the performers who were usually young actors rather than trained singers. I also wrote a short overture for *Cinderella*, the first of several that I would write in the coming years. We met up at 10.30 on Saturday December 10 at Blackhorse Road Underground station in East London where we bundled into a somewhat decrepit transit van, which also had the set and costumes, and drove to Dunfermline. It was good to be on the road again for a few weeks; it was almost like being back in D'Oyly Carte although these journeys up and down the country in the middle of winter were more than a little stressful at times.

The cast were an interesting lot. Most of them were new to me, but we did have former D'Oyly Carte chorister Guy Matthews playing Prince Charming. The ugly sisters (Primrose and Charisma Hardup) were played by a duo called Alvis and O'Dell who kept us all in fits of laughter during the 400-mile journey to Dunfermline with tales of things that had happened to them in the business (many of these were almost certainly embroidered), but I found later that they were funnier off-stage than on. Prone to much ad-libbing, some of their *risqué* asides went down like the proverbial lead balloon with the somewhat staid Dunfermline audiences. Baroness Hardup (and Fairy Godmother) was Daphne Neville who also kept otters and who had written about one of them which was called Bee; our Cinderella was Laura Collins whose father, Leslie, was an agent. Essentially an actress, Laura was a lovely 'Cinders', but she had a vocal range of about three notes. Despite this she somehow managed to get through the musical numbers that she had. Baron Hardup was played by Denis Nelson who was prone to 'corpsing' at the drop of a hat, and the Dandini was Marc Seymour. Buttons was played by Alan Moore who had appeared in *Z Cars* and *Nearest and Dearest* but was perhaps best-known as Dr Fletcher in the TV series *Owen MD*. Alan also directed. For me it was a new and quite different side of the business.

The 'orchestra' consisted of me and a drummer. People often complained about our small orchestra in D'Oyly Carte (particularly sparse in string numbers), but it is easy to forget that this costs money. The pantomime was a low-budget affair, and there wasn't even money available to have a double bass which would have added some depth. But Dunfermline's Carnegie Hall had a very good piano.

The set and costumes had all come from the old Fol-de-Rols stock, courtesy of Phillip's father Hugh Charles, and much of it had seen better days. I recall many of the cast (even the men) busy with a needle when costumes began to fray and literally come away at the seams. We all stayed in the same digs (a bit of a crush) with Mrs Jean Spiden at the Eloro Guest House in New Row which was quite near the Carnegie Hall where we performed (Andrew Carnegie was born in Dunfermline). Next door to the Hall was the Carnegie Music Library. Some of its stock had belonged to the Scottish composer David Stephen (1869-1946), a former Director of Music to the Carnegie Trust, and I managed to get copies of one or two interesting items including an arrangement for organ of one of Sullivan's piano pieces *Twilight*.

The older dancers in these Charles Haley pantomimes were called the Jenny Set, and the younger ones, the Jenny Babes, named after Jennifer Haley who also wrote most of the scripts. The Dunfermline group, which we rehearsed on December 11, was in the capable hands of Audrey Mortimer who had been one of the famous Bluebell Girls. The show ran from December 12-18, and while there were some afternoon matinées there were also morning shows at 09.30. Getting into the theatre for these was quite a trial; singers don't like to perform in the morning. Guy Matthews had an early entrance, and almost immediately he had to sing "The Loveliest Night of the Year": hard at 09.45, and also somewhat inappropriate at that time of day although as it was December it was often still quite dark. We also had a pony to pull the carriage, and while this is an added attraction, especially for children, it can be a problem in a theatre as the animal has to be properly looked after; sometimes there isn't much space backstage to accommodate it. There is, too, the constant worry that if it feels stressed while onstage it might produce some unwelcome extras, but I think it behaved itself during the two weeks. One day, we had an indoor football match.

Cinderella at Dunfermline – the football team.

Top: Marc Seymour, Denis Nelson, Guy Matthews; bottom:
Laura Collins, David Mackie (with Glasgow University scarf –
see Chapter 3, p. 75), Daphne Neville.

When we finished in Dunfermline on Saturday December 18
we had to strike the set, get it and the costumes into the van,
and drive overnight to Barnstaple where we had to rehearse
the new Jenny Set and Jenny Babes (this time from the Diana
Slocombe and Joan Spear School of Dancing) on Sunday. We
had been told that if we didn't get there by lunchtime the girls
would be sent home, and we would have to open the show on
the Monday with no rehearsal. I think we made it that year,
but on a subsequent journey down we had a puncture
somewhere in Devon which held us up; I also recall snow on

at least one of those journeys: hardly surprising in late December. This was my first visit to Barnstaple. We performed at the Queen's Hall in the main street. One of the local stage crew went around everywhere, backstage and outside, in bare feet which was quite bizarre. Further down the main street was a pub that we frequented: it had an unusual and very old-fashioned bowling alley which was much used. We didn't perform on Christmas Day (a Sunday that year), and several of us had our Christmas lunch in a hotel. There was one more week, finishing on the Saturday (New Year's Eve); we then had to pack up and get back to London.

III – 1984

The tour ended with a week at Ealing Town Hall which had poor facilities both onstage and in the dressing-rooms. Not being a theatre the stage had no appreciable depth, and while we had a proper carriage in both Dunfermline and Barnstaple we now had to make do with a wood and hardboard cut-out: it was, to say the least, somewhat embarrassing. The girls here were from the Joyce Butler School of Dancing. But this year turned out to be the last time the touring pantomime played in Ealing, and for the next few years it was just Dunfermline and Barnstaple. The pantomime ended on Saturday January 7. For all its shortcomings, particularly the drive from Dunfermline to Barnstaple in the depths of winter, it was another string to my bow, and it was more useful experience. I was hoping that I might be offered another one in December, assuming that nothing else came along. It had been a short run (just four weeks: we toured for forty-eight weeks with D'Oyly Carte), but long runs of anything were now very rare. In a later pantomime I worked with Paul Matthews who had been in D'Oyly Carte in the 1950s, and he told me that at one time he might only ever do a pantomime and a summer season in the course of one year.

Rehearsals for the pantomime would start around October with the show running until Easter; then there would be a short break before rehearsals started for the summer season. This, in turn, would run on until the end of the summer, and soon after that, following another short break, rehearsals would start for the next pantomime: changed days indeed.

Despite the various concerts with former colleagues it had been hard trying to find a way forward after the closure of D'Oyly Carte, but at last things seemed to be moving: we had formed London Airs, I had just done a pantomime, and our first tour for Byers, Schwalbe would be starting in February. I still hadn't sold my flat in Eastbourne, but Ross and Ginny Jenkins now had a spare room ready in their basement, and I would soon be moving into London where I hoped to find even more work. The weeks after the pantomime were again fairly quiet, but I came to realise that as December was often the busiest month in the free-lance world January was often the quietest. I did make one other useful contact, and that was with a fellow-pianist (and another Scot) Kenneth Barclay. I had been introduced to him by my cousins in Hampshire, June and Ron Millar, who were much involved with the Petersfield Musical Festival where Ken had been an accompanist. He was the pianist for a group called the Parlour Quartet (similar to our London Airs group) which specialised in Victorian and Edwardian evenings. When I was touring with D'Oyly Carte I didn't have much opportunity to meet people, but when I moved into London I saw Ken regularly, and this led to other work. He was on the music staff of a group called Opera Players Ltd which I later joined; as we both enjoyed playing piano duets we also formed a duo called the Gentlemen Duettists.

I had been on tour with D'Oyly Carte for much of the time that I owned my flat in Eastbourne, but I did make some friends and contacts in the town, and on one of my last social evenings there I attended a Burns Supper held by the Eastbourne Scottish Association at the Sandhurst Hotel on January 25. There were two concerts with the ex-D'Oyly

Carte group at the end of January, one in Leeds and one in Sevenoaks, and on January 30 we had a rehearsal at Kenneth Sandford's house in Ealing for the forthcoming Byers, Schwalbe tour of the United States (we didn't play in Canada on this first tour).

Shortly after this I moved into Ross and Ginny Jenkins' house in Hackney with my personal belongings (they had a piano which was useful as I couldn't bring mine). As my flat had not yet been sold I went back to Eastbourne from time to time. When I bought the flat in 1980 I had no furniture, and I quickly had to find some basic items. My mother, who spent much of her time in salerooms, sent some things from Scotland, and I gradually acquired other things, including the piano, in Eastbourne; I was later given a three-piece suite by my new neighbour Dorothy Walden. Once the flat was sold I would have to decide what to do with it all. Our old family home in Greenock had an attic, and every time I went back I took some of the books, music and records that I was still acquiring. This was a useful way of storing it although the gradual accumulation resulted in a problem some years later. But my Eastbourne days were now over, and the next stage of my life was about to begin.

Chapter 2 – Early days in London

I – 1984

There wasn't much immediate work in London, but I had various things to attend to such as collecting American dollars from the bank. I had also been told to get an international driving licence for the Byers, Schwalbe tour as we would sometimes have to drive ourselves from one venue to another. There was a Magic of D'Oyly Carte concert on Sunday February 12, the day before we flew out to America. It was always good to be busy, but why did engagements have to be so close together? This was another aspect of 'feast or famine'. Our departure day began somewhere on the M6 as we travelled back after our concert at the Palace Theatre, Manchester. There wasn't time for much sleep as we had to be at Heathrow on Monday for an 11.30 flight, but we all duly turned up. It was good to be back in the United States again, my first visit since 1978. We landed at Boston and went immediately to Avis car hire to pick up our transport. This had been organised by the Byers, Schwalbe office, but they had only booked one car. Vivian Tierney had left us on arrival as she was staying with friends in Cape Cod, but it was still with the greatest difficulty that we managed to get five of us and our luggage into the car (some of the luggage was on the roof), despite the fact that in those days most American cars were much bigger than our own. We then had to get to Wakefield RI, a difficult journey with very heavy traffic round Boston. Ken Sandford did the driving, and he coped very well.

The accommodation in Wakefield was not in one of the standard chains like a Holiday Inn or Day's Inn but in a lovely old building, the Larchwood Hotel.

These tours were very different to the ones we had undertaken with the full D'Oyly Carte Opera Company. We were essentially a concert party performing solos, duets and concerted numbers in evening dress; there was no scenery although the singers occasionally had hand-held props. I accompanied on the piano. Sometimes we had an orchestra, and occasionally we had the backing of a chorus for some of the numbers. Another difference was that while D'Oyly Carte had only played in large cities (or at specific venues where a large audience might be expected, such as at Saratoga Springs NY) we were able to play in smaller towns, some of them quite remote, that could seldom attract large-scale touring companies; we also played in a number of universities and colleges. This first tour lasted for two weeks during which we visited a number of states that I hadn't been in when we toured with D'Oyly Carte in 1978. Returning regularly over the next sixteen years I managed to notch up forty out of the fifty states.

Our later tours were organised along similar lines, and they all involved a good deal of travelling. Some of our journeys were by car (if the distance between venues wasn't too great), but more often they were by air, and sometimes we flew with airlines that few of us had heard of; occasionally we were in very small aircraft such as the 15-seater Beechcraft 99 turbo-prop. Another feature of these tours was meeting up for breakfast to discuss our plans for the rest of the day. Breakfast was nearly always 'out' somewhere, seldom in any of the hotels. The standard could vary quite considerably, depending on where we were, but you could often get a very good meal (with limitless refills of wonderful coffee) in the unlikeliest of places: on that first tour I had an excellent one in a Woolworths breakfast bar for all of $1.95.

The first concert, which I played for, was in the Fine Arts Recital Hall at the University of Rhode Island where we had a very enthusiastic reception. It was late in starting, and we didn't finish until 22.45; by the time we got back to the Larchwood Hotel at 01.00 we found that we had been locked out. We rang the bell, and a kind guest let us in. The second concert, sponsored by the duPont Company, was with the Delaware Symphony Orchestra in the Grand Opera House, Wilmington DE, and I was looking forward to it as I had understood that I was to conduct. However, on arrival at Wakefield I had received a phone call to say that it (and a second concert) would be conducted by their resident conductor Stephen Gunzenhauser: apparently he was contracted to conduct at least two 'popular' concerts during the season. Doug Schwalbe, who had turned up for our first concert, apologised profusely: he said that he had only just learned of the change. It was obviously a disappointment for me, but it wasn't the last time that I found myself in a similar position. It was also slightly alarming as we didn't know how Stephen Gunzenhauser would cope with some of the more idiosyncratic ways that our artists performed this repertoire. I had to go through all of the pieces with him to warn him of changes that were not apparent from a perusal of the score; this obviously helped, but there were still a few tricky moments.

The concert was repeated a few days later for the Harford Symphony Association at the C. Milton Wright High School in Bel Air MD, and this was more assured. In the programmes for these I was listed as a soloist, and I had to fend off a few awkward questions as to my exact position in the group. Of the six names in the Bel Air programme four had the wrong spelling: Kenneth Sanford [sic], Allstair [sic] Donkin, Lorrain [sic] Daniels and David Malkie [sic]. Before the concert we were invited to relax at the home of Mr and Mrs J. Preston McComas who gave us a very nice buffet lunch. He had been in the UK from 1944-46, and she, a former piano student at the Royal Academy of Music, had been a 'GI bride'. Between these orchestral concerts there was one in Charlotte NC; it was held in the NCNB Performance Place which was an old

Baptist church (appropriately in Spirit Square) of the 'box' variety with a very good Baldwin piano. Inside the piano were the signatures of many people who had played it; these included Dave Brubeck, Lionel Hampton, the avant-garde composer George Crumb and the duo Ferrante & Teicher. I added my name to the list. On returning from a meal after this concert we passed some very odd business signs: Charlotte Extermination Company, Pillow Centre of the World and Unfinished Furniture Store. You could only be in America.

The fifth concert was at James Madison University in Harrisonburg VA. The reception here was muted, but a member of the audience, a friend of Geoffrey Shovelton, came back to our hotel afterwards, and he kindly bought us a bottle of champagne which cheered us up somewhat. The following day we had no less than three flights to get us to Rock Island IL where, by contrast, we had a standing ovation from the audience who obviously knew the G&S repertoire. The concert was held in the Circa 21 Playhouse. After this we were in Detroit MI where I met up with cousins from Greenock who had settled in the United States many years before. Our concert on February 24 was presented by Brethren Productions. It was in the Orchestra Hall, and there was an audience of some two thousand who also gave us a standing ovation. But it coincided with another event across the road at the Detroit Civic Center - Prayer and Community Unity with Muhammad Ali. I don't know who got the bigger audience. From Detroit we flew to Pittsburgh PA from where there was another flight, in a Beechcraft 99, to State College PA. This was extremely uncomfortable, and both Vivian and Lorraine came off looking very much the worse for wear. It was snowing when we arrived, and the hotel reminded me of the one in the film *White Christmas*. The concert, part of the Schwab Concert Series, was at the Schwab Auditorium, Pennsylvania State University where we had another rather muted reception. Afterwards, we had a second bottle of champagne: we treated ourselves to this one.

Our final concert was in New York NY, this one being a benefit performance for the British American Educational Foundation at Hunter College Playhouse. While we were here (we generally avoided large cities on these tours) I took the opportunity to visit the Pierpont Morgan Library with its vast G&S collection. I saw the manuscript full score of *HMS Pinafore* and the surviving copy of the solo part of Sullivan's cello concerto that I had recently reconstructed. I also paid a second visit to the Empire State Building, my first being in 1978 during the D'Oyly Carte tour of the United States and Canada. We always took advantage of any social occasions that might arise, and after the New York concert I saw G&S enthusiasts Jesse and Rochelle Shereff whom I had met on the 1978 tour. On our last day we had breakfast at Macy's; after this we went to the Byers, Schwalbe office located at their prestigious One Fifth Avenue address, comparable to D'Oyly Carte's equally prestigious address (which was 1 Savoy Hill when I joined the Company in 1975 although this was later changed), and met Doug Schwalbe and his secretary Cathy. We then had lunch in a nearby restaurant which had been decorated with fittings from the former Cunard liner RMS *Caronia*. We arrived back in London on February 28; we already knew that a further tour had been planned for October. This was certainly very promising. It was also good financially as we earned more than we would have earned with a similar series of concerts at home: for this first tour I received $2,000. We hoped there would be many more tours.

Among the first engagements on my return were two music hall evenings. One was in Cirencester, and the other was in a pub, the Crown & Horns, in East Ilsley just north of Newbury in Berkshire. This was another new venture for me, and it had come about through Laura Collins, the 'Cinders' in the Charles Haley *Cinderella* pantomime that I had recently done: one of Laura's favourite numbers was *The Boy I Love is Up in the Gallery*, made famous by Marie Lloyd. We did a number of these concerts in various venues. One of them was a pub (latterly called the Water Rats) in Gray's Inn Road, near King's Cross station; we performed there in a small back room that had a stage and a piano. I was now introduced to yet another set of performers who specialised in this type of entertainment which was still popular, partly as a result of the TV programme *The Good Old Days* (1953-83) with the actor Leonard Sachs (1909-1990) as the chairman. We never worked with him, but many of our concerts were chaired by another music hall veteran whom Laura knew: Johnny Dennis (1940-2016), an actor who was also a cricket announcer known as 'the voice of Lord's'. I greatly enjoyed these evenings. The pianist often has to improvise and invariably play 'til ready' for some of the performers, and I learned a lot from doing these concerts.

Around this time, and thanks to the pianist Ken Barclay, I started to work for Opera Players Ltd which was run by the indomitable and charismatic Elisabeth Parry (1921-2017) from a large house in Wanborough, Surrey to which one was occasionally invited for a social gathering. Elisabeth had been a singer herself, making her operatic début at Glyndebourne in 1947 as Lucia, the maid in Britten's *The Rape of Lucretia*; during the Second World War she had even been a 'forces' sweetheart'. I also met Peter Gellhorn (1912-2004), the company's music director since its foundation by Elisabeth in 1950. Peter, a fugitive from Nazi Germany, had held posts at the BBC, Glyndebourne Festival Opera, Sadler's Wells Opera and the Royal Opera House, Covent Garden. Opera Players had two distinct groups: London Opera Players and London Chamber Opera. The former presented productions in English of the standard repertoire such as Mozart's *The Magic Flute* and Rossini's *The Barber of Seville* and *La Cenerentola* (a very different *Cinderella* to the one I had recently done for Charles Haley Productions); these were performed with orchestra, the conductors being either Peter Gellhorn or Charles Farncombe (1919-2006), an expert on Handel's operas who had founded the Handel Opera Society.

London Chamber Opera presented a range of one-act operas which usually had just three principals and no chorus, and these were given with piano accompaniment. There were orchestral accompaniments available, but they were seldom used, and it was as a pianist with the Chamber Opera that I was mainly concerned although I often had to play for Opera Players rehearsals as well. These were held at the Friends' Meeting House in Hammersmith. Among the Chamber Opera's repertoire were Mozart's *The Impresario*, Sullivan's *Cox and Box* and Donizetti's *Rita*, a work I had not come across before; there were also operas by Antony Hopkins (1921-2014): *Three's Company*, *Hands Across the Sky* and *Dr Musikus*. The accompaniments for these were rather difficult, and I thought they were sometimes unnecessarily complicated. Antony Hopkins turned up one day at a rehearsal for *Three's Company*, and I tentatively asked him about a section that, to me at least, was almost unplayable. "Oh, I just splash about there", was his reply. So much for all the time I had spent on trying to get the passage right.

You can never have too many contacts in the free-lance world, and now, as mine were increasing, the year continued with a bit of this and a bit of that which, despite the usual gaps when there wasn't any work, was quite encouraging. As well as introducing me to Ken Barclay, my cousins in Hampshire also introduced me to the composer Michael Hurd who lived in the same village, Liss. Michael had written a cantata *Mrs Beeton's Book* for the 1984 Petersfield Musical Festival (he also wrote the lyrics). It was for ladies' choirs and piano duet; knowing that Ken Barclay and I had formed a piano duo he invited us to take part in the performance on March 23 which he conducted. It lasted for about thirty minutes, and it was part of a programme called *A Victorian Entertainment*. This also included part-songs by Elgar and Mendelssohn, and Ken and I played about twenty minutes' worth of duets: the overture to *Zampa* by Hérold

(1791-1833), *Morning Dewdrops* by Sydney Smith, a composer I would be more closely associated with later, and two pieces, *Germany* and *Italy*, from an album called *From Foreign Parts* by Moritz Moszkowski (1854-1925). Moszkowski wrote brilliantly for both piano solo and piano duet: as a pianist himself (not all composers are) his writing for the instrument is superbly idiomatic and always lies 'under the fingers', even when difficult, as well as being both tuneful and harmonically interesting. These duets are not heard very much nowadays, but they are always a delight to play, and we usually included some of them in our concerts. The Petersfield Musical Festival was a one-off 'gig', but work of any kind was always welcome, and it was good to see my cousins again.

Another connection was renewed when I did two concerts for Tom Round and Donald Adams' group Gilbert & Sullivan for All: one in Heswall on April 12 (we had entertained at the Golf Club there when I was with D'Oyly Carte) and another in Weston-super-Mare on May 12.

But the next major event was my first tour for London Chamber Opera which ran from May 24-28 and consisted of five performances each of Donizetti's *Rita* and Mozart's *The Impresario*. The first of these was in Ripon at the College of Ripon and York St John, and we then moved up to Scotland, the first concert there being at the Edinburgh University Staff Club in Chambers Street. We were to have had an orchestra here, but for some reason this had been changed, and as in the other concerts the operas were given with piano accompaniment: yet another disappointment. I had recently been thwarted in conducting concerts in the United States, and I was beginning to think that I was destined never to conduct anything again. But at least I did act as the musical director in Edinburgh, albeit (as usual) 'at the piano'. We then played at the Lochgelly Centre in Lochgelly, Fife, at Loretto School in Musselburgh and finally at the Theatre Royal, Dumfries. Accommodation had been arranged for us over the five days, and so we didn't have to organise that ourselves.

I worked for London Chamber Opera for a number of years, but that was one of the few tours that I did: most of the other engagements were single performances. These were often in halls in villages or small towns as the company's policy was to take opera to places that would not otherwise have the opportunity to see these pieces (not unlike the Byers, Schwalbe tours with dates in smaller towns in the USA and Canada). One incident I recall when working for the group happened in London. Opera Players owned an Austin Maxi that I had to drive from time to time to pick up scenery or costumes. I was on one of these errands when I noticed that the fuel gauge was just coming on to 'empty'. When the gauge on my own car reached 'empty' there was quite a decent reserve which would enable you to get to a filling station in time to replenish, and I assumed that there would also be some reserve in this car. I was near Waterloo station, and I remembered that there was a filling station not too far away on the New Kent Road. I headed for that, but I soon realised that when the gauge read 'empty' it really meant 'empty'; to my horror (on, of all places, the Elephant and Castle roundabout) the car just stopped: it had run out of petrol. Luckily, I was now very close to the filling station, but I still had to push the car. What may seem like a level road when you are actually driving may well be part of a slight incline (which this turned out to be), and getting the car to the filling station was an experience I didn't ever want to repeat. The disruption to other traffic was bad enough then: I hate to think what mayhem it would cause today. But, as someone once said, "it's all part of life's rich tapestry".

June began with another new connection; this was my first encounter with Spaghetti Opera at Terrazza-Est, an Italian restaurant where live opera was presented by two singers and a pianist. Part of a chain called Mario & Franco Restaurants it was situated near the Fleet Street end of Chancery Lane. The artists performed on a twenty minute on/twenty minute off basis, and as well as being paid they were fed during the evening which was an added bonus. The waiters also joined in by banging their trays at the end of each number; it was a very lively atmosphere. On this occasion I had been asked by one of the Chamber Opera singers Alison Truefitt to deputise for another pianist, but I hoped that it might lead to more of the same; eventually it did. Different artists performed each night, and many singers and pianists were involved.

The following day, Lorraine Daniels, our mezzo-soprano in the various groups I was now involved with, was married to Brian Patient who worked in the City of London, and I played the organ. I had never had organ lessons although I had played occasionally over the years, but while we were touring permanently with D'Oyly Carte it wasn't possible to play anywhere regularly, even if one wanted to. Now, however, I wasn't on the road all the time, and for the foreseeable future I was settled in London; it occurred to me that I might try to get an organist's job somewhere to add some regular work to whatever free-lance work might come my way; eventually this also happened.

A few more G&S concerts followed, and then, for the last two weeks of June, I had a holiday: the first I had had since 1979. In my somewhat precarious financial situation a holiday was the last thing on my mind, but this one came about through an offer I couldn't refuse. Ken Barclay, my piano duet partner, and his friend Clive Simmonds, neither of whom could drive, had been thinking of taking a holiday on the continent, visiting a number of places and hopefully meeting up with an old friend of Ken from Edinburgh, Lorraine Thomson, who had married and was living in Italy. To do all of this without being able to drive would have involved much planning, but I was then asked if I would like to join them - and would I take my car? They offered to pay for the petrol and for all my accommodation, and I only had to bring whatever money I would need personally. I still had the Renault 16 which I had bought after the 1979 tour of Australia and New Zealand, and I thought that having a French car might be useful if anything went wrong on the continent. It was an ideal opportunity to have a holiday, and I was happy to be the chauffeur.

This holiday lasted for two weeks. We spent the first night in Paris; after we had found our hotel we went out for a meal. We took the car into the centre of the city, but parking was very difficult. Many cars were parked on the pavements, and I parked there too when I found a space. After our meal we walked back to the hotel, leaving the car along with many others. The following morning I was horrified to find that it was the only one there – with a clamp on the wheel. We then had to go to the police station where Ken, who spoke French, told them that we were tourists who hadn't understood the parking situation, and we were just at the beginning of a holiday. The upshot was that the police agreed to release the car on payment of the fine; that done, we thankfully left Paris.

We spent a few leisurely days getting to the South of France, using only the older roads and staying at various *pensions*, and we eventually arrived in Grasse, famous for its long-established perfume industry. There was a square in the town which seemed to consist of nothing but restaurants, and we had a memorable meal in one of them, sitting outside under a canopy on a lovely warm evening. Next day we had a morning in Cannes (it was very hot) before moving on through Nice and via one of the Corniche roads above Monte Carlo to Genoa where we picked up another of Ken's friends who had flown over from Canada. From there we drove to La Spezia where we turned inland and stayed for one night in a typical hill-top village. We then travelled on again, by-passed Milan and met Lorraine and her husband Ernest Shore at Grantola near Varese in the North. This is close to the Swiss border and Lake Maggiore. We drove along the lakeside next day. It was lovely, but it was very slow going as there was a lot of tourist traffic. We stayed in Grantola for another couple of nights before moving on via the Valle d'Aosta to the Mont Blanc Tunnel between Italy and France. (Some years later there was a serious fire in that tunnel with great loss of life.) The last few days were spent travelling up through France, and finally we were back in London. It had been a wonderful opportunity to see France and Italy, something I could not have afforded to do myself at that time.

We were now almost into July, and I had to pick up the various threads of my free-lance career. One of the first concerts, on June 30, was with my friend the tenor Sandy Oliver: it was in memory of a friend of his, the potter Pamela Nash, who had died of cancer. Pam and her husband 'Bunny' Collyer (also a potter) had originally lived in Hampstead, but they had moved out of London and had bought the disused railway station at Winchelsea (trains still ran through): with plenty of space it was an ideal place for them. Sandy and I saw Bunny again in July. There were also numerous rehearsals and several concerts with the various groups I now worked with: it wasn't a lot of work, but at least something was happening fairly regularly. An unusual occurrence at this time of year was another pantomime *Puss in Boots*. This was not a Charles Haley production: it had been arranged by Laura Collins, and it was in aid of the NSPCC. There were just two performances, both morning ones (shades of Dunfermline): one in Stevenage on July 7 and the other in Erith on the 14th.

My flat in Eastbourne had not yet been sold, but my neighbour Dorothy Walden wrote to me regularly with bills that I had to pay or share, or about problems with insurance; there was even an opportunity to purchase the freehold which we and the ground floor residents all declined.

On July 30 Geoffrey Shovelton and I saw Doug Schwalbe prior to our second US tour. Doug was a member of the East India Club in St James's Square, and we met him there: I thought that it was strange for an American to be a member of such an eminent English club as he presumably wouldn't be in London very often to take advantage of membership. August was a quiet month which was faintly alarming, but I got used to the summers being quieter: much of what happened in the free-lance world took place in the winter months. At the end of August I went up to Scotland again; on the way I stayed for one night with Harold and Hazel Oakley in Appleby Magna. On Sunday September 2 there was a G&S concert which Gordon MacKenzie had organised; this took place at Barrfields Pavilion, Largs as part of the Largs Viking Festival. There were six principals, myself and a local chorus among whom was an old school friend Renwick Adam, the brother of Norman with whom I had shared a flat in Glasgow. A few days later, on September 5, there was a London Airs concert, this time in Greenock Arts Guild where I had taken part in G&S performances when I was at school. It was good to be on that stage again.

While I was in Greenock I visited a couple in Hamilton, Billy and Margaret Skelly, whom I had first met during my D'Oyly Carte days. Billy was a member of a well-known family in the motor trade in Glasgow, and Margaret was a G&S aficionado who had introduced herself at the stage door after one of our performances, having discovered that I came from Greenock. We became very good friends. In his youth Billy had taken part in the TT races on the Isle of Man, and they eventually settled there. On the way back to London I stayed again with Harold and Hazel Oakley. Seeing friends up and down the country when I was being paid to do the travelling was one of the great pleasures of the somewhat nomadic existence I had chosen for myself: "mixing business with pleasure", as my Uncle John, himself an inveterate traveller, had often said.

On September 14 I had to deputise for Ken Barclay at one of the Parlour Quartet concerts. The quartet consisted of Ken and singers Maureen Keetch, Sylvia Eaves and Robert Carpenter-Turner. Robert was also a photographer. These concerts consisted almost entirely of old ballads, a genre that was very much to my own taste, and the format was similar to our own London Airs concerts (there was one of those in October at Uckfield). September had also seen G&S concerts in Tunbridge Wells and Wimbledon, a Two of Hearts (Geoffrey Shovelton and Vivian Tierney) in Codsall and, early in October, another concert for Geoffrey's cousin Irene in Bolton; once again Vivian was with Geoffrey. It all seemed to be developing quite nicely, and we were about to start a second tour for Byers, Schwalbe with the same artists: Vivian Tierney, Lorraine Daniels, Kenneth Sandford, Geoffrey Shovelton, Alistair Donkin and me.

As in February this tour was preceded by a Magic of D'Oyly Carte concert; it was even at the same venue in Manchester. And so the first day (October 14) began again 'somewhere on the M6': this time just north of Birmingham. We didn't get back to London until 03.00, and so again there wasn't very much sleep that night. But we all managed to get to Heathrow by 11.00 for a 12.50 flight. The tour was shorter by one concert than the February tour, and our first date was in a small town, Iola KS. We flew first to O'Hare Airport, Chicago IL where we caught another flight to Kansas City MO; we then had to hire a car. This was worse than before as there were now six of us. We had very little idea of where we were going, and to make matters worse it started to rain heavily. Eventually we saw lights in the distance, but we took a wrong turning and ended up in a field of wheat. The journey was beginning to assume the proportions of a Kafkaesque nightmare, with more than a passing reference to Alfred Hitchcock, but we finally made it to Iola where we performed at the Bowlus Fine Arts Center as part of the Cultural Attractions series. In the United States our 'theatre' and 'centre' were usually spelled 'theater' and 'center' although sometimes I came across the English spelling.

Our hotel here was the Crossroads Motel which caused some amusement as *Crossroads* was the name of a legendary British TV soap opera which was still running (it was set in a fictional motel in the Midlands, and it ran from 1964-88). The agency had provided Geoffrey Shovelton, as the leader of the group, with a substantial sum of money (some $2,500) to be distributed to us as subsistence, and Geoffrey thought that he must put this into the motel safe rather than keep it in his room. "Oh my", said the lady at the desk, "that will have to go into the freezer". Thinking that this was an unfamiliar American term Geoffrey said "I've never heard a safe called that before". "No", said the lady, "it's not the safe. It really is the freezer. If anyone breaks in we reckon that's the last place they would look for money". Next day, having retrieved this very cold wad of notes from the freezer, we set off for Emporia KS (a bigger town than Iola) some sixty miles to the north-west. Stopping on the way for refreshment we had some strange looks from other patrons in their ten-gallon hats, jeans and spurred boots: we were obviously not 'locals'. We drove across the endless flat plains of the American Mid-West, and while this was interesting in its own way I was glad that it was part of the tour and not a holiday that I had paid for myself. The concert in Emporia was for the Emporia Arts Council, and it was held in Lowther Middle School North. The dressing-rooms here were rather uninspiring, and the audience was again subdued, but the hall had one of the best pianos I had yet encountered. We then drove to Lincoln NE. Just into the state we stopped for lunch; I had a runza (similar to a Cornish pasty) which was apparently a speciality of Nebraska. The concert in Lincoln, which was well received, was presented by Abendmusik: Lincoln in the First Plymouth Church, a large building with every sort of amenity including a gym. We then flew to Washington DC where we performed in the Baird Auditorium at the Natural History Museum as part of the Smithsonian Resident Associate Program [sic]. While in Washington we met up with Donald Adams who would shortly be singing in Lehar's *The Merry Widow* at the Kennedy Center. Any so-called glamour in this profession can be off-set by loneliness when you are away from home, particularly if you are on your own; Donald was delighted to see us.

Our next concert was in the enormous E.J. Thomas Performing Arts Hall at the University of Akron in Akron OH.

There was a wonderful Baldwin piano here, and we got a standing ovation. We then flew out to California where we did the last three concerts. The first of these was at Victor Valley College, Victorville, in yet another Performing Arts Center. (Victorville is home to the Roy Rogers-Dale Evans Museum, complete with a stuffed Trigger, which we visited.) The second concert was in the University Theatre at the University of California in Riverside, part of their Performing Arts Presentations, and the last one, sponsored by Ambassador College, was in the Ambassador Auditorium in Pasadena for the Ambassador International Cultural Foundation. I managed to phone Joe and Ducelia Contreras (friends of my cousin June in Hampshire) whom I had met on the 1978 tour, and we met again earlier on the day of the concert; we were then joined by Neil Downey, whom I had also met during the 1978 tour, and his friend Carol whom I had not previously met.

The founder and president of Ambassador College was Herbert W. Armstrong, then still alive at ninety-two, originator of the Radio Church of God and the magazine *The Plain Truth* which was given away free (presumably he made his fortune from something else). The Auditorium was a spectacular building in a lovely setting, constructed with the finest materials: our dressing rooms had carpets that seemed inches deep, and the taps on the wash-hand basins were gold-plated. Joe, Ducelia, Neil and Carol came to this last concert as did Michael and Mary Anne Scheff, another couple I had met in Long Beach CA in 1978. They all came round afterwards to say goodbye, and for a brief moment I was with many of the people I had met on the 1978 tour. Socialising like this was one of the great joys of touring; this was equally so at home if I was out of London. But there was one further surprise at Pasadena.

Coming out of the stage door after the concert I was amazed to see Linda Wood, a G&S aficionado from Glasgow. Linda was also a great fan of *Star Trek*, and she had come to Los Angeles with a group of like-minded enthusiasts. She had also contacted Lillias Gilbert Jones (who was apparently related to W.S. Gilbert), the secretary of the Los Angeles branch of the Gilbert and Sullivan Society, and Lillias had told her that we were appearing at the Ambassador Auditorium. Linda immediately expressed an interest, and Lillias managed to get a ticket for her. Yes, it's a small world.

The Ambassador concert was our last one, but it wasn't quite the end of our second Byers, Schwalbe tour. On the last day, October 29, we had to get up early to drive to Hollywood to do a short recording session. We had agreed to do this for some event that was to take place later, and they only wanted part of the famous trio from *Ruddigore* "My eyes are fully open to my awful situation" which is notoriously difficult to perform as it is one of Gilbert's 'patter' songs which are usually sung as solos by the comedy baritone. Alistair Donkin (as Robin Oakapple) didn't have much difficulty with it, and Lorraine Daniels (as Mad Margaret) also coped very well, but Kenneth Sandford (as Sir Despard Murgatroyd) had a heavier baritone voice and always found it difficult to get the words out. He had performed the role many times, and he had managed to find a way round its difficulties, but the man in charge of the recording session wasn't satisfied, and we had several shots at it: from his control box we would hear his encouraging words "C'mon, Kenny baby" in the hope that there would not be yet another 'take'. Mercifully, we finally got it 'in the can'. We then departed for the airport where we boarded a half-empty plane, arriving back in London the following morning. It had been another very enjoyable tour. It was our second tour in one calendar year, but the February one had been towards the end of the 1983-84 season, and this one had been at the beginning of the 1984-85 season. We had tentatively been booked for the 1985-86 season, but we might not go until 1986. If we didn't have a tour in 1985 (and this is eventually what happened) my next year's income would almost certainly be less than this year's, whatever other work I managed to find.

Shortly after our return Geoffrey Shovelton and I had a meeting at the Savoy Hotel with Victor Emery, a former Canadian Olympic gold medallist who was now an executive director of the Savoy group. The Savoy was one of a number of leading hotels of the world whose directors would meet every so often in one of the hotels for a conference; that hotel also had to provide some cabaret. But this time a tour of several of these plush establishments in West Germany and Austria was being planned, and it was the Savoy's turn to provide some entertainment. Victor, who was married to Jennifer, daughter of Sir Hugh Wontner (whom we all knew through his involvement with the D'Oyly Carte Opera Trust), was given the job of organising it, and it occurred to him that he might devise something based on the history of the Opera Company and its connection with the Savoy, Richard D'Oyly Carte being the common factor. He then asked Albert Truelove, Dame Bridget D'Oyly Carte's private secretary, if he could suggest someone who might be able to help him with this, and Albert suggested Geoffrey who said that he would be pleased to do it, but he would also need an accompanist. And so I had another very interesting and enjoyable experience although this didn't begin until the end of November.

I then had a taste of something that would become a regular part of my work (the nearest thing to an actual job in my free-lance career), a tour of hospitals in the East Midlands where we entertained the patients at venues in and around Northampton, Leicester, Nottingham and Derby. This was not organised by the company that I later worked for, but I got involved with it through members of the G&S group The Magic of D'Oyly Carte. I didn't possess an electronic keyboard at that time, and I don't recall anyone lending me one for the tour: it used to be the norm for hospital wards to have pianos. But on one occasion we couldn't see a piano, and we asked if they had one. "It's down at the end of the ward under that cover", was the reply, and this rang alarm bells as there were numerous potted plants on the cover which looked as if they hadn't been disturbed for many a long day. We took them off gingerly and removed the cover, only to find that the instrument was completely useless: it was full of dust, and most of the strings were missing. If I had had an electronic keyboard with me I would of course have used it, but on that occasion I could only take a back seat while the group sang unaccompanied.

Immediately following this tour I had another concert with Geoffrey Shovelton in Bolton. Most of these concerts, organised by his cousin Irene, took place in a local church, but this one was in the Library Theatre in the centre of the city, a small venue that was ideal for concerts of this type. As usual, we stayed with Irene, but I had to be back in London by the Sunday evening as one of my duties at the Jenkins' home was to act as a child-minder, particularly for their daughter Katy, and I had to stay at the house all day on the Monday. Later that week there was a Magic of D'Oyly Carte concert in Plymouth, and this was followed by a week of concerts in Swansea. Here, the group was joined by a former D'Oyly Carte principal soprano Pamela Field who had left the Company in 1975, just before I joined, but I had already met Pamela as she had come back as a guest artist in our last London season, 1981-82. I had a very bad cold that week, and I sat snuffling at the piano every night. At times like these I would console myself by saying that at least I could still play: singers with such a bad cold would inevitably have to cancel their performances. But it was still particularly annoying as Geoffrey and I were about to start our grand tour of some of Europe's leading hotels.

I had had some memorable experiences during my time with D'Oyly Carte, particularly on the five-month tour of the United States and Canada in 1978 and the four-month tour of Australia and New Zealand in 1979; this single week, from November 26 to December 4, was equally memorable. We performed in Frankfurt, Düsseldorf, Hamburg, Munich, Salzburg and Vienna. We had been told that initially we were to be kept out of the way so that our first appearance would be a surprise although from our second appearance onwards it would become apparent that we were actually part of the group; so we had to travel separately at first. We flew to Frankfurt and waited in the baggage claim to retrieve our cases. Passengers who had got off with us (the plane was going on to Vienna) collected theirs and departed; Geoffrey and I were now the only two there, but our cases still hadn't appeared. The carousel stopped and we looked at each other in dismay. What now? We then went to an official, who fortunately spoke English, and told him what had happened. "Your tickets, please" (brusque but efficient). He looked at them and said "But you are booked through to Vienna". "Oh, yes, well...", we said, "we are flying home from Vienna, but we have to start our week here". It appeared then that the Savoy had booked return tickets to Vienna, and we hadn't bothered to look at them closely or we might have spotted this. "Wait there", said the official, and so we dutifully sat down and waited. Then the carousel started up again, and eventually the two cases appeared. I had nothing but admiration for the baggage handlers who had to find the cases and get them off the plane, presumably delaying its departure in the process. I suggested to Geoffrey that we should let the cases do a lap of honour on the carousel, but common sense prevailed, and we quickly retrieved them and set off for our first destination, the Schlosshotel [sic] Kronberg, some miles to the north-west of the city.

The hotel, a vast edifice, had been built for Queen Victoria's eldest daughter Victoria, the Princess Royal, who had been married to the Emperor Frederick III and was the mother of Kaiser Wilhelm II. Being out of the city it had escaped wartime damage, and for some years, from 1945, it had been taken over by the Americans. Of the hotels we performed in this was the only one at which we also stayed. For a leading hotel of the world the rooms were certainly up to the latest standards of comfort, but the public rooms seemed to be just as they would have been in Victoria's time. There was a wonderful library, half of whose books were in English; among these was a two-volume set *The Gurneys of Earlham,* a history of the famous banking family mentioned by Gilbert in *Trial by Jury:* "At length I became as rich as the Gurneys". The cabaret started with Victor Emery giving a short history of the Savoy Hotel and its connection with Gilbert and Sullivan, and then, at the appropriate moment, Geoffrey and I made our entrance. The first numbers were, naturally, some of the tenor arias from the Savoy Operas, but Geoffrey later took the opportunity to regale the guests with arias by Verdi and Puccini and also some Irish songs, all of which went down very well.

Next day we headed into Frankfurt where we boarded a train for Düsseldorf. We travelled via Wiesbaden and Mainz before heading northwards alongside the Rhine to Coblenz, Cologne and finally to Düsseldorf. The hotel we performed in, the Breidenbacher Hof, was elegance personified; it had a stunningly beautiful lounge in blue, grey and gold. After our performance we began to meet some of the Savoy directors and their wives who had now realised that we were part of the group. Other guests included the Finnish Ambassador from Bonn (at that time the provisional capital of West Germany) and the local British Consul. We then went back to our own hotel, the Vossen am Karlsplatz. The following morning, after an early breakfast, we were off again on another train journey, this time to Hamburg, via Duisburg, Essen, Gelsenkirchen and Münster. All of this, for each of us, was an added attraction in addition to being paid to undertake this somewhat unusual assignment. The hotel in Hamburg was the famous Vier Jahreszeiten (Four Seasons) on the Inner Alster, then basking in the glory of being the top hotel in Europe. It was certainly very impressive. We were at the Alster-Hof which was perfectly adequate.

On Thursday November 29, now fully integrated with the group, we all flew to Munich: the hotel we performed at here was another Vier Jahreszeiten, and it was very close to ours which was the Platzl. In the audience for our performance that night were some of Europe's nobility, the guest list including one baron, one prince and three princesses as well as dignitaries of one sort or another. We stayed longer in Munich than in any of the other cities, and the Friday and Saturday were free so that we were able to see something of it; Geoffrey even managed to get himself an audition with a Herr Wolfgang Stoll to whose office we went on the Friday morning. We then did a bit of sightseeing. In the evening, with the rest of the group, we were given a tour of the Residenz (wonderfully restored after wartime bombing) and then saw some ballet in the Residenz Theatre, a lovely baroque gem whose internal fittings were original, having been removed before the bombing.

The next day, Saturday, was December 1, and we did more sightseeing although it was hardly the tourist season. Following another early breakfast we boarded a coach for a tour of the iconic castles of Linderhof and Neuschwanstein, creations of the unfortunate King Ludwig II of Bavaria. After Linderhof we made an unscheduled stop at Oberammergau (another bonus) and after this we stopped at the famous baroque Wieskirche - 'the church in the meadow' - which had survived the war but was now being threatened by vibrations from jet planes: flying over it had been banned. Then it was Neuschwanstein, perhaps the most iconic castle of all. I couldn't believe how lucky we were to have been doing these performances in hotels that neither of us could have afforded to stay at while effectively also having (as Frederic Lloyd, former general manager of D'Oyly Carte, would have said) "a paid holiday". We got back to Munich at 18.00. There was no performance that night, and the West German part of the tour was now over.

On the Sunday we travelled by coach to Salzburg where we arrived in the afternoon in time to have a guided tour of the city. We stayed at the Elefant Hotel and performed at the Goldener Hirsch Hotel, the audience again including more nobility, among them two princesses and a countess. The latter seemed genuinely interested in offering us some engagements, but, as so often in these situations, nothing came of this. The room that we performed in had a low vaulted ceiling. It was atmospheric and charming in its own way, but it was not very good to sing in, particularly when the cigars got going; in situations like that the singer also has to keep the audience's attention when he or she is introducing items, often through loud conversation. This is never easy, and I'm always glad that I just sit at the piano on these occasions.

December 3 was the last day. I managed to see a little more of Salzburg in the morning before we set off on another coach for Vienna. We didn't see much of the scenery as it was very foggy, but we did pass the huge monastery at Melk on the Danube (I was to visit it many years later). At around 12.30 we pulled unto a layby where, to our astonishment, we found a huge picnic set out for us. This consisted of Hungarian goulash, rolls and sandwiches, beer, wine and Schnapps, the latter very comforting on a bitterly cold day (everyone was well wrapped up; many of the ladies were in fur coats). It was a nice idea, but it did rather smack of British eccentricity. Unfortunately, the unisex toilet at the layby was one of the most primitive I have ever come across: it was a far cry from the five-star hotels we had recently visited.

We arrived in Vienna sometime after 15.30. It was beginning to get dark, and we didn't see very much, but I remember driving past the Opera House. Geoffrey and I were staying at the appropriately named Hotel Amadeus just a couple of blocks away from St Stephen's Cathedral which I managed to visit briefly. The last venue, the Palais Schwarzenberg, was perhaps the most fascinating of all. It had been a palace at one time, but it was now a hotel. We performed in a very large dining room-cum-music room which occupied one whole wing of the building; the piano, a Bösendorfer, was one of the best yet. Once again we had nobility in the audience: one count, two countesses and Fürst

Schwarzenberg (Fürst, I think, translates as prince or sovereign) of the family who still owned the building. With the brilliance of the surroundings, and in such exalted company, we endeavoured to give of our best that night. After the concert some of us were given a tour of the basement, now a very modern kitchen, by none other than Fürst Schwarzenberg himself. It had been a truly wonderful week, and we were now given one of the Savoy hand-outs, a Royal Worcester ashtray with a representation of the Lord Chancellor (*Iolanthe*) on it.

We flew home the following morning at an ungodly hour. I hadn't seen much of Vienna, but that was a small price to pay for spending such an interesting week in wonderful surroundings (very nice if you can afford it) and seeing how the wealthy live. We touched down just after 09.00, and after travelling up from Heathrow we called in at Methodist Central Hall, Westminster where London Airs was rehearsing a new show that we were to perform in about a week's time. In my absence Fraser Goulding, former musical director of D'Oyly Carte, was standing in as pianist, and it was good to see him again. For some reason, however, this concert was cancelled. The Savoy seemed very pleased with what we had done, and we hoped that we might be used again. But now it was time for another pantomime with Charles Haley Productions: rehearsals began a few days later.

The next pantomime was *Aladdin*, again at the Carnegie Hall, Dunfermline (December 14-22) and the Queen's Hall, Barnstaple (December 27-January 5, 1985): thankfully, Ealing had been dropped as a venue. We had a completely different cast this time, but I didn't keep in touch with any of them afterwards. In Dunfermline there were two days when we had three shows - at 09.30, 14.00 and 19.00 - and on another two days, although there were only two shows, the first one was again at 09.30, the second at 19.00. An afternoon off was one thing, but four shows at 09.30 was hard for everyone, even for the pianist. We arrived in Barnstaple on Sunday December 23, and we had a welcome break of a few days over Christmas before the performances started.

II – 1985

I had kept in touch with the Molesworth-St Aubyn family at Pencarrow, and when I told them that I would be at Barnstaple again they invited me to spend New Year's Day with them at their other seat Tetcott Manor which was at Holsworthy in Devon and not too far from Barnstaple. This was another very pleasant break. The pantomime finished on Saturday January 5, and we headed back to London. I think I knew by now that there would not be a Byers, Schwalbe tour this year, and this would result in a definite drop in income; I could only hope that other work would materialise to help fill the gap. It was quiet again after the pantomime, but there was always something else including more child-minding for Ross and Ginny Jenkins. I also paid a visit to the dentist. It was useful to have time to attend to these things, and even shopping was easier if you could do it on a weekday and not at the week-end, but the fact that I was free meant that I wasn't working, and that was always a worry. Thanks to Ginny Jenkins I did get a rather unusual job, namely to be a guinea pig at the local hospital where they wanted volunteers to help test a new drug. It involved being at the hospital for most of the day (there were four days in all between January and February), and you had to make sure that you didn't have any alcohol the night before. Sometimes we were just given placebos. There was some payment for this: not a lot, but anything was welcome as there was just one concert that month. But the good news was that my flat had finally been sold, and on January 24 I went down to Eastbourne to spend a last night there in preparation for the removal of my goods and chattels to London on the 25th (not how a Scotsman wants to celebrate Robert Burns' birthday) by the well-known firm of Pickfords who had been operating since the eighteenth century and who were immortalised by W.S. Gilbert in *Iolanthe*: "He's a Parliamentary Pickford – he carries everything!" (Could I have chosen anyone else?) Ross and Ginny had agreed to take some of my furniture, but the rest had to go into storage. Now I could look for a flat of my own.

There were a few more concerts in February, and there was yet another one-off occasion when Geoffrey Shovelton, Vivian Tierney and I went to the Isle of Wight to provide some entertainment for Iona Molesworth-St Aubyn's mother's ninetieth birthday. Iona had met Vivian and me at Pencarrow in 1982, but the tenor then had been Meston Reid: this time it was Geoffrey who came with Vivian, and they gave one of their Two of Hearts programmes. Iona's mother was the widow of Admiral Sir Francis Tottenham. She lived at Bembridge in a house which had a central hall with a balcony; this was ideal for some of the numbers. After our performance we joined Lady Tottenham and the other guests for a meal. It was my first visit to the Isle of Wight, and it was a very pleasant week-end.

The year I joined the D'Oyly Carte Opera Company, 1975, was the centenary year of *Trial by Jury*, Gilbert and Sullivan's first big success. In the years left to the Company we marked the centenaries of the next four operas: *The Sorcerer* in 1977, *HMS Pinafore* in 1978 (in San Francisco), *The Pirates of Penzance* in 1979 and *Patience* in 1981. The Company closed in February 1982 before the centenary of *Iolanthe* in November of that year, but we celebrated this at Pencarrow in July. Following *Iolanthe* came *Princess Ida* which, despite its wonderful music, had never been as popular as some of the others, and I don't recall much in the way of a celebration of its centenary in 1984. But now, in 1985, we had come to the centenary of *The Mikado*, easily the most popular of all the operas, and although D'Oyly Carte had ceased to exist it was felt that some sort of 'official' recognition was due.

A Centenary Luncheon, organised by the D'Oyly Carte Opera Trust, was held in the Lancaster Room at the Savoy Hotel on Saturday March 16 (the actual centenary was on March 14), tickets being available only to subscribers to the Friends of D'Oyly Carte. The event was attended by some four hundred and seventy people, some from overseas, among whom were Lord Wilson of Rievaulx (the former Prime Minister Harold Wilson, a keen G&S aficionado) and Margaret Philo, a former D'Oyly Carte principal mezzo from the 1920s who was now in her mid-eighties. Sir Hugh Wontner gave a speech, saying that the day was "a momentous theatrical occasion", and after the meal came the entertainment. This had been devised by Albert Truelove and Cynthia Morey (a former D'Oyly Carte principal soprano) and included the main numbers from *The Mikado*. The performers were dressed in the old D'Oyly Carte costumes, and one guest said that it brought tears to his eyes to see, just once more, so many familiar faces in these equally familiar costumes. I had earlier received a letter from Albert asking me if I would take part, and I was more than happy to be involved. Albert, Cynthia and I met beforehand to discuss the details, and we had a short rehearsal at 11.00 on the Saturday morning. Everyone who took part had been a member of D'Oyly Carte. Albert and Cynthia had managed to secure the services of former principals Tom Round and Valerie Masterson as Nanki–Poo and Yum-Yum, but all the other performers were from my time in the Company. The two other 'little maids' were Jane Metcalfe as Pitti-Sing and Caroline Tatlow as Peep-Bo; Jill Pert was Katisha, Patrick Wilkes was the Mikado, James Conroy-Ward was Ko-Ko, Bruce Graham was Pooh-Bah and Alan Rice was Pish-Tush. Once again I was 'at the piano'.

Shortly afterwards, I received two letters. The first, dated March 19, was from Dame Bridget D'Oyly Carte who, sadly, was already terminally ill. It said:

Dear Mr Mackie,

I am so glad that you were able to accompany and control the concert for the Centenary Luncheon on Saturday which I know everybody enormously enjoyed.

With my very best wishes,

Yours sincerely,

Bridget D'Oyly Carte.

The second letter, dated Tuesday [March 19], was from Albert Truelove. It said:

Dear David,

Thank you so much for doing such a splendid job last Saturday & keeping the whole show together in such a fine way. I'm sure the audience didn't realise how little rehearsal you had. I was very proud & happy with the result.

Once again many thanks.

Yours sincerely,

Albert.

Almost a month later I received another letter, this time from Sir Hugh Wontner, which came with a small memento of the occasion. It had been a splendid afternoon, and although it didn't lead directly to any other work it somehow made us all feel that D'Oyly Carte was still alive and kicking.

Albert Truelove was a somewhat Dickensian character, physically not unlike one's idea of Samuel Pickwick. His office desk was perhaps the untidiest I have ever seen - even worse than my own. It was covered in a mountain of papers which doubtless concealed any number of important documents waiting to be attended to. But there was also a sign which read "A cluttered desk is a sign of genius". He was certainly a one-off, and it was thanks to him that another door now opened for me.

Knowing that we were all looking for work Albert had suggested that I join the Concert Artistes' Association (CAA) in Bedford Street where I might be able to make more contacts. From the latter part of the nineteenth century there had been many groups of entertainers (minstrel shows and concert parties) at seaside resorts, often dressed as pierrots and often performing outdoors (a scene in the film *Brighton Rock* (1947) shows just such a pierrot group). The artists who worked in variety were usually performing in theatres up and down the country all the year round, but when the holiday season ended the concert artistes (with an 'e') would come into London to look for other work. This wasn't always forthcoming, and there were many cases of hardship among performers. It was partly to help alleviate this that the CAA was formed in 1897: it has a benevolent fund for members in distress. But it was also a useful meeting place where performers could relax while 'resting'. Later, a tradition evolved of members giving concerts in the Club on a Monday evening. At these concerts the front row was reserved for agents who might be looking for new acts; many a young member would be pleased to get a foothold on the ladder following a Monday evening appearance. These concerts were still being given when I joined the CAA (although by that time there were few agents present), and I played for many of them, invariably having a meal in the Club beforehand. There were no fees for the acts, but the pianist was always given a token 'consideration' although you tended to spend most of that in the bar afterwards.

The walls of the bar were covered with photographs of former members and presidents, many of the latter well-known to me from radio, film and television such as Jack Warner and his sisters Elsie and Doris Waters ('Gert and Daisy'), Arthur Askey, Cyril Fletcher (of the *Odd Odes*), David Nixon and Leslie Crowther among others, but I also got to know many of the current members, among them Pamela Cundell (Mrs Fox in *Dad's Army*) and Jack Haig of *Allo Allo!* ("It is I, Leclerc!"). Jean Fergusson (Marina in *Last of the Summer Wine*) was also a member as was Barbara Newman, a small lady whose speciality was playing the goose in *Mother Goose* pantomimes: she designed a goose skin for herself. One former president I just missed meeting was Leslie Sarony who had died in February at the age of eighty-eight: he had been one half of the Two Leslies (with pianist/singer Leslie Holmes) in the 1930s and 1940s. At home we had old recordings of him singing his own comic songs, and I even had sheet music for some of them; as this material belonged to a much earlier period I assumed that he had died many years before. As the concert parties thinned out and there was more variety, the distinctions between the CAA members became blurred, but variety itself had all but vanished when I joined. Nevertheless, there was still some of it around, and I found myself playing for various groups and individuals, often at afternoon performances put on by some of the London boroughs.

Apart from the work that I found through the CAA I also made some life-long friendships, particularly with Kay Laing, Vivienne Jay and Conrad Leonard. Kay was a pianist who had played in a piano duo with another lady Vera Manwaring [sic], and Vivienne was a singer and actress who often appeared in advertisements, always a lucrative area of the business. Vivienne's husband Gerald was not a performer, but he too became a good friend. Conrad was one of the most remarkable men I have ever met, and one of the few people to have lived in three centuries: born in 1898, he died in 2003 at the age of one hundred and four. He was a pianist, composer and former conductor of shows; he had also worked for the music publisher Lawrence Wright who published many of his songs including *I Heard a Robin Singing*, inspired by the singer Sylvia Robin who adopted it as her signature tune.

Shortly after joining the CAA I bought a book called *Stage Struck*. Written by one of the members, Chris Wortman (a name hitherto unknown to me), it told of his life as an entertainer. He had appeared in just about every aspect of the business including music hall, concert party work and the legitimate theatre, and he had played the eponymous title role in the famous musical comedy *Mr Cinders*, much of whose music, including the hit number "Spread a little happiness", was written by Vivian Ellis. He was also much in demand as the dame in pantomime. Some years later, for the CAA's centenary, another member Larry Parker produced a book called *But – What Do You Do in the Winter?* Both of these told of areas of the world of show business that were appealing more and more to me but of which there now seemed to be less and less. But there was still enough left to help my career along, and this continued for a few more years.

There were more music hall concerts in April followed by another short London Chamber Opera tour with dates in Macclesfield, Lancaster and Huddersfield; this was followed by more music hall. Then came another hospital tour with dates in the East Midlands, Norwich, Ely, St Albans and Swindon with the ex-D'Oyly Carte group that I had worked with on a similar tour in November 1984: this was under the auspices of an organisation called SHAPE. I was certainly getting around the country.

Shortly before this, on May 2, Dame Bridget D'Oyly Carte died. The granddaughter of Richard D'Oyly Carte, she was the last of that particular line of the family, and there was much speculation as to whether she had left money to reform the Opera Company. I was glad that she had lived long enough to see the centenary of *The Mikado* in March, but her death did seem to be the end of an era.

Next, another door opened, thanks this time to Geoffrey Shovelton. When Geoffrey was with Scottish Opera he met and befriended the baritone Michael Maurel who in 1983, with his wife Brenda Stanley (a soprano who also produced for Opera Players), had purchased a restaurant called Chatts in St Leonards-on-Sea (part of Hastings since the nineteenth century). It had been owned by Gerald Chatterton (from whom the name derived) and his wife Louise Denny, a fellow-musician whom I got to know well, but Gerald had died in 1981, and Louise had decided to sell the property. When

Michael and Brenda came to look at it they asked if they could sing something (somewhat to Louise's astonishment), and they found that with its high ceiling it was ideal for conversion into an operatic wine bar: it was perhaps the only restaurant that ever changed hands on account of its acoustics. The name was changed to Il Boccalino, and performances were duly given (Geoffrey was involved in a number of these): the Maurels and their son Paul lived in the flat upstairs. The productions were on a limited scale as there wasn't a great deal of room (and just an old upright piano), but the venture had been successful, and Michael and Brenda decided to broaden the scope by introducing a lighter element. The piece they had chosen to do was the long-running American musical *The Fantasticks* by Tom Jones and Harvey Schmidt, and they were looking for a musical director who might be interested. They asked Geoffrey if he knew of anyone, and he kindly suggested me. I went down to St Leonards on May 27 to meet Michael and Brenda and discuss the project.

I knew little of *The Fantasticks* beyond the famous number "Try to remember" which had been a big hit when the show opened in New York in 1960, but I soon discovered its delights. There were other wonderful numbers such as "Soon it's gonna rain", "They were you" and "Plant a radish", but its entertaining script was a revelation: essentially the story of a boy, a girl, their fathers and a wall it also contains other colourful characters such as Henry, an old Shakespearean actor, and his sidekick Mortimer who specialises in death scenes. Henry was played by Anthony 'Tony' Bateman, a well-known actor with many television appearances who was also a member of the Players' Theatre; he also directed the production. I met him in London on May 31 after collecting a vocal score from Weinberger. Mortimer was played by a local man Fred Nash who was well-known to the Hastings/St Leonards audiences. The girl, Luisa, was Fiona O'Neil, a singer I was to work with again, and the boy, Matt, was played by Paul Maurel. The two fathers, Hucklebee and

Bellomy, were Frederick 'Fred' Westcott and Simon Brotherhood, and the narrator, El Gallo, was Erik van Rekum. It was not only my introduction to Il Boccalino but one of the most enjoyable productions I have ever been involved in.

The Fantasticks wasn't staged until July/August, but I was kept busy with various engagements in June. Harold and Hazel Oakley's daughter Christine was married on June 8, and for this I made an arrangement of the old Irish tune *Slane*, sung to the hymn "Be thou my Vision", to which I added a descant; there was also another hospital tour in the North from Whitehaven across to Newcastle.

I had finally managed to find a flat in Islington, at 6 Mildmay Grove, which was very close to where I had been living in Hackney. I had paid £20,000 for my Eastbourne flat in 1980, and I had sold it for £30,000 just five years later; I was now paying £32,000 for this one. Given that I still had no regular source of income I was very lucky that all of this happened during the 1980s when property values were rising rapidly, and I am still grateful to Nationwide for its confidence in my ability to find enough work to enable me to keep up the payments. The completion date was June 20, and the removal took place on July 4 (appropriately Independence Day) just after the hospital tour in the North although my piano had to be moved separately the following Tuesday. The flat was barely a third of the size of my Eastbourne flat, but I now had a home in London.

Chapter 3 – A new home

I – 1985

My new home was the second floor of an early Victorian terraced house which had been converted into flats. Originally, my floor consisted of just two rooms: a main room at the front, which was the full width of the building, and a narrower room at the back. The remaining space was taken up by the staircase. To make the flat into a self-contained unit a kitchenette was inserted into the staircase side of the front room and a bathroom was made out of part of the back room. But the bathroom was in the middle of the flat, and it had no window. It was not the full width of the back room, and the remaining space became a square 'entrance hall' each of whose sides was no wider than a door. The staircase wasn't particularly wide either, and it was with some difficulty that the piano was hauled up. It had to go into what was now a very small bedroom; after the generous space that I had had in Eastbourne it was all a bit of a tight squeeze.

I didn't have much time to get used to this shoe-box as there were various things to attend to. I also had to play at the CAA on July 8 and at another concert in Wolverhampton on the 13th. Shortly after that there were daily rehearsals in St Leonards for *The Fantasticks* followed by a week of performances from July 27-August 3. A local paper, the *Hastings & St Leonards Observer*, gave the performers 'eleven out of ten'. It was ironic that I had not performed there during my two years in Eastbourne: now that I was in London I found myself going down regularly as this was just the start of a long association with Il Boccalino. Shortly after I began work on *The Fantasticks* I was asked if I would stay on and be the pianist for Puccini's *La Bohème* with Brenda Stanley as Mimi. I was more than happy to do this although I had not played for very much opera (I had only just started to work for London Chamber Opera), and I had much to learn. But it was more good experience, particularly as I had recently been veering towards an even lighter side of the business than G&S.

All this extra work didn't mean that I was travelling up and down every day: one of the features of the set-up at Il Boccalino was that performers would be put up 'for the duration', either at the wine bar itself or with one or other of its many patrons. I had accommodation at St Michael's Hospice in a small cell-like room which was comfortable enough if somewhat Spartan. It was, however, bigger than my new bedroom at Mildmay Grove. There was an adjacent kitchen where I could make my own breakfast, and it was there that I learned how to use a microwave oven although my first attempt at scrambled egg was not very successful. The wine bar at Il Boccalino also had a kitchen, and one of the features of performances there was that food would be served during the interval. This was usually just pasta and salad, but it was always very welcome, and as there also seemed to be an inexhaustible supply of red wine the second half of whatever was being performed would invariably go with quite a swing.

There would be more work in St Leonards, but after *La Bohème* I was back in London, settling in to my new flat and taking whatever jobs came along. There were also rehearsals at the CAA for *A Victorian Evening* (which included dialogue) with London Airs. This was to be in Greenock where we had performed in 1984. On this second visit Gordon MacKenzie organised an evening at Largs Golf Club of which he was a member. Gordon's first wife had died shortly after

D'Oyly Carte closed in 1982, and in 1986 he married Beti Lloyd-Jones, also formerly with D'Oyly Carte. Back in London I met the cellist Julian Lloyd Webber (brother of Andrew, now Lord Lloyd-Webber). He had heard about my reconstruction of Sullivan's cello concerto from Sir Charles Mackerras, and I discovered that he had known about the original and had earlier expressed a hope that it might be brought back to life one day. The concerto was indeed another project that was making some progress although essentially it was now out of my hands. Sir Charles had my second version, and he was making various changes to it prior to publication by Weinberger.

There was another Spaghetti Opera evening at Terrazza-Est; this time I was playing for Geoffrey Shovelton. That gradually became a regular date, but not in Chancery Lane as the restaurant had moved to a basement at 109 Fleet Street near Ludgate Circus. I always enjoyed these evenings as we were fed as well as being paid: we often had pasta e fagioli soup as a starter, and that was a meal in itself. There was also a female singer, usually a soprano, and Geoffrey wasn't always the male singer, and so I got to know quite a number of artists, and my knowledge of the operatic repertoire increased by leaps and bounds. One thing that had stopped by the time I started to do these regularly was the banging on trays by the waiters after each item: this had been a feature of the evenings when the restaurant was in Chancery Lane.

There were several customers who came specifically for the opera, and there was one man from the Netherlands who would get very annoyed if other customers were talking too loudly and obviously not listening to the music. "Please be quiet!" he would say (fairly regularly and quite audibly) if it was a noisy evening. Sometimes there were office parties celebrating something or other, and these could become quite boisterous (I remember one group throwing bread rolls at each other) making it difficult for the singers. On one occasion Geoffrey had just finished singing "Nessun dorma" from

Puccini's *Turandot* (hardly the quietest of arias) when someone from a particularly noisy group came up and said "Could you sing 'Nessun dorma'?" "I've just sung it" said Geoffrey, pointedly. I really felt for the singers in these situations; I don't know how they kept going. They would often walk round the restaurant while performing, and if it was a really noisy evening I would have great difficulty in hearing them myself although that was exceptional; sometimes it was very quiet. But it was always good fun to be there, and we got to know the manager, Luigi, very well. Being in Fleet Street we were often among the first to hear of some major news item as many journalists dined at Terrazza-Est, and they would tell Luigi what would be appearing in the following morning's papers; Luigi would then pass this on to us.

I also got some work with New Sadler's Wells Opera as a répétiteur. One of the operas was Verdi's *La Traviata* which I didn't know well, but the other one was *HMS Pinafore* which I did know: the first rehearsals took place in September. Shortly before this Ken Barclay and I played some duets at one of the lunchtime sessions in the foyer of the Royal Festival Hall. There was now plenty of variety in what I was doing, and I was thinking less and less of trying to find a full-time job. But all of these activities would have to continue if I was going to survive as a free-lance performer, and there was no guarantee that any of them would do so. I was back at Il Boccalino in St Leonards at the beginning of October for more performances of *La Bohème*, and this was followed by more rehearsals at Sadler's Wells. Then came another hospital tour, this one for West Midlands Artlink, with dates in Whitchurch, Birmingham, Oswestry and Hanley, and there were concerts with The Magic of D'Oyly Carte in Ramsgate and Southend. I also played for Studs and Bustles, a quartet formed by my D'Oyly Carte colleague Jane Metcalfe which consisted of former Company members.

At the beginning of November Geoffrey Shovelton and I had another meeting with Victor Emery at the Savoy. This was to discuss a second promotion for the hotel following the success of the tour in West Germany and Austria in 1984; again we were to provide some cabaret. But this time it was to be five days in Rome, and we would be in just one venue: the Roma Inn. I hadn't been to Rome, and it was yet another chance to combine business with pleasure. Geoffrey felt the same way, and we were more than happy to take it on. We flew to Rome on Tuesday November 12: no problems this time with baggage. We were surprised to see a large number of Japanese on the plane (November wasn't the tourist season), but it turned out that they were Catholic priests who were presumably on a pilgrimage to St Peter's. As usual, we were in a smaller establishment: the Hotel Portoghesi in the Via dei Portoghesi. We were only performing in the evening, and so we spent each day sightseeing. The Pantheon and the Piazza Navona (supposedly the centre of Rome) were both quite near our hotel, and we also saw the Castel Sant'Angelo, the Colosseum, the Trevi Fountain and the huge Victor Emmanuel monument. We even managed to get into St Peter's where I was surprised to see, just inside the main entrance, the monument to the Royal Stuarts: Charles Edward ('Bonnie Prince Charlie'), his father (styled James III) and his brother Henry who eventually became a cardinal.

Our first performance at the Roma Inn was on November 13. As he had done before, Victor Emery gave a short history of the Savoy, and then Geoffrey and I came on to do our bit. Later, again as on the previous tour, Geoffrey sang non-G&S numbers, this time Italian arias and Neapolitan songs. The second evening was slightly different. The piano had been moved to the other side of the stage, and the audience was nearly all American; this was useful as there wasn't a language problem, and they were more at home with G&S. We were not due to fly back until the 17th, and we had already been informed that we were not staying on in Rome but were going down to Positano on the Amalfi Coast south of Naples. This was an added bonus. We were not quite sure what else we would have to do, but we were prepared for anything.

On November 15 we met up with Victor and his wife Jennifer who were staying in the Grand Hotel whose standard equalled that of the Savoy; we also met Jennifer's brother Julian Wontner who was then living in Venice. After lunch, Victor, Jennifer, Geoffrey and I set off for Positano in a BMW that Victor had hired. We drove past the famous Monte Cassino Abbey (restored after war-time bombing) and eventually arrived in Naples, unfortunately just as the sun was setting. During an unsuccessful attempt to find Pompeii we got involved in a classic traffic jam: lines of cars converging at a hub from which several roads radiate, with us in the middle of it and horns blasting continuously. But we managed to get out of this, and we finally arrived at Positano. The hotel, Le Sirenuse, had been in the family of the man who greeted us (a marchese whose name was Aldo Sersale), one of three brothers who were now running it, for about two hundred years before becoming yet another leading hotel of the world. Geoffrey and I still didn't know what we would have to do, but the hospitality was so good that we just went along with it. Later, as we expected, we were summoned to the piano, but this time it was rather more informal. We were told that we might be appearing on Italian TV the following day, but nothing came of this; there was also going to be a trip to Capri, but that didn't happen either. We were given cod Italian names here: Geoffrey, whose middle name was Richard, became Riccardo Veltoni; I became Davide Mac-a-Roni.

David Mackie and Geoffrey Shovelton at Positano, Italy.

Positano, built into a huge cleft in the cliffs, was originally a fishing village, and at one time, before a road was contrived from the cliff top, it could only be approached by sea. The houses are all at different levels, seemingly one on top of the other, and the hotel, covering a large area, had several floors connected by endless flights of stairs. Next day, after breakfast, we were joined by Julian Wontner; we then went down to the beach where Julian took a photograph of Geoffrey and me. The beach was deserted at that time of year, but it was still fascinating to be there. We then came back to a magnificent lunch. There were about a dozen varieties of pasta, and there was a dessert table the like of which I had not seen in any of the hotels we had previously been in. It was such a magnificent display that those who had a camera photographed it before anyone started to eat anything. After this there was another informal session round the piano. One of the brothers played something; he and I then improvised a duet version of *Never on Sunday*. This informality suited Geoffrey whose voice was showing signs of strain, and he didn't sing. He was hoping to perform in the evening, but his voice had gone, and I had to step in by playing Neapolitan songs. Everyone joined in, and it didn't matter that Geoffrey couldn't sing as this trip to Positano was an addition to what we had originally been asked to do. Our last night there didn't finish until about 01.00.

On November 17 we said our goodbyes (to Victor and Jennifer as well as to our hosts) and set off in a Volvo for Naples where we had to catch a train to Rome. We were standing at one end of the large concourse when I noticed a lady at the far end who seemed to be interested in us. She eventually started to walk across (I couldn't have guessed what was coming), and to my amazement she said, in a strong Scottish accent, "Is that a Glasgow University scarf you're wearing?" Indeed it was. We had a brief conversation, and it turned out that she had been teaching science for a year at an American college in Naples. We then got our tickets, but we had to pay even more on the train itself as it turned out to be a luxury international service. When we got to Rome we were accosted by a taxi driver who persuaded us to let him take us to the airport, but he charged us more than twice what we had paid the driver who brought us into the city when we arrived. After a short verbal tussle we simply split the difference, gave him the money and walked away, the driver still yelling after us that it wasn't enough. But we reckoned that he wasn't an official driver, and he still did well enough out of it. I always hate situations like that, but Geoffrey didn't waste much time with him.

Our flight home was very full, the previous flight having been cancelled, and I'm quite sure that one of the passengers was none other than Terry Waite, the then Archbishop of

Canterbury (Robert Runcie)'s 'special envoy' who had helped to free several hostages and was himself held hostage for several years. If it wasn't Terry Waite it was certainly his double.

It had been another wonderful experience (yet another paid holiday), but apart from a number of subsequent single evening engagements in London it was the last such trip for us although I daresay the Savoy directors and their wives continued to enjoy the delights of these luxurious establishments.

I had previously been asked to play at Il Boccalino again at the end of December, and for the first time I found myself having to say no to something else, in this case another pantomime: an enviable position to be in, no doubt, but perhaps this would be the last time I would be at the wine bar, and having declined an offer from Phillip Charles I might not be asked to do a pantomime again and might end up with neither. But these situations would arise from time to time, and you had to bear other possibilities in mind when accepting any offer of work. Sometimes these would be financial considerations. I can't recall if I would have had more money for a pantomime, but I had already committed myself to Il Boccalino. Rehearsals started in St Leonards at the end of November.

There were more performances of *The Fantasticks*, some of which were in Eastbourne, but Fiona O'Neil wasn't available, and the Maurels were looking for a substitute. I had met an American singer Dorothy Maddison who was living in London, and as it was an American show I suggested that she might be approached. Dorothy was delighted to do it, and she was well received. There were also performances of *The Beggar's Opera*. Both were done several times throughout December, but I was back in London for Christmas as Ken Barclay and I were playing as the Gentlemen Duettists once again at the Festival Hall: this time it was an early evening session from 18.00-19.00. I then went down to

St Leonards for more work at Il Boccalino. We ended with two performances of *The Fantasticks* on New Year's Eve at the unusual times of 18.30 and 22.00. Thankfully, despite not having a Byers, Schwalbe tour to boost the finances, it had been a good year with some interesting developments.

II – 1986

Inow had several potential sources of employment, and these provided work, if at first intermittently. I was at Il Boccalino again on January 2, and there were various G&S and London Chamber Opera performances during the first three months. If I was free on a Monday night I would go to the CAA for the evening's entertainment by members, even if I wasn't playing there. It was always interesting to watch the performers, particularly those older members who had spent a lifetime in the business with a ten-minute act that they performed night after night up and down the country on a variety bill. One such was Jack 'quick on the draw' Crosbie who would come on to the stage with a large artist's pad. He would chat to the audience and tell jokes, all the while drawing something on the pad. A particular joke might have two contrasting characters in it, perhaps an old sailor with a beard and a Russian with a typical fur hat. At the punch line Jack would hold up the pad, and there would be the old sailor - polite applause. Then he would turn the pad upside down, and the drawing became the Russian with the hat - even more applause. Jack's wife Gladys was a Queen Mother look-alike. The first time I was in the bar at the CAA I saw what I thought to be a photograph of Her Majesty Queen Elizabeth the Queen Mother. I asked someone why it was there and was told "That's not the Queen Mum, it's Gladys Crosbie". There was a remarkable similarity.

If I was the pianist for the evening an act like Jack Crosbie's would only require me to play the performer on and play him (or her) off again, but I might have to play for singers, comedians (who often included songs in their acts), accordionists, trick violinists and others: 'variety' summed it up perfectly. There was seldom much rehearsal, and I was playing one night for an accordionist who had arrived late and just had time to hand me the music (in a manuscript book as it so often was) before he was 'on'. "It's quite straightforward", he said. "No repeats. Just keep going". I did as instructed, and it was indeed going reasonably well until I turned a page and was faced with a blank sheet of manuscript paper. There wasn't any more music, but the accordionist was still playing, and I had to attempt to busk at the keyboard to follow him. Luckily it was Scottish country dance music with which I was familiar, and we somehow finished together. I told him afterwards that the music just stopped halfway through, but he seemed to have no idea that it was incomplete. I wondered how other pianists had coped with it. On another occasion I was given music that had been folded up and put into the artist's inside jacket pocket. It was also held together with sticky tape, and when it was unfolded it wouldn't sit properly on the piano; for most of the time I was playing with one hand and holding the copy open with the other. At yet another concert I was handed a sheet with no music on it, just a series of letters (C-G-C and so on) which was simply a chord sequence that I was expected to 'fill out'. This was quite normal, but it was still very new to me: 'in at the deep end' indeed, but it was more useful experience, and you just had to keep going.

The stage at the CAA was very small, and there was a baby grand piano at one side (stage right). If I was playing for magicians such as Ali Bongo or Billy Wand I thought that being so near them I would see how they managed their tricks - like pouring liquid into a rolled-up newspaper - but of course I never did: the sleight of hand, even at close quarters, was amazing. Among many other people that I got to know at the CAA were fellow-Scot Kenny Gibson, Mary Morland (whose grandfather had been Edwin Adeler of Adeler and Sutton's Pierrots: her mother, Gwen Adeler, had also appeared in these shows as a pierrot) and comedienne Joy Graham who sang comic songs such as Joyce Grenfell's *Stately as a Galleon*. Joy was friendly with Frankie Vaughan's wife, and one night when Frankie was appearing at the Theatre Royal, Drury Lane she took me over to the theatre where I met both of them. Despite being a big name in those days he was very down-to-earth and approachable.

The first three months of 1986 were fairly quiet (as usual) although I gave a talk to the Sir Arthur Sullivan Society of which I would eventually become a vice-president, but it suddenly became quite busy in April. We had known for some time that there would be another Byers, Schwalbe tour which would include Canada for the first time; the première of the joint reconstruction of Sullivan's cello concerto by myself and Sir Charles Mackerras was also looming and was to take place in London. But this would be during the G&S tour, and I wouldn't be able to attend - a clash of dates of which there are so many in the free-lance world. However, there was to be a second performance in Manchester after I got back from North America, and I hoped that I would be able to attend that.

Our third Byers, Schwalbe tour with The Best of Gilbert and Sullivan began on April 1 when we flew to Boston MA. Our personnel was the same as before – Vivian Tierney, Lorraine Daniels, Kenneth Sandford, Geoffrey Shovelton, Alistair Donkin and me – although the team would change from time to time as these tours continued. We carried no scenery, but the individual artists might have an occasional hand prop such as a fan for *The Mikado*: as Archibald Grosvenor in *Patience* Ken Sandford had a large blonde wig which looked wonderfully incongruous with a dinner jacket. But Lorraine also had imitation pistols for a scene from *The Pirates of Penzance*. At Heathrow they had shown up in her luggage which she was asked to open by a large and intimidating policeman. She then had to take the 'guns' out and explain that they were props for a scene in an opera. The explanation was accepted although the policeman retained a stony face throughout. Lorraine was then allowed to keep the props, but she had to sign a receipt for them, and they had to travel in the hold. I can't think what the reaction to this would be today, but it was bad enough then: and on April Fool's Day.

This was the longest tour yet: just over three weeks. The day after our arrival we met Royston Nash, the musical director of D'Oyly Carte when I joined in 1975. Having tried to find permanent work at home since leaving the Company in 1979 he was now conducting several orchestras in Massachusetts. It was good to see him again. Our first two concerts were in Boston on April 3 and 4. They were part of the Wang Celebrity Series, and they were held in the Jordan Hall of the North Eastern Conservatory of Music: Doug Schwalbe came up from New York for the first one. We now had to drive south to New Bedford MA, and we hired a minivan which had adequate seating for six and also much more luggage space. The concert at New Bedford was part of the Merrill Lynch International Series; it was held in the Zeiterion Theatre, and it was followed by a very nice reception. After New Bedford we flew to Washington DC for two concerts in the Baird Auditorium at the Natural History Museum where we had performed in October 1984. While we were there we met David and Ann Stone and Ralph MacPhail, Jr., G&S experts whom I got to know well over the years, and their first words were "Dame Bridget's will has just been published". We might now find out if she had left money to get the D'Oyly Carte Opera Company on the road again. A New D'Oyly Carte Opera Company was indeed formed, and an advertisement for the post of general manager soon appeared in the press, applications to be in by August 14, 1986. The position was eventually held by Richard 'Dick' Condon who had been the general manager of the Theatre Royal, Norwich.

After Washington we had our first concerts in Canada with dates in Lethbridge and Calgary in Alberta. We flew first of all to Calgary, via Omaha NE and Salt Lake City UT (a distance of not far off two thousand miles), where the rest of the group took another flight to Lethbridge: I had to stay in Calgary as our concert there was with an orchestra, and this time I was going to conduct it. I rehearsed the orchestra at the Calgary Centre for the Performing Arts during the afternoon of April 8, and I then had to drive to Lethbridge as our concert there was that same evening: it was presented by the University of Lethbridge Students' Union at the University Theatre. I asked someone if it would be difficult to get to Lethbridge, and I received what was probably a stock answer: "You can't miss it. There's only one road". He was right, but I then had to find the venue, and I didn't get there until 19.45. The rest of the group were anxiously awaiting my arrival, and I had just enough time to change before the concert started, as they so often did, at 20.00.

The following day I had a more leisurely drive back to Calgary. I had a wonderful view of the Rocky Mountains, and I stopped briefly at Fort Macleod (so many Scottish connections in Canada) where I wandered round the old stockade. Back again in Calgary I was interviewed in a CBC studio by Liz Palmer, originally from the UK, who had worked for the BBC; when I got to the Centre for the Performing Arts I was interviewed again, this time by David Gell, originally from Calgary but who had also worked for the BBC. This was all rather like the 1978 tour of the United States and Canada. I hadn't conducted an orchestra since the *Gilbert & Sullivan Afloat* performances in Sunderland in 1982, but I did know how our artists were going to perform, and it all went very well. The second flautist, Phillipa Waugh, had actually played in the D'Oyly Carte orchestra although not in my time. The concert was in the Jack Singer Concert Hall which seated some eighteen hundred people.

The next two concerts were in Portland ME. These were with the Portland Symphony Orchestra in the City Hall

Auditorium, but again I had to step aside in favour of their regular conductor Bruce Hangen. The first concert went well enough although again, as with Stephen Gunzenhauser in Wilmington DE, there were ragged edges that were unavoidable in the circumstances. It is almost impossible to do a concert of this type on one rehearsal when the orchestra and conductor are not familiar with the music and, more specifically, the artists' own distinctive way of performing. While I would never have achieved the status of either Stephen Gunzenhauser or Bruce Hangen I was still able to conduct the concert in Calgary without the inevitable mishaps in Wilmington and Portland simply because I was as familiar with the music (and its interpretation) as the artists themselves. And I had to rehearse the orchestra *without* the singers: the orchestra only saw them for the first time at the concert. This was a point that I was keen to put to Doug Schwalbe if there were going to be further concerts with orchestras: letting someone else conduct them with just one rehearsal could result in poor performances that might jeopardise future engagements. As in Wilmington the second concert was better for having had a trial run, but that only proves the point I'm making: by the second concert each conductor was becoming familiar with the music and the artists.

The next three concerts were in Cedar Falls IA (in the twelve hundred-seater UNI Auditorium at the University of Northern Iowa, UNI Artists Series), Sioux Center IA (in Dordt College Chapel Auditorium, another twelve hundred-seater, sponsored by Allied Concert Services) and Hesston College KS (part of the Hesston Performing Arts Series and held in the Yost Center, a thirteen hundred-seater that doubled as a sports arena). The flights between Cedar Falls and Sioux City (via Minneapolis MN) were in small planes, and when we arrived we found that four of our cases were missing as all of our luggage would not fit into one of these planes. The girls had an extra case each for evening dresses, and one of the missing ones was Vivian's dress case; mine contained my toilet bag, shaving gear and all of the music. At Sioux City we hired a twelve-seater van and drove some fifty miles north to Sioux Center. Luckily, we were not performing that evening, and the cases arrived the following morning, but I resolved that from then on I would always keep the music folders in my hand luggage.

We travelled from Hesston to Detroit MI where we were met by Harry Benford, Professor of Naval Architecture and Marine Engineering at the University of Michigan and a keen lover of G&S, who had organised transport for us to Jackson MI for our next concert at the Potter Center Music Hall at Jackson Community College. Harry and his wife Betty had founded a support group FUMGASS (Friends of the University of Michigan Gilbert and Sullivan Society) which published a journal GASBAG (Gilbert and Sullivan Boys and Girls). They came to the concert with some other people from Ann Arbor MI, and we saw them again on a future tour. I also met my cousins, Jim and Pat, whom I had seen on the first tour in February 1984. I spent some time with them, but I nearly missed the concert as they said that they would take me there but then got lost: we finally arrived at the venue just ten minutes before the concert was due to start. The singers were understandably worried at my non-appearance (and so soon after my similar late arrival at Lethbridge), but the sponsor was beginning to tear his hair out. The day of our concert in Jackson, Sunday April 20, was the day on which our joint reconstruction of Sullivan's cello concerto had its première at London's Barbican Hall with Julian Lloyd Webber as the soloist and the London Symphony Orchestra conducted by Sir Charles Mackerras.

The final concert on this tour was at Pike's Peak Center in Colorado Springs CO, sponsored by the Colorado Springs Chorale. This was the opening event of a five-day Gilbert & Sullivan Festival which included two performances with the Chorale of Sullivan's cantata *The Golden Legend*, conducted by Donald P. Jenkins, on April 25 and 27. Geoffrey Shovelton and Vivian Tierney were singing in these along with John Ayldon who had just arrived from London. Also in Colorado Springs with his wife Joy was Robin Wilson, son of Lord Wilson, the former Prime Minister Harold Wilson, who had been a D'Oyly Carte trustee since 1975. Like his father, Robin was a keen G&S fan, and he was the driving force behind these performances of *The Golden Legend*. He gave a talk on the morning of April 22 which I attended. After our concert that evening we went our separate ways. Geoffrey and Vivian stayed on for the performances of *The Golden Legend*, Alistair Donkin went to Texas, and Ken Sandford, Lorraine Daniels and I went back to London, arriving at Heathrow in the morning of April 24. It had been an excellent tour.

One downturn in the gradual build-up of work was that I had now severed my connection with the group calling itself The Magic of D'Oyly Carte. Having been run initially by Gordon MacKenzie, latterly in association with Second City Management, the group was now being run by its members, and as a new broom sweeps clean I found that there were a number of changes, one of them being that my services as the musical director were no longer required. I might have been able to stay on as the second pianist, but I declined to do this. Luckily, there were plenty of other opportunities to continue with G&S, and I also felt that if I couldn't maintain a hold in the free-lance world without one specific source of work then I shouldn't be in the business at all. Ken Sandford and Alistair Donkin were both heavily involved in the running of the group, and it was always awkward when we were doing the Byers, Schwalbe tours. If they wished to discuss their future plans they tended to do this out of my presence; at breakfast they would often sit at a separate table leaving Vivian, Lorraine, Geoffrey and me to occupy another table. I was sorry not to be doing the concerts, but I could only hope that other work would be forthcoming to fill the gaps.

On Sunday April 27, just three days after we returned from the Byers, Schwalbe tour, I was in Manchester to hear the second performance of the cello concerto, part of an all-Sullivan evening. Julian Lloyd Webber was again the soloist, but the orchestra this time was the Manchester Camerata, and the conductor was Brian Wright. The concert opened with the overture to *The Yeomen of the Guard* followed by the concerto. The second half consisted of excerpts from *The Pirates of Penzance*; this was introduced by none other than Donald Adams who also sang the Pirate King. Frederic was sung by Philip Creasy who had been a D'Oyly Carte chorister in our last season (1981-82), and Mabel, by Sandra Dugdale who had been a guest artist with us during that same season. Major-General Stanley was sung by Patrick McGuigan whom I didn't know. Hearing the concerto for the first time was quite a thrill, but it almost didn't happen. The soloist enters after a 30-bar introduction; as Julian played his first note the string broke, and he had to leave the stage to get another one. Once this had been attended to, the performance started again and continued without a hitch. The concerto was recorded by Julian Lloyd Webber with the London Symphony Orchestra conducted by Sir Charles Mackerras. Later, there were further recordings.

At the beginning of May I received a phone call from Dione Livingstone, an actress who had written a couple of two-hander plays about the women in the lives of Chopin and Liszt. In these, Dione would play the lady concerned ('George Sand', born Amantine-Lucile-Aurore Dupin, in the Chopin and the Countess Marie d'Agoult in the Liszt), and she had found two pianists who had taken on the task of not only playing when appropriate but also acting the part of each composer: Oliver Williams as Chopin and Jonathan Cohen as Liszt. Dione had now written a third play, this time about Brahms and Clara Schumann, and she was looking for a third pianist. I don't know how she got hold of my name, but clearly she had no idea if I looked remotely like Brahms (I don't) or if I could act. I was a bit concerned about my ability to learn the dialogue, but I decided to stretch myself by accepting the challenge. And of course I also had to play some music: she even wanted to have part of Schumann's relatively unknown violin concerto which I had to write out from having listened to a recording. I managed to avoid playing some of Brahms's more densely written pieces, but it was the dialogue that I found difficult: when we did the play I had to have bits of it written on the music and other bits lying on the piano. But in the end it was quite an enjoyable, if rather different, experience.

The year continued as usual with a London Airs concert in Swindon in June, London Chamber Opera performances, Spaghetti Opera at Terrazza-Est and Monday nights at the CAA where on one occasion I played for a fellow-Scot Glen Hayes who had appeared regularly in *Take the High Road*.

I was soon working again for Michael and Brenda Maurel. While continuing with the serious opera performances at Il Boccalino *The Fantasticks* had been such a success that they decided to do more lighter fare, and this time they chose *The Pirates of Penzance*. Feeling that they needed more space they moved to George Street Hall in Hastings, but the only way they could get a licence for alcohol was to open it as a club, and at some £60 per annum for membership this was not as popular as Il Boccalino; sadly, it ultimately failed. For the moment, however, *Pirates* went on at the end of June and into July. But there were also rehearsals for the next production which was to be *The Boy Friend*. This very successful show had first appeared in 1953, and among the younger cast was Larry Drew who played Bobby van Heusen. Now, over thirty years later, Michael and Brenda asked Larry to take part in their production, this time as the older Lord Brockhurst; they even persuaded John Heawood, a Canadian who had choreographed the original production, to get involved. Also in the cast was the actress and singer Sheila Mathews [sic] whom I met in London in July. Later, I had to drive John Heawood down to Hastings for rehearsals, and it was interesting to hear him talk about his life in the business. He had even appeared in the Brent Walker film of *Iolanthe* (in a non-speaking, non-singing role) which was made after D'Oyly Carte closed in 1982. *The Boy Friend* opened on August 23 and ran for a week.

Before this, at the beginning of August, and with some of the artists I had met at the CAA, I went down to Babbacombe in Devon to do some music hall, but when we got there we found that there had been poor publicity for it and there was a very small audience: scarcely more than ourselves. We were told that we could cancel the performance, but having driven a long way we said that we would do it. The manager, the box-office lady, the janitor and the ice-cream girl all came in to swell the ranks, and the show went very well, something that often happens in a situation like that.

Early in September my friend Martin Delgado (son of Alan with whom I had worked on *Have a Nice Day!*) was married in the Ukranian Cathedral in Duke Street, London. It was an interesting service, and, one I had not experienced before. This was just one of many social occasions that I was able to attend as I was now living in London. As a free-lance musician I could organise my life round events such as this even if it meant turning down the offer of a job on a particular day although even with all of the contacts that I had made there were still many days when I wasn't working.

Saturday September 13 was another interesting one-off when I went to Althorp, home of Earl Spencer (the father of Diana who was now the Princess of Wales), to play for some entertainment which consisted of excerpts, with dialogue, from *The Mikado*. This had been organised by John Gale, a friend of Geoffrey Shovelton, who lived near Althorp and knew the Spencers well. Our group consisted of Patricia Cope, Judith Buckle and Caroline Tatlow as the 'three little maids', Geoffrey as Nanki-Poo and Adrian Lawson as Ko-Ko. The Gales kindly provided us with lunch, and we then rehearsed before moving to Althorp. We were given a room to change in, and we were told that it had been Prince William's nursery. Earl Spencer, who had had a stroke some years before, and his wife Raine (daughter of the novelist Barbara Cartland) were an excellent host and hostess, and we were very well looked after. I would be there again.

There was another concert with Geoffrey, this time in Codsall in Staffordshire on September 20, and the following day I was again at Appleby Magna where there was a triple celebration for Harold and Hazel Oakley's Ruby Wedding, Harold's eightieth birthday and the christening of their daughter Christine and son-in-law Simon's son Tom. (The Oakleys later moved to Guernsey to be closer to Christine and Simon who lived on Jersey.) This was followed by a London Airs concert in Bolton on the 26th and rehearsals for Dione Livingstone's new play about Clara Schumann and Brahms which she had called *Clara and Old Prickly* (Brahms frequently visited a Vienna café called the Red Hedgehog). The first performance was in Burgh House, Hampstead, on Sunday October 5; with my dialogue written out everywhere I managed to get through it without too much difficulty.

A week later I started working for Andrew Meadmore. Andrew was the son of Norman Meadmore, a former stage director for D'Oyly Carte. Later, having worked initially with Tom Round and Donald Adams, Norman set up The World of Gilbert and Sullivan. Andrew, one of four brothers, now ran the company, renamed London Savoyards, and regularly presented G&S productions in London. I never got the opportunity to conduct any of these, but I did get regular work as the répétiteur during rehearsals. A number of my former colleagues also worked for Andrew, but there were other regulars, both principals and choristers, that I soon knew well. One was the soprano Katie Morrell whom I would meet again when I returned to Scotland, and another was the bass John Megoran with whom I shared an interest in river steamers although for John it was more than an interest. His father was the well-known marine artist Winston Megoran, and aside from his singing (he had studied at London's Guildhall) he had always wanted to go to sea; when I met him he already had qualifications to sail as the master of smaller domestic passenger vessels. He latterly ran, and was master of, the paddle steamer *Kingswear Castle*, but he had also sailed as master of the paddle steamer *Waverley* on which I had been an assistant purser in 1961. My first work for Andrew Meadmore was three days of rehearsing *The Pirates of Penzance*.

Around this time, although I can't remember how it came about, I started to do some teaching at the Academy of Live and Recorded Arts (ALRA), founded in 1979 by Sorrel Carson, which was housed in part of the Royal Victoria Patriotic Building on the edge of Wandsworth Common. As usual, I didn't find the teaching particularly satisfying, and this job didn't last very long.

Towards the end of October I played for Michael Wakeham who had been in D'Oyly Carte from 1958-61. I had already met Michael as he was a friend of Conrad Leonard. They were both masons, and I was now beginning to play regularly at masonic functions. The entertainment at these came after the particular lodge's business which was usually the installing of a new master. The singer (often a lady) and I would wait outside until we were invited to enter, but as several of the men I played for were masons themselves they would sometimes go in before we were due to perform, and they would take me in too, introducing me to the lodge as 'worshipful brother Mackie'. And so I got a hint of what went on at these meetings although I wasn't supposed to be there. (My grandfather had been a master-mason, but my father had never shown any interest in the subject: if he had been a mason he might have persuaded me to become one.) Many of the lodge meetings were held at the Connaught Rooms in Great Queen Street, and I discovered that the manager there was André Eldon-Erdington who had organised our 'sing for your supper' visits to the Arts Club in Dover Street when I was with D'Oyly Carte. One of the singers I worked with regularly was Niven Miller, a fellow-Scot.

Another contact I made around this time was with the Hepburn Starey Blind Aid Society which met on Thursday afternoons to provide an hour's music for blind and partially blind members. The concerts were organised by the accompanists – Ken Barclay, Geoffrey Vince or Linda Ang - who worked on a rota system depending on who was available. There would be a singer or an instrumentalist, and the accompanist would also play a couple of solos. My introduction to this came about through deputising for Ken. Later, I took over from him, and later still I became the sole organiser. On that first occasion I played for a lady whose name was Dorothy Copeland. The concerts were originally held at the New Gallery Centre in Regent Street, but they were latterly given at St Columba's Church of Scotland in Pont Street. Tea was served afterwards; this was organised by a number of ladies, several of whom were also Scots.

On December 1 I did my last teaching at ALRA, and this was followed by more work for Andrew Meadmore, this time for *The Mikado*: these rehearsals were held in St Gabriel's Church Hall in Pimlico. I only did three days, December 2-5, as I was about to do another pantomime *Dick Whittington and his Cat* for Phillip Charles. Ealing had been dropped from the touring schedule after my first pantomime in 1983-84, but we were still on the Dunfermline/Barnstaple circuit, and we travelled up to Dunfermline on Friday December 5 for a week's rehearsal which started on the Saturday. The show ran from December 12-20; once again there were early morning performances at 09.30 which we hated. Audrey Mortimer was still providing the dancers, and among this year's cast were Paul Twain and Elaine Harrison who would also take part in next year's show, a fairly unusual occurrence in these Charles Haley pantomimes. During the week's run we had another indoor football match on the afternoon of the 17th.

Another member of this year's cast was Ralph Meanley who was primarily a singer rather than an actor, again a fairly unusual thing in these pantomimes. Ralph was particularly fond of old ballads like *The Road to Mandalay*, and as I enjoyed them too (we performed some in our Victorian programmes with London Airs) we decided to keep in touch after the pantomime to see if we could take this idea any further. Ballad concerts had been very popular in the early years of the twentieth century; perhaps we might reawaken interest in them.

After the last performance we had to strike the set, pack it and the costumes into the van, and head south to Barnstaple in time to rehearse the other team of dancers on the Sunday morning. We opened in Barnstaple on December 22 and played for three days with a matinée on Christmas Eve. Again we had our Christmas lunch in a pub, but we also had a free day on Boxing Day, and we were able to relax more than usual. We then had another seven performances including a matinée on the 31st. At the end of another year, having made even more contacts, I could afford to be quietly optimistic that I could keep going as a free-lance performer, but with mortgage repayments and a car to run there was never going to be much money left over for any luxuries.

III – 1987

The year began with the last four pantomime performances. Was this going to be the pattern from now on? It was the third time in four years that I had been in Barnstaple over the holiday season: not that it was a holiday for us although I was more than happy to be working. We ended the run on Saturday January 3, and I headed back to London. January was busier than usual as I had a full week working for Andrew Meadmore (*Ruddigore* this time), a number of Terrazza-Est engagements and some Opera Players rehearsals; I also played at the CAA. Early in February we had our fourth Byers, Schwalbe tour with eleven concerts in the United States and just one in Canada; we now had our first change of personnel as Vivian Tierney had earlier indicated that she would not be coming on this tour. She was doing very well in the operatic world, and she had three major roles in 1986. We were sorry to lose her, but we had to find a substitute, and we were lucky to acquire the services of Sandra Dugdale. We were all supposed to be ex-members of D'Oyly Carte, and Sandra, strictly, was not. But she had been a guest artist with the Company in its last season, and that seemed to satisfy Byers, Schwalbe. She had also been in several of the Brent Walker films of the Savoy Operas.

Geoffrey Shovelton and Douglas Schwalbe at the
East India Club, London.

Our first two concerts were in Washington DC at the Baird Auditorium in the Natural History Museum on The Mall where we had previously performed. I had often been amused by the various attempts to spell D'Oyly Carte, and I had to smile again at a notice in our hotel which read 'Welcome Doyle Car' [sic]. From Washington we moved to Andover MA where the concert, part of the Classical Ruby Series, was held in the J. Everett Collins Center for the Performing Arts, a vast auditorium which made dialogue and fast numbers very difficult. We slowed it all down. We were then taken out for a meal by a couple who were in charge of finance at the venue. They seemed very pleased with us, not just as performers but as people, saying that some of their artists had demanded everything but had given very little: a nice compliment. The next stop was at Burlington VT (in the fourteen hundred-seater Flynn Theatre for the Performing Arts) where Sandra's "Poor wandering one!" (*The Pirates of Penzance*) went so well that she had to come back onstage to acknowledge the thunderous applause, the first time that had happened to any of the singers. Burlington was followed by Oneonta NY where the concert, for the Oneonta Concert Association, was in the Oneonta High School Auditorium: quite a good hall but not a very good piano. The journey to Oneonta involved a flight from Boston with Catskill Airlines. We couldn't find a check-in desk for them, and no-one seemed to have heard of them. Alistair Donkin spoke to an official, but he hadn't heard of them either. Eventually someone told us that Catskill had been taken over by Continental; as we set off to find them he added "Look out for a man in a flying helmet and a long white scarf!" We did find the desk eventually, tucked away in a remote corner, and it made us realise just how vast the whole air network is in the United States. We were often in small planes, but by not flying very high we had good views of the countryside. Being early February there was a lot of snow which made the constant travelling quite difficult at times.

Our next concert was for the Arts Council Inc. in Gainesville GA, held in the Pearce Auditorium. Georgia was the furthest south I had been on the east side of the United States. Then came two concerts with orchestra, both of which I conducted. The first of these was in Columbus OH for the Columbus Association for the Performing Arts, held in the wonderful Ohio Theatre, and the second, our only concert in Canada, was at the Roy Thomson Hall in Toronto, Ontario for the Corporation of Massey and Thomson Hall. The day we arrived was the coldest day of the year so far, but despite the temperature the performance that evening was possibly the best one we had yet given on these tours. Some members of the orchestra had played for D'Oyly Carte on the 1976 and 1978 tours of North America; at least one of them remembered me. While we were here I met yet another cousin from Greenock who had emigrated many years before; we caught up on family affairs.

The remaining concerts on this tour were in the United States. The first of these was at Monmouth IL, presented by Monmouth in the Arts in Monmouth College Auditorium which had a very good Steinway piano. Next, we were in Quincy IL (in Quincy Senior High School for the Quincy Civic Music Association), Flint MI (in the University of Michigan's four hundred-seater Flint Theatre which was just the right size for us) and finally St Joseph MI on the east shore of Lake Michigan. The journey from Flint was in a Greyhound coach, and it took all of five hours, luckily with a 20-minute comfort stop. We passed through Kalamazoo whose name I knew from the song *I've Got a Gal in Kalamazoo*.

This final concert had been organised by the all-female Civic Benefit Club, and it took place in Lakeshore High School Auditorium which seated about eleven hundred people. The piano here was particularly difficult, and I had to play everything fairly loudly just to ensure that the notes sounded: at the rehearsal I had discovered that any attempt at subtle playing resulted in half of the keys sticking. Despite this the concert went quite well, and there was another reception afterwards. We were always treated well on these tours, particularly by sponsors (the ladies here had been among the friendliest group we had yet encountered), and as a parting gift we were given some souvenirs of St Joseph. On the flight back we found that we were travelling with the Academy of St Martin-in-the-Fields who had been on a ten-day tour around Chicago and Milwaukee. We arrived on Monday February 23, and I immediately had to go to a rehearsal of

HMS Pinafore which Andrew Meadmore was putting on. I didn't get home until 19.30, but as I was required every day that week I didn't fully relax after the tour until the Saturday. I also had to play at a masonic function on the Thursday, and I went to the annual CAA Ball on Sunday March 1. I was certainly keeping busy although sometimes there were just too many engagements one after the other: 'feast or famine' again, but you had to take what work was offered or someone else would do it. I wasn't complaining.

Many of my sources of income had now been established, and these were the basis of my future working life. With the closure of D'Oyly Carte in 1982 Andrew Meadmore's London Savoyards productions were very popular, and *HMS Pinafore* was presented no less than three times in 1987, in February, March and September. *The Mikado*, easily the most popular of the operas, was given in April, and *The Pirates of Penzance*, one of the top three, was presented in August. There was also a performance of *The Gondoliers* in June with the usual week's rehearsal at St Gabriel's Church Hall in Pimlico and some extra rehearsals at Hammerton Hall in Stockwell.

Andrew used some well-known singers such as Forbes Robinson and Johanna Peters, and also a number of people from D'Oyly Carte such as principals John Ayldon and Tom Lawler and some former choristers, but every so often he would ask someone for whom it was a new experience. One was the actor Norman Rossington whose face I knew from having watched countless old films. For the *Gondoliers* production Andrew had asked Norman to take on the role of the Duke of Plaza-Toro, and he asked me if I would give him a separate coaching session. Norman duly came round to my tiny flat in Islington, and we went through the Duke's music. After a few shots at his Act 1 song "In enterprise of martial kind" with its tongue-twisting verse endings of which the first is "That celebrated,/Cultivated,/Underrated/Nobleman…" he said "I can't do this. I'll have to tell him to get someone else".

I forget who did do it, but Norman Rossington didn't add the Duke of Plaza-Toro to his c.v.

Another opera group that I played for occasionally was Beaufort Opera whose regular pianist was Margaret Eaves, the sister of Sylvia Eaves who was the soprano in Ken Barclay's Parlour Quartet group. I would meet Margaret again some years later. From time to time I also played at another Italian restaurant called Parco: it was a similar situation to that of Terrazza-Est. You never knew where you might be asked to play, even if just once, and I always tried to take on anything that was offered, even if the payment wasn't particularly good, as one job often led to another. It was one way to build up a portfolio of contacts, and you had to try to present yourself as someone who was willing, able, reliable and, particularly, a good sight-reader - a very useful accomplishment in the situations I often found myself in, standing in for singers at short notice without having any idea as to what they might be performing.

Much of this work was in London, but there were also regular dates further afield. I was in Manchester twice in 1987 for meetings of the Gilbert and Sullivan Society. The second occasion, on September 5, was their fifty-fifth anniversary dinner at which I had to propose the toast The Immortal Memory of Gilbert and Sullivan. There were also Two of Hearts concerts with Geoffrey Shovelton and Vivian Tierney, the first one in Bolton in February, organised by Geoffrey's cousin Irene, and a second one in Urmston in November organised by Valerie Bailey, a fan of D'Oyly Carte whom I got to know well. Trips out of the capital were always very welcome.

As well as the regular work there were the usual one-offs from time to time. There was no foreign tour this year for the Savoy Hotel, but Geoffrey and I were asked to perform at a function at the Berkeley Hotel (part of the Savoy group) in London in January. This was more like our performances at

Terrazza-Est, and Geoffrey sang a wide variety of songs. There were other similar dates. Apart from the concerts on the two previous Byers, Schwalbe tours I still wasn't doing any regular conducting, but in April I was asked to take a rehearsal of the Reading Symphony Orchestra. They were playing the fifth symphony by Glazunov (1865-1936); that was quite an experience after G&S.

But perhaps the most interesting one-off was a performance of *Trial by Jury* at the Mansion House on May 8. The then Lord Mayor, Sir David Rowe-Ham (a keen lover of G&S), played the Judge, being listed in the programme as Mr Richard Whittington. The Plaintiff was played by Patricia Cope who was married to Andrew Meadmore. Although not ex-D'Oyly Carte, Patricia had sung most of the leading soprano roles in Andrew's G&S productions. Geoffrey Shovelton was the Defendant, and Michael Wakeham, the Counsel for the Plaintiff. Michael's wife Anne Stuart (again not ex-D'Oyly Carte) played the First Bridesmaid, and John Ayldon and John Banks (both ex-D'Oyly Carte) played the Usher and the Foreman of the Jury respectively. The Associate was Christopher Walford (not ex-D'Oyly Carte). The chorus consisted of a large number of mainly ex-D'Oyly Carte personnel, some of them from well before my time; they were listed collectively with the instrumentalists and me as Chorus and Orchestra of The Opera House, Threadneedle Street under the direction of Mr David Mackie. The performance was staged by Cynthia Morey, and the set and costumes were provided by Albert Truelove. The evening, part of the Lord Mayor's Year of Office, was in aid of the Prince's Youth Business Trust Appeal with tickets at £50.00 to include a champagne reception with a buffet supper following the performance. That was certainly one of the highlights of the year; it was also one of Albert Truelove's last involvements with his beloved G&S as he died in August. The music at his funeral was all by Sullivan; Meston Reid, former D'Oyly

Carte principal tenor, sang the well-known aria from *The Yeomen of the Guard* whose words are so often sung or quoted on such occasions: "Is life a boon?/If so, it must befall/ That Death, whene'er he call,/Must call too soon". There was a memorial service for Albert at the Savoy Chapel on November 9.

I was still doing arrangements as and when required, and I had been asked by London Chamber Opera to rearrange the orchestration of Mozart's *Bastien and Bastienne*. I was to keep the original string parts as a string quintet and turn the two oboes and two horns (with, in one number, two flutes in place of the oboes) into a wind quintet of flute, oboe, clarinet, bassoon and horn. Whatever I was doing during the day I could always burn the midnight oil to do any writing, and this occupied me for a month between April and May. The performance was given with Sullivan's *Cox and Box* at the Reading Festival on June 9, the performers being Ian Kennedy, Robert Bateman and Christine Page (Christine becoming *Mrs* Bouncer in *Cox and Box*) with Ken Barclay conducting.

Another writing project was connected with Sullivan's cello concerto. The full score had been published concurrently with the first performance in 1986, but I had also been asked by the publishers, Weinberger, if I would prepare a piano reduction. I had completed a version by February 1986, but as he had told me to thin out my original reconstruction of the concerto Sir Charles Mackerras also told me that I should thin out the piano reduction. I remember him saying that apart from making it easier to play you should never put too much of the original into a reduction. "Make them buy a full score!" The second version was ready by the beginning of March 1986, but it was not until May of this year that it was finally published.

At the beginning of May I received a letter from Clare Lambert, the honorary secretary of the Gilbert and Sullivan Society, asking me if I would be willing to be nominated as a vice-president of the Society. She assured me that there were no duties involved, and I was more than happy to let my name go forward. Another letter in June confirmed my appointment which brought the number of vice-presidents up to ten.

Having thought that I had given up teaching I was persuaded to take on one pupil, a gifted boy named Jeffrey Hampton who was about ten years old and who had apparently been composing since he was three. He would often play his own compositions and arrangements as well as pieces by, among others, Mozart and Rachmaninov. At first I went to his parents' house in St John's Wood, but they ran a school at Kenton in North London, and later I taught him, and some of the other pupils, there. This lasted a little longer than my teaching at ALRA. In 1995 Jeffrey was involved in a road accident which frustrated his hopes of becoming a musician, and I received a letter from a lawyer asking me to assess how well he might have done had the accident not happened. I duly replied to this, but I never heard what happened to him or if he was able to take up a musical career.

It was always good to meet other artists, many of them ex-D'Oyly Carte. I had already met Cynthia Morey who was married to clarinettist Tony Jennings. They were good friends of John Reed, and through Cynthia I also met another former D'Oyly Carte principal John Fryatt when I played for them at a concert at the Merchant Taylors' Hall in Threadneedle Street in November. Also performing that night were Michael Wakeham, whom I already knew, and the soprano Ann James (not ex-D'Oyly Carte) who sang with the English Heritage Singers at Grim's Dyke, W.S. Gilbert's former home near Stanmore, where I would later work regularly. Another singer, Richard Suart, whom I met through Opera Players Ltd, later became very well-known in the G&S world as a leading exponent of the comedy baritone roles such as Ko-Ko in *The Mikado*.

In July I saw Ralph Meanley who had been in the recent pantomime, and we began to prepare a programme of old ballads and to think about how we might present it. There were many such meetings, and so began a collaboration that lasted for some twenty years. Ralph was a great admirer of the Australian singer Peter Dawson (1882-1961) who, although he had recorded some serious songs and operatic arias, was particularly famous as a ballad singer, his performances characterised by a down-to-earth approach and impeccable diction.

The year continued with a succession of the regular dates - Meadmore productions, Terrazza-Est, teaching Jeffrey Hampton and other pupils at his parents' school, and appearances at the CAA - but every so often there was something different. In June I had been elected a vice-president of the Gilbert and Sullivan Society, and in October Patricia Cope and I gave a recital for the Society.

Aside from music, the most memorable event (for the wrong reason) was the great storm during the night of October 15-16. When I went to bed the windows were rattling, and I remember thinking "It's a bit windy tonight", but characteristically I slept through it all. When I woke up next morning I went into the bathroom, switched on the light and thought that a bulb had gone. I then went into the living room, switched on my transistor radio and discovered that there had been a storm which had caused a great deal of damage across much of southern England. It wasn't a faulty light bulb in the bathroom: the electricity was off. Later, I walked from Islington into the centre of London, and I saw the extent of the damage to property and also to cars, some of which had been hit by falling trees or masonry. Luckily, there was very little damage to our property, and my own car was all right.

G&S week-end at Newby Bridge. L-r: Geoffrey Shovelton,
Vivian Tierney, Alistair Donkin, David Mackie,
Lorraine Daniels, Kenneth Sandford.

There was a G&S week-end at the Swan Hotel, Newby Bridge
in Cumbria from November 6-8 for which we managed to
assemble the original Best of Gilbert and Sullivan group, and
the next pantomime was *Goldilocks and the Three Bears*. This
year we had Paul Twain and Elaine Harrison who had been
in the previous pantomime, and we also had Jackie Pallo
Junior who, like his father, was a wrestler. Many sports
people, certainly at that time, liked to do a turn in pantomime
although their performances invariably showed deficiencies in
acting or singing. But it was always good publicity, and, in
fairness, their presence helped to draw in the crowds: Jackie
was perhaps the nearest thing to a 'star' in this production.
Once again we drove up to Dunfermline to rehearse for a
week before the show opened on December 11: it ran until the
19th with several of the dreaded 09.30 performances. But
there was something new this year as we didn't immediately
drive overnight to Barnstaple: instead, we had a week at
Airdrie Town Hall, mercifully with no 09.30 starts. We had a
break on Christmas Day (a Friday) which enabled me to get
back to Greenock, and we finished on the Saturday with two

performances before heading off to Barnstaple where we ended the year with another seven performances. There was one regular attendee here who always sat near the front and whom I got to know quite well.

But this year Barnstaple was memorable for two things, the first of them very amusing. Paul Twain was an identical twin, and as his brother had come to visit him they decided to play a trick on the audience. They had found a more or less identical costume, and at the end of one scene Paul walked off stage right and the brother immediately appeared stage left, giving rise to a gasp of astonishment from the audience with audible murmurs of "How did he do that?"

Next, there was something much more serious. Elaine Harrison, who also choreographed the show, played Goldilocks. In a scene near the end of Act 1 she comes into the bears' cottage and sees three bowls of porridge, three chairs and three beds. Having tasted the porridge and tested the height of the chairs she then feels sleepy and decides to lie down on one of the beds. These beds folded for convenience in packing, but one of the hinges had come loose, and just as Elaine lay down on the bed it collapsed, and one of her arms was caught in it. She somehow managed to get up and finish the scene, luckily with just minutes to go, but when she came off as the curtains closed she fainted in the wings. I think her arm was just very badly bruised, and as far as I remember she managed to finish the performance (we never had understudies for these shows) although she had to go to the local hospital for treatment later. But it must have been extremely painful.

IV – 1988

Once again the year began with the last pantomime performances. The opening months of 1988 seemed to be a re-run of 1987 as I came back from Barnstaple to more work with Andrew Meadmore and, at the beginning of

February, our fifth tour of the United States and Canada for Byers, Schwalbe. Just before this I gave a talk to the Sussex Gilbert and Sullivan Society in Brighton, adding one more contact to a growing list. The tour, our longest yet with sixteen concerts, took up most of February; the group was again Sandra Dugdale, Lorraine Daniels, Kenneth Sandford, Geoffrey Shovelton, Alistair Donkin and me. We flew to Buffalo NY, via New York, on Friday 5; it was snowing heavily when we arrived. We hadn't expected this, and on the Saturday Geoffrey and I took a cab to a shopping mall (it was too cold to walk) where I purchased ear muffs and a pair of snow boots. The concert in Buffalo was on the Sunday afternoon, presented by the QRS Arts Foundation at the Kleinhans Music Hall; following a reception we then had to hire two cars and drive into Canada. With all the snow, driving conditions were atrocious, and there were cars abandoned by the roadside. We were almost the only traffic venturing out in such weather, and we were given some strange looks at the border crossing. There were two concerts in Ontario, in Guelph and Brantford. The first one was presented by Guelph Music Club in the War Memorial Hall which looked more like a church; the evening was enlivened by the presence of a bat that had got into the building and occasionally flew round the stage. The Brantford concert was sponsored by the Capitol Theatre which had very poor backstage accommodation including a row of three toilets that looked like cells: one had no lock, one had no light and the third had no door handle.

We then had three concerts in America. The first one, sponsored by Rockhurst College, Kansas City MO, was held in the Mabee Theatre which seated just over three hundred. It was still very snow-bound when we arrived, and we were booked in at a Comfort Inn under the name D'Ogly [sic], yet another amusing variation on D'Oyly Carte. The second and third concerts were at the delightful Opera House, Woodstock IL (seating some four hundred and thirty) where we were part of yet another Performing Arts Series. There were delays in getting to Woodstock due to the bad weather, and the first concert was late in starting. Both shows were well received. We then had to go back to Canada for a concert at Thunder Bay, Ontario in the Community Auditorium (seating some fifteen hundred); we had to fly from Chicago IL to Minneapolis/ St Paul MN to get a flight to Thunder Bay.

The day this tour started, February 5, we had just landed at New York before getting our flight to Buffalo when I discovered that I seemed to have lost some of the air tickets that we always received from Byers, Schwalbe. This was most embarrassing, and the office had to get more tickets: every so often on our travels a FedEx (Federal Express) van would arrive with replacements. I couldn't think how I had come to lose them; I hoped that the office could claim something back. However, while we were waiting in the airport lounge at Chicago for the flight to Minneapolis/St Paul Sandra Dugdale, who had been looking through her own tickets, suddenly said "Oh dear, here are your tickets, David". Quite how they came to be with hers will probably never be explained, but at least they had now surfaced, and this would save the office any further bother.

We then flew to Minneapolis/St Paul, but unfortunately there wasn't much time to get the connection, particularly as our tickets said Air Canada when it turned out to be Air Ontario, and by the time we had worked out where to go we had missed the connection - the only flight that day. It was fortunate that the concert wasn't until the following night, but we had to get accommodation (along with two other men who had also missed the flight) in a Rodeway Inn, a standard but comfortable motel. We had heard that of four concerts planned for this season two had already been cancelled, presumably because of bad weather, and we felt that we must get there despite having been held up. Luckily there were no more problems although it was so cold when we arrived that we couldn't get out of the plane because the door had frozen. But we were given a warm reception when we finally walked on to the platform; we also had a standing ovation, possibly for just managing to get there.

The final concerts on this tour were in America, the first being for the Artist Series of St Olaf College, Northfield MN held in the college's Skoglund Auditorium (the Scandinavian influence was very obvious in this state). Then came two concerts at the Ordway Music Theatre in St Paul MN where we were part of a Distinguished Artists Series. In the city we saw the famous ice sculptures which even now, despite the cold, were beginning to melt. The first concert was on February 17 at 11.00, an unusual time. On the 18th we did a preview in a shopping mall at 11.45 to publicise the second concert, and later that afternoon we recorded a Best of Gilbert and Sullivan tape that was to be broadcast on a *St Paul Sunday Mornings* programme the following month; on the 19th we did the second concert at the normal time of 20.00. Next, we were part of The Artist Series at Wheaton College, Wheaton IL, *alma mater* of the evangelist Billy Graham. We were well looked after here, but the atmosphere was a little rigid; the group had been told to tone down the dancing in order to avoid offending anyone. But there wasn't much of it onstage anyway: just some basic movement that was always referred to as 'two D'Oylys and a Carte'. Even the normally ebullient Geoffrey Shovelton seemed cowed by the restriction. The concert was held in the Edman Memorial Chapel.

From Wheaton we moved to Middletown OH where we performed at Miami University as part of an Artist and Lecture Series held in the Dave Finkelman Auditorium. The concert here, which was on a Sunday, was at 15.00; we then had to speak to some singing students and their teachers. Neil Downey, whom I had first met in Washington DC in 1978, and then in Pasadena in 1984, was here on business; it was good to see him again. Later that evening one of the Brent Walker films of the Savoy Operas, which were made just after D'Oyly Carte closed in 1982, was shown on TV: appropriately it was *Patience* in which Sandra Dugdale was the eponymous heroine. After Middletown we were in St Louis MO where we gave two concerts in the lovely wood-panelled Sheldon Concert Hall which had the reputation of being one of the finest lecture halls in the country, if not the world. As a more intimate venue it was ideal for us; the man in charge, Walter Gunn, was particularly helpful. The concerts were presented by The Sheldon and the Saint Louis Opera Guild, and rather than being put up in a hotel we were offered accommodation in various homes. Geoffrey and I stayed with Mrs Emma 'Em' Ware and her daughter Nina in a rambling old house; Lorraine and Sandra were with another daughter who lived not very far away. On these tours there were several occasions when we were accommodated in private houses. This didn't always please everyone, but Geoffrey and I enjoyed our stay with 'Em'; I kept in touch with her for many years. We also met her friend Kay Applegate whose late husband George had been another G&S aficionado.

We had a free day before our concerts, and we did some sightseeing which included the famous Gateway Arch (surely one of the wonders of the modern world) which is a memorial to the pioneers of the Old West, many of whom started their trek west from St Louis. We managed to get to the top, in a series of tiny carriages seating just five people, from where there were wonderful views. The first concert went very well; next day Geoffrey and Sandra were interviewed for a radio programme. We listened to this later in the car just before the start of the second concert which was even more successful than the first one: we had a wonderful reception from the audience. Our few days here had certainly been a highlight of the tour.

When we were in hotel rooms I watched a lot of TV including the infamous *Gong Show* which I had first seen on the 1978 D'Oyly Carte tour of North America; the religious programmes too were morbidly fascinating. There was Dr Robert Schuller in his Crystal Cathedral. The previous year, for a commitment of $500 per annum, you would receive

a model of a golden eagle and become a member of Dr
Schuller's Eagles' Club; this year you would get a reproduction
of a painting of an eagle. But he was dignity personified
compared to some of the other 'televangelists'. Another one
was Jimmy Swaggart, and around this time came the revelation
of his marital misdemeanours which he publicly admitted in a
vast auditorium, packed to overflowing, with his wife and
family sitting demurely on the front row. I couldn't envisage
such an embarrassing spectacle happening in Britain. On the
evening of our arrival in St Louis the news was still all about
Jimmy Swaggart. Kay Applegate's comment was "Well, we've
had Watergate and Irangate; now we've got Holygate". Em
and Nina Ware were also quite scathing about the whole
religious scene in the United States.

The penultimate concert was in Springfield MO, and it was
with the Springfield Symphony Orchestra which I conducted.
This was held at Evangel College in the Evangel Chapel
Auditorium. The last concert was at Iowa State University,
Ames IA in the Stephens Auditorium, a huge modern hall
seating almost two thousand. It was leap year, and we flew
home on February 29 (Frederic's birthday and the pivot of the
plot in *The Pirates of Penzance*), an appropriate date for a
G&S group.

I was soon into another round of the regular dates although
few of these matched the remuneration of the Byers, Schwalbe
tours. But every job was welcome, and as usual there was
always something different. Opera Players was putting on
Donizetti's *L'Elisir d'amore*, and some of the rehearsals, which
I played for, were held at Charles Farncombe's house. There
was a London Airs concert in Oxford at the end of April, and
another Meadmore *Pinafore* at the beginning of May.
The Mario & Franco Restaurants group now included Villa
Claudius in Broadway which was just outside New Scotland
Yard; like Terrazza-Est it was also in a basement. You went in
to what appeared to be a glass cubicle on the pavement and
then went down a spiral stair to the restaurant. We still

performed at Terrazza-Est, but we were at Villa Claudius on its opening night, May 31.

With everyone trying to further his or her own career it was becoming difficult to keep our London Airs group together, and it was eventually wound up. Altogether we did twenty-one concerts in nineteen different venues. I was sorry to see it go, but I could now accept that this was a normal part of the free-lance world and that hopefully there would be other work in its place. We had all enjoyed these concerts, particularly as they were in costume: that was very unusual for me. I wore my splendid Victorian tails again on numerous occasions.

Around this time I made what was to be perhaps the most far-reaching contact to date when I started to work for The Council for Music in Hospitals (as it was then called: 'The Council for' was later dropped from the title). One of the singers I met at the CAA was Judith Baxter who had successfully auditioned for Music in Hospitals; we did many of these concerts together. Another singer was Caroline Dixon whom I also met at the CAA. Caroline had once played Eliza Doolittle in a long-running tour of the United States in one of the many companies formed after the production of *My Fair Lady* in 1956. She now ran a small group called the Pantheon Singers, and I played for them at their Music in Hospitals (MiH) audition. At that time it was quite usual for the concerts to be given by a small group, but later, with mounting costs (the organisation is a charity), they were often given by just one singer (or sometimes an instrumentalist) and an accompanist. The Council for Music in Hospitals had been founded in 1948, and I was still working for it when it celebrated its seventieth anniversary in 2018. Most of my early concerts were single ones, but I was soon doing a number of tours, usually with Judith or with members of Caroline's Pantheon Singers.

I also made two other useful contacts this year, the first of them being with the BBC. I had previously written to them to see if there was any possibility of conducting one of the *Friday Night is Music Night* concerts which had been running for many years. I had not had a reply, but it was the very act of writing that enabled something else to happen. In the 1960s the BBC had broadcast all of the Savoy Operas in a series that involved the former D'Oyly Carte comedy baritone Peter Pratt: I remember listening to them when I was living in Glasgow. Unbeknown to me a second series had already been underway for some time: the operas were in the hands of Robert Bowman, a BBC staff producer, with Sir Charles Mackerras in charge of the music. This new series was progressing slowly as Sir Charles, with a busy international career, was not always available for recording sessions; with five operas still to be done Robert Bowman reached the age of sixty at which point he was compulsorily retired and went to live in the West Country. He could have continued on a free-lance basis, but bringing him up to London would have been awkward and expensive, and Sir Charles was still not always readily available. The BBC now decided that the series had to be finished quickly: another of its staff producers would take Robert Bowman's place, and the musical side would be in the hands of one or more of its staff conductors. Tim McDonald agreed to become the producer, but he also said that he would like to have someone who knew something about the Savoy Operas as an assistant; my letter about possibly conducting a *Friday Night is Music Night* (which included my c.v. with the D'Oyly Carte connection) was lying on his desk. And so began my brief but enjoyable 'career' with the BBC.

The second contact I made was with The Royal Society of Musicians of Great Britain (to give it its full title: it was usually referred to simply as the Royal Society of Musicians or just the RSM), a charity founded in 1738 as the 'Fund for Decay'd Musicians': Handel was a founder Member [sic]. I had been asked by D'Oyly Carte's principal cellist Andrew Adams if I would like to become a Member of the Society (Andrew had been elected a Member just two years earlier). Monthly meetings were held on a Sunday in the Society's splendid premises (in which other musical organisations also had their offices) in

Stratford Place just off Oxford Street, and as I was living in London I was able to attend many of these. I was then elected to the Court of Assistants that ratified grants awarded by the Governors to needy musicians. When the business had been concluded there was always a glass (or more) of wine, the vintages chosen by fellow-Member and wine connoisseur John Leach; after these Sunday meetings at Stratford Place I would float home on a cloud, having once again been combining business with pleasure. It was only some years later that I was made aware of the Society's particular association with Arthur Sullivan of which more anon. The Society eventually moved to a smaller property in Fitzroy Square.

Another most enjoyable event (again a one-off) was a cruise. I had been asked to be the musical director for a series of G&S performances on the MV *Astor* which was sailing from Harwich to Bergen and then up the coast of Norway to Honningsvaag and the North Cape. This had been organised by Michael Heyland, former D'Oyly Carte producer, and we were to give abridged performances of the three best-known operas - *HMS Pinafore*, *The Pirates of Penzance* and *The Mikado* – with, on the last night, a complete performance of *Trial by Jury*. Those taking part were Geoffrey Shovelton, Michael Rayner, Adrian Lawson and Patricia Leonard (all ex-D'Oyly Carte) with soprano Patricia Cope: it was listed in the ship's publicity as *Gilbert & Sullivan Go To Sea!*

For the first three productions we cut out long passages of chorus work but kept most of the remaining music and practically all of the dialogue; we had a running time for each opera of about an hour and a quarter. For *Trial by Jury* we were hoping that we could persuade some passengers (and any crew who might be interested) to be the jury; I was to attempt to teach them the music during the two weeks that we were on the ship. On June 15, the day before we left Harwich, we had a rehearsal for the first opera *Pinafore*. Adrian Lawson played Sir Joseph Porter, but occasionally he also had to play Dick Deadeye, and there were some hilarious moments as he switched from one to the other with suitable *ad libs*. We thought this might add something to the performance, and we decided to make a feature of it.

We assembled at Harwich the following day, and we were allocated cabins. We had our first meal on board at 21.30; by that time we were at sea. As temporary members of the crew we had to have instruction in safety drill, and we were also expected to sit at table with the passengers. This was fine at the beginning, but we gradually found that the amount of food on offer was just a bit too much (we were there to work; we couldn't just sleep off big meals every day by relaxing on deck chairs), and so we excused ourselves and began to have meals with the crew. These were more than adequate if somewhat less filling. We also found out that we would be performing in the Astoria Lounge. The area itself wasn't too bad, although quite small, but there was a terrible noise from the air-conditioning. We asked if it could be turned off, but we were told that this was impossible as there was only one switch for the whole ship; so we had to put up with it.

MV *Astor* at Bergen, Norway. L-r: Geoffrey Shovelton, Adrian Lawson, Patricia Leonard, Michael Heyland, Michael Rayner, Patricia Cope.

On June 18 we had our first taste of sightseeing (one of the great pleasures of cruising) and saw something of Bergen. This included a trip on the funicular railway to one of the vantage points above the town. As usual on a large liner we were just one item in the entertainment on offer; the previous evening we had attended the international cabaret which was very good. We now met some of the performers, and we persuaded one or two of them to take part in our performances. Chief among these was Lia Linda, a singer from Belgium; one of the dancers, Lydia Badia, also volunteered to take part. Another performer was a Polish pianist, Bogdan Kulakowski, who gave several recitals which usually included the music of Chopin. He was very good, but he also played when afternoon tea was served daily in one of the lounges, and this was far less successful as he didn't have the lighter touch required for it. I could not have given the recitals that he gave, but I would have been better at the tea sessions, and I said to Michael Heyland that I would have been quite prepared to take this on as well. Michael said that playing during afternoon teas would have been part of the pianist's contract, but it would probably have clashed anyway with our G&S rehearsals and performances.

We were now beginning to get to know some of the passengers, one of whom was a man from Miami who had made a fortune in real estate and who had recently retired aged just forty-five. There was also a retired dentist from Bearsden who was something of an amateur musician and who had had lessons at my old college, the Royal Scottish Academy of Music and Drama, known in his day as the Athenaeum. His conversation was peppered with phrases like "gee blooming whiz" and "by golly gosh". There were also many Germans on the cruise as the ship had started out in Hamburg before sailing to Harwich where we had joined it. As we sailed up the Norwegian coast there would be regular information over the tannoy system, and this would often be along the lines of "The town you can see on the starboard side was almost completely destroyed by the Germans during the war". I thought this was somewhat undiplomatic (no political correctness then) as most of the German men on the ship were of a certain age, and some of them might well have been stationed in Norway during the war. But no-one seemed to be in any way offended by these announcements.

On June 19, at 16.45, we had our first performance: this was *HMS Pinafore*. As we feared, we could hardly hear ourselves for the noise of the air conditioning, but it seemed to go down well enough. Adrian Lawson made the most of his joint portrayal of Sir Joseph Porter and Dick Deadeye which got quite a few laughs. The performance was followed by the inevitable socialising. As we sailed north, and it stayed lighter for longer, there was also some photography at 01.00 and later. Next morning we found ourselves at Svartisen, at the head of a fjord, in bright sunshine and with a brilliant blue sky. As always there was plenty of time for sightseeing and relaxing, but we still had to rehearse, and after breakfast we turned our attention to *Pirates* before going ashore at 11.00. There wasn't much obvious habitation other than a few isolated farms, but we walked up to a glacier which was the local attraction: with its ice-blue colour it positively sparkled on such a lovely day. The journey back down the fjord to the open sea was quite breathtaking; I was hoping that cruising might feature as one of my regular earners, but sadly this wasn't to be. We did hear later that the almost perfect weather was quite unusual: apparently there were only about half a dozen such days in the year.

On the following day, June 21, we had our first chorus rehearsal for *Trial by Jury*. Ten people turned up, and they did their best although some had obviously never done anything like this before. There were some English and American passengers, and we even had Karin Paquay-Bruck, the cruise director (Karin had a very good voice), and her assistant Andy Whitehouse. There was also a lady from Ely, Elisabeth Bradley, who was giving needlework classes as an on-board activity.

Elisabeth enjoyed G&S, and she could read music which was a great help. When she heard about the clerihews that Geoffrey Shovelton and I had produced she suggested that she might prepare some embroidery patterns based on them. We kept in touch with Elisabeth after the cruise, and she produced two designs, one based on John Wellington Wells (*The Sorcerer*) and the other on Ko-Ko (*The Mikado*), but this was yet another idea that never quite got off the drawing board. I did, however, compose a further series of clerihews whose subjects were the entertainers, including ourselves, and some members of the ship's crew. The chorus rehearsal was followed later by our performance of *Pirates*, also at 16.45, which, for various reasons, was a little less successful than that of *Pinafore*.

We were not rehearsing all day for our performances, and we had plenty of time to enjoy the shipboard amenities which included deck games such as quoits and shuffleboard; you could also walk (or run) round the deck for exercise. By now we were at Honningsvaag (at the extreme northern tip of Norway), and it was light all the time. Most of the passengers went off to see the North Cape, but many of them found it disappointing as a tourist complex was being built there; they thought this rather spoiled it. We sailed away at 02.30 in broad daylight. I wondered how anyone living there could get used to this. It was all rather weird, but it was certainly very beautiful. I had been given an inside cabin, and at first I was a little disappointed, but as we sailed further north I was very glad that I had it as it was easier to sleep in the darkness: those of the group who had outside cabins found it more difficult, even with the curtains drawn.

The next opera was *The Mikado* for which we had a rehearsal on June 22; during this I nearly fell asleep. Like so many, I had stayed up late every night watching the other performers in the cabaret and then enjoying not only the endless daylight but drinks and buffet meals that were served into the small hours. There was always an idea at the back of my mind that "I'll go to bed when it gets dark", which of course it never did; I think it was all beginning to catch up with me. There was an extra cabaret that night, a Pub Night with the Belgian singer Lia Linda who was going to take part in *The Mikado*. Michael Rayner and Adrian Lawson had somehow managed to get in on the act with Adrian playing the guitar. This all finished at about 01.00, and as I staggered off to bed I saw another ship coming towards us: it looked remarkably like ours, and I began to think I had been imbibing rather too freely. But it turned out that this ship was the original MV *Astor* which had been sold to the East Germans and was now the MV *Arkona*. It had then been decided to build an almost identical ship (ours) which retained the name *Astor*.

As temporary members of the crew we had boat drill at 10.15 on June 23; this involved standing around for some time before we were mustered. I was stationed on life raft 16 along with Michael Heyland, but we didn't really achieve anything, and if there had been an emergency few of us would have known what to do. It was very cold, and we shivered somewhat on deck. We then had a late breakfast followed by another *Mikado* rehearsal. There was now quite a swell. Geoffrey Shovelton and Patricia Cope found it awkward trying to do the famous 'kissing duet', and there were a few near misses; dance steps also proved difficult. The swell affected Patricia who suffered from sea sickness. In the afternoon we had another rehearsal for *Trial by Jury* which wasn't too bad considering that most of the chorus couldn't really sing, and few of them could read music. I had to take this rehearsal standing at the piano, and as the ship was rolling considerably it was quite difficult, not to say amusing: the weather was not exactly what we had expected on Midsummer Day. In the evening there was a fancy dress competition which was won by a couple dressed as a chicken and an egg. The second prize went to a group who called themselves 'the emergency crew' while the third prize was taken by a lady who appeared as the North Cape; there were also other eccentricities that were equally entertaining. It was all part of the cruising experience.

We reached Trondheim, a smaller town than Bergen, on June 24, and we were able to go ashore. In the afternoon we had a rehearsal for *Mikado* with our cabaret singer Lia Linda taking the part of Peep-Bo in the 'Three little maids from school' number. She was very good. Next day, we arrived in Geirangerfjord: stunning scenery on an epic scale and again with perfect weather. Two other liners, the *Pacific Princess* and the *Funchal*, were also there: it must have been difficult to manoeuver in such a tight space. There was a barbecue lunch on deck, and there was also a band playing. It all seemed too good to be true. Were we really 'working' here? We went on shore and climbed up above the fjord for some stunning views before coming back for another *Trial by Jury* rehearsal. We heard later that the *Pacific Princess* had had a very rough crossing from Harwich on the 21st.

On June 26 we had another rehearsal for *Trial* followed by our performance of *Mikado*, slightly earlier at 16.30. This was perhaps the best of the three, and having Lia Linda as Peep-Bo was an added attraction. The audience lapped it up. Later that night there was another cabaret in which members of the crew performed. One man played the spoons, and another, the guitar. The ship's doctor played the flute, and two girls sang "I know him so well" from *Chess*; there was also a ballet with four men dressed as women.

We were now travelling through the Kattegat to Copenhagen which we reached on the 27th. After breakfast we rehearsed *Trial* again. I had played for the other three performances, but as we now had a chorus we felt that it might be a good idea if I conducted this one, and we asked the Polish pianist Bogdan Kulakowski if he would play. He agreed to do this, but as with his sessions during the afternoon teas he seemed to have little idea of the style. Despite having had a number of rehearsals for *Trial* it still wasn't right, and the performance was just two days away. After the rehearsal I went ashore with Michael Heyland to see something of Copenhagen.

There were morning and afternoon rehearsals for *Trial* the following day before we reached Kiel at about 17.00. A farewell cocktail party was held later in the Astoria Lounge. We passed through the Kiel Canal as we were having dinner, and it seemed strange to be looking out at cattle grazing in fields as you sailed along. There was a final cabaret that evening with most of the performers, including Lia Linda, puppeteers and illusionists, taking part; all compèred by the effervescent bi-lingual MC Thomas Kasper from Hamburg.

June 29 was our last full day, and the performance of *Trial* was to take place that evening. We had a final rehearsal in the afternoon, and I was quietly confident that it would be all right - if the chorus remembered to come in. Thankfully, Bogdan at last seemed to have got the measure of the piece. Having docked briefly at Cuxhaven we were now sailing across the North Sea, and there was a slight swell. I was hoping it wouldn't be too bad or Patricia Cope might feel ill again. We had dinner at 20.30 followed by our performance of *Trial by Jury* at 22.15. By now the swell was quite noticeable, and Patricia wore something on her wrist to help her combat any queasiness. It all went remarkably well: the chorus kept their heads and got most of the entries. The ladies had made hats out of old nautical charts, and these were held on with bows: one lady had tied her bow on the top of her head, and it looked as if she had toothache. But it was good fun, and everyone enjoyed it. Afterwards, we had another party during which we signed programmes in the usual theatrical way. Geoffrey Shovelton used his calligraphic skills to prepare certificates for everyone who had taken part, and these were given out after the performance. Not surprisingly I didn't get to bed until 03.00.

We docked at Felixstowe at around mid-day on June 30, but we had to wait until the passengers had disembarked before we could leave. When we came to pay our on-board expenses we were delighted to find that our drinks bills had been cancelled. We said our farewells, collected our passports and headed for home. I got back at 16.30. It had been fun doing the shows, particularly rehearsing *Trial by Jury*, but it really had been yet another paid holiday. As I couldn't afford holidays I was more than grateful for this opportunity to see another part of the world. But a repeat of this was not to be as the *Astor* had already been sold to the Russians (becoming the *Fedor Dostoevskiy*), and G&S was not likely to figure as part of *its* on-board entertainment in the coming years. (The ship later reverted to the name *Astor*, and at the time of writing was still afloat.) Several of our group did work for other cruise lines, but I never got the chance to be part of that. Cruising was now very much a growth industry in the entertainment profession, and I would have had to go as the accompanist for a group (as with *Astor*) as I could not have auditioned as a solo pianist, even if I could have coped with afternoon teas. But another Byers, Schwalbe tour was coming up in October, and there would hopefully still be plenty of other work at home.

The next three months consisted of a succession of jobs within the framework that I had now established: Spaghetti Opera at Terrazza-Est and Villa Claudius, teaching Jeffrey Hampton and the other pupils at his parents' school, another *Mikado* for Andrew Meadmore and more jobs for Music in Hospitals in Norfolk, Hertfordshire, Devon and Somerset as well as many in and around London. While the performances were much the same everywhere the venues were always different, and that was an added interest. Originally in hospitals, as the name implies, concerts were now also given in hospices, nursing homes and day centres; there were even occasional visits to prisons. I particularly remember one concert at Broadmoor Hospital (high security). Security was extremely tight, and as I had a nail file in my top pocket I had to leave it at the front desk. "You'd be surprised what they can get hold of", I was told. The concert took place in a hall, with many staff in attendance. The audience was well-behaved and clapped politely after each number, but the atmosphere was somewhat tense.

I continued to make new contacts, and in August I began playing for Valerie Masterson, former principal soprano with D'Oyly Carte before embarking on a distinguished international career. At first I only played for her pupils, but later we did a number of concerts together. There was also a concert at Spains Hall in Essex, organised by Lorraine Daniels, and one in Bolton organised by Geoffrey Shovelton. Geoffrey was now working regularly with Patricia Cope and me and we called ourselves Lyrical Allsorts: I had suggested 'Lyricous' Allsorts, but this was firmly stamped on. On one occasion we provided some entertainment at Barker's in Kensington.

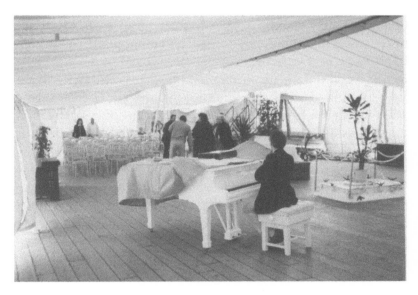

Rehearsal for *HMS Pinafore* on HMS *Belfast*.
The *Astor* group with Michael Buchan (centre).

Aside from the regular dates you never knew what might come up, and one-offs were always a welcome change from the routine work. One such was a performance of *HMS Pinafore* on HMS *Belfast* on September 15. This was for Hambros Bank, celebrating their move to new premises at 41 Tower Hill. It was organised by Michael Heyland, and the cast was our MV *Astor* group with the addition of Patricia Leonard's husband Michael Buchan, a former D'Oyly Carte chorister.

The 1980s was a time of sharply rising house prices, and even my tiny flat in Islington had doubled in value in just three years. I was now thinking of trying to find a bigger flat although that wasn't easy as all property was becoming more expensive. But Islington (which is fairly central) was definitely on the up as a desirable place to live, and I thought that if I moved further out I should be able to find a bigger flat more cheaply. The three friends I had made at the CAA (Conrad Leonard, Kay Laing and Vivienne Jay) all lived in South-West London: Conrad in Wimbledon, Kay in Sutton and Vivienne (and husband Gerald) in New Malden. And so partly to be nearer to them, and partly to get something bigger (although I still had to increase my mortgage), I moved to 187a Worple Road, Raynes Park on Friday October 7, 1988. Once again I was indebted to Nationwide for having confidence in my ability to find enough work, and it was with some satisfaction that I was able to tell them that we were about to start our sixth Byers, Schwalbe tour of the United States (we were not in Canada this time). Shortly before the move to Raynes Park I went back to Scotland for a few days, and while I was away there was a break-in at Mildmay Grove. There wasn't much taken, but I had to get a new door at great expense, something I could ill afford.

Raynes Park was an area that I didn't know, but it was close to Wimbledon where we had played when I was with D'Oyly Carte. The nearest Underground station was at Wimbledon: the end of one branch of the District Line. Sometime after I moved in I arranged to give some coaching lessons to a singer who had contacted me by phone. I asked him if he knew where Raynes Park was. "Oh yes", he said, "no problem". I waited and waited, but he didn't turn up. Eventually the phone rang again. "Sorry", he said, "I'm at Rayners Lane". This is near the end of the Piccadilly Line in North-West London, a different area entirely. That was one job that fell by the wayside, and, one singer I spoke to but never actually met.

Chapter 4 – Another new home

I – 1988

I was to remain at 187a Worple Road for almost twenty years before I finally moved back to Scotland in 2007. It was part of a block consisting of a row of shops with houses above (I had lived in a similar property in Wembley in 1976 when I first joined D'Oyly Carte). Our house, the last one at the Wimbledon end of the row, had been divided into two flats: mine was immediately above the shop which was a pharmacy. Next to it, at the corner of Worple Road and Pepys Road, was a filling station. The flat was certainly bigger than the one in Mildmay Grove, but not very much bigger. The living room, again with a kitchenette contrived out of one end, was about the same size. The bedrooms were both small, but at least there were two of them. The bathroom was quite large, and it was out of proportion to the rest of the flat which is often the way with conversions. I found that the gas central heating wasn't working, but I had no time to deal with this or even to settle in properly as we left London for our sixth Byers, Schwalbe tour four days later on Tuesday October 11.

The line-up for this tour was the same as for the fourth and fifth tours: Sandra Dugdale, Lorraine Daniels, Kenneth Sandford, Geoffrey Shovelton, Alistair Donkin and me. We flew first to New York with Air India and then to Washington DC where we stayed in the appropriately named Savoy Suites Hotel: apparently it was an old re-vamped Howard Johnson. The first two concerts were again in the Baird Auditorium in the Natural History Museum. We were getting quite used to it by now. As these were not until October 13 and 14 we had some time for sightseeing, and Sandra and I went to Georgetown and then to Washington Cathedral. Built in Gothic style (the Americans must have felt that their capital ought to have something that looked mediaeval) the cathedral was begun in 1907 and was still unfinished in 1988. When we left Washington on the 15th we found that we had been booked into the hotel under 'British Embassy'. I hope the Embassy wasn't asked to foot the bill.

The next two concerts were sponsored by SUNY (State University of New York) Fine Arts Center, Stony Brook NY, and they were in the eleven hundred-seater Main Theatre. There was a short programme for children in the afternoon, and, a standard one in the evening (co-presented by Rankin Realty, Inc.). During the evening show I contacted yet another cousin from Greenock who was now living on Long Island. We then flew to Allentown PA for a concert in Allentown Symphony Hall, another lovely old building: it had footlights, a rarity in theatres by now. This concert had been sponsored by the Community Music School, Emmaus PA. After that we were back in New York. The last part of our journey (from Philadelphia) was by train on an Amtrak Metroliner, the only time we travelled on one. The concert was at Columbia University, sponsored by the School of the Arts, in the Kathryn Bache Miller Theatre, but there had been poor publicity for it, and we played to just some fifty people, perhaps the smallest audience we had yet experienced. A compensation for this was an after-show party in Doug Schwalbe's elegant apartment overlooking Central Park.

Our next concert was at Middlebury VT, but we had to fly first of all to Burlington VT where we had given a concert on the fourth tour in February 1987. As we touched down at Burlington I heard a timid lady ask one of the cabin crew if we were at Miami: she had somehow landed up on the wrong flight and, like the man I was to have coached in Raynes Park, was going in the wrong direction. We were picked up at the airport and driven to Middlebury through some lovely countryside that reminded me very much of Scotland; at that time of year we also had the wonderful Fall colours. The concert here was part of the Middlebury College Concert Series, and it was given in the Mead Chapel. We then had three concerts in Maine with the Portland Symphony Orchestra: we had worked with them on the third tour in April 1986 with conductor Bruce Hangen. (Kenneth Sandford, whose real surname was Parkin, was listed in some publicity here as Kenneth Parker.) They now had a Japanese conductor, Toshiyuki Shimada, and again I had to step aside as he had been contracted to conduct the concerts. Bruce Hangen hadn't been particularly familiar with G&S, and I wondered how much less familiar a Japanese conductor would be with the material. We met for a rehearsal on the day that we arrived, and like Stephen Gunzenhauser with the Delaware Symphony Orchestra on our very first tour Toshiyuki also said that he would have been happy if I had been conducting. We didn't get through all of the material, but luckily there was a second rehearsal next day. However, despite these two rehearsals the first concert (in the Margaret Hopkins Merrill Gymnasium at Bates College, Lewiston ME, some twenty miles north of Portland) wasn't very good. For reasons I have stated elsewhere this didn't surprise me, and there were more 'glitches' (as they say in the USA) here than in any of the concerts we had done in the previous five tours. There were two more concerts with the orchestra which were in Portland itself, in the City Hall Auditorium, and these got progressively better as Toshiyuki became more familiar with the material. During these concerts I set up a stall for the sale of the tapes that we had made from the *St Paul Sunday Mornings* programme on our fifth tour in February. We had already sold a good number of them at the other venues, and this added considerably to our fees for the tour. After the third concert we went out for a meal with Toshiyuki and his wife Eva, a Czechoslovakian pianist; Toshiyuki kindly paid for this.

We then had two free days in Portland. It rained on the first day, but on the second day I decided to take a trip into Portsmouth NH to add another state to my growing list of those that I had visited. I went there by Greyhound coach, and I had a pleasant enough day, but on the return journey the coach that was to have left at 15.55 didn't turn up until 17.25 having had to wait at Boston for a delayed connection from New York; in fact, the coach that arrived was an extra one put on at Boston, and the driver didn't even know what had happened to the other one. I finally got back to Portland at 19.00 to find that the others were about to go out for a meal. It was just as well that it was a free day as I might have been even later; it was also a salutary warning not to attempt any more such trips away from base if we had a performance in the evening.

There were three more concerts on this tour. From Portland we moved to Grantham PA on October 26. When we went out for breakfast next morning, as we usually did, I found an item on the menu called scrapple which I hadn't yet come across. (Grits was another delicacy we encountered somewhere. It was all part of the learning curve.) The concert was part of Messiah College Cultural Series, and it was given in the Miller Theatre, Climenhaga Fine Arts Center. After this we flew to Milwaukee WI. Wisconsin was another new state for me. When visiting any town or city I tried to see as much of it as I could, even if this was shortly before a concert, but I was often on my own as the others preferred to rest before singing. It was extremely cold, but I did manage to get down to the edge of Lake Michigan which was about ten blocks from our hotel. The concert here, the first of a Great Artists Series, had been organised by the University of Wisconsin – Milwaukee School of Fine Arts, but it took place in the Pabst Theater, yet another lovely old building (c.1895, and presumably built by, or having some connection with, the famous brewery firm established there in 1844) which had been hired for the occasion. We then moved to Fremont OH for the last concert which had been arranged by the Arts Council of Sandusky County and took place in Fremont Junior High School. (America's nineteenth president, Rutherford B. Hayes, died in Fremont in 1893. His house had become a museum, but I didn't have time to visit it.) As we had found on previous tours it was often in the smaller venues that we encountered the best hospitality, and here we met Michael and Elizabeth Curry, originally from England, who laid on a splendid party for us. I had pumpkin pie which I had not tasted before. I kept in touch with Michael and Elizabeth who later moved back to England. And that was the end of another successful Byers, Schwalbe tour. The following day, October 31, we were driven to Cleveland OH for a flight to New York. From there we got our flight to London (once again with Air India), but not before several muddles over travel had been sorted out. Ken Sandford found that he didn't have a return ticket from New York, and Sandra Dugdale wasn't sure if she would be able to fly as she had earlier intended staying on for a few days and had a ticket dated November 3: she might have to pay extra to come back with us. But we also discovered that we had come out from London on October 11 with tickets dated October 31, and we were now trying to get back on October 31 with tickets dated October 11. I don't know how this wasn't spotted originally, but there clearly wasn't the same attention paid to these things in the 1980s. Somehow we all made it on to the plane; we even managed to get Sandra on board with her ticket dated November 3. I don't think that would happen with today's heightened security. We arrived at Heathrow at 08.30 the following morning.

I still continued to be fascinated by the quirkiness (to me at least) of so much American TV, particularly *The Gong Show*. On one episode during this recent tour there was a five-year old who did impressions of John Wayne and Mae West. He was introduced by the incorrigible Chuck Barris who said of this would-be star that "he first knew that he was stage struck when he did an impression of Niagara Falls in his uncle's lap".

(The child got nine out of ten for his efforts and was not, as so often on this bizarre show, 'gonged off'.) Even the weather forecasts had their own way of putting the information across. One weather chart said that the North-West would have 'harmless clouds' with the Mid-West having 'a messy day'; on another day the weather was going to be 'splendid', 'golden sunshine' or 'nice!' depending on where you lived.

And the Sunday religious programmes didn't disappoint either: Dr Schuller, in his Crystal Cathedral, was now offering a 'blessings basket' (but hurry while stocks last). There seemed to be at least one channel entirely devoted to religion, but if you watched it long enough you realised that much of the content was repeated over and over again. One very over-the-top programme called *The Gospel Bill Show* was dressed up to look like a Western. The eponymous Bill was a sheriff who sat at a table on which there was a large Bible; anyone coming to him for help was told to meditate according to God's Word. It was all very strange, but, like *The Gong Show*, endlessly fascinating. Thanks to the wonders of technology you can now see these programmes in the comfort of your own home, anywhere in the world, but this has removed the fun of anticipating them when you could only see them in the country in which they were produced.

Shortly after our return there was another concert for Father Paul Lenihan, now the army chaplain at Tidworth Barracks in Wiltshire. The venue was the Garrison Theatre at Tidworth; the singers were tenor Meston Reid, baritone Clive Harré and mezzo-soprano Patricia Leonard (all ex-D'Oyly Carte) with soprano Ann James. Paul Lenihan also sang in some of the items. It took place on November 5 and was appropriately called *Sparklers & Crackers*.

This was followed by another round of evenings at Terrazza-Est and Villa Claudius and more concerts for Music in Hospitals. Most of the latter were with Caroline Dixon, and we were often joined by the tenor Noel Drennan, an engaging Irishman who kept us amused on long journeys with endless jokes and impressions of John Wayne and James Cagney. (He would have done well on *The Gong Show*.)

On November 20 I conducted a concert in Stafford with the Midland Concert Orchestra and Stone Choral Society. This also involved Patricia Cope, Geoffrey Shovelton, Kenneth Sandford and Alistair Donkin. Later in the month I was back in Scotland for concerts at the Civic Theatre, Ayr, and I had a few days in Greenock. Incredibly, having just moved to another flat, I was burgled again while I was away, and this time more was taken. It was a particular shock to come home to a second break-in.

In December there was a concert for Music in Hospitals in Colchester, and for this we had three singers: Caroline Dixon, Noel Drennan and Carole Mudie. Carole was the daughter of Michael Mudie (1914-1962), a talented conductor who had worked at Sadler's Wells and Glyndebourne: his early death cut short a promising career. Her mother, Elizabeth Aveling, had sung opposite Richard Tauber in his operetta *Old Chelsea*. Following this concert we were in Cornwall for two days, and this was followed by concerts in Cirencester and Swindon with Noel Drennan and Judith Baxter, and in High Wycombe with Judith and Caroline. I couldn't complain that I wasn't busy or that I wasn't getting variety in the work, the venues, or my fellow artists.

In my early days with Music in Hospitals we often performed in what had been large Victorian mental asylums (as they were then called). They were built in the country, deliberately away from urban areas, in many acres of land where the residents could roam at will if they were fit enough: I remember one near Cardiff where I saw a man in his pyjamas walking about outside; there were also sheep grazing in the grounds. There were several of these buildings around London itself, but their days were numbered as attitudes had changed since Victorian times. If we paid a return visit to one of them we would sometimes find that much of the surrounding land had already been sold off for commercial building, and housing schemes would be springing up. But these asylums had at least been built with amenities for entertainment, and they often had a separate theatre, or hall, with a stage and dressing-room accommodation; there was usually a grand piano (invariably out of tune) on the stage. On one occasion, somewhere in the Midlands, we turned up for a concert in just such a building to find no-one there, neither patients nor staff. At the appointed time, still with not a soul in evidence, we started our concert, and eventually the sound attracted an audience of sorts who drifted in and out during the performance. At the end we just packed up and went away. We had not even seen a member of staff, but, in fairness, this was an exceptional case.

If we had a full week's tour in a rural area (I particularly remember one tour in the West Country) we would sometimes be put up in what had originally been nurses' quarters in older hospitals. As most staff now had their own transport they would operate daily from home, and these buildings had become redundant: they were sometimes quite Spartan, but they were otherwise perfectly adequate. We usually did two concerts a day, one in the afternoon and one at around 18.30 or 19.00. After that we would go back to our quarters with some food and drink and spend a convivial evening: Noel Drennan was good company on these occasions. It wasn't so easy to do this in private accommodation which we had to organise ourselves from lists provided by Music in Hospitals although we could claim that back along with travel expenses.

The New D'Oyly Carte Opera Company finally opened this year with productions of *Iolanthe* and *The Yeomen of the Guard*. Among the cast were former principals from the old Company – Gillian Knight and Vivian Tierney - and former choristers Gareth Jones, Jill Pert and and Philip Creasy (in principal roles) and Pamela Baxter and Guy Matthews, but its approach to the productions was very different from the traditional approach of the old D'Oyly Carte: some of these productions moved quite a long way from that tradition and were not always universally appreciated. I never worked for the New D'Oyly Carte, but I continued to work with G&S. The new company also performed other repertoire, including Offenbach's *Orpheus in the Underworld*, but in the end it too had to close.

As well as getting a reasonable amount of work I was now settling in to my new home and ironing out the initial problems: getting the gas central heating working and getting a new phone installed. December brought further concerts out of London, as far afield as Maidstone and Blythe Bridge. I had to have an electronic keyboard for many of the Music in Hospitals concerts as not every venue had a piano. At that time I didn't own a keyboard, but MiH had one or two which were available to the pianists. As I did many concerts for them I finally kept one permanently in the flat; I occasionally used it for other work although I tried to avoid that in case anything happened to it. I also bought an amplifier for it which I still use. On December 15 I was in Warwick in the afternoon, but I had to be back in London for Spaghetti Opera at Villa Claudius in the evening; the following day I had to be in Taunton and then Bristol where we stayed overnight before another concert in Wincanton on December 17. This was definitely 'feast' and not 'famine', and all of that just before yet another pantomime which was *Cinderella*: I had now come full circle as this was the first pantomime I had done in 1983. But this year we were only in Barnstaple. We rehearsed from December 19-23 and opened on Christmas Eve for a two-week run.

II – 1989

The first week of the year was the last week of the pantomime, and I was back in London on Sunday January 8 in time for the first RSM meeting. There was a hospital concert in Stotfold in Bedfordshire where I played for Vince and Rita Starr, and later in the month there was another *Pinafore* for Andrew Meadmore. Work continued throughout

February. Carole Mudie, with whom I had done concerts for Music in Hospitals, had formed a duo with alto Carol Leatherby which they called Sweet and Low (in the free-lance world artists have to make work for themselves), and I did a concert with them in Frinton; shortly after this I played for Caroline Dixon's Pantheon Singers who were doing an afternoon music hall for Lambeth Borough Council. There were many of these concerts throughout London, mainly with pensioners in mind, but gradually the various boroughs began to cut back on them, probably for financial reasons. In March there were concerts in Norfolk and Essex, and there was a hospital tour in the Midlands, but towards the end of the month there was a welcome return to the United States with just over a week in New York: not another Byers, Schwalbe tour this time but courtesy of the BBC.

There were still five operas to be prepared and recorded for the G&S series that the BBC would eventually broadcast over several months; these were *The Sorcerer*, *Patience*, *Iolanthe*, *Utopia Limited* and *The Grand Duke*, and it was my brief as musical associate to assist the new producer Tim McDonald with all aspects of both the text and the music to try to get versions that were as authentic as we could manage, particularly with regard to reinstating passages of dialogue and musical numbers that had been deleted for one reason or another. I was even able to present them with my own reconstruction of the Duke's song "Though men of rank may useless seem" (*Patience*), the melody of which had been lost although, rather oddly, the orchestration still existed. Once they had been prepared, the operas were recorded at the BBC's studios in the old Golders Green Hippodrome (often referred to as 'the Happydrome') where G&S friends of mine told me they had seen D'Oyly Carte perform: it was obvious that it had been a theatre as the balcony had been retained in more or less its original condition. (Similarly, when the Theatre Royal in Glasgow was converted into studios for STV in 1957 the outline of the balcony could still be seen clearly.)

Patience was conducted by Ashley Lawrence, and the other four were conducted by Barry Wordsworth whom I got to know quite well. Of these five operas the manuscript full scores of *Patience* and *Iolanthe* remain in the UK. The score of *Utopia Limited* has been lost, but those of *The Sorcerer* and *The Grand Duke* were then in private hands in New York, owned by the G&S scholar John Wolfson. I told Tim McDonald that I knew John, and he said "Well, perhaps he will let you see these manuscripts". And so, having contacted John and obtained his co-operation, I was sent to New York for just over a week from March 19-27.

One of the secretaries at Byers, Schwalbe managed to get me an artist's rate at the Excelsior Hotel where we had stayed the previous October when we gave a concert at Columbia University, but I spent much of my time at John Wolfson's home in central New York studying Sullivan's original full scores of *The Sorcerer* and *The Grand Duke*. Although never as popular as *The Pirates of Penzance* or *The Mikado*, *The Sorcerer* had been performed regularly by the D'Oyly Carte Opera Company (there was a new production by Michael Heyland in 1971) and most of its textual and musical problems had been ironed out. But I did find a section of recitative preceding Constance's first aria "When he is here" which had been deleted. A slightly different version of the text was printed in earlier libretti, and it may have been performed in the original production, but the music was a complete surprise. This was a good 'find', and it was just the sort of thing that Tim McDonald was looking for to give added touches of authenticity to the series.

The Grand Duke had not been performed professionally since its original production in 1896 (apart from a concert performance during D'Oyly Carte's centenary season in 1975), and there were innumerable problems with both the text and the music. The hand-written band parts (which had also been used in D'Oyly Carte's recording of the opera in 1976) were full of mistakes, and although I had tried to eliminate as many of these as possible during the recording sessions (my first with D'Oyly Carte) I hadn't had time to correct all of them. I had brought a set of band parts with me, and my main task now was to attempt to edit them in the time available. We were hoping that the work I was doing for the present recording would finally do some justice to the opera. I couldn't attempt anything similar with *Utopia Limited* as the full score had been lost: before I left London we even made efforts to trace its whereabouts since its last known sighting although we were not successful. It has not yet surfaced, and it may have been destroyed, but aficionados live in hope.

My New York trip wasn't just all work: it was in fact something of a social whirl, and I saw a number of the friends I had made through my association with G&S including Jesse and Rochelle Shereff. I had a meal with them at their home where we were joined by another mutual friend Harry Forbes. Fredric [sic] 'Ric' Woodbridge Wilson, curator of the G&S collection at the Pierpont Morgan Library, treated me to lunch one day, and on another day I was introduced to Howard McGowan, a fan of the old D'Oyly Carte. We dined out that evening at Chateau Ruggero (where I had oysters Rockefeller) and he showed me some G&S photographs from the 1960s of Valerie Masterson, Donald Adams and the conductor Isidore Godfrey, known as 'Goddie'. I also paid a visit to the Byers, Schwalbe office where I finally met Monty Byers and was able to catch up on progress towards further tours: they were hoping to have one in October, and another one was planned for 1990.

To thank him for letting me work on the scores of *The Sorcerer* and *The Grand Duke* I had been told to take John Wolfson out for a meal courtesy of the BBC. We went to the Helmsley Hotel, one of a number of properties owned by Harry and Leona Helmsley who had just been charged with tax evasion (he, at eighty, was considered too frail to stand trial; she, at almost seventy and known as 'Queen of Mean', was fined and given an eighteen-month prison sentence). I also took a train to Stamford CT, adding another state to the growing number that I had visited.

On what was to have been the last day, March 26, I met up again with Howard McGowan who introduced me to a lady who sang in the Metropolitan Opera Chorus, and we had yet another very nice meal. When I got to the airport I found that my flight with Virgin Atlantic had been cancelled, and I had to be put up overnight in a rather plush Radisson hotel. I managed to get up at 05.00 on the 27th as I was to catch a 'jet express' to the airport at 06.00, but there was now another hitch. It was to take three of us, but the other two had the only voucher for it, and they left early without waiting for me despite my name being on the list. The 'jet express' (it turned out to be a limousine) eventually came back, but as I now had no voucher for the journey I had to pay for it myself. How I cursed those two! Luckily I had enough of my allowance left, but this journey to the airport, with tolls, still came to $78.00. I finally got to London at about 21.45, and it was nearer midnight before I got back to Raynes Park. It had been an enjoyable week, and, a great opportunity to examine Sullivan's original scores in detail. There was much of interest to add to the recordings.

I didn't have much time to relax on my return as I was due at the BBC at 14.30 the following day, and I was there for the next three afternoons and evenings. Also, the regular work that I had been doing soon started again: concerts for Music in Hospitals, masonic functions (at one of which I played for Vivienne Jay's niece Claire Rutter who was now becoming well-known), rehearsals for *La Cenerentola* for Opera Players, and another *Pirates* for Andrew Meadmore. I also played regularly for Valerie Masterson's pupils. But even with all this activity I was only just keeping my head above water financially, and I couldn't afford to turn down any offer of work - however poor the remuneration. Spaghetti Opera at both Terrazza-Est and Villa Claudius were now also regular events, usually with Geoffrey Shovelton and Patricia Cope.

Aside from Spaghetti Opera we three did yet another concert for Geoffrey's cousin Irene in Bolton.

Work on the BBC G&S series continued apace, and in April, thanks to my D'Oyly Carte connection, I was able to consult Sullivan's original manuscript full score of *Iolanthe*, at that time owned by the D'Oyly Carte Opera Trust. Tim McDonald came with me, and we were allowed to see it at the Savoy Hotel, a privilege not granted to everyone who asked to see it. (The D'Oyly Carte archive, including the manuscript full score of *Iolanthe* is now in the British Library.) During the week of May 15-18 there were rehearsals for *The Grand Duke* at the Hippodrome in Golders Green (later, there was a recording session in Studio 4 at Maida Vale), and in June there was a week of *Pinafore* rehearsals for Andrew Meadmore: no getting away from G&S, but I was very thankful for it.

On May 27 I played again for Sandy Oliver when he gave a recital at the Burgate Festival. There were some taxing accompaniments in the first half, among them Roger Quilter's *Love's Philosophy* and Frank Bridge's *Love Went a-Riding*, and I was glad to relax with some lighter fare in the second half which included Noel Coward's *A Bar on the Piccola Marina*.

I was also rehearsing for a rather unusual concert which was yet another one-off. Through the pianist Ken Barclay I met a number of people who also enjoyed Victorian music; among them were Robert 'Bob' Wilson and Brian Rees whose particular interest was the pianist, composer and teacher Sydney Smith (1839-1889): I had played his duet *Morning Dewdrops* with Ken Barclay at the Petersfield Musical Festival in 1984. Bob and Brian had managed to acquire copies (or photocopies) of every one of his compositions (running into the hundreds), most of these for piano solo or duet although there were also a few songs. Sydney Smith's music, once described as 'brilliant nothings', had never been highly thought of by serious musicians, but it enjoyed an enormous vogue in its day. Many of his compositions were fantasias on popular operas such as Gounod's *Faust* and Mozart's *Don Giovanni* (the latter dedicated to Arthur Sullivan), but the majority were original pieces, often with French names or subtitles (*de rigueur* in Victorian times) such as *The Fairy Queen* (*Galop de Concert*) or *La Harp Éolienne* (*Morceau de Salon*). Titles like *Fairy Whispers* and *Fountain Spray* have not helped his posthumous reputation, but this overlooks the fact that the pieces are all very well written for the instrument, and although not always easy they invariably lie 'under the fingers': it is obvious, as in the works of Moszkowski, that the composer was a pianist himself. But he also had a genuine gift for melody, a talent which is not given to everyone, even to greater composers, and is too often undervalued.

On July 19 we presented a centenary tribute to this much maligned figure: *Mr Sydney Smith and his Times - 1839-1889*. We had assembled a number of artists, both singers and pianists, and there were even spoken interludes between the musical items. The pianists were Anthony Saunders, Nicola Billington and me; the singers were Maureen Keetch and Angela Vernon Bates (both of whom sang with the Parlour Quartet), Carol Leatherby (of Sweet and Low) and Leon Berger (who, like me, would become a vice-president of the Gilbert and Sullivan Society). The spoken interludes were delivered with some verve by Leo Aylen. We gave this concert in the suitably Victorian surroundings of Leighton House in Kensington (built in 1866), home of the artist Frederic, Lord Leighton. The majority of the items were by Sydney Smith (piano solos, duets and one song), but there were also songs by Mendelssohn, Sullivan and other Victorian composers well-known in their day: Alice Mary Smith (no relation), Paolo Tosti, Theo Marzials and Wilhelm Ganz. One of the highlights was *Qui Vive* (yet another French title) by Ganz in an arrangement for three performers at one piano: great fun. We ended with Sydney Smith's piano duet *Sleigh Bells – a Canadian Reminiscence* which, although played by Anthony Saunders and me, involved the entire company as Ken Barclay had added some words in French to the middle section.

The singers also had tambourines, and they marched round the stage as they sang. The audience loved it, and we had to do part of it again. It was a delightful evening, and I was glad that someone had recorded it: I acquired a copy, and I still play it from time to time. It is a pity that so much of this music (well-written, tuneful and quite unpretentious) has fallen from favour, but this could be said of much of the words and music of any age; even the Savoy Operas do not attract the audiences that they used to although the work that author and composer wrote away from each other has received more attention in recent years thanks to the efforts of the W.S. Gilbert Society and the Sir Arthur Sullivan Society.

The year continued with the usual engagements, but with an emphasis on the G&S series at the BBC. I was also playing occasionally at Grim's Dyke, and there were more concerts of music hall and variety. These were sometimes with Laura Collins whom I had met when I did my first pantomime, but I also worked with Carole Mudie and Judith Baxter who were usually joined by comedian Marty Swift whom I had met at the CAA. Marty was tall, and he bore a passing resemblance to the actor Basil Rathbone whose credits included a number of Sherlock Holmes films made in the 1930s and 1940s. As a London tourist attraction Marty could often be seen dressed as the great detective (with Inverness cape, deerstalker and pipe) at the entrance to Baker Street Underground on Marylebone Road: doubtless some people thought he really *was* Sherlock Holmes - or even Basil Rathbone.

Marty sometimes did an act as the comedian Max Miller (considered *risqué* in his day) in which he would sing Max's famous number *Mary From the Dairy*. I had to notate this for him from a recording; also the song *When Can I Have a Banana Again?* He wrote songs himself which were all on wartime themes, such as *Sitting In the Shelter* and *Come Along and Quickly Join the Queue*, and again I had to put these down on paper after he had sung them over to me. There was also a monologue called *While Passing a Coal Mine* for which I had to write suitable underlying music. It was in the style of the Western Brothers (Kenneth and George: they were actually cousins), a well-known variety act. Another man at the CAA, the Punch and Judy expert Percy Press lll, asked me to notate a 'vent' (ventriloquist) number with the intriguing title *When the Gizzy Gungle Gees are Gizzy Guzzing*.

August saw a week of *Mikado* rehearsals for Andrew Meadmore, and after that I met John Wolfson who had come over from New York: he was interested to hear how the G&S series was progressing. I then managed to have a week's holiday in Normandy with some friends (things were looking up). I didn't take my car this time, but we hired one while we were there; we managed to see Mont-Saint-Michel and the Fort de la Latte where part of *The Vikings* (with Kirk Douglas, Tony Curtis and Janet Leigh) was filmed in the 1950s: an early use of a genuine location.

Shortly after my return Tim McDonald told me that the series was more or less ready, but they needed some interval talks; could I do them? At first I thought he simply wanted me to write them, but then I realised that he also wanted me to read them. There wasn't much time left, but luckily I had most of the written material on the Savoy Operas at home, and by sitting up into the small hours I was able to get them done. Tim gave me a free hand to write what I wanted, and I also had the pick of the BBC's library of recordings to illustrate the talks. The thirteen surviving operas (minus *Thespis* (1871) for which only a little of the music has survived) were given in chronological order; they now went out on Sunday afternoons on Radio 2 in twelve programmes between October 1 and December 17. The series even made the front page of *Radio Times* for the week of September 30-October 6 with a photograph of a lady in Japanese costume holding an open fan covering the lower part of her face. On the fan was printed "G&S from A to Z/ Radio 2 presents the complete Gilbert and Sullivan – and finds a long lost aria (or two)".

The first programme consisted of a double bill of *Trial by Jury* and *The Sorcerer*. This meant that I had to provide two talks with illustrations, and in the first one Derek Hammond-Stroud and I performed *Little Maid of Arcadee* (the one number from *Thespis* which had been published separately) with Gilbert's original words. In the second talk, as *The Sorcerer* was one of the operas whose manuscript scores I had studied in New York, we introduced some unfamiliar excerpts such as the original ending to Act l (a reprise of "Eat, drink, and be gay"), the original opening to Act ll ("Happy are we in our loving frivolity"), both of which we did with piano accompaniment, and the hitherto unknown extension of the opening recitative, beginning "Ah, dearest daughter", with the original string parts.

Writing these interval talks was fun, if nerve-wracking: with so many G&S experts likely to be listening I was hoping that there wouldn't be too many howlers followed by indignant letters pointing out the mistakes. But I got off lightly on both counts. I was still slightly in awe of being asked to do this, not ever having had any test to see if I would come over well enough on air, but they must have had confidence that I could do it. However, writing the talks was nothing compared to the first attempt at recording them. I was in a studio in the depths of Broadcasting House in Portland Place, and I sat in a cubicle from which I could see Tim McDonald and another man who was in charge of the recording. There was communication via headphones, and when the red light came on I was to start speaking. I was also told not to worry if I made any mistakes: if I had to stop for any reason I was to go back a few lines and pick it up from there. This seemed straightforward enough, but the ground beneath this area of London is criss-crossed by several Underground lines, and, as I soon found out, it is pretty obvious when the trains are running. I wasn't long into the first talk when I became aware of a distant rumbling, but as I hadn't yet made any mistakes I wasn't sure what to do and kept on reading. Almost immediately I was told to stop until the rumbling had ceased, to go back a few lines and start again. This happened numerous times, which didn't exactly help my confidence, and I thought that the end result, if we ever managed to get it finished, would sound dreadful with all these terribly obvious breaks. But I hadn't reckoned on the BBC's highly efficient equipment and expertise in these matters, and when I listened to the transmission I was amazed to find no sign whatever of the trouble we had had during the recording. I seem to recall that we used this studio again, but we also used other studios with less distracting outside interference.

The talks were recorded in sequence (occasionally two at a time), some of them well before the transmission of the opera concerned: those for *The Pirates of Penzance* and *Patience* were recorded on October 9, the day after the *HMS Pinafore* transmission, and those for *Ruddigore* and *The Yeomen of the Guard* on November 10, two days before the transmission of *The Mikado*. The talks seemed to go down well, and as the series progressed I began to get some appreciative letters which was very encouraging. During my talk for *Ruddigore* (transmitted on November 19) I played Webster Booth's recording of "Take a pair of sparkling eyes" (although this is from *The Gondoliers* which was transmitted on December 3, just four days before its centenary), and I had a very nice letter from his widow Anne Ziegler thanking me for playing it. Webster Booth had been in D'Oyly Carte from 1923-27, listed then as Leslie W. Booth.

There was one further development from the G&S series when I took part in a short *Victorian Interlude* accompanying the tenor Bonaventura Bottone in Henry Leslie's setting of *Annabel Lee* and Sullivan's *The Lost Chord*: this was effectively a 'filler' following the transmission of *The Pirates of Penzance* on October 15. The programme also marked Sydney Smith's centenary, and Nicola Billington played Smith's *Arlequin et Colombine* which she had played at our concert at Leighton House. Nicola and I then joined forces for the duet

Morning Dewdrops which I had played with Ken Barclay in 1984 and more recently in July with Anthony Saunders. Due to lack of time only the opening of this was heard, partly as background when the items were announced at the end.

Other work continued throughout these three months. On October 3 I had the pleasure of playing for Gillian Knight, former D'Oyly Carte principal contralto, at a Gilbert and Sullivan Society meeting; later that month I met Arthur Parry, a former D'Oyly Carte chorister, when I played for him at a masonic date at the Connaught Rooms. Many of my masonic dates were with the tenor Niven Miller who had made a name for himself as a Scottish entertainer in Canada. Niven was a mason, and he now sang mainly at masonic functions. Many of these were in London, but some were as far afield as Bournemouth and Eastbourne. It was good to have this regular work, particularly as there was no pantomime this year.

The Charles Haley pantomimes had been running in Barnstaple for some time, and although there was a different one each year the scripts, mainly written by Phillip Charles's wife Jennifer, had an obvious family resemblance. Even in the few years that I had been doing them we had repeated *Cinderella* which had been my first one for them. Phillip rang me one day to say that Barnstaple had decided that they wanted a change, and my services would not be required. But he did say that as he put on various other shows he might well be in touch at a later date. That was some comfort at least.

Luckily there was plenty of other work, again often involving a great deal of travel: there were two concerts with Judith Baxter, one in Scarborough (an Ivor Novello programme) and one in Haverfordwest in Pembrokeshire, and there was one in Chiddingstone Castle in Kent with a group of singers that I had played for occasionally. Following the transmission of the BBC's *The Gondoliers* on December 3 there was a week of rehearsals for the same opera which Andrew Meadmore was putting on at the end of its centenary week. On December 5 I recorded the talk for *Utopia Limited* which was transmitted on December 10, and on the 12th I recorded the talk for the last opera *The Grand Duke* which was transmitted on December 17. It had been a fascinating experience to be the musical associate for the series and to write and deliver the talks, and I wondered if I might be able to capitalise on this and get some more work at the BBC. But there was nothing immediately forthcoming.

As there was no pantomime I took the opportunity to go back to Scotland for Christmas, but I had to come back to London on Boxing Day to play for rehearsals for yet another Meadmore production, *Pirates* this time, which was to take place early in January. And there was a return visit to Althorp for a final concert in that last week. Geoffrey Shovelton wasn't available, and the singers were Patricia Cope and the baritone John Cunningham. We entertained a large number of guests at the Spencers' Christmas party; we ate with them (this doesn't always happen when you perform at functions), and we were generously included in the Christmas gifts. I received a very nice piece of Waterford crystal and a bottle of 1988 Bourgogne Blanc bearing the Althorp label with the legend 'selected for Earl Spencer'. Like the bottle of 'Greenock' wine that I brought back from Australia in 1979 I still have the Althorp bottle. It was a delightful evening, and, a splendid way to round off not only the year but the decade of the 1980s. After a slow start with the closure of D'Oyly Carte in 1982 I seemed to have found my feet as a free-lance artist. What would the next decade bring?

Interlude

The Savoy Operas of W.S. Gilbert and Arthur Sullivan fall neatly into three periods: early, middle and late; curiously, each period also falls neatly into a separate decade. The early period was in the 1870s starting with *Thespis* (1871), most of the music of which has been lost. This was followed by *Trial* by *Jury* (1875), *The Sorcerer* (1877), *HMS Pinafore* (1878) and *The Pirates of Penzance* (1879). The next opera, *Patience* (1881), may be seen as the first of the middle period; it was followed by *Iolanthe* (1882), *Princess Ida* (1884), *The Mikado* (1885), *Ruddigore* (1887), *The Yeomen of the Guard* (1888) and *The Gondoliers* (1889): the bulk, in fact, of their joint productions. The 1880s had therefore seen the full flowering of the formula that was now instantly recognisable as 'G&S'; during this period the impresario Richard D'Oyly Carte had also built the Savoy Theatre which opened on October 10, 1881 with *Patience*, and the Savoy Hotel which opened on August 6, 1889 during the run of *Yeomen* and not long before the first night of *The Gondoliers* on December 7. This opera ends, somewhat ambiguously, with the words "We leave you with feelings of pleasure!" although at the time neither Gilbert nor Carte had any desire to bring to an end a partnership that had brought so much success to all of them, even if Sullivan felt that he could do little more in that particular field. But there was every reason to expect, or at least hope, that there was more to come.

And what did the decade of the 1890s bring? First of all there was the famous 'carpet quarrel' (over expenses for a carpet in the theatre for which Carte had expected both Gilbert and Sullivan to pay a share) which resulted in the break-up of the partnership. Sullivan may have been glad to get away from both Gilbert and the general style of comic opera (despite his gifts being eminently suited to it and to which, indeed, he returned) to concentrate on other things (particularly his grand opera *Ivanhoe* (1891)), but he and Gilbert were persuaded by Richard D'Oyly Carte to come together again for *Utopia Limited* (1893) and *The Grand Duke* (1896). These two operas alone constitute the late period, but neither has held the stage, and so, from an overview of the entire G&S canon, this late period was not exactly a great success for either of them.

Having been with D'Oyly Carte for seven years I had come to know all of this history, and I was fascinated by the various periods of the operas and how neatly each period fell into a separate decade. I was now wondering if my own career, such as it was, might mirror this in terms of both work and the decades of the 1970s, 1980s and 1990s. I had joined D'Oyly Carte in 1975 (the centenary year of *Trial by Jury*, Gilbert and Sullivan's first real success), and as author, composer and impresario had progressed during the 1870s I too had progressed during the 1970s, in my case from répétiteur to chorus master and associate conductor, and with the added bonus of tours of the United States and Canada (1978) and Australia and New Zealand (1979). The D'Oyly Carte Opera Company closed in 1982, and the remainder of the 1980s was for me, therefore, hardly comparable to the success of G&S throughout the 1880s, but by 1989 I had at least achieved something in the free-lance world, and there was no suggestion that this, like the G&S partnership in the 1890s, might falter in the 1990s and ultimately fail. Perhaps I was becoming somewhat paranoid about it all, but I still entered 1990 with bated breath.

Chapter 5 – Into the nineties

I – 1990

My first job in 1990 was a final rehearsal on January 2 for the Meadmore *Pirates*. I wasn't involved in the performance, but I was rehearsing on the 3rd for something else. Our Sydney Smith centenary concert at Leighton House the previous July had been such a success that we felt we must do something similar, and so we presented *Wilhelm Ganz and his Circle – 1833-1914*, again at Leighton House, on Friday January 5 (we had performed Ganz' sparkling *Qui Vive* in an arrangement for six hands at one piano at our Sydney Smith concert). This time the singers were Angela Vernon Bates, Sylvia Eaves and Leon Berger. Nicola Billington and I were the pianists, and Leo Aylen introduced the items. The following evening there was a *Gilbert and Sullivan Gala* at St David's Hall, Cardiff with the BBC Welsh Symphony Orchestra and the Chorus of Welsh National Opera conducted by Gareth Jones. The singers included Bonaventura Bottone whom I had accompanied in the BBC *Victorian Interlude*; the presenter was the newsreader Richard Baker. I didn't take part in this concert, but I had been asked to provide background notes for it, and they kindly sent me a copy of the programme. The concert included excerpts from *The Yeomen of the Guard*, but despite my spelling this correctly it came out, as so often, as *The Yeoman* [sic] *of the Guard*. I was to write programme notes again.

On January 24, at the Victoria and Albert Museum ("Oh, South Kensington!"), there was a lecture on Oscar Wilde given by Geoffrey Squire; this was followed by excerpts from *Patience* introduced by Michael Heyland. Those involved were myself, Lorraine Daniels, Gareth Jones and Adrian Lawson. This was followed by concerts for Music in Hospitals, Spaghetti Opera at Terrazza-Est, masonic dates and yet another Meadmore production, *Pinafore* again, at the end of February.

Geoffrey Shovelton, David Mackie and Deborah Clague at Terrazza-Est under the watchful eye of another well-known tenor.

Like me, Geoffrey Shovelton had moved from East Sussex into London, and following the break-up of his marriage he had met the American soprano Deborah Clague who soon became his regular partner in concerts for Music in Hospitals, at Terrazza-Est and elsewhere, and who would eventually become part of our North American tours. They also sang for Simon Gilbert who organised concerts under the general heading of Spun Gold; again these were usually concerts of lighter music. Geoffrey and Deborah introduced me to Simon, and I did some work for him: another string to the bow. On March 17 we took part in the Golden Jubilee celebrations of Airborne Forces at Manchester Airport: the singers, in wartime uniform, were in a boxing ring, and Deborah sang a wonderful Harry Warren song *At Last*. But Geoffrey and I were about to get involved in what for me was a particularly unusual one-off; this came about through Father Paul Lenihan, the Roman Catholic chaplain at Tidworth Barracks, who had asked me to make a setting of The Reproaches (Psalms) to be performed on Good Friday at Tidworth.

Of all the music I have written perhaps upwards of ninety per cent of it has been arrangements and orchestrations of existing pieces such as hymn tunes, Christmas carols or folk songs; there are also reconstructions of lost works by Sullivan, principally the cello concerto but also the Duke's song from *Patience*, Captain Corcoran's song from *HMS Pinafore* ("Reflect my child, he may be brave") and Mountararat's song "De Belville was regarded as the Crichton of his age" from *Iolanthe*. The little original work that I have done has usually been lighter and mainly pastiche, as in the songs that I wrote for Alan Delgado's *Have a Nice Day!* This was going to be something quite different. I knew nothing about the Roman Catholic Church, its liturgy or its music, but I agreed to make a setting. Geoffrey, a Roman Catholic himself, would be singing it, and so I was able to consult him as the piece progressed. I kept it all very simple and tonal (for those who understand these things), and it occupied me for a month between February and March. It began with the words "My people, what have I done to you? How have I offended you? Answer me". I also set a hymn at the end to words beginning "Faithful crown above all other", but this wasn't sung.

On March 19 we presented our Best of Gilbert and Sullivan programme at the Cliffs Pavilion, Southend-on-Sea, and two days later we began our seventh tour of the United States (again, we were not in Canada) from March 21-April 6. It was not the last of these tours, but we already knew that it would be the last one for Byers, Schwalbe. The first tour, in February 1984, had consisted of nine concerts, and this had built up over the years: there were sixteen concerts in our fifth tour in February 1988. It had all seemed so promising, but the fifth tour turned out to be the peak: there were twelve concerts on the sixth tour in October 1988, and now we were back to where we started with just nine. The agency had been having difficulty in finding dates for us, and the tour planned for October 1989 had already been cancelled; the Byers, Schwalbe organisation itself was undergoing some changes, with Doug Schwalbe and Monty Byers parting company, and so we had to go. This was worrying as the tours were very good for us financially, but we felt that we now had enough experience of travelling around North America to perhaps get another agent interested. For the moment we could only enjoy this one as we had enjoyed the first six.

Once again we had a slight change of personnel. Vivian Tierney had been our soprano for the first three tours, and Sandra Dugdale, for the next three. Sandra was unable to be with us again, and Patricia Cope joined us (the earlier requirement of being ex-D'Oyly Carte had now been waived): as before, the others were Lorraine Daniels, Kenneth Sandford, Geoffrey Shovelton, Alistair Donkin and me. This tour started with a slight blip as Patricia and Lorraine found that their tickets (which had been supplied by the Byers, Schwalbe office) were in their own names which they used on stage, but their passports were in their married names, and so they had to get new tickets. This accomplished, we set off. The first concert was in the Roberts Auditorium at Rhode Island College in Providence RI, part of their Performing Arts Series. The audience loved it; they bought some forty of the tapes that we had made from the *St Paul Sunday Mornings* broadcast in 1988. The second concert was at the Franciscan Life Center (Visiting Artists Series) in Sylvania OH, and it was here, in taking my change of clothing from the hotel, that I discovered that I had done the classic trick of bringing one shoe from one pair and another shoe from a second pair. Luckily I was already wearing a pair of black (although not patent) shoes, and I had to wear those for the concert, but I only had one black sock (as I kept one in each shoe), and I had to wear the socks that I already had on – and they were white. I just hope that no-one took much notice. Some of the people we had met at the concert in Fremont OH on our last tour in October 1988, including Michael and Elizabeth Curry, were here, and we had drinks with them afterwards. My cousins Jim and Pat (originally from Greenock) and their children also came, and when the Fremont party had left we all went out for a pizza: all, that is, except Ken Sandford who had broken a tooth and didn't think that he could cope with anything crusty.

From Sylvania we moved to the Opera House in Woodstock IL where again we had performed on a previous tour. This concert was a special benefit for the fourth annual Mozart Festival. Our digs here were in the Bundling Board Inn. I didn't know what this name referred to, but apparently 'bundling' was an old tradition in some parts that allowed sweethearts, and possibly others, to lie together on a bed – fully clothed, of course, to discourage intimacy. Hope springs eternal. From Woodstock we moved to Ann Arbor MI where we played in the Michigan Theater, a wonderful old vaudeville building which had recently been renovated. Although we had made strenuous efforts everywhere to make sure that any advertising avoided saying that we were the D'Oyly Carte Opera Company we were billed here as "D'Oyly Carte sing Gilbert and Sullivan – thanks to Applied Dynamics"(!) Another odd feature of this tour was that in the programmes for each concert Patricia Cope's name became Penelope Cope on the title pages although it was listed correctly on the pages which gave the artists' biographies. This was obviously a Byers, Schwalbe office blunder which hadn't been picked up.

While we were in Ann Arbor we were treated to lunch by G&S aficionado Harry Benford and his wife Betty. Harry wanted to pick our collective brains for the forthcoming revised and enlarged second edition of his book *The Gilbert and Sullivan Lexicon* which appeared in 1991; we were duly credited in the acknowledgements for having explained the meanings of some twenty terms in the G&S libretti which had been causing him some difficulty. (The first edition had appeared in 1978, and a third edition, further revised and enlarged, appeared in 1999. Geoffrey Shovelton provided illustrations for all three.) We also met 'Em' Ware from St Louis MO with whom Geoffrey and I had stayed during the fifth tour in February 1988. We left Ann Arbor on March 20, but Geoffrey had slept in. He hurriedly threw all his things together, and we set out for Detroit Airport, but he then discovered that he had left a yellow folder behind; amongst other things it contained his British Airways ticket to get him back to London. Hopefully it would be forwarded to him in Washington. (Everything happened to Geoffrey. On the fourth tour in February 1987 he left a coat at Boston's Logan Airport, but we came back through the airport the following day, and he was able to pick it up.)

We then flew to Florida, another state that I had not yet visited. Even at 23.00 you were aware of a quite different, wonderfully balmy, atmosphere. It rained next day, but the locals welcomed this as there had been something of a drought. There were two concerts here, the first one in the Ira M. McAlpin Jr. Fine Arts Center at the Indian River Community College, Fort Pierce FL where once again we had an orchestra which I was able to conduct. This went well considering the orchestra's almost total lack of experience and unfamiliarity with the music: many were still at High School, and the group had never played together before; it didn't even have a name. The following day, April 1, there was a reception at the British Consulate General in Miami where we met a number of British people, including some British Airways employees, who lived and worked in Florida. We also managed to do some sightseeing; this included a one-and-a-half-hour tour of the city with a laid-back guide who told us that there were three ways of pronouncing Miami: My-ah-me (the standard one used by most Americans), Me-ah-me (used by the Cubans, Miami being only ninety miles from Cuba) and My-ah-ma (used by the locals). One lives and learns. The second concert was for the Miami-Dade Community College/Wolfson Campus (part of the 6PM Series) in association with the Gusman Center for the Performing Arts. The building had possibly the best acoustics I have ever come across. It also had an unusual feature in that the two areas either side of the proscenium arch were quite different: in every theatre that I have been in, either as a performer or a patron, this part of the house has presented a symmetrical façade to the audience. There was an excellent Baldwin piano here; the Gusman was certainly a highlight of our final Byers, Schwalbe tour.

When we arrived in Florida we hired two cars at the airport, one of which I drove. There was an extra charge for leaving them in the hotel car park, and, a very complicated way of getting them out again: this involved obtaining a card at the hotel desk to prove that you had paid. Having done this I handed over my card to the lady who was on duty at the car park exit. She looked at it for a while and then gave me a blank stare; next, she consulted a very long list of room numbers and eventually said "You workin' for the Government?" I said that we were guests who had just checked out and had been told to hand in the card. She looked puzzled, shrugged her shoulders, and then said "OK. You go". I forgot to ask the others later if they had gone through the same procedure.

After this episode we travelled north again for two more concerts at the Baird Auditorium in Washington's Natural History Museum. The man in charge, Marc Overton, was always pleased to see us. There were many G&S enthusiasts in and around Washington, and we always did well there; we sold almost one hundred tapes over the two nights. Doug Schwalbe turned up for the second concert, our penultimate one with Byers, Schwalbe, and he treated us to a meal afterwards. It was a very pleasant way to end our association with him. Thankfully, Geoffrey's folder had now arrived.

The last concert was in Olean NY, a town in the far west of the state near the border with Pennsylvania (the local airport, Bradford, is in Pennsylvania). This concert was part of the Friends of Good Music Concert Series, and like so many on our previous tours it was in a school, Olean High School. It was something of an anti-climax after our concerts in the Baird Auditorium; we were also feeling the strain of having been on the road for two weeks, but we pulled ourselves together, and it seemed to go down well. We then had a get-together in the hotel and divided the spoils. As well as our fees from Byers, Schwalbe we also had some $430 each from the sale of the tapes. We then finished off the evening with some drinks, and we reminisced about the seven tours that we had done. It was quite something to have been associated with two organisations (D'Oyly Carte and Byers, Schwalbe) whose addresses had been respectively I Savoy Hill, London and One Fifth Avenue, New York. Doug Schwalbe sent a round-robin note to each of us which said "Many thanks for our years together, the fast planes (and the slow ones), the snow storms and the sunny days...rain or shine you made each of the concerts memorable for thousands of people in the United States".

We flew home the following day (Bradford-Pittsburgh-London) with mixed feelings. There was disappointment that there would be no more tours for Byers, Schwalbe (not least from the financial point of view), but there was every reason to hope that another agent might take us on. We had done seven tours in seven years, and we had plenty of practical experience of being 'on the road' as well as having a product to offer that was still popular; we also had the D'Oyly Carte connection which was an added draw. Some of the people we had met, such as Marc Overton in Washington and Walter Gunn in St Louis, seemed keen that we would return, and we could only hope that they or others might be able to put us in touch with an agent. We would just have to wait and see.

The end of the last Byers, Schwalbe tour, Bradford PA.
L-r: Lorraine Daniels, Geoffrey Shovelton, David Mackie,
Alistair Donkin, Patricia Cope, Kenneth Sandford.

Back in London life carried on as usual. By now I had made enough contacts to ensure a steady trickle of work although the possibility of no more North American tours was worrying. But the regular work was always supplemented by something different. One such event, just a week after our return, was the performance of The Reproaches at Tidworth Garrison Roman Catholic Chapel as part of the Good Friday liturgy on April 13. Despite the ominous date it went off without a hitch, and Paul Lenihan seemed pleased with it.

Then came a week of concerts for Music in Hospitals in the North-East: we were in Morpeth, Winlaton, Newcastle, Prudhoe, Harrogate and York. Driving there from London took a long time, and I always thought that it would be more sensible (and economical) if these northern tours were done by artists from Scotland. But this rarely happened. However, the advantage of being in an area far away from London was that we tended to remain there longer, often for an entire week with ten or more concerts. For this tour we travelled on the Monday; the concerts ran from Tuesday to Friday.

With Scotland being organised separately, under its then director Nella Kerr, it followed that they had their own artists, but there were exceptions to this. Soprano Maria Arakie and baritone Glenn Wilson of Connaught Opera in London, for whom I played on a number of occasions, often performed in Scotland as well as throughout England and Wales. Maria's performances were characterised by several changes of dress (in a programme that lasted for just an hour and a quarter) and this was an added attraction for the audiences. Glenn was also a qualified psychologist, and as such was occasionally interviewed on television.

At the end of April I gave a talk to the Norwich branch of the Gilbert and Sullivan Society which was billed under a quotation "My taste for a wandering life" (*Ruddigore*): singularly appropriate for my nomadic existence. John Balls (secretary) and Arthur Barrett (chairman) of the Norwich branch were among many people I got to know through the various Gilbert and Sullivan Societies. Angie Arnell and John Penn (who eventually married) were prominent in the parent Society in London; others included David Edwards of the Sussex branch, Linda Wood in Glasgow and Tony Joseph, who had written an excellent history of the D'Oyly Carte Opera Company, of the Bath branch. But I was perhaps closest to the Manchester branch (these branches eventually became Affiliated Societies), many of whose members - Norman and Grace Beckett, Jean Dufty, Sheila Taylor, Ray Walker and David Walton among many others - I had first met in my early days with D'Oyly Carte. The line "In Friendship's name!"

(*Iolanthe*) neatly sums up what the world of G&S has meant to so many people over such a long time.

There was another concert at Tidworth in May, again at the Garrison Theatre, organised by Paul Lenihan. It was called *Melodies for Ethiopia*, and it was to raise money for the famine there. Paul was quite a character. Sadly, he died not long afterwards at too early an age. In June there was a week's tour for Music in Hospitals in Wales although the final concert was in Birmingham; in August there was yet another tour, this time with Sweet and Low (Carole Mudie and Carol Leatherby), which was in Norfolk and Suffolk. In September I was back in Wales, not for Music in Hospitals this time but for the Gwynedd Inter-federation Women's Institute: an evening of music hall in Criccieth on the Lleyn Peninsula with Carole Mudie, Judith Baxter and Marty Swift. That was a long journey for just one performance, and we stayed overnight before returning to London. Through Judith Baxter I had also met the singer Alan Lamb who did a lot of teaching. I sometimes played for Alan's pupils and even took classes for him, not in singing but in rudiments. Alan was another useful contact. In October, London Chamber Opera were in Chipping Sodbury, and Geoffrey Shovelton and I were again in Bolton, this time with Patricia Cope, where Geoffrey's cousin Irene had arranged yet another concert. We always travelled up on the Friday, did the concert on the Saturday and travelled back on the Sunday: yet another 'business with pleasure' mixture, these week-ends were a welcome opportunity to get away from London. I got to know quite a few people in Bolton.

The next big event came about through my school friend Peter Morrison who had become well-known as a singer, not only in Scotland but in Australia, New Zealand, Canada and the United States. He often worked with the soprano Marilyn Hill Smith with whom he had recorded several *Treasure of Operetta* albums, and I was delighted when he asked me if I would accompany them at a performance at St James's Palace on Tuesday November 13 to take place in the presence of Her Royal Highness the Princess Royal. This year was the fiftieth anniversary of the Battle of Britain, and the short concert, billed as *A Musical Soirée*, was part of an evening with dinner being held on behalf of the Royal Air Force Benevolent Fund's Reach for the Sky Appeal. There were other performers, including the pianist John Lenehan, but our contribution was, not surprisingly, from operetta and musical comedy with items from Kalman's *The Gipsy Princess*, Monckton's *The Arcadians* and Lehar's *Giuditta* and *The Merry Widow*. The concert, which was held in the Picture Gallery, was introduced by the well-known BBC personality Raymond Baxter. We then had dinner, the artists being allocated various tables. Seated at ours was Michael Bentine, the writer, comedian and former Goon (along with Peter Sellers, Spike Milligan and Harry Secombe), who had been in the RAF during the Second World War. He was quite as entertaining off-stage as on with an almost non-stop supply of stories and jokes. Afterwards, we were introduced to Her Royal Highness at an informal reception; she was charming and relaxed and spoke of her own musical experiences while at school. In keeping with the spirit of the Appeal the artists donated their services. It was another memorable evening. Shortly after this I was in Scarborough again with Judith Baxter, this time for a Rodgers and Hammerstein programme, and at the end of the month there was a third concert at Leighton House. This one was called *Mr Sullivan in the Salon*. The main item was a performance of *Cox and Box* (music by Sullivan and libretto by Frank Burnand (1836-1917)) in its original full-length version, but we also did some Victorian ballads including several by Gerard Francis Cobb, a composer with whose work I would be more closely associated later. I presided at the piano and introduced the items; the artists were Robina Vallance, Leon Berger, Christopher Davies and Ian Kennedy.

There was to have been a concert in Northampton on December 3 with soloists and a military band for which

I re-fashioned an arrangement of *Good King Wenceslas* that I had first made in the 1960s. Unfortunately this was cancelled, and so I went up to Scotland for a few days, coming back at the end of the week for a welcome string of jobs with the various artists I now worked with regularly.

There was still no word of any further tours of North America, but after a year's break I was now about to do another pantomime for Charles Haley Productions; this time I wouldn't be in Dunfermline or Barnstaple but in Bexhill-on-Sea, in the famous De La Warr Pavilion, an iconic Art Deco building dating from 1935 and winner of a competition instigated by the 9th Earl De La Warr: it has featured in many TV programmes such as *Poirot*. (The architects, Erich Mendelsohn [sic] and Serge Chermayeff, also designed Nimmo House in Buckinghamshire in a similar style: it was later bought by Dame Bridget D'Oyly Carte who renamed it Shrubs Wood; it too has appeared in *Poirot* and other programmes.) The pantomime this year was once again *Cinderella*, my third for Charles Haley Productions. Our Fairy Godmother was Ann Emery, half-sister of the comedian Dick Emery.

I had to arrange digs in Bexhill, and I found a room above a café which was directly opposite the stage door area of the Pavilion. This was obviously handy, but unfortunately it had no toilet facilities. It wasn't a problem during the day as I was in the theatre most of the time, but I still can't think why I decided to take it as this situation clearly presented problems, particularly during the small hours: I draw a veil over how I coped with it. I can't believe that anyone would advertise a room without basic amenities today (or indeed if they would get any takers), but I put up with it 'for the duration'. There was a car park at the stage door for the Pavilion staff which I used; coming back later one night I was followed in by a police car. It was with some difficulty that I managed to persuade them that I was the musical director for the pantomime, that I was using the car park legitimately, and that my digs were in the café across the road. We opened on

Christmas Eve (which was a Monday), but there were no performances on Christmas Day, and I was able to get back to London. Performances started again on Boxing Day, and after the Saturday performances there were two free days so again I went back to London. We were at Terrazza-Est on the 31st from 20.30 until 01.00, and we sang *Auld Lang Syne* at midnight. And so another year came to end.

II – 1991

Once again, the first week of the year was the last week of the pantomime. Bexhill was closer to London, and it was much more convenient, but how long would this new contact last? Back in London there was plenty of other work, and for a while there was something each day, but gaps soon started to appear. This was a perpetual worry. I then met Joseph Vandernoot who had been the conductor of a performance of Sullivan's *Ivanhoe* in 1973 which had been recorded and issued the following year. It was the first complete recording of the work; the cast included people that I already knew or would eventually work with. I saw him a couple of times, but despite our mutual link with Sullivan and my experience with the Savoy Operas he thought that while I might know something about operetta he didn't think I knew enough about opera, and he didn't give me any work. This was disappointing, but other things were on the horizon although we still didn't have an agent for further North American tours. I also had to sign on again.

Geoffrey Shovelton had often worked with the singers David Winnard and his wife Mary Illing who regularly put on shows although I never worked with them as an accompanist. But David also had a job at Methodist Central Hall, Westminster. Geoffrey told me that David had had an assistant, but he was currently without one and was looking for someone to fill in for two days a week until the Hall could get a permanent replacement. I said that I didn't know much about secretarial work, but I would be quite happy to help out if I could. And so in February I met David and Mary for the first time. The job was then explained to me; it turned out to be more than just sticking on stamps and being a general dogsbody. First of all, I was to get to grips with double-entry bookkeeping which I never quite mastered; I was also introduced to the new (to me) world of computers which I couldn't understand at all: it was many years before I acquired a computer myself. David and Mary lived in Cheam; David used to drive into London, and he would pick me up at an ungodly hour of the morning as he liked to get in before the roads got too busy. My efforts didn't add very much to the running of the Hall, but, as always, the extra money was useful. The job didn't last very long, and I was quite relieved when a permanent assistant was appointed.

Another source of income, stretching back some years to my university days, was copying music by hand; I did this occasionally for Novello and Co. When I was at Birmingham University one of the senior lecturers in the music department was the composer John Joubert (perhaps best-known for his setting of *Torches*), and being 'on hand' it was convenient for Novello to let me be the copyist for a piano score of his bassoon concerto. When it was published he gave me a copy which he kindly inscribed with the words 'our joint handiwork'. But technology was taking over, and this somewhat laborious job could now be done by machines such as Sibelius (which I didn't have). Soon, my services would no longer be required, but I currently had a deadline of March 1 for Novello. One of the last pieces I worked on was *Metropolis* by Adam Gorb (1992).

I then had an introduction to English National Ballet when I played for one or two rehearsals thanks to an old college friend David Frame from Bridge of Allan who had become a conductor of both ballet and opera: he was apparently highly thought of in the former medium. This was only a brief interlude, and it didn't lead to anything, but it was more useful experience. David unfortunately had a serious drink problem which may have hastened his early death in 1999.

I always tried not to turn away any work, even if it wasn't particularly well paid, in the hope that it might lead to something else: you can never have enough contacts in the free-lance world, and a small fee is better than no fee. But, as Captain Corcoran says in *HMS Pinafore*, "...the line must be drawn somewhere". Clive Harré, principal baritone with D'Oyly Carte, and a member of our London Airs group, told me that he had once been offered a job; when he asked what the fee was he was told "It's £10.00, but you'll get a cup of tea". I think Clive declined that offer.

Two new ventures began early in the year. First of all, Terrazza-Est introduced a Gilbert & Sullivan evening every Monday, starting on April 8, with Geoffrey Shovelton, Patricia Cope and me. This was fine for G&S fans, and particularly for some of Geoffrey's many female admirers, but it wasn't always appreciated by the regular clientèle who expected at least some Italian opera, and it was eventually changed to a more general evening.

Shortly after this started I was offered a part-time job at the BBC. It was only for one day a week, but that suited me very well. I was working at Elstree in a large warehouse that contained a vast amount of music, mainly arrangements of single numbers and incidental music for radio shows. The heyday of radio was in the late 1940s and throughout the 1950s with shows like *Take It from Here*, *Life with the Lyons* and *The Goon Show*; there were others which were built around one individual such as *Ray's a Laugh* (with Ted Ray), *Hancock's Half-hour* (with Tony Hancock) and *Hip Hip Hoo Roy* (partly written by Spike Milligan) with the comedian Derek Roy, a big name at that time. There were also variety shows like *Variety Bandbox* (hosted by Derek Roy) and *Up and Coming*.

I grew up in the 1940s and 1950s, and I heard many of these shows on 'the wireless'; so it was fascinating to see all of this music. I even found the original manuscript of *Balham*,

Gateway to the South which appeared in a variety programme in the late 1940s and was later issued on a Peter Sellers album. There were also extended items such as the music for a complete radio pantomime (*Dick Whittington*) by Ernest Longstaffe, and I found one of Leslie Baily's famous Scrapbooks (*Scrapbook for 1899*) which contained a script of the show. This was broadcast in 1949, fifty years after the events it portrayed. The sets of incidental music were perhaps the most interesting, some items being very short. One of these was *Elephant Walking Music* which was a mere six bars. I began work at Elstree on April 15.

My brief was to reduce the bulk of the material by throwing out as much as I could, but there were criteria for disposal. If there was a full score and a set of parts I could throw out the parts as another set could be prepared if the arrangement or the incidental music was ever used again (the former was perhaps possible, the latter somewhat unlikely). If there was no full score I had to keep a set of parts, but if there were three first violin parts I could keep one and throw out the other two. I don't know if photocopying machines were available at the time, but I never found any such material. If three first violin parts had been required each was written out separately: the BBC must have had an army of copyists as well as its many arrangers. I was also told to retain what were termed B1 arrangements which were for 5 saxophones, 8 brass, strings and percussion (and usually also with a rehearsal piano part, vocal copy and what was called a control copy). I was further told to use my discretion in retaining what might be termed borderline cases such as arrangements for 5 saxophones, 8 brass and percussion which (without the strings) seemed to be a first cousin to the B1 arrangements. There were supposed to be arrangements listed under New World Orchestra, but I never found any of those; I had also been told to keep everything issued from 1970 onwards, but I didn't get as far as that. With all these conditions and restrictions I did wonder if the amount I was allowed to discard would make any appreciable difference.

There were literally thousands of arrangements which were all numbered. They were in old paper orchestral bags which were often covered in dust and literally crumbling away with age. In sifting through the music, whatever was being retained had to be transferred to cardboard folders which, it was hoped, would have a much longer life. The bulk of what I was to deal with extended from numbers 50,000 to 79,521. Another hand (or perhaps several) had begun the work although the earliest one that I could find was 69 with the next one being 220. This proceeded, with gaps, to 29,661, and so I started at 29,662 and continued up to 30,000. After this there was another gap as numbers 30,001 to 49,999 were either missing or stored elsewhere, and I started again at 50,000.

Then there were the arrangers themselves, and I was given a list of those whose work was to be retained as found. Among them was Stanley Black, a big name in broadcasting, who had also written much film music. Others in this list were Ray Jones, David Francis, Robert Farnon, Wally Stott (who later became Angela Morley, an early case of transgender), Robert Docker, Leon Young, Frank Cordell and Arthur Wilkinson. Among the many staff arrangers were Alan Yates, Peter Akister, Arthur Sandford and Malcolm Lockyer; another name that cropped up regularly was Bruce Montgomery: like Stanley Black, he too wrote much film music. I soon got to recognise their manuscripts, some much neater than others. One man, whose name I have forgotten, produced extremely artistic manuscripts, invariably in ink (many arrangers just used pencil) and often with neat illustrations. In one of these, an arrangement of Irving Berlin's *A Fella With an Umbrella*, the manuscript had little umbrellas all over it; in an arrangement of some Christmas music the title was drawn in block letters with snow on the top of each letter and sprigs of holly at the beginning and end in green and red ink. This particular manuscript was a work of art, and I thought it was a pity that it was languishing in this warehouse: perhaps no-one but myself had seen it since its first performance in the studio.

Apart from the effort involved in the actual arrangement he must have spent much time simply decorating the title page. I hope that it may still be in the BBC archives.

The job lasted for almost three years. I usually went up to Elstree on a Monday, but occasionally I went on another day if other work came along. Later in the year it suited me to be there on Mondays as I would soon be making another contact in North London that involved regular Monday evenings. The warehouse was right beside the *EastEnders* set, and I often saw the actors in the canteen and was eventually on nodding terms with some of them, particularly June Brown who played Dot Cotton. In those three years I managed to thin out and re-bag about 3,000 items, and I calculated that it would take another eighteen years to cover the remainder. But eventually I was told that the job would cease. I don't know if anyone took over: perhaps the remaining items are still waiting to be thinned out.

Some of the arrangements from the late 1940s were done on manuscript paper made from old wartime maps of Yugoslavia with staves ruled out on the reverse side. There was clearly still a paper shortage at that time, but in some of the later arrangements it was obvious that quality manuscript paper had become available again, and it was used in a rather wasteful manner. Even in short items, such as the six-bar *Elephant Walking Music*, a full sheet of manuscript would be used for each instrument, the bars taking up perhaps only the first two staves, and if an instrument wasn't playing in the arrangement a full sheet would still be used simply to write *tacet* at the top. But it was a fascinating experience to be working with what had been perhaps the major part of broadcasting before television took over from radio.

With the BBC and Methodist Central Hall work I now had another two regular jobs in my portfolio. Neither turned out to be permanent, but the former certainly outlasted the latter. At the end of April I attended the funeral of Michael Maurel whom I had met at Il Boccalino; with his death that contact came to an end. One of the singers I had met there, Maxine Symons, who had sung Musetta in the production of *La Bohème*, introduced me to a man from Mauritius, Michel Ballet. Although not a musician himself Michel was very fond of opera, and he used to arrange for singers to go out there to perform: Maxine and others from England had already done this. Unlike even the '£10.00 and a cup of tea' job I don't think there was any payment involved, the bait being "But you're getting a free trip to Mauritius!" I'm sure that I would have accepted such an offer, but although I saw Michel Ballet from time to time I was never asked to go. Perhaps pianists were not required.

As well as working I was able to see friends regularly. Among these were Ken McAllister, a fellow-student from my days at the RSAMD who had played in the D'Oyly Carte orchestra, and Margaret Bowden (from the D'Oyly Carte office) and her husband Ken. Through G&S I had also met Hilary and Sheila Tangye (related to the author Derek Tangye), two sisters with a formidable knowledge of the opera world who lived in Barnes: Hilary compiled crossword puzzles on G&S themes. They had several cats, one of which was called Mr Bunthorne (after the 'fleshly poet' in *Patience*).

In April there was an *Astor* reunion in Ely at the home of Elisabeth Bradley although not all the artists who had taken part in the G&S performances in 1988 were able to come. I also saw Ceinwen Jones, the widow of Bert Newby who had been the business manager when I joined D'Oyly Carte in 1975. Ceinwen had formerly been in D'Oyly Carte as a chorister, but I met her when she came with Bert on the 1978 tour of North America, and I kept in touch with her after Bert died in 1979. It was through Ceinwen that the next major step came.

When I was looking for suitable employment after D'Oyly Carte closed I decided that whatever happened I would not work with amateur societies. I had been with a professional company for seven years, and I felt that with that experience

I should to be able to find similar employment in the professional world: perhaps D'Oyly Carte would just be the prelude to a glittering career in the theatre. But I soon realised that this was not going to happen. I had been very lucky in getting into D'Oyly Carte; the reality now was that beggars couldn't be choosers. Other colleagues had taken up work with amateur societies, and as these groups paid both producer and musical director my attitude quickly changed. But having accepted that this would be another useful source of income and a chance to conduct works other than G&S I found that it was easier said than done. I couldn't just oust someone but would have to wait until a vacancy arose; even then there was no guarantee that I would automatically be appointed anywhere. And so for some years this particular area of work eluded me until, thanks to Ceinwen, I now became the musical director of Manor House Hospital Operatic Society.

Amateur operatic societies, particularly those that did G&S, often tried to get former members of D'Oyly Carte to be their producer or musical director. Ceinwen had been involved with Manor House for some years although she was not currently producing for them. But she knew that they were looking for a musical director, knew that I was looking for work, and knew that the idea of a former assistant musical director of D'Oyly Carte would appeal to the Society. And so on Wednesday August 7 I had a preliminary meeting with Stuart Killen who was the chairman of the executive committee. This was at his office which (appropriately, given my association with D'Oyly Carte and the Savoy Operas) was at Savoy Hill House. A month later, on Wednesday September 4, I went to Stuart's house in Hampstead Garden Suburb to meet other members of the Society. Earlier that day I visited Ceinwen who lived fairly near the Killens (Stuart's wife Carolyn usually had a part in each show) and close to the Institute in Central Square where the Society gave its productions.

Manor House Hospital Operatic Society had been founded in 1954 by Jesse Huggins, a bank manager who was also well-known in London as a singer, and Muriel Woodall who produced the shows for many years. The aim was to encourage operatic and musical talents in the Hampstead area and also to raise money for Manor House Hospital which stood on North End Road opposite Golders Hill Park. In return for its donations the Hospital allowed the Society to rehearse on its premises. The piano there was among the worst I had ever come across although we eventually managed to get another one. After rehearsals a number of us would repair to a nearby pub, the Hare and Hounds, for the usual refreshments; later, we would sometimes go the more famous Old Bull and Bush.

And so I now had another source of income. The performances were nearly always in May; rehearsals took place throughout the winter and spring. Like many societies Manor House started off doing just Gilbert and Sullivan, their first show being *The Pirates of Penzance* in 1955, and it was not until 1970 that they did their first non-G&S productions: Edward German's *Merrie England* and Julian Slade's *Salad Days*. After that they returned to G&S, but they also did other operettas, and they occasionally ventured into the world of musical theatre. Being close to Golders Green the Society had a high proportion of Jewish members, and when they did *Fiddler on the Roof* in 1988 it sold to packed houses. By now they had settled into a pattern of G&S one year and something else the following year. Their latest production (April-May, 1991) had been *The Mikado*, and my first show, in May 1992, would be *Oklahoma!*; I was looking forward to it as it would be a different experience after so many years of G&S. The rehearsals took place on Monday evenings, and this fitted in very well with my day at Elstree for the BBC although I now had to drop Monday performances at Terrazza-Est. Before my début with Manor House in *Oklahoma!* the Society gave a concert in the Hospital on Monday October 7. I had to take a dinner jacket to Elstree that day.

It was good to be able to conduct a number of shows (mainly operettas) other than G&S, but the Society also had a healthy social life, and I became very friendly with several people, particularly the Huggins family. Jesse Huggins had died some years before, but his wife Eileen, who had taken part in many of the productions, was still to the fore, and two of her sons, Paul and Simon, were still living at the family home in Finchley. The house was often the venue for parties after the last performance of the show on the Saturday night, and I usually stayed overnight after these. On the Sunday we would go out to visit country pubs or historic houses, and I much appreciated this new social element in my life. Another friend I made there was Ella Gaskins, a German lady who had been in her teens at the end of the Second World War and who eventually came to London. Given the circumstances of Jewish oppression in Germany I was always surprised that one of Ella's closest friends in the Society was one of the Jewish members Judith Rosen.

Mondays were now fully occupied, but if I was offered other work I could go to Elstree on another day. During one busy week when I had to rehearse on the Monday for an Opera Players production in Grantham on the Wednesday I decided to go to Elstree on the Friday, but when I got there I found that there was no light in the building: not surprisingly it was Friday the 13th. On another occasion I had to go to a Manor House rehearsal following an afternoon concert for Music in Hospitals. As I hadn't had anything to eat I decided to get something at Golders Green. I went into a café and ordered a cheese roll, but as it was late afternoon the roll was now rather hard; as I bit into it the lower half of one my front teeth simply disintegrated. I had no time to try to get to a dentist, and I had to go straight to Manor House Hospital to take the rehearsal. The gap in my tooth made speaking difficult; incongruously I was still in my dinner jacket. When I eventually got to a dentist he managed to give me a temporary repair, but at the time of writing I still have this 'temp' and it has been one of the best pieces of dental work I have ever had.

Most of the contacts that I had made continued to provide a steady amount of work, but there were also other jobs, often far out of London. One of these, on a Sunday in August, was at Dinmore Manor in Herefordshire with Geoffrey Shovelton, but despite being so far away I had to drive back after the concert as I had to be at Elstree on the Monday. Another concert, a G&S one, was in Leeds in September, not in the Grand Theatre where we had played with D'Oyly Carte but in the famous, and much smaller, Leeds City Varieties. On this occasion I stayed with my former colleague Paul Seeley in Bradford for two days. The bed that I was sleeping in was very soft, and when I tried to get up I found that it had affected my back and I could hardly move. Walking was almost impossible, but I managed to stagger out of the house although every movement was extremely painful; I could hardly bend to get into the car. As a result, I was late for the afternoon rehearsal: so late, in fact, that the other artists informed the police that I hadn't turned up (this was in the days before mobile phones were the norm) and they set out to try to find me. When I finally arrived at the theatre, still walking very slowly and painfully, I had to lie on the floor for quite some time. By the evening I was just about able to sit at the piano, and the show went ahead as planned. I have always had intermittent back problems, and you never know when you are going to get a spasm. But it was still a pleasure to have played at this venue, well-known to lovers of *The Good Old Days*.

Some of my contacts didn't produce very much work, and some eventually ceased altogether, but there was always something different. At the beginning of August there was a G&S concert at Melvyn Tarran's Oak Hall Manor in what had been part of the Sheffield Park estate in East Sussex: Sheffield Park and Garden is now a National Trust property. I had first met Melvyn in 1976 when D'Oyly Carte played at the Theatre Royal in Brighton. There was a restaurant at Oak

Hall Manor, but there was also a hall with a stage for performances, and there were two rooms for Melvyn's growing collection of G&S memorabilia which was almost certainly the largest of its kind after that of the Pierpont Morgan Library in New York. Along with former members of D'Oyly Carte, and also with other artists who were now making their names in G&S, I did many concerts for Melvyn, and I got to know him and his wife Kay very well.

There was another concert in Bolton with Geoffrey Shovelton and Patricia Cope, and two for John Gale (who had organised our concerts at Althorp) in the churches at Whilton and Spratton in Northamptonshire. I also worked from time to time with Wes Macrae, an entertainer I had met at the CAA. Wes was essentially a comedian, and our 'gigs' were often in working men's clubs, usually far out of London. There was invariably a lot of noise which made it difficult for Wes as he moved round among the customers, and it was also difficult for me because although he had a microphone I couldn't always hear him. In those days many people were still smoking, and these evenings were often quite a trial. At one venue I was up on the stage as I had to use the band's keyboard. There was a separate music stand which was right at the edge of the stage, and halfway through one number the stand collapsed and fell off the stage, leaving me to busk my way through the rest of the song with no music: never a dull moment, but all good experience.

I was still much involved with G&S, and I gave a number of talks to various Gilbert and Sullivan Societies: there was one in Bath in October, one in London in November and a return visit to Norwich in December. I had started to give talks about G&S, or Sullivan specifically, while still in D'Oyly Carte, and this is an aspect of my work that has remained constant over the years.

My cousins June and Ron celebrated their Ruby Wedding in November. They held the reception at the Spread Eagle Hotel in Midhurst in West Sussex, and I spent a pleasant couple of days there. June was my blood relative, but Ron was related to the famous Goossens family of musicians as his uncle, Norman Millar, formerly Sir Thomas Beecham's secretary, was married to Sidonie, the renowned harpist and sister of Marie, Leon and Eugene (another brother, Adolphe, was killed during the First World War). Earlier, in September, 'Sid' had given her last performance at the Last Night of the Proms shortly before her ninety-second birthday. Born in 1899, she died in 2004 at the age of one hundred and five; like Conrad Leonard she was one of the few people to have lived in three centuries. It was interesting to have this connection, admittedly rather distant, to such a distinguished member of the musical profession.

Ron, who had dental practices in Petersfield and Waterlooville, asked me if I could arrange some entertainment for the Petersfield Rotary Club, and so Geoffrey Shovelton and I duly obliged in December: occasions such as these invariably included a very nice dinner. Shortly before this there was a combined Chamber Opera and Opera Players evening for Newark-on-Trent Music Club commemorating the bicentenary of Mozart's death with *Bastien and Bastienne* and *The Impresario*. But soon I was in Bexhill again for another pantomime, *Dick Whittington* this time, and again the second time I had done it. After the 'no facilities' digs I made sure that I found more suitable accommodation. This year we had Michelle Collins from *EastEnders* as Dick.

We had a week of rehearsals before opening on Monday December 23. There was a matinée on the 24th, and I then went back to London for Christmas, but we were in business again on Boxing Day with two performances. During the run I saw some of the people I had met at Il Boccalino in nearby St Leonards including D'Oyly Carte's former principal mezzo Jane Metcalfe, fellow-musician Louise Denny and the local vet John Pybus and his wife Sue: mixing business with pleasure again. There was no performance on New Year's Eve, and so I went back to London for more socialising; this time there was a party at the home of my Greenock friends Peter McCrorie and his wife the singer Linda Esther Gray. It was a good end to another year.

III – 1992

O nce again the year started with the final week of the pantomime; after this I was back in London to continue a round of various musical activities including making up for two days lost at Elstree while I was in Bexhill. A milestone was coming up in just under two months: it would be ten years since D'Oyly Carte closed on February 27, 1982, and I had already spent more time away from it than I had spent in it. But despite not having another full-time job I had managed to keep going as a free-lance artist, and I had found that as long as there was some work coming in, from whatever source, it was actually quite a pleasant way of earning a living although there was always the fear that one or more of these contacts would simply not be there any longer. This had already happened with the Byers, Schwalbe tours of the United States and Canada (the best contact so far), and there was still no sign of another agent being interested. But this year was to bring other work.

It is not always easy to remember how some of this started, but much of it came via other musicians, word of mouth as usual being an important factor. One such contact, however it came about, resulted in my playing for a number of ballet classes for young children run by Chelsea Ballet Schools. Early in January I started to play for a group that met in St Barnabas Parish Hall in Dulwich Village. I enjoyed these sessions as you had to be able to improvise (something I always had to do in the pantomimes) as well as playing specific pieces. Not everyone, even an otherwise competent pianist, is able to improvise at the keyboard, but this was something I could do, and it turned out to be a useful accomplishment. Some of the younger children's classes were more like games than actual ballet lessons; I might be playing fairy music one minute and then switching to something sinister if the big bad wolf or 'Mr McGregor' made an appearance. And of course I had to watch the children as they danced around: in these situations you have to be able to play without actually looking at the keyboard. Again, not everyone can do this.

The ballet classes were a welcome addition to the job at Elstree and rehearsals for Manor House, but there was still plenty of other work. In January there was a Lyrical Allsorts concert in Seaford, and in February there was a third visit to Scarborough with Judith Baxter, this time with a Noel Coward programme. I had also been asked by the Sir Arthur Sullivan Society if I would reduce the orchestration of Sullivan's *Te Deum Laudamus* (1900) which had been commissioned to celebrate the anticipated end of the Boer War. It was Sullivan's last completed major work, but he died in November 1900 without actually seeing an end to the war which came in 1902. The *Te Deum* was now to be recorded in Ely Cathedral, and I went up to meet the conductor Paul Trepte who was in charge of the music there. I also saw Elisabeth Bradley from the MV *Astor* and her husband Derek.

Many of the ballet classes were now in private schools in West London although others were held outside school hours in church halls. One of them was run by a lady who with her twin sister had been the first of several sets of twins who featured in advertisements for a well-known brand of home permanent wave: "Which twin has the Toni?" Although I normally only saw Elisabeth who ran these classes, the twin, Priscilla, turned up once at an end-of-term party. Now in their sixties they were still almost indistinguishable.

April was a busy month. There was a recording session for Sweet and Low with Carole Mudie and Carol Leatherby; shortly after this we did a concert in London. I also did *The Forties Show* in Wellingborough with Marty Swift and Judith

Baxter, and I attended the Manchester Gilbert and Sullivan Society's sixtieth anniversary on the 24th; I also had to give a talk the following morning and play at a concert in the evening. Sometime previously I had been offered the post of music teacher at Norbury Manor High School for Girls by the headmistress Kathleen Jones, the wife of Brian Jones whom I knew through the G&S world, but I turned it down and suggested my college friend Sandy Leiper as a much more experienced teacher. Sandy took the post, and he was now organising a week-end for the school choir at Slindon College near Arundel in West Sussex. He asked me if I would help him run it which I was happy to do. That was enjoyable and certainly different.

I had also been asked to write programme notes for a booklet to go with a videogram release of Australian Opera's production of *The Gondoliers*. This had come about through a recommendation from Peter Kemp of the Johann Strauss Society: Peter was married to Marilyn Hill Smith, and I had played for Marilyn and Peter Morrison at St James's Palace in 1990. I was happy to take on work like this as I could do it at any time, often in the small hours.

In May there was another *Clara and Old Prickly* with Dione Livingstone at Eye in Suffolk where once again I attempted to portray Johannes Brahms with my obvious Scottish accent. As we didn't do this play very often I never fully learned all the bits of dialogue that I had to deliver, and each performance was always a bit scary.

After this it was Manor House Hospital Operatic Society's production of *Oklahoma!* As it was my first non-G&S show I was a bit apprehensive about it, but from my own point of view it went off without any hitches. But many in the company were not too happy about it as they were used to doing operetta: they would welcome a return to G&S next year. Several new people had joined the Society for this production, but many of them didn't come back, either because they didn't get a part or because they didn't like G&S. At one time, if you auditioned for a part and didn't get it, you stayed with the society and sang in the chorus even if you didn't like the particular show. Now, if people didn't get a part (or didn't like the show) they would often audition with another society, but this was mainly the case with new people who had joined: most of the members had been there for many years, and the old loyalty was still very much in evidence. A good social life also helped to keep the group together. For this production I had a small orchestra which had been named The David Mackie Ensemble; it became something of a gimmick to change the name every year.

Wednesday May 13, during the run of *Oklahoma!*, was a busy day. This was the one hundred and fiftieth anniversary of Arthur Sullivan's birth, and there was a celebratory afternoon tea with a birthday cake at the Savoy Hotel; once again I was 'at the piano', this time providing suitable background music. Among those present was Arthur Jacobs who had written the most recent biography of the composer (1984). A revised and enlarged second edition had just appeared, and he kindly autographed a copy for me. Earlier that day, at the Royal Academy of Music, there had been a lunchtime concert of music by Sullivan (and also Dvořák) to celebrate the sesquicentennial, and later, in July, the Post Office issued five commemorative stamps. Designed by Lynda Gray they depicted characters from *Yeomen*, *Gondoliers*, *Mikado*, *Pirates* and *Iolanthe*.

Immediately after *Oklahoma!* (on Sunday May 17) Sullivan's *Te Deum Laudamus* was recorded in Ely Cathedral under the famous octagon at the crossing. Several other choral numbers by Sullivan were also recorded, and the tape was issued under the title *That Glorious Song of Old*.

June was fairly quiet apart from visits to Elstree and some ballet classes, but it also saw a round-robin letter from Geoffrey Shovelton to say that an agent in the United States, with whom he had been in touch since February, was interested in setting up a tour for us. This was very good news; it was the start of our association with Joanne Rile Artists Management,

Inc. of Jenkintown PA. Further letters followed. One gave possible dates in October/November 1993: still some way off but very encouraging. We now had to provide new photographs and updated biographies; we also had to fill in visa forms. In August we had some publicity photographs taken at Gawsworth Hall in Cheshire. This venue was chosen because some members of the group were singing in a production there. Alistair Donkin was in these photographs, but shortly afterwards he decided to leave the group to concentrate on producing and directing for amateur societies. Lorraine Daniels wasn't able to travel up for the session, and we had to find a substitute; Caroline Tatlow, who had been a chorister with us in D'Oyly Carte, kindly obliged. One of these photographs was eventually used for publicity despite the fact that Alistair and Caroline would not be part of the group.

The agents had been worried to learn that Alistair had decided to leave, but Geoffrey assured them that his replacement, John Ayldon, would be more than adequate. John had not played the comedy baritone roles, but he had agreed to replace Alistair on condition that he wouldn't have to sing the fast 'patter' number "I am the very model of a modern Major-General" (*The Pirates of Penzance*) which was one of Alistair's specialities. He did sing the Lord Chancellor's "When you're lying awake with a dismal headache" (*Iolanthe*) although he was happier with the less taxing numbers such as "When I was a lad I served a term" (*HMS Pinafore*). But he could also sing numbers from the baritone roles he had played so successfully for many years in D'Oyly Carte, and we could now have items that we had not so far been able to include in our programmes. One of the most successful of these was "When a felon's not engaged in his employment - " (*The Pirates of Penzance*) in which John could involve the audience; another was "Take my advice - when deep in debt" (the 'roulette song' from *The Grand Duke*). Even if Alistair had stayed, Geoffrey would have welcomed John into the group, but this would not have been possible for financial reasons. The fast patter numbers always went down well, but John was more versatile, and we now had a useful compromise.

Work continued as before while these arrangements were going on, and yet more doors opened. In August I started working with First Act Opera, a group run by John Nuding and Elaine Holden. One of their regular performers was Judith Buckle who had sung in the *Mikado* concert at Althorp in 1986. The first date was at the Café des Amis at Crossbush (also near Arundel), and this entailed a long drive which cut into the fee, but if I didn't do it someone else would. On August 15 they presented an open-air performance of *Carmen* at Tonbridge Castle and I had to stand in for another pianist. There was also an *Opera & Song Dinner Concert* in the Archbishop's Palace at Maidstone in October. Next day I had to play for Larry Barnes - 'The Viceroy of Versatility' - whose daughter Katie was a great G&S fan who often came to our performances at Sadler's Wells. Larry was a performer in the old music hall tradition. When he was younger he did a Houdini escapology act, but he had given that up before I met him. He often sang a number made famous by the music hall star Gus Elen - *If It Wasn't For the 'Ouses In Between* - and while singing it he would be tearing a newspaper. At the punch line (which is also the title of the song) he would open out the paper which had now been transformed into a row of little houses. Larry was also the Pearly King of Thornton Heath, and it was a treat to see him in his regalia. With its many buttons the jacket was extremely heavy.

Manor House returned to G&S after *Oklahoma!* The next production was to be *The Yeomen of the Guard*, and rehearsals started in October. But Manor House was also my introduction to a second operatic group, the Philbeach Society, which had been founded over thirty years before when a group of friends started singing Christmas carols in Philbeach Gardens in Kensington. One of the members of Manor House also sang with Philbeach, and when a vacancy arose there for a musical director I found myself with even more work. Manor House rehearsed on a Monday, and Philbeach, on a Tuesday, and so there was no clash. Philbeach did some G&S, but they also ventured into musicals and other shows. In September I had received a letter from their president Helen Edwards confirming my appointment as musical director for a 'participative concert performance' of *The Mikado* which took place on Saturday December 5 at the Amadeus Centre in Maida Vale. Philbeach also planned to do a production of *Patience* the following year.

I continued to see the baritone Ralph Meanley, and over many a pint in his local in North London we mapped out our plan to present concerts based on the ballads that we both enjoyed performing. But I was soon in Bexhill again for the next pantomime, another *Goldilocks*. Rehearsals began on Tuesday December 15, and we opened with two performances on the Saturday and a matinée on the Sunday. With just one performance on the 24th I was able to get back to London for Christmas, but we were in Bexhill again for two performances on Boxing Day followed by another Sunday matinée on the 27th. While I was in Bexhill I got to know a lawyer named Bill Llewellyn. Bill was another G&S aficionado who introduced himself one night in the bar after the show; I later met his wife and family. We kept in touch for some time, but like Paul Lenihan he too died at an early age.

IV – 1993

Once again the year began with the last performances of the pantomime. There were four of them in two days as January 1 and 2 this year were a Friday and a Saturday: you were certainly kept busy during the pantomime season. On the Sunday (as in the previous year) I saw some of the friends I had made at Il Boccalino in St Leonards before going back to London. I was now into my second decade of free-lance work; hopefully I had made enough contacts to enable me to keep going.

In the middle of January I began to play the organ regularly, something I could not have done while I was touring with D'Oyly Carte. This was in St John's Church in Robin Hood Lane, Kingston Vale, not far from where I lived. I had previously met the vicar who told me that his wife, who was a piano teacher, wanted to take up the organ but thought that it would be a good idea if she could share the duties with someone. This suited me very well as it meant one Sunday on/ one Sunday off, and we could always swop Sundays if I had to be away, for example in Bolton with Geoffrey Shovelton. If we did more tours of North America I might be away for several Sundays in a row; in that event she would do a full month, and I would do the following month. I didn't tell the vicar that I too was a pianist rather than an organist, but I did now have the opportunity to go along to the church at any time to do some practice; this was particularly useful for pedal work, the one aspect of playing that always gives pianists most bother when they take up the organ.

The one drawback at St John's was that there were two services each Sunday although sometimes the attendance in the evening was barely half a dozen. But occasionally I would have to play at a wedding, and that was yet another fee. This new job lasted for some time until the vicar was defrocked, having committed some misdemeanour. For the moment, his wife was allowed to remain in the vicarage, but she felt that she couldn't show her face in the church, and so for a brief period I had to play every Sunday. I didn't want to do this permanently, and the new incumbent wanted to have a choir which would have meant another week-day evening for rehearsal, and so someone else was appointed. But it had been more valuable experience as well as being another regular source of income. From then on I only played as a deputy until I came back to Scotland in 2007.

Later in January rehearsals began for the Philbeach *Patience* while Manor House was rehearsing *Yeomen*: G&S still much to the fore. W.S. Gilbert famously wrote to Sullivan after the first night of *The Gondoliers* in 1889 that his music "...gives one the chance of shining right through the twentieth century with a reflected light". That light was still burning when the D'Oyly Carte Opera Company closed in 1982, but as the century drew to a close it became apparent that interest in these masterpieces was waning, with much less prospect of the light shining right through the twenty-first century. Nevertheless, G&S was still a major part of my working life, and with another agency in the United States taking an interest in The Best of Gilbert and Sullivan there was every expectation that it would continue to be a source of employment.

I was still playing regularly for Valerie Masterson's pupils, and I met her own teacher Eduardo Asquez (Vivian Tierney was another of his pupils). I also continued to give talks, mainly about G&S: one at the Lensbury Club in London in January, and another for the Sussex Gilbert and Sullivan Society in February. John Nuding and Elaine Holden, who ran First Act Opera, also provided work from time to time, mainly in Sussex or Kent, with concerts in Arundel, Brighton and Eastwell Manor at Ashford; they even organised a riverboat cruise for which an electronic piano had to be hired. Another singer I met was Susan Clements who sang with Vivace Opera; I was the musical director with them for *A Gilbert & Sullivan Gala* in London in February. Susan also sang at Terrazza-Est.

In March I attended a thanksgiving service at St Clement Danes, Strand, for Sir Hugh Wontner who had died in November. A former Lord Mayor of London, he had been a trustee of the D'Oyly Carte Opera Trust, and his daughter Jennifer was married to Victor Emery who had organised the European trips for Geoffrey Shovelton and me in 1984 and 1985. Sir Hugh had also been the honorary president of the Glasgow Gilbert and Sullivan Society, and I now received a letter from Linda Wood inviting me to accept this position which I was very happy to do.

Following the week-end at Slindon College in 1992 we paid a return visit in April with Sandy Leiper's choir from Norbury Manor High School for Girls; at the end of April Manor House began its run of *The Yeomen of the Guard* at the Institute, Hampstead Garden Suburb which finished on May 1: the orchestra's name had been changed to The David Mackie Sinfonietta. On May 11 I played for Anthony Scales of First Act Opera in a programme he had devised called *Around the world (again!) in 50 minutes*. (Presumably he had already presented one called *Around the world in 50 minutes* although I hadn't played for that.) This was a lunchtime concert, part of a series presented by Westminster Libraries, at the Victoria Library in Buckingham Palace Road. I then played for Donald Adams on May 15 and 16 at Oak Hall Manor when he presented *Donald Adams in Concert*.

There was more G&S when Philbeach did *Patience* in Victoria Embankment Gardens (appropriately just a stone's throw from Richard D'Oyly Carte's Savoy Theatre and Savoy Hotel) in June as part of a series of performances by various groups (under the general heading of Open Air Opera) presented by Alternative Arts, an independent arts organisation supported by Westminster City Council. This was just before the run of the show at the Polish Theatre in Hammersmith. In this production we performed my reconstruction of the Duke's song "Though men of rank may useless seem" which we had included in my interval talk during the BBC transmission of the opera in 1989.

I then went up to Scotland, and on the way back I stopped off at Cambridge to play for Donald Adams again on June 26. Doyen of countless G&S performances in D'Oyly Carte and later with Gilbert & Sullivan for All he was now in his sixties, and despite having spent most of his working life with G&S he had recently embarked on a new career in the opera world: later this year he would be playing Mumlal in Smetana's *The Two Widows* for ENO at London's Coliseum. He told me that this Indian summer came as quite a surprise to him, and having dealt almost exclusively with English in the Savoy Operas he found it hard to sing in other languages, particularly the Eastern European ones. As a poor linguist myself I had to agree that we had been lucky in D'Oyly Carte having to deal only with a smattering of foreign phrases such as "Buon' giorno, signorine!/Gondolieri carissimi!" in *The Gondoliers*. It was a pleasure to see Donald again, and, to play for him.

In July I played for Sandy Leiper's choir at Uckfield in East Sussex, and in October I accompanied Valerie Masterson at the Palace Theatre, Newark-on-Trent: I had been there with Opera Players in 1991 to commemorate the bicentenary of Mozart's death. Valerie's programme ranged from Handel and Mozart to Ivor Novello and Noel Coward.

I continued to see friends and colleagues socially, among them Dr Percy Young, who had been my external examiner at Birmingham University in 1974, and his wife Renee: I occasionally stayed with them in Wolverhampton. Percy was now working on a critical edition of *HMS Pinafore* for Broude Brothers. I also made new friends, among them Ed and May Edmans who lived at Maidstone. They were not musicians themselves, but they were great music lovers. They had befriended many of the artists that I worked with, and every so often they would give parties to which these singers and pianists would be invited, and at which they would also be expected to perform. Artists are often reluctant to get too involved with fans, but there are always exceptions, and Ed and May's parties were legendary. My first visit to their house was in September; at the end of October we began our long-awaited second series of tours of North America.

Chapter 6 – Another agent

I – 1993

Our introduction to Joanne Rile Artists Management, Inc. came through Ralph MacPhail, Jr. who pronounced his name Rafe as in the character Ralph Rackstraw in *HMS Pinafore*. He was then Professor of Theatre, Communications and English at Bridgewater College VA. He was also Director of Theatre at the College, and he had used the Rile Management to get attractions for the Lyceum Series of concerts there. A leading authority on the Savoy Operas, I saw him regularly in London when he brought students over from America. He had previously mentioned the Riles to Geoffrey Shovelton who had then successfully contacted them in February 1992. This long-awaited resumption of The Best of Gilbert and Sullivan was our eighth tour, and it was the longest so far (almost a month, from October 26 to November 23) with nineteen concerts. Once again we had a change of personnel which now consisted of Deborah Clague, Lorraine Daniels, Kenneth Sandford, Geoffrey Shovelton, John Ayldon and me. As Geoffrey and Deborah were now together it was inevitable that she would become our next soprano. She had not been in D'Oyly Carte, and she had not had much experience of G&S, but with Geoffrey's expert guidance she soon became familiar with the soprano roles. Just prior to the tour, on September 25, they were married. With a new soprano, a new bass-baritone and a new programme we had a rehearsal for the tour in a church hall in

Kingsthorpe, Northampton (where Geoffrey and Deborah now lived) on October 9.

We flew to Seattle WA on October 26 (Washington was another new state for me). The first concert, sponsored by Key Bank of Washington and others, was in the Pantages Theatre, Broadway Center for the Performing Arts in Tacoma WA on October 28. The second one, the following evening, was in the Washington Center for the Performing Arts in Olympia WA: this was for the South Puget Sound Community College, presented as the first of Five Extraordinary Evenings. Many of our concerts were sponsored by colleges who would hire local theatres for the performances. Next day we flew to Los Angeles CA, passing over Mount St Helens which had erupted in 1980: it looked as if it was still smouldering. At Los Angeles we hired two cars from Alamo. "Remember the Alamo!" was the famous cry, and we certainly had cause to remember this company. We then drove north to San Luis Obispo for our third concert, presented by Questa College Public Events and held in Questa College Auditorium: we were described in the programme as Stars of the London Musical Stage. The audience here seemed unfamiliar with the material and didn't know when to laugh or clap. Socially, I met up with Joe Contreras. I had first met Joe and his wife Ducelia (a friend of my cousin June) in Long Beach CA in 1978, and I had met them again at Ambassador College CA on our second Byers, Schwalbe tour in 1984. Ducelia had since died, but Joe had driven up from Long Beach to come to our concert. It was on the return journey to Los Angeles that we had our accident.

It was October 31 - Hallowe'en: an appropriate day although it was a pleasant enough journey down; we even passed a Cord, a rare American car. It was a Sunday, and as we got closer to Los Angeles the traffic began to build up; it was almost at a standstill when we got into the city, partly due to road works. We were about three miles from our destination when it happened. Geoffrey, Deborah and Lorraine were in the first car; Deborah was driving. I was in the second car, directly behind it, with John Ayldon and Ken Sandford. John was driving, and I was in the front passenger seat half watching the traffic and also doing some map-reading. I happened to look up from this and saw that Deborah's car had braked. It wasn't very far in front of us, and I suddenly realised that we weren't slowing down. In an involuntary reaction I yelled "John, stop!" I don't know if his attention had wandered, but he then jammed on the brakes which I had previously noted were rather spongy. But to no avail: the car didn't stop, and we crashed into Deborah's car. There didn't appear to be too much damage to it although it had received such a jolt that its boot (or trunk, as they call it in North America) wouldn't open. But the front of ours had definitely crumpled, and we discovered that my passenger door wouldn't open. This was all bad enough, but in running into our other car we had propelled it into the car in front which was a brand new BMW. Apart from a few minor scratches there didn't seem to be too much damage there either, but the owner was none too pleased. We had taken out insurance, and we exchanged details before limping on to the Alamo depot.

In all of this I don't know who came off worst. I think I was the only one who drew blood as my hand hit the dashboard causing a scab from a previous minor injury to break, leaving a blood stain on the map. Ken said that he felt some whiplash; Lorraine, in the back of the first car, would have been closest to the impact, and she may also have been similarly affected. When we finally got to the depot I was fearful for the reaction as we limped into the yard, but I was taken aback by the casual attitude of the staff - "Hi there! You guys OK? How ya doin?" Ken Sandford said that he thought this sort of thing happened all the time (the crash, not the laconic greeting), and as we were dealing with the paperwork another damaged vehicle arrived – on the back of a lorry. "Remember the Alamo!"

We then moved to Brookings SD (South Dakota being yet another new state for me); for part of the journey we again hired two cars, from National this time. We were at Brookings for three days with just one concert for the Brookings Chamber Music Society in the Doner Auditorium at South Dakota State University where there was a very appreciative audience. The piano was a Wurlitzer, a name more often associated with cinema organs. Our free time here, although welcome, was marred by the news of the death, from a heart attack, of our former colleague Meston Reid, principal tenor with D'Oyly Carte from 1974-82, aged just forty-eight. Ironically, he had died on October 31, the day of our accident in Los Angeles.

Next, there were concerts in Peoria IL and Schaumburg IL. The first of these was at the Peoria Civic Center, presented by the Amateur Musical Club, where the audience of approximately six hundred, which included a contingent from the Mid-West Gilbert and Sullivan Society, was scattered throughout yet another vast two thousand-seater auditorium. The response seemed lacklustre although they apparently enjoyed it: one response afterwards was "Gee, that was impressive!" We also had competition from the American country singer Reba McEntire who apparently pulled in ten thousand in the Civic Center Arena next door. We left Peoria in a light flurry of snow for our next venue, the Schaumburg Prairie Center for the Arts, the concert sponsored by the Village of Schaumburg. The audience here was one of the best so far. But this theatre seated just four hundred and twenty, and it was full. The intimacy of a small theatre invariably helped our performances, particularly as this enabled people who were not familiar with the Savoy Operas to catch all the words. Our programmes were a mixture of solos, duets and ensembles which were sometimes preceded by the appropriate dialogue, and in some of the vast auditoria that we played the dialogue was often lost.

From Schaumburg we moved to Washington DC for a further two concerts (matinée and evening on a Sunday) at the Baird Auditorium in the Natural History Museum. We didn't always have a new programme for every tour although we did have one this time which was useful as we came here regularly. But the audiences seemed to be happy with whatever we gave them, and every programme invariably included familiar items, even if presented in a different order. We always enjoyed being here, but we were in one of the seediest hotels we had encountered anywhere, an Econo Lodge (luckily only for one night), and we were happy to move on to our next destination.

Geoffrey Shovelton, a born raconteur, always introduced the various numbers at these concerts, often two or three at a time, and he would also tell stories of the things that had happened during our constant touring with D'Oyly Carte. One concerned a mid-week matinee of *The Mikado* in which Geoffrey played the hero Nanki-Poo. We were in Bournemouth; it was a hot summer day, and there was no air-conditioning in the theatre. The audience consisted mainly of pensioners, most of whom would have had a good lunch and were now half asleep. The performance got under way; there was an occasional titter and a smattering of applause here and there, but otherwise it was fairly quiet. Then, in a scene with the heroine Yum-Yum, Geoffrey delivered his line "But we are quite alone, and nobody can see us". Before Yum-Yum could reply an old man on the front row shouted out "I can see you!" and this got the biggest laugh of the afternoon.

The next few days after Washington were quite hectic. First of all there were two concerts in Virginia. For the first one we drove virtually the whole length of the state on Route 81. This took over six hours, but it was a delightful journey through the Appalachians with the Blue Ridge Mountains on one side. We passed towns called Glasgow and Edinburg [sic] and chuckled at a few more signs: Carlos O'Kelly's Mexican Café, a large truck labelled Mobile Chapel and a curious notice that read 'Hear rocks sing'. Our destination, close to the borders of Tennessee and North Carolina, was Emory and Henry College where the group was billed as Historic D'Oyly Carte Soloists. We played at the Kings Center in

Emory in a large gymnasium that wasn't ideal for us, particularly as regards the dialogue. But we still got a standing ovation. Afterwards, a lady told us that her husband had played for D'Oyly Carte on one of its North American tours. The following morning we gave a seminar for some students before driving about two thirds of the way back to Bridgewater College where we were to perform at Cole Hall as part of the college's Lyceum Series.

Ralph MacPhail, Jr., our contact here, and his wife Alice provided us with a very nice meal at their home where we were joined by Harry and Betty Benford from Ann Arbor MI, Em Ware from St Louis MO and Kay Applegate who was now living in North Carolina. When Ken Sandford knocked at the MacPhails' door it was opened by their teenage son Alexander. "Hello, I'm Ken Sandford", said Ken. "I know", said Alexander. "I grew up in this house listening to you on records". Ken was a heavy smoker, and Ralph decided to put the cigarette ends in a plastic bag for his collection. But Alice was too quick for him: she had already consigned them to the dustbin. Thwarted! Such is the collecting mania, as I know only too well myself.

After the concert in Bridgewater we had to drive another hundred miles back to Washington DC where we arrived at 01.00. We then had to return the cars and catch a flight to Atlanta GA at 05.45 so there was very little sleep at the hotel that night: barely a couple of hours; I believe John Ayldon didn't bother going to bed at all. We finally arrived at Tampa FL; we then had to hire another two cars to drive across the Courtney Campbell Causeway to Clearwater (Gilbert would have loved that alliteration) where we performed in yet another vast two thousand-seater auditorium, the Ruth Eckerd Hall, to what appeared to be a full house. It was presented by PACT, Inc. and was described as an Adults-at-Leisure Concert. Luckily it was a matinée, and we then finally had a free evening. A recommended restaurant was the Key West Grill which specialised in fish, and at last we were able to relax over a wonderful meal. The following day we flew to Fort Lauderdale FL where we performed at the Broward Center for the Performing Arts, once again billed as Stars of the London Musical Stage. There were two auditoria here, and we had been booked to perform in the Au-Rene Theater seating some two thousand eight hundred, but as ticket sales had only reached about five hundred we transferred (thankfully) to the Amaturo Theater which seated about six hundred and fifty. This concert was on November 11, Armistice Day, but it was a balmy day with a lovely blue sky: so different to a typical Armistice Day at home.

The final section of this tour took us back to the North-East for another seven concerts. The first of these was in yet another Performing Arts Center, this time at Stockton State College, Pomona NJ; here we finally met Joanne Rile and her husband. We then drove north to the Bardavon Opera House in Poughkeepsie (pronounced P'keepsie) NY where we shared the concert with a local Gilbert and Sullivan Society: they opened our programme with a selection from their next show *The Pirates of Penzance*. Their presence, and that of their friends, made for a very good audience. Afterwards, we had to stay onstage and answer questions about D'Oyly Carte. Next, we drove north to Albany NY where the concert, for Siena College, Loudonville NY, was at the Empire State Performing Arts Center, an oddly-shaped building called The Egg which seated about six hundred. After the concert we met Elizabeth Burgess who had been a chorister in D'Oyly Carte from 1949-51 and who had played Fleta (*Iolanthe*) and Inez (*The Gondoliers*).

There was much driving in this last section of the tour; Deborah and I did most of it. From Albany we drove to Lancaster NH for our next concert at White Mountains Regional High School in Whitefield NH. This was presented by the Noyes Lecture Fund. Driving through these New England states was very pleasant, even in November, and Lancaster was a lovely small town, the sort of place, as locals told us, where you could leave your car door unlocked and the engine running while you went into a shop. It was here that we met not only Deborah's mother and stepfather but her own father James Clague who had travelled up for the concert. Typically, in a High School, the piano was not very good, and there was a lack of suitable dressing-room accommodation, but, as so often in these venues, we had a wonderful audience who responded enthusiastically.

Our next concert was at the Tilles Center for the Performing Arts in Long Island University at Brookville NY. After our delightful drive to Lancaster, traffic free for much of the way, we now had to negotiate heavy traffic as we came into New York via Mamaroneck, where we came to a standstill, and the toll bridge at Throgs Neck which took us on to Long Island. Once again we were in a huge two thousand-seater auditorium (with particularly difficult acoustics), and on this occasion the singers were miked: otherwise I don't think any of the dialogue would have been heard. While we were here I saw my cousin Mina from Greenock who had lived on Long Island for many years.

The penultimate concert was in Wayne NJ at the Rosen Auditorium, YM/YWHA of North Jersey. In the audience was a contingent from the New York Gilbert and Sullivan Society including Jesse and Rochelle Shereff whom we now knew well. (Other New Yorkers that I got to know and kept in touch with were Hope and Jay Yampol and Harry Forbes. Harry, like Ralph MacPhail, Jr., made regular trips to London, and I usually managed to see him when he came over.) It was in Wayne that the accident-prone Geoffrey Shovelton walked into a glass door. His nose bled profusely for some time before the flow was staunched with the aid of some ice.

Our final concert was in the Carver Hall at the Kenneth S. Gross Auditorium, Bloomsburg University, Bloomsburg PA, on Sunday November 21. The piano here was excellent (a Knabe, a make I hadn't come across before), and the concert went very well: a good end to our first tour for Joanne Rile.

Our last day, November 22, was the 30th anniversary of John F. Kennedy's assassination in 1963, and there was much about this on daytime TV; it also happened to be the 93rd anniversary of Sullivan's death in 1900. We flew home overnight in the knowledge that the tour had been a success, and the Riles had given us tentative dates for another tour in February/March 1995: a little way ahead but still something to look forward to. Hopefully there would be even more tours in the future.

We arrived back in London on November 23. The more I did these North American tours the more I realised that I was never going to get used to jet lag, and it was always worse coming back, particularly if you flew overnight. But I had a Philbeach rehearsal that evening, and so there was no time to try to adjust by going to bed. There was a Music in Hospitals concert at Fareham on the Wednesday, and there were ballet classes on the Thursday. On the Friday there was the first of four BBC days I had to make up at Elstree: no rest for the wicked, but I was happy that I was coming back to work and not to days of doing nothing.

Having done G&S (*The Yeomen of the Guard*) this year, Manor House's next production was to be Offenbach's *La Belle Hélène* for which principal auditions were now being held. The piano at the hospital was so bad that it was decided to try to find another one, and I was dispatched to Forest Hill in South-East London to look at one. It wasn't perfect, but anything was better than the one we had, and so I said I would take it. The lady who was selling it was the widow of a band leader, and she also offered me a large quantity of music which I somehow managed to pack into my car. It consisted mainly of popular songs of the 1940s and 1950s which were often difficult to find, and it was very useful as I was now regularly playing lighter music at the CAA and elsewhere.

Philbeach gave another 'participative concert performance', this time of *The Gondoliers*, at the Amadeus Centre on December 4, and as Christmas approached I found myself conducting a group from the Society who always sang

Christmas carols in St John's Wood, either in one of the main thoroughfares or in the Hospital of St John and St Elizabeth. If we were at the Hospital we would have mulled wine and mince pies afterwards, but it wasn't always pleasant performing out of doors at that time of year, particularly if it rained or snowed. Earlier in the year I had had a phone call from Phillip Charles to say that there would be no pantomime at Bexhill this year. As virtually all of these shows had been written by Phillip's wife Jennifer there was an undoubted similarity between them; I think Bexhill, like Barnstaple, had finally said "Thank you, but no thank you". With no show this year I was able to see my mother at Christmas: she had now moved to a flat in Skelmorlie, North Ayrshire. I didn't do a pantomime again until I moved back to Scotland.

With another Elstree to be made up I came back to London for the last week of the year; I also played for a concert at Grim's Dyke. Although it was W.S. Gilbert's last home it had been designed for the painter Frederick Goodall by the architect Norman Shaw, and it is therefore one of the very few buildings that has a Blue Plaque with no less than three names on it. The concert was on December 31, and so I saw in the New Year there. It was a venue that was to become much more familiar to me just a few years later.

II – 1994

Although the pantomimes appeared to have come to an end I wasn't too worried as I was getting used to the workings of the free-lance world, and I now had various sources of employment. Like the pantomimes, any one of these sources might dry up, but something else would usually take its place. On January 15 I played for a group called Quintessence who gave a G&S concert in Frinton. At the end of the month John Nuding and Elaine Holden's First Act Opera gave two evenings at the Towngate Theatre, Basildon with a programme called

Mr Gilbert & Mr Sullivan: the old D'Oyly Carte was represented by Lorraine Daniels, John Ayldon and myself, and the new company by the soprano Lesley Echo Ross and the tenor David Fieldsend. Lorraine and I also took part in two concerts in October, one in Saffron Walden, Essex and another in Streatham, London.

Manor House rehearsals for *La Belle Hélène* had started on January 10, and Philbeach rehearsals started on January 18. Their next production was to be *The Threepenny Opera* (by Bertolt Brecht and Kurt Weill) in April. But Philbeach was also involved in something that promised to be even more interesting, namely the next BALOE performances. This acronym stood for British American Light Opera Exchange, an ongoing relationship with the Village Light Opera Group of New York (VLOG) which had started in 1976 with VLOG coming to London to join Philbeach in a performance of *The Pirates of Penzance*. The following year Philbeach went to New York for a joint production of *HMS Pinafore*. This exchange had also happened in 1982-83 and 1988-89, and it was about to happen again. The show was to be Rodgers and Hart's *The Boys From Syracuse*, based on Shakespeare's *The Comedy of Errors*, and the performances would be in New York in August. One of the traditions of this joint enterprise was that the visiting group's conductor would conduct the show, and so I would be the conductor in New York, something I was very much looking forward to. A London group, Centre Stage, was presenting it at the Steiner Theatre in February, and we all went along to see it.

The now well-established pattern of work continued much as before, but it was always changing; one of the casualties of this year was the BBC job at Elstree. I couldn't always get there on a Monday, and my last visit was on Wednesday March 23. I was sorry to lose that one.

On April 10, a Sunday, the Gilbert and Sullivan Society celebrated its seventieth birthday with a concert in the Savoy Theatre which included excerpts from all the Savoy Operas as well as some rarely heard works by Sullivan and Richard D'Oyly Carte. The artists, all ex-D'Oyly Carte, were Valerie Masterson, Gillian Knight, John Ayldon, Gareth Jones, Geoffrey Shovelton and me. This started at 15.00, but patrons could also have a pre-theatre luncheon at the nearby Simpson's-in-the-Strand where a full three-course meal with coffee could be had for what now seems the absurdly small sum of £15.00. Shortly after this, at the end of April, Philbeach staged three performances of *The Threepenny Opera* at the Amadeus Centre, and in May came Manor House's week of *La Belle Hélène*, again at the Institute, Hampstead Garden Suburb. This was my third show for Manor, and also my third producer Shane Collins, a larger-than-life character who stayed with Manor House for five years. The 'orchestra', now reduced because of financial constraints, was listed as The Marabar Quartet with Alan Gout - Piano. For the first time the other players were also listed individually. In July, Philbeach again gave two concert performances for Open Air Opera at Victoria Embankment Gardens, this time of *The Gondoliers*.

One of the pleasures of this life style was that no two weeks would be the same. I hadn't played for Andrew Meadmore for some time, but work for Music in Hospitals was increasing. This was usually just a single concert on any one day in or near London, but there were also tours which might last for a week with ten or more concerts: there was one in June with Judith Baxter and Noel Drennan which covered Bromsgrove, Fleetwood, Lytham St Anne's, Manchester, Blackpool, Lancaster Moor, Leeds and York. On two separate tours, each with concerts in the Worcester area, I stayed with an old friend Ian Matthew who was now teaching at the Royal Grammar School Worcester.

Geoffrey Shovelton and Deborah Clague (now Mrs Geoffrey Shovelton) also worked for Music in Hospitals, and I did three tours with them this year. There was one in July covering Birmingham, Liverpool, Lancaster and York, one in August which took us as to Wakefield, Morpeth (the furthest north in

England I ever got with MiH), Prudhoe, Newcastle and York, and one in Wales in December where we did three concerts on each of four consecutive days in Caerphilly and in and around the valleys north of the town. One day, in one of the valleys, we couldn't find a particular care home, and we stopped to ask someone for directions. "Oh yes," was the reply, in a strong Welsh accent, "it's just up the hill there [pointing]. You can't miss it". So up we went - and missed it: we had to ask a number of people before we found it. Another artist I met through Music in Hospitals was the flautist Mark Underwood with whom I would later do an interesting Channel Islands tour.

Life wasn't all work, of course, and there were plenty of social activities. (There were also several relationships over the years, but it will perhaps be kinder to draw a veil over these.) Early in January, thanks to Sandra Dugdale, I was invited to a party in a fascinating house in Hampstead called The Convent where, as so often, I had to do some accompanying: one of the guests at the party was the actress Stephanie Cole. I went up to Scotland in March and attended two events which were part of an eightieth birthday tribute to Frederick Rimmer who had been Professor of Music at Glasgow University when I was a student there in the early 1970s. The first of these was a lecture on the recently discovered *Messe solennelle* by Berlioz; this was followed by its first Scottish performance. The following day there was another concert which featured a former fellow-student from the RSAMD, Patricia MacMahon, accompanied by one of my former university lecturers Kenneth Elliott. There was also a third concert, but I missed that one as I had to drive back to London. But it had been a pleasant diversion from the normal routine.

My former D'Oyly Carte colleague Paul Seeley was married on June 25. Among the guests were former D'Oyly Carte artists Jon Ellison, Beryl Dixon, Fred Sinden (Beryl's husband) and myself; also Shelagh Fawcett from the wardrobe department. Later in the year, on November 25, I was in

Cambridge to attend a performance of Elgar's unfinished opera *The Spanish Lady*, a reconstruction by Percy Young from the composer's sketches: this was part of the Cambridge Elgar Festival. It was good to see Percy and his wife Renee again. These were two very pleasant occasions, but there were sadder moments too. There was a memorial service at St Paul's, Covent Garden on February 21 for our D'Oyly Carte colleague Meston Reid who had died suddenly in October 1993; on October 12 I attended the funeral of Leonard Osborn, former D'Oyly Carte principal tenor, who had latterly been director of productions from 1977-80 during my years with the Company.

But the highlight of 1994 was undoubtedly the production of *The Boys From Syracuse* in New York. We flew out on Saturday July 23, and we were there for two weeks, the show running for three days from August 4-6 at the Fashion Institute of Technology's Haft Auditorium (thankfully, the auditorium was air-conditioned as it can be stiflingly hot in New York in August). Some of the VLOG cast were known to some of the Philbeach cast from previous BALOEs, but with lots of rehearsals we all got to know each other fairly quickly, and I made some new American friends that I kept in touch with, among them the show's director and choreographer Nathan Hull. I don't recall much sight-seeing this time, but I did manage to get to St John's Cathedral: a vast building, and still incomplete (as was Washington Cathedral when I visited it in 1988), it was known locally as St John the Unfinished. But there was a lot of socialising, particularly in an Irish pub, well into the small hours. Prior to starting rehearsals I had known only two numbers from *The Boys From Syracuse* - "Falling in love with love" and "This can't be love" - but there were other numbers which were equally good such as "He and she" and the wonderful female trio "Sing for your supper". Conducting in New York certainly made up for the lack of a tour for Joanne Rile this year, and it was a useful addition to my c.v.

Back in London there were two concerts that I was looking forward to. These were with Ralph Meanley, and they were essentially ballad concerts: we were hoping that they might be the first of many. Once so popular (the music publishing firm of Boosey & Co. had been promoting ballad concerts since the 1860s) these songs had gradually gone out of fashion, and it was something of a leap of faith to think that we might encourage people to listen to them again. But we both felt that many of them were really excellent, and it was a pity that they were rarely heard now. We were not the first to try to revive interest in this repertoire. A number of artists had made recordings of Victorian and Edwardian ballads throughout the 1970s, among them Benjamin Luxon and Robert Tear who together sang on two albums with André Previn as the accompanist; also Stuart Burrows (accompanied by John Constable) and Felicity Palmer (again with John Constable). The Parlour Quartet, for whom I deputised occasionally, produced two albums, and Tom Round, former principal tenor with D'Oyly Carte, also produced one.

In no way pretentious, ballads usually tell a simple story (often quite an amusing one), and the best of them have engaging and memorable settings. Many of Sullivan's songs (such as *The Distant Shore*, to words by W.S. Gilbert) can be classed as ballads, but there were other less famous composers, well-known in their day but virtually forgotten now, for whom, particularly if they had a melodic gift, the ballad was a natural mode of expression. One such was Sullivan's contemporary Stephen Adams (1844-1913) who wrote *The Holy City*, but there were many others such as Wilfrid [sic] Sanderson, W.H. Squire and Kennedy Russell; also Haydn Wood (1882-1959) who wrote *Roses of Picardy*, and Eric Coates (1886-1957), 'the uncrowned King of Light Music', who wrote *Bird Songs at Eventide*. Many of these ballads were written by women, among them the composers Frances Allitsen, Amy Woodforde-Finden and Liza Lehmann, and lyric writers such as Georgiana Hubi Newcombe. But no-one, male or female, ever matched the prolific Fred E. Weatherly (1848-1929), a barrister who wrote literally hundreds, perhaps even thousands, of lyrics.

Ralph and I were now close to getting our ideas into a more practical form; what became known as Bentley Concert Productions (from the area Bentley in Walsall, Ralph's home town) began life at one of our social meetings, this one at the Orange Brewery in Pimlico (where the excellent beer was brewed on the premises) in June of this year. These concerts would be based on the repertoire of the Australian singer Peter Dawson whom Ralph greatly admired, and at first we had two programmes: *Shipmates O' Mine* (the title of one of Wilfrid Sanderson's ballads), which was a concert of sea songs (as befitting a salt-water nation), and *Rolling Down to Rio* (the title of Edward German's setting of one of the poems in Kipling's *Just So Stories*), which was a more general selection of songs and ballads. Our inaugural concert, *Rolling Down to Rio*, was at the Gladys Child Theatre, Southgate College in North London on September 24 although we had tried out some of the numbers the previous week at a nursing home also in North London. We opened with *On the Road to Mandalay*, the famous setting by Oley Speaks of one of Kipling's *Barrack-Room Ballads* (originally entitled just *Mandalay*), a 'must' in any ballad concert, and included some more serious numbers such as Vaughan Williams' *The Vagabond*. We finished with W.H. Squire's perky *A Chip of the Old Block*, and as an encore we did one of our own favourites *When the Sergeant Major's on Parade* by Ernest Longstaffe who had latterly held a position at the BBC and whose radio pantomime *Dick Whittington* I had found in the archives. I always played some suitable solos at these concerts, such as Elgar's *Salut d'amour* or Rubenstein's *Romance*. I was happier just accompanying, but as in the Music in Hospitals concerts I had to give the singer a rest from time to time.

Our second concert was *Shipmates O' Mine*, and we thought it would be a good idea to try to arrange this for

Trafalgar Day (October 21, a date that would assume more importance for us as the years went on), and to try to find a suitable venue in which to present it. And so we duly gave the first performance of this programme on the famous tea clipper *Cutty Sark* at Greenwich. We opened with *The Fishermen of England*, a stirring number from Montague Phillips' light opera *The Rebel Maid*, and finished, appropriately, with Sanderson's *Shipmates O' Mine*, a fine song in its own right. For an encore we did Arne's *Rule, Britannia!* in the authentic version revived by Sir Malcolm Sargent and sung at the Henry Wood Promenade Concerts. My solos this time were *Gondola Song* (one of Mendelssohn's *Songs without Words*) and a piece called *Steamboat Polka*. As there was no piano on board we had to hire an electronic keyboard. These were the only two concerts in 1994, but Bentley Concert Productions was now well and truly launched.

Throughout the year, and in my own time, I had been involved in a project for the Canadian Children's Opera Chorus who had asked me to prepare a children's version of *The Pirates of Penzance* (there had been performances by children of *HMS Pinafore* in 1879-80 and of *Pirates* in 1884-85). I was able to leave much of the writing for the ladies as it stood, but the writing for the men all had to be written in the treble clef; there were also numerous alternatives to high or low notes. The choral writing had to be reduced to its harmonic essentials, invariably in three parts: soprano 1, soprano 2 and alto, sometimes with the notes realigned. The famous unaccompanied "Hail, Poetry" chorus was quite difficult, but I managed to retain four parts for most of it. This occupied me from February 4 until September 7.

I continued to be kept busy with the two operatic societies, ballet classes, masonic dates, Music in Hospitals, organ playing and other work; I also continued to play regularly for Valerie Masterson. In November I played for Judith Buckle who had sung with us at Althorp in 1986: this was yet another Spaghetti Opera at a restaurant in Bromley called Caligula.

It proved to be a one-off, but I did play for Judith again. On December 3 Philbeach presented *Iolanthe*, another of its participative concerts, and on the 19th Geoffrey Shovelton, Deborah Clague and I gave a concert for the Eastbourne Ashridge Circle. It was good to be in Eastbourne again. After the Welsh tour for Music in Hospitals in December I went up to Scotland for Christmas, but I was back in London by the 29th. I missed the pantomimes, but more for the fun of doing them than for the financial reward. Now that Ralph Meanley and I had got Bentley Concert Productions off the ground we were looking forward to what the next year might bring.

III – 1995

The year started with a flurry of activity. I was still playing at St John's Church, and as January 1 was a Sunday I had to play for two services. I then went to a New Year party in Wimbledon. On January 3 I went up to Manchester to give a talk to the Gilbert and Sullivan Society, and at the end of the week we made a second recording with our group The Best of Gilbert and Sullivan. This was deemed necessary as we would shortly be starting a second North American tour for Joanne Rile, and we needed to have a recording to sell at our concerts that represented the group as it now was. The first recording was made in 1988 using the master tape from our *St Paul Sunday Mornings* broadcast in St Paul MN. Vivian Tierney had left by then, and the line-up had been Sandra Dugdale, Lorraine Daniels, Kenneth Sandford, Geoffrey Shovelton, Alistair Donkin and me. Sandra had now been replaced by Deborah Clague, and Alistair, by John Ayldon, but we still had Lorraine, Ken, Geoffrey and me. This second recording, like the first, was a tape, and it was also issued under the group name The Best of Gilbert and Sullivan, but when it was later made available as a CD we added the subsidiary With Heart and with Voice, a quotation from *The Sorcerer*. It was recorded at Nene College, Northampton on Friday January 6. We later discovered that one number ("If you go in" *(Iolanthe)*) had been omitted from the sleeve note in the tape: this was rectified in the CD. As with our first tape the art work was done by Geoffrey Shovelton.

Rehearsals for the two operatic societies started again the following week. Manor House was now doing *Ruddigore*; Philbeach was planning a double bill of Gilbert and Sullivan's *Trial by Jury* and Joseph Horovitz's clever spoof oratorio *Horrortorio*. But there was also the forthcoming visit of the Village Light Opera Group from New York for the reciprocal BALOE to be held this time in London: the show, to be conducted by Ron Noll of VLOG, would be Offenbach's *Orpheus in the Underworld*. Other regular work, such as the ballet classes and Music in Hospitals, also started again, and there was a concert with Lorraine Daniels in Stowmarket at the beginning of February. Shortly after that we were off again to the United States for our ninth tour. The line-up for this one was the same as for the previous one, and now also as in our second recording: Deborah Clague, Lorraine Daniels, Kenneth Sandford, Geoffrey Shovelton, John Ayldon and me.

The tour lasted from February 10 until March 6 and consisted of fifteen concerts. There had been nineteen on the previous tour although this was still a good number. But that first tour for Joanne Rile proved to be the longest of the entire series, including the Byers, Schwalbe tours. This time we also had much more driving than before, presumably to save money on air fares. We flew first to John F. Kennedy Airport in New York, and we then had to get another flight to Washington DC. As we walked through the airport we saw much renovation work; there was a sign that read 'Pardon our dust', another amusing Americanism. As we checked in for the second flight the lady looked at my ticket and said "I've heard that name. You famous? An actor, huh?" I told her that I was a musician, but she wasn't likely to have heard of me unless she was a G&S fan or had perhaps attended one of the performances of *The Boys From Syracuse* in New York the previous year. Neither alternative seemed to ring a bell, and she said "I'll go home and sleep on it". Needless to say, I never found out if I had a famous namesake. But it isn't a particularly common name.

When we arrived at Washington we found that the Riles had only made provision for us to have one car, and cars were now getting smaller: there was no way in which we could possibly fit ourselves and our luggage into one. We phoned the Riles who said that they couldn't afford to hire two cars, particularly as we would be doing a lot of driving. On previous tours we had sometimes been picked up by sponsors who would arrive in a seven or eight-seater minivan, and we asked the Riles if we could have one of those, but still they refused. It seemed an impossible situation until we realised that the difference was only $20 per day, and as this was cheaper than hiring two cars we decided that we would hire a minivan and pay the difference ourselves: this worked out at just under $3.50 per person per day. It was an unfortunate start to the tour, but we had solved the problem.

We opened at the now familiar Baird Auditorium in Washington with two concerts, the first being the one hundredth concert since we had started at the University of Rhode Island in February 1984. We had a new programme for this tour, and we were a bit apprehensive about it, particularly as Deborah Clague was not so familiar with the material. It didn't settle down until the second half, and we all made mistakes of one sort or another, but the second concert was better, and it improved with repetition as we went along. From Washington we moved to the Grand Opera House, Wilmington DE: we had appeared there on our first tour in 1984, the singers performing with the Delaware Symphony Orchestra. We didn't have the orchestra this time, but we did have a chorus formed from five G&S groups in the area: if we had known how good they were, and how well they knew the music, we would have used them more. But we also discovered that one of the singers was a former D'Oyly Carte chorister John Dennison who had been with the Company for a year from 1956-57. We were delighted to meet him, and we altered the programme slightly to let him sing the solo "This the autumn of our life" in the opening chorus of *The Yeomen of the Guard*. We also added, as an encore, "Once more *gondolieri*", the closing section of Act ll of *The Gondoliers*, to give the excellent chorus one more chance to shine. Afterwards, there was a reception in one of the oldest houses in Delaware, supposedly dating from 1690. It had been a very good evening.

We then had a series of concerts in colleges and universities. The first of these was at Lynchburg College at Lynchburg VA, the concert being held in the college's Snidow Chapel. Ralph MacPhail, Jr. from Bridgewater College VA, who had introduced us to Joanne Rile, came to the concert with his wife Alice. The next concert was in the Johns Auditorium at Hampden-Sydney College at Farmville VA, some fifty miles away. I drove on this leg of the tour, in freezing rain, which took us through the famous Appomattox where, at the end of the American Civil War, General Robert E. Lee surrendered to General Ulysses S. Grant (a future president of the United States): a sign as you entered the town read 'Where our nation united'. It was always frustrating not to have time to stop at such places, but it was at least interesting to have been there. Hampden-Sydney College turned out to be all-male, but there was an all-female college nearby called Longwood, and so we didn't just have an all-male audience. Few of the students seemed to know much about G&S, but the concert went over well. There was a reception afterwards, and when we got back to the hotel Geoffrey Shovelton had another accident, banging his head on the van's rear door.

Next morning Geoffrey seemed to be all right, and we set off for South Carolina, now the thirty-second state I had been in. The concert here was in the Belk Auditorium at the Presbyterian College, Clinton SC, the venue being a proper theatre. Again we got the impression that not many of the audience seemed to be familiar with G&S. It was still raining when we drove from Clinton to Rock Hill SC for a concert at Winthrop University: this was held in the Byrnes Auditorium which seated no less than three thousand five hundred, the largest venue we had yet played. We also had a very large chorus of over two hundred, drawn from four separate choirs. The soloists had to have microphones which they didn't like, particularly as they weren't working properly, but the concert went down well. In yet another howler the programme listed an excerpt from *The Yoeman* [sic] *of the Guard*.

We then travelled to Brevard NC for a concert, part of yet another Performing Arts Series, in the Dunham Auditorium at Brevard College which was right in the middle of this delightful small town. For our accommodation here we were given a four-bedroomed house in the college grounds. This would have meant some rearranging and some sharing, but as smoking was not allowed in the building Ken Sandford and John Ayldon both elected to find accommodation elsewhere; the remaining four of us now had plenty of room to spread out. As it was a Sunday the concert was an afternoon one. The following morning I was surprised to see a white squirrel in the garden. These squirrels were a unique feature of Brevard, but apparently they had originally come from Hawaii. Next day we gave a short concert/lecture at 09.00 in a local school before setting off for Sumter SC. (Fort Sumter, where the Civil War started in 1861, is at Charleston SC.) The concert here, for the Sumter-Shaw Community Concert Association, was in the Patriot Hall. As we had found at other venues the audience didn't seem to realise that you could laugh at comic opera.

The next two concerts were in Oklahoma. Having done a lot of driving recently we were now airborne again, flying from Charlotte NC to Oklahoma City OK via Dallas/ Ft. Worth TX, two more new states for me although Texas was the third state that I had just 'touched down in' to change planes. We were certainly getting around America. We hired another minivan in Oklahoma City and drove some sixty miles north to Stillwater OK. The weather was very pleasant. Despite having done *Oklahoma!* with Manor House I was only now realising what those pioneers were faced with on this flat and seemingly endless terrain. It is awesome country. The concert at Stillwater, presented by Allied Arts, was in the Seretean Center Concert Hall at Oklahoma State University where we had an excellent audience of some six hundred who seemed to be familiar with the repertoire: their enthusiasm carried us along.

Next day we drove from Stillwater to Shawnee OK on a road that was almost dead straight, but with a few undulations to relieve the monotony. On the way we passed a scrap yard for old cars. In the UK, with limited space, these would usually be piled one on top of another: out here, with so much space, the cars were simply parked in rows as in a car park. Many of them, red with rust, dated back to the 1930s; it would have been a treasure trove for vintage car collectors. We somehow missed signs for Shawnee and ended up in Tecumseh (Civil War General William T. Sherman's middle name although he wasn't born here), but eventually we found our way back to Shawnee. With everything so spread out it was difficult to know if you were actually in a town or not. Our hotel was in an area called Biscuit Hill which was on the outskirts. This was even more spread out and really was at the back of beyond. I tried to go 'downtown' for an hour, but there was almost nothing to see except endless space. The concert here was in the Raley Chapel, Yarborough Auditorium (a two thousand five hundred-seater) at Oklahoma Baptist University, and again we had an excellent audience. We were to have been in a smaller hall, but the demand for tickets had exceeded its capacity, and so we moved into the larger one. Among the audience were Overton and Suzette Shelmire from Texas, great fans of D'Oyly Carte whom I had met briefly in Washington DC during the 1978 tour of North America. Overton had just written a book about his life, and he kindly presented each of us with a signed copy. I discovered that as a child in the 1930s he remembered meeting his great-grandfather who had fought in the American Civil War (1861-65) - a fascinating link with history.

Our short stay in Oklahoma was one of the most unusual of all our visits to various parts of the United States, adding to our growing experience of this amazing country which is really a vast continent. The sense of space was overwhelming; it seemed to be yet another place where doors might be left open when people went out, and engines left running when they went into a shop. "We're in the middle of nowhere. Nothing ever happens here", was a comment we heard several times. It was, therefore, a great shock, shortly after we got back to the UK, to hear of the terrorist attack on the Alfred P. Murrah Federal Building in Oklahoma City on April 19, 1995 which resulted in one hundred and sixty-eight deaths, over five hundred injuries and much other damage. What remained of the building was later demolished, a memorial being created on the site. Until the attack on the World Trade Center in 2001, of which it was in some ways a forerunner, it was the worst terrorist attack in the United States. Nothing was quite the same in Oklahoma after that.

The morning after our concert in Shawnee we were up at 06.30 in time to see a spectacular Oklahoma sunrise. We then flew north-east to Toledo OH where we stayed in the Toledo Radisson Hotel, rather expensive at $135 a night but we had a special rate of $45. We stayed there because our concert was being held in the hotel's ballroom. It seated some two hundred, but with a low ceiling it had poor acoustics. Nevertheless, the concert went well, and we had a standing ovation. Among the audience were Michael and Elizabeth Curry whom we had first met in Fremont OH on our sixth tour in October 1988 and who had also come to our concert in Sylvania OH in 1990.

There were just three more concerts: in Ashland KY, Marion IL and New York; once again we had a minivan. It had been snowing, but the weather improved as we drove south. Shortly after leaving Toledo we stopped at a Denny's restaurant where I had a Grand Slam breakfast: two of everything for a mere $1.99 (it was just as well that we would be flying home soon). Kentucky was the thirty-fifth state I had been in. This was something of a milestone, but the following day I drove into the adjacent West Virginia, the only one in the North-East that had so far eluded me: that brought my total to thirty-six. The first of the remaining concerts was in the Ashland Community College Auditorium, presented by Artists in Concert. We should have had a local choir here, but they didn't turn up, and so we did our standard programme which went down very well: the piano was an excellent Baldwin. Next day we drove to Marion IL where the concert was in the Marion Cultural and Civic Center, part of their Patron Series. The concert went well, but the piano, a Steinway this time, was not so good. The audience included Em Ware and Walter Gunn and his wife from St Louis MO; we were delighted to see them. Next day, we set out for New York.

The journey took two days as we first had to drive back to Toledo where we spent the night after returning the minivan. The following day we boarded a Greyhound coach: this was just the second time the group had travelled on one. The last concert was at the Golden Center for the Performing Arts, Queen's College at Flushing NY. The auditorium, seating some two thousand one hundred, was again rather too big for us, but we did our best with it. The printed programme listed mezzo-soprano Lorraine Daniels as a soprano, bass-baritone John Ayldon as a tenor, and baritone Kenneth Sandford as a bass-baritone, but by now we were used to mistakes: in the programme for the concert in Bel Air MD, on our first tour in 1984, four of our six names were spelled wrongly, and *The Yeoman* [sic] *of the Guard* was a recurring feature. The audience here included many of our New York friends, and we were able to see them afterwards: it was a nice way to end the tour.

I was back in London on March 7, and the regular work started again: much of it not perhaps as exciting as a North

American tour but always very welcome. And as usual there was plenty of variety: Philbeach's two-night run of *Trial by Jury* and *Horrortorio* was from March 31-April 1 at the University College School Theatre in Hampstead, and on April 9 there was another concert at Melvyn Tarran's Oak Hall Manor at Sheffield Park with Cynthia Morey and John Fryatt. It was always good to see Melvyn's ever-growing G&S collection which eventually included a Broadwood grand piano that had belonged to Sullivan's mistress Fanny Ronalds: it was virtually identical to our own family piano that was now in my mother's flat in Skelmorlie (and taking up most of the lounge).

The week of May 15-20 saw Manor House's *Ruddigore*. The band hadn't been reduced any further, and it was listed this year (with a slight change) as The Marabas [sic] Quartet with Pam Bray - Piano. I took the opportunity to use the original overture, and I arranged it as a piano quintet which seemed to work quite well: it was certainly something of a novelty. Manor then held a fortieth anniversary dinner in June. In September there was a G&S evening in Lincoln Cathedral that was not very successful. The dialogue and fast 'patter' numbers were simply lost in the vast space although it was still good to be performing in one of the great glories of English mediaeval architecture.

Lorraine Daniels and her husband Brian had decided to try to organise some work for us, and they set up Lorian Enterprises, the name coined from their Christian names. This resulted in a number of engagements, some of them for educational or fund-raising events, including concerts in Stowmarket in February, Peterborough in May, Helmingham in June, Kings Lynn in July (with just Lorraine and John Ayldon but with pupils from a local Primary school) and Saffron Walden in September with Lorraine, John, Deborah Clague and Geoffrey Shovelton.

Peter Pratt, former G&S comedy baritone (from whom John Reed, who was playing those roles when I joined D'Oyly

Carte in 1975, had taken over), died on January 11. I attended his funeral on January 19, but later in the year, on May 22, there was a memorial service for him at St Paul's, Covent Garden at which I had to accompany the sextet "I hear the soft note of the echoing voice/Of an old, old love, long dead - " (*Patience*). I had met Peter a few times although I didn't know him very well, but I did get to know his widow Patience (named after the opera's eponymous heroine) whose father was the former D'Oyly Carte principal baritone Leo Sheffield (1873-1951). At Oak Hall Manor, on September 10, Melvyn Tarran presented a joint tribute to Peter Pratt and Leonard Osborn who had died the previous year. Another death, after a long illness, was that of Gordon MacKenzie on August 25, and I was in Greenock for his funeral on August 29.

There were two concerts with Valerie Masterson this year. The first of these was in March when Valerie was the guest artist at a celebrity concert in Dudley with the Gentlemen Songsters Male Voice Choir. The second concert, in October, was in Valerie's hometown of Birkenhead. There was also a return visit to Dinmore Manor with Geoffrey Shovelton in August and *An Evening with Noel Coward* with Judith Baxter at Moreton Pinkney in Northamptonshire in September.

The Village Light Opera Group of New York arrived in London in July for the BALOE exchange with Philbeach following our performances of *The Boys From Syracuse* in 1994; three performances of *Orpheus in the Underworld* were given at the Questors Theatre in Ealing from August 3-5. As usual, these were conducted by the visiting musical director (VLOG's Ron Noll), and I took a back seat. During the rehearsal period prior to the performances we took our visitors to the Houses of Parliament where we had tea on the terrace overlooking the Thames.

Ralph Meanley and I were hoping that our new venture, Bentley Concert Productions, would produce more work, and from just two concerts in 1994 we had five this year although the first one wasn't until October 21 (Trafalgar Day): another performance of our nautical *Shipmates O' Mine*. The first *Shipmates O' Mine* had been on the tea clipper *Cutty Sark* (also on Trafalgar Day), and we now persuaded the authorities in Portsmouth to let us do this one on HMS *Warrior* (1860), Great Britain's first iron-clad battleship. In the first *Shipmates O' Mine* I played a piece called *Steamboat Polka*, but I had recently acquired a copy of Vaughan Williams' *Sea Songs* which seemed more suitable, and so I played that instead. We were delighted to meet Captain Fraser Morgan of *Warrior* whose maxim was "Don't ask awkward questions"; there was also Captain John Wells, chairman of the Warrior Association who, I discovered, lived in the same village in Hampshire as my cousins and knew them well. Whatever else we managed to do, we now hoped that we could do a Trafalgar Day concert every year, either on a ship or at least somewhere with a maritime connection. Earlier in the year, on May 13 (Arthur Sullivan's birthday), we had planned to present another concert on *Cutty Sark*: it was to be called *At Her Majesty's Pleasure*, and it was to consist of songs and ballads that were popular at the time of Queen Victoria's Diamond Jubilee in 1897. Unfortunately it didn't happen although a poster was prepared for it, but as I was now free, and thanks to Valerie Masterson, I found myself playing for a session with British Youth Opera.

Ralph and I were now working on a third programme, this one based entirely on settings of Kipling's *Barrack-Room Ballads* by the forgotten composer Gerard Francis Cobb (1838-1904), an almost exact contemporary of Sullivan. Among the earliest music that I acquired while still at school was *The Scottish Students' Song Book* published by the well-known Glasgow firm of Bayley & Ferguson (long popular, it first appeared in May 1891 and could still be bought new in 1958 when I got my copy). Divided into sections, the first two songs in the section *Soldier Songs and Sea Songs* were *For to admire* and *Back to the Army again*, settings of Rudyard Kipling's words by Gerard F. Cobb of whom I knew very little other than a brief entry at the back of the book under the heading *Notes about some Contributors*. Even as a schoolboy, and without knowing why, I was greatly taken with these songs as they seemed to stand out among many others in the book. Little did I realise then how much they would eventually mean to me. I later became aware that the texts were two of Kipling's *Barrack-Room Ballads* which had obviously appealed to Cobb as he made some twenty settings in all. I had found some of them in second-hand shops, and I was becoming ever more interested in the man and his music: he too had a genuine melodic gift. I also found other songs that he had written, among them *Cavaliers and Roundheads* and *The Scent of the Lilies*.

I mentioned Cobb, and the few settings that I had acquired, to Ralph, and I discovered that he knew of him through the repertoire of his idol Peter Dawson, the Australian baritone. One of the most popular of the *Barrack-Room Ballads* was *Mandalay*, best-known in Oley Speaks' famous setting. But Cobb had also made a setting of this poem as had the composers Charles Willeby and Walter Hedgcock, and Dawson (no mean composer himself with his equally famous setting of Kipling's *Boots*) had arranged a *Mandalay Scena* using all four settings. Ralph liked the settings I had found, and we decided to see if we could acquire all of them and make another programme devoted entirely to them. We got all the missing ones from the British Library, and we were now preparing our new programme. For a title Ralph suggested *Thank You, Mr Atkins* which is a line from another of the ballads *Tommy*. By chance, a modern edition of the *Barrack-Room Ballads*, edited by John Whitehead whom we were to meet and befriend, had just appeared. John had also written an article *The 'Barrack-Room Ballads' as Treasure Trove* for the March 1995 edition of *The Kipling Journal* which was very helpful.

Shortly after our performance of *Shipmates O' Mine* on HMS *Warrior* we gave it again at the Kirkgate Centre,

Cockermouth on October 26. An old university friend of Ralph, Richard Evans, who lived near Cockermouth with his wife Angela and family, had suggested that we contact the Kirkgate Centre, and Richard and Angela kindly put us up for a few days. Ralph and Richard had long enjoyed hill walking, and so I had to borrow some boots while we were there as we went out for some healthy exercise in that lovely part of the country. It was another week-end of business and pleasure.

Feeling that our somewhat male-orientated programmes needed the female touch we then asked Lorraine Daniels to join us in some lighter programmes covering just about everything from Victorian ballads and Broadway hits to light opera and operetta; we even had a Christmas programme. But our next concert (on December 2 at the Library, Saffron Walden) was a general programme called *Perfect Harmony* which we later adopted as a title for the group.

Following this we did a lighter version of *Shipmates O' Mine*, also with Lorraine, which we called *The Fleet's In* from the song *The Fleet's In Port Again* by Noel Gay. This was a cabaret performance, part of an evening at the Royal College of Art in Kensington Gore on December 15. We decided to do it in costume, and we managed to get naval uniforms from an official shop in Portsmouth: we used them in subsequent performances. Ralph became a captain (complete with scrambled egg on cap), and Lorraine had a Wren officer's uniform, but I was a humble matelot with a 'jumper/seaman's RN/class ll' although whoever had owned it had acquired three gold stripes on his left arm. We were doubtless committing some punishable offence and liable to be hung from the yardarm if caught, but no-one ever challenged us, and the uniforms certainly added much to the performances. Lorraine and I would ever afterwards refer to Ralph as 'the captain'. Three days later, Ralph and I recorded *Shipmates O' Mine* at Nene College, Northampton where our second Best of Gilbert and Sullivan tape had been recorded: the art work for this tape was also done by Geoffrey Shovelton.

Three days after that we repeated *The Fleet's In* at the Royal College of Art. That was the fifth and last Bentley performance of 1995, but we had paid a visit to Bateman's (Kipling's home in East Sussex, now a National Trust property) in November to arrange a concert there in 1996. The Trust's man in charge, David Fox, proved extremely helpful.

To put Bentley Concert Productions on a more business-like footing we had administrative help from Clive Simmonds whom we had both known for some time. We also received help from Sandy Leiper, mainly with regard to recording and acquiring a portable keyboard. With no pantomime I was kept busy with concerts for Music in Hospitals: there were even concerts on Christmas Day and New Year's Eve. I wasn't able to get up to Scotland, but some cousins looked after my mother at Christmas. And so another year came to an end.

Chapter 7 – Towards the millennium

I – 1996

With no pantomime it was another quiet start to the year. We had the first Manor House rehearsal on January 8. After *Ruddigore* in 1995 it would be a non-G&S work this year. I had been consulted on the choice, and I would have suggested Edward German's *Merrie England*, one of the most popular light operas and one I had always wanted to conduct, but Manor had done it in 1970 and also in 1988. I didn't think that they would want to do it again quite so soon, but I suggested another of German's light operas *Tom Jones*. This is not as well-known as *Merrie England*, but the story is familiar, particularly through Tony Richardson's 1963 film starring Albert Finney and Susannah York, and German's music is well up to the standard of *Merrie England*. Perhaps the best-known number, which was often heard in BBC programmes such as *Friday Night is Music Night,* is the waltz song "For tonight, for tonight/Let me dream out my dream of delight", a number that Patricia Cope often sang at our Terrazza-Est evenings: it is similar to the waltz song from *Merrie England* "O who shall say that Love is cruel". Two other numbers, "Dream o' Day Jill" and "If love's content" were also popular at one time. I had some difficulty in persuading the Society to do *Tom Jones*, but they eventually gave in, and once they were familiar with the music they enjoyed it.

Life continued as usual throughout the rest of January and into February with work and social activities. One day in early

February I saw another of my Greenock cousins, Winifred, who with her husband Peter now lived in Hillingdon in Middlesex. Many years before, they had lived in the top flat of a building in Gerrard Street, London W1: it was above a jeweller's workshop. I stayed there as a child in the 1950s when the area was not, as now, the heart of the capital's Chinatown. I think they only rented the flat then, but I wonder what it might be worth today. When I was there one of the hits of the day was *The Little Shoemaker* sung by Petula Clark. We heard it regularly on the radio.

At the end of February we began our tenth North American tour, the third one for Joanne Rile and with the same line-up: Deborah Clague, Lorraine Daniels, Kenneth Sandford, Geoffrey Shovelton, John Ayldon and me. It was shorter than the first two (just ten concerts), and this was worrying as it seemed to be following the pattern of the Byers, Schwalbe tours, but we were still more than happy to be doing another one. The tour began with two concerts in Texas. This time we flew from Gatwick, arriving first of all at Houston where we took another flight to San Antonio. It was surprisingly warm for February although that may be normal in Texas. We then hired the by now customary minivan and drove to our hotel. To help reduce the costs we had been asked if we would share rooms here, and Geoffrey and I shared as did Deborah and Lorraine. Our first concert, on February 22, was at Kerrville TX, some sixty miles north-west of San Antonio, in the Kerrville Municipal Auditorium. This was for the Kerrville Performing Arts Society, and it was well received by an enthusiastic audience. We now had a programme which included excerpts from all thirteen surviving Savoy Operas from *Trial by Jury* to *The Grand Duke*. This time I had a solo, opening the second half of our programme with the ebullient cancan-like dance from *The Grand Duke,* a piece of clever pastiche by Sullivan.

The following day we set off for Conroe TX, some thirty miles north of Houston. This involved a long journey during which we went through Fredericksburg with its Admiral Chester Nimitz (Second World War Commander in Chief, US Pacific Fleet) Museum; we later passed the Lyndon B. Johnson Natural History Park near Johnson City before stopping for a late breakfast at the wonderfully named Dripping Springs. We were now seeing something of this enormous state, having previously just 'touched down' at Dallas/Ft Worth to catch another flight to Oklahoma City on our 1995 tour, and we often heard the Texan expression "Y'all have a good day!" The concert at Conroe was for the Montgomery County Performing Arts Society, and it was held in the Crighton Theatre. This also went down very well. In the audience were Overton and Suzette Shelmire whom we had previously met. Afterwards, they laid on drinks and a splendid supper in their hotel room. They were keen that we might perform in Dallas TX on a subsequent tour, but sadly this never happened.

Next morning we had an early start to catch a flight to Phoenix AZ, yet another new state for me although again it was just a 'touch-down'. But it brought my total to thirty-seven. We were now on our way to Pepperdine University at Malibu CA where we performed at the Smothers Theatre, the concert being presented by the Pepperdine University Center for the Arts. I say 'we', but this was another orchestral concert for which I had to take a back seat: the Pepperdine University Community Symphony Orchestra was conducted by its music director Thomas Osborn. February 25 was a Sunday, and so this concert, like many Sunday ones, was in the afternoon. There was a rehearsal in the morning, and it was everything that I had predicted. The conductor was a competent musician, but you cannot assimilate such an amount of unfamiliar music, performed in a very specific way, in just one rehearsal. We had a different programme for orchestral concerts, the first half opening with the overture to *Iolanthe*, and the second, with the overture to *Patience*. The concert wasn't too bad, but there were moments when I knew that the conductor was just trying to follow the singers before giving cues, and this really doesn't work. The conductor has to know what is happening, and he has to give a clear beat to the orchestra: something I learned myself in D'Oyly Carte. Most of the players were inexperienced students, and there were several rather scary moments. Many in the audience would not have noticed some of the 'glitches', but I certainly did. Joe Contreras, whom I had last seen in San Luis Obispo, was also at this concert, and I sat with him and a friend of his, Fran, in the audience. Afterwards, I met the sister of one of Manor House's long-standing members. She and her husband kindly invited me to dinner, but I had to decline the offer as I was seeing Joe and Fran. Someone else who was at the concert was John Welch, a former chairman of the Gilbert and Sullivan Society in London who had lived in California for a number of years: a small world indeed.

Our next destination was Vancouver, British Columbia for the only Canadian concert that we did for Joanne Rile. We got there by way of a stop at Reno NV, bringing my state count to thirty-eight. Getting through Customs was fairly easy, but Immigration took very much longer, leaving us in various stages of anger, boredom or resignation. The concert was in North Vancouver; it was for the North Shore Community Concert Association and was held in the Centennial Theatre where there was an excellent Steinway piano. It went very well, and the audience loved it, but all too soon we were packing up to travel back to the United States without having had any time for sightseeing. We were back at the airport less than twenty-four hours after our arrival, and there was the same endless paperwork and delay; we even had to pay $10.00 to get out: this was apparently an 'airport improvement tax'. It all seemed out of proportion for just one concert.

Our fifth concert was in Portland OR where we were part of the twenty-fifth season of Music Matinees [sic] presented by the Reed College Music Associates at Reed College Commons. (We had previously performed in Portland ME; Oregon was now my thirty-ninth state.) Despite being called a Music

Matinee this was an evening concert described in the programme as 'A gala concert with the stars of the D'Oyly Carte'. It was well received. On the way back to our hotel we passed another deliciously dotty sign that read Rub-a-Dub Dog Wash - Pet Wash 'n Dry. We were now halfway through the tour.

The sixth concert was in St Joseph MO (we had performed in St Joseph MI on the 1987 Byers, Schwalbe tour). St Joseph is at the extreme western edge of Missouri on the eastern bank of the Missouri River, but we stayed some miles further south in a Best Western in Leavenworth KS on the western bank of the Missouri as that was where the seventh concert would be; we were there for three days. It was leap year, and our concert in St Joseph was on February 29, an auspicious day in the G&S world (we had flown home on that day after the February 1988 tour). The concert was for the Performing Arts Association of St Joseph; it was held in the Missouri Theater, a real gem with quasi-Eastern decoration including Assyrian-style lions on the proscenium arch. The piano was a Mason & Hamlin; the audience, although numbering some eight hundred, was somewhat subdued.

Next day, March 1, we gave our concert in Leavenworth presented by the Saint Mary College Community Cultural Council (more alliteration) in the college's Xavier Theatre. The piano was a Howard, another make I had not yet come across; the programme listed me as David Mackle [sic]. (I once received a letter addressed to Mr D. Wackle.) Among the audience were Em Ware and Walter Gunn from St Louis MO. As so often on these tours there was a reception afterwards, and we had a chance to catch up with Em and Walter. Next day we flew to Little Rock AR, and I entered my fortieth state. We had some trouble with the car hire as the Rile office had failed to organise one, but we finally got another minivan from Avis. From our hotel, which was near the airport, we had to drive some sixty-five miles to the concert venue: the Woodlands Auditorium, Ponce de Leon Center, Hot

Springs Village. The piano this time was a Baldwin with an excellent action.

The last two concerts were once again at the Baird Auditorium in Washington DC, presented by the Smithsonian Associates: both concerts were on March 3 which was a Sunday. We often had travel days on these tours giving us time to get to a town or city without having a concert on the same day, but on this occasion we had to get a very early flight from Little Rock to Atlanta GA before getting another flight to Washington where we finally arrived at mid-day with our first concert at 15.00. We were met at the airport by Deborah's mother Nona and stepfather Gard who had kindly hired a car for us; we then went straight to the venue. The matinée was a sell-out and was extremely well received. There were a few empty seats at the evening performance, but it too was very well received; we also sold about seventy-five tapes. And so our tenth North American tour ended. We had covered a lot of ground, perhaps comparable only with the tour I did with D'Oyly Carte in 1978.

Back in London the regular dates began again, the routine varied every so often by something different. On March 13 I played for Cynthia Morey and John Fryatt at a Gilbert and Sullivan Society evening at the Friends' Meeting House opposite Euston Station. This was a programme of excerpts from *The Sleeping Beauty of Savoy*, a pantomime with text and lyrics by Cynthia and John set to Sullivan's music; it was a replacement for a concert at the Players' Theatre that was to have celebrated the centenary of *The Grand Duke*, the last, and least known, of the Savoy Operas (the Sir Arthur Sullivan Society presented a centenary concert performance in Oxford in June). In April our North American group, minus Ken Sandford and billed as Stars of Gilbert & Sullivan, gave a concert at the Plaza Centre in Southend-on-Sea.

I was also rehearsing with Ralph Meanley as our new venture, Bentley Concert Productions, seemed to be taking off. There had been two concerts in 1994 and five in 1995; by the end of this year we had done thirteen which was very encouraging. The first of these, on March 19, was in Ilford Town Hall for the Redbridge Music Society; it was closer to a recital with items from a well-known volume of Italian songs and arias, some Handel, Mozart and Schubert, and songs from our programmes *Rolling Down to Rio* and *Shipmates O' Mine*. It was recorded by the Society's chairman Colin Pryke.

Our next concert, *Shipmates O' Mine*, was on April 27 at the Historic Dockyard Church at Chatham for the Friends of Chatham Dockyard; this was a further development of our idea to present this concert in naval or maritime settings. It wasn't particularly well attended, but it was well received, and we hoped that we might return at some future date. John Megoran, whom I had met through the Meadmore productions, was in the audience. As 1996 was the four hundredth anniversary of the death of Sir Francis Drake, and one of the songs in *Shipmates O' Mine* was *Drake's Drum*, we hoped that we might be able to present this programme at Buckland Abbey in Devon where Drake had lived for some years, but unfortunately this wasn't possible.

The next Bentley concert wasn't until June, but I was now well into rehearsals for Manor House's production of *Tom Jones* and Philbeach's *Fiddler on the Roof*. At the beginning of May there were two dates as part of the Banstead Arts Festival: on the 3rd I gave a talk on D'Oyly Carte and G&S, and the following evening there was a concert with our North American group, again billed as Stars of Gilbert & Sullivan. The run of *Tom Jones* took place at the Institute, Hampstead Garden Suburb from May 14-18. I had managed to get an extra player, a double bass which gave added weight, bringing the band up to six. This year it was called The Fielding Ensemble; from now on its constantly changing name usually had some relevance to the show being performed. The pianist this time was Margaret Eaves whom I had previously met. Shane Collins, the producer, had rewritten the story, and this affected the order of some of the numbers so that the musicians and I were constantly turning pages forward and back which was a bit confusing. On one evening, about five minutes before the end, the stage lighting broke down resulting in a rather lame ending to this particular performance.

On June 13 Ralph Meanley, Lorraine Daniels and I gave a concert in the Cramphorn Theatre in Chelmsford as part of *Aria - a Month of Opera in Essex*. This was virtually a re-run of a programme we had presented the previous December as *Perfect Harmony*, the name we had devised for concerts that were generally lighter than *Shipmates O' Mine* and *Rolling Down to Rio*. The following week Philbeach gave four performances (June 20-22 including a matinée) of *Fiddler on the Roof* at the Polish Theatre, Hammersmith. It was a show that always attracted full houses.

On June 24 I went to a memorial concert at the Coliseum for Donald Adams who had died at the age of sixty-seven; on June 30 Michel Ballet asked me to play the organ at a Requiem Mass for his fellow-countryman Sir Gaetan Duval QC who had once been the Deputy Prime Minister of Mauritius. Maxine Symons, who had introduced me to Michel Ballet, also sang during the Mass.

The next Bentley concert was at Leighton House in Kensington (where I had previously taken part in concerts celebrating Sydney Smith, Wilhelm Ganz, Sullivan and others) on July 6. This was the first performance of our new programme *Thank You, Mr Atkins* which consisted entirely of Gerard Francis Cobb's settings of Rudyard Kipling's *Barrack-Room Ballads*. The poems (including the famous *Mandalay* and *Gunga Din*) describe army and imperial life in the late nineteenth century. We thought highly of both words and music, and we felt that these songs, very popular in their day, should be heard again. We had been working on the programme for some time, and we had performed some of the settings at our concert in Ilford in March.

Following our preparatory visit to Bateman's in November we gave the second performance of *Thank You, Mr Atkins* there on July 20. There is no suitable room at Bateman's for a concert, and so it was held out of doors; we were lucky that we had a well-nigh perfect evening for it. David Fox, who was in charge at Bateman's, was married to Johanna Angermeyer who had written a fascinating book *My Father's Island* about her German family's time in the Galapagos Islands from the 1930s, and she gave my mother, who had come down for this concert, a signed copy that I now have.

Concert at Oak Hall Manor. L-r: David Mackie,
Fiona O'Neil, the Hon. Mrs Mitchell Anderson,
Cynthia Morey, Mark Hathaway.

At the end of July I took part in another concert at Melvyn Tarran's Oak Hall Manor at Sheffield Park. Devised by Cynthia Morey, it told the story of Isabel Jay (1879-1927) who had been a principal soprano with the D'Oyly Carte Opera Company in the late 1890s and who later starred in many Edwardian musical comedies. Taking part were Cynthia and myself, soprano Fiona O'Neil, whom I had worked with in *The Fantasticks* at Il Boccalino, and baritone

Mark Hathaway whom I had not met but was to meet again, somewhat unexpectedly, more than a decade later. Among the audience was Isabel Jay's daughter Celia, the Hon. Mrs Mitchell Anderson (then in her nineties: she died the following year), who was much involved with the Sussex Gilbert and Sullivan Society.

On August 10 Ralph and I did another *Rolling Down to Rio*, this time in a splendid baroque church at Great Witley, Hereford and Worcester: the church was regularly used for concerts. The following day we met John Whitehead and his wife Ella who lived near Ludlow. John's recent edition of the *Barrack-Room Ballads* had been very helpful to us in preparing *Thank You, Mr Atkins*, and we kept up a correspondence with him until his death in 1999. Bentley Concert Productions certainly seemed to be taking off, but we remained cautious about future developments: we were, after all, trying to resurrect interest in songs that many would have said had had their day. But for the moment it all looked promising.

At the end of August, following a short tour for Music in Hospitals, I met up with Ralph again for a visit to the Isle of Man. This had come about through Billy and Margaret Skelly who had mentioned us to their friends Malcolm and Jan Kelly who organised concerts and events on the island. We did two concerts there: the first one was at the Arts Centre, Port Erin on August 23. Among the audience were the well-known Scottish singer Moira Anderson and the Bishop of Sodor and Man, Noel Jones, and his wife (the Bishop of Sodor and Man is mentioned in Colonel Calverley's tongue-twisting song in *Patience* "If you want a receipt for that popular mystery,/Known to the world as a Heavy Dragoon"); we were also interviewed for Manx Radio by Geraldine Jamieson. This concert was basically *Shipmates O' Mine* with some G&S, but Ralph wisely didn't attempt the Colonel's song. We gave the second concert the following evening. It was similar to the more general programme we had given in Ilford, and it was held in Baldhoon House on the outskirts of Douglas overlooking the Glen Roy valley. The evening began with a champagne reception in the conservatory, and this was followed by the concert which took place in a magnificent indoor swimming pool whose décor included pillars, classical statuary and murals: it was given in the presence of the island's Lieutenant Governor Sir Timothy Daunt and his wife. Both concerts were in aid of the Manx Housing Trust, and between them they raised over £5,000. We stayed with the Skellys, and we were very well looked after; we also managed to visit the Great Laxey Wheel. Shortly after we got back to London, and with the help of Sandy Leiper, we recorded items from *Thank You, Mr Atkins*.

September saw the start of the operatic society rehearsals; both had returned to G&S. Philbeach was planning another of its concert performances in December, this time of *The Sorcerer*, and Manor House was planning to do a full production of *Princess Ida* in 1997. These two were less well-known than most of the others, and I was always pleased to be doing them again. But before *Ida* happened I managed to persuade Manor House to do a concert version of *The Grand Duke* in its centenary year. I had tried to persuade them to do a concert version of the penultimate opera *Utopia Limited* when it celebrated *its* centenary in 1993, but I got the inevitable reaction - "Oh, no-one knows that; no-one will come" - and so we didn't do it. I felt that if they wouldn't do *Utopia* they certainly wouldn't do *Grand Duke*, but to my surprise they agreed. It was, for most of them, completely unfamiliar material. I also wrote an article *Centenary Thoughts on 'The Grand Duke'* for *Gilbert & Sullivan News*, vol. ll, no. 7, November 1996.

Other work continued; there were G&S concerts, masonic dates and a Midlands tour for Music in Hospitals that covered Lichfield, Birmingham, Coventry and Worcester. Ralph and I also purchased a keyboard so that we could perform in venues that didn't have a piano. The make, a Daewoo, surprised me as I had hitherto only associated the name with cars. It wasn't the best instrument I had ever played, but it was (just) portable although the keyboard had to be unscrewed from the stand, and it took both of us to lift it. It also had a rather heavy action, but it did serve its purpose.

I also made another G&S connection; this was with a group called New Savoyards of London who presented fully costumed excerpts from the Savoy Operas. Formed in 1985, it was run and directed by Gareth Gwyn-Jones who also narrated the programmes. Ralph Meanley was one of the many singers they used, and so I knew of them; when their accompanist Hilary Morgan (whom I would meet later) was indisposed Ralph suggested me, and I played for them at a concert in Swindon on September 28. On that occasion I got a parking ticket in the car park near the theatre, having mis-read the instructions on the notice board. But I thought that the wording, typically in small print at the bottom, had been very misleading, and I queried the fine and managed to get it reduced.

I was now playing regularly for the Hepburn Starey Blind Aid Society that met in St Columba's Church of Scotland in Pont Street on Thursday afternoons; I shared this work with pianist Linda Ang although eventually I became the sole organiser of the concerts. I had to find a performer for each programme, and I used many people who worked for Music in Hospitals: among them were singers Patricia Sabin and Jane Webster, violinist Mary Kennard and flautist Mark Underwood. Another singer, not from Music in Hospitals, was Sylvia Clarke whom I later introduced to the world of G&S. Ralph Meanley sang too, and if we were doing a new programme we would try it out there. I always played a few pieces myself, and I built up a repertoire which was also useful for Music in Hospitals.

The next Bentley concert was a return to the Kirkgate Centre in Cockermouth where we gave a new G&S programme on October 4: we later called it *Ballads, Songs and Snatches* after a line in *The Mikado*. Two further concerts which were to have taken place at the Wynd Theatre in Melrose unfortunately failed to materialise despite much initial planning, a not uncommon occurrence. We stayed with Ralph's friends Richard and Angela Evans, and again we did more hill walking. One of the smaller lakes near Cockermouth had a pub at one end, and the idea was to start there, walk round the lake and then go into the pub. The weather wasn't particularly good when we started, but at least it was dry. However, we had just reached the half-way point when the rain came on, and by the time we got to the pub we were all soaking wet. We went in to an already steaming foyer and dried out by an open fire before ordering our drinks. But it was still a very pleasant week-end.

We did *Shipmates O' Mine* again on October 21. This was our third Trafalgar Day concert, and we felt that we had now established a 'tradition' for it, but as we couldn't find another ship, or venue with a nautical connection, it was done at the Players' Theatre in London. There were several changes to the programme including the insertion of sea shanties for the audience to sing; we also had a song called *Gallant Webb* (words by Mr Fox, music by Charles Westren [sic]) which had been written in the early nineteenth century to celebrate a contemporary but now forgotten naval engagement with the French. It had been found in the British Library by a descendant of Lieutenant Webb (who commanded the English ship), a Mrs Luckham, who had somehow heard of us and had written to us about it. We discovered that Mrs Luckham was the widow of the distinguished actor Cyril Luckham.

November was a G&S-orientated month with two performances of Manor House's *The Grand Duke* on the 16th and 17th, the first one in a church and the second one in a care home, and auditions for *Princess Ida* in 1997. There were also numerous concerts for Music in Hospitals including two tours in December: a three-day one taking in Bristol, Bath, Wincanton and Swindon, and a full week in the North from the 16th to the 21st that covered Lancaster, Liverpool, Bebington, Longton, Lancaster Moor, Fleetwood and, on the

Saturday, Corby and Stamford. We saw much of the country doing these tours, but driving at the end of December could be arduous with uncertain weather.

There were three more Bentley concerts this year. The first of these was another *Thank You, Mr Atkins* which played to a very small audience at The Nave, Uxbridge on October 31; the last two were in December, the first being a last-minute request from the Ashridge Circle in Eastbourne as other artists had backed out. This was on December 2, and we made it a three-hander with Lorraine Daniels; we kept it on the lighter side with G&S and numbers from various shows and musicals. The last one was more of a cabaret, and it was for an organisation called the Arts and Heritage Club, an off-shoot of the Theatre-goers Club. This was at the Runnymede Hotel near Windsor on Christmas Eve, but we were only required to provide entertainment from 17.00-18.15.

On December 14 there was a concert for Frinton Arts & Music Society with Carole Mudie and Carol Leatherby, and I even had a job on Christmas Day, this time with Geoffrey Shovelton and Deborah Clague, at Cobham; in the following week there was a masonic date on New Year's Eve. It had been a good year with more new contacts; hopefully they would continue to provide work.

II – 1997

O nce again the year started quietly, and although I was getting used to this it always made me nervous. I was still paying off a mortgage, and any cessation of work, even for a few days, meant that a tighter grip had to be kept on the purse strings. The first job, a Rodgers and Hammerstein evening with Judith Baxter, was at Staines on January 7; the following day I was in Bristol for Music in Hospitals: feast or famine. After that it began to settle in to the familiar routine. Rehearsals for Manor House and Philbeach began, and while

I was in familiar territory with Manor's *Princess Ida* I knew nothing of Philbeach's next presentation *Dick Daredevil*, a new show with words by Phil Willmott and music by Steven Markwick: part of a Guinness New Musicals scheme it had had its première in 1996 but had not yet been published. Philbeach had planned to do *Kiss Me, Kate*, but this had fallen through, and they were looking for something else. The Society's president had seen a performance of *Dick Daredevil* during its initial run and had thought that it might be suitable for them; they had struck a deal with Phil Willmott which included the set (an enormous wireless) and the costumes. Philbeach was the first amateur group in the country to perform this show; in that sense the Society was always a bit more adventurous than Manor House. The music was in a fairly straightforward idiom, but it still required many extra rehearsals as no-one knew it, and, as so often, not everyone in the Society could read music. It was the same at Manor House, and teaching the music for shows was often quite a struggle.

Ballet classes started towards the end of January, and there were several Music in Hospitals jobs although no tour yet (there was a full week's tour at the end of July starting in Sheffield). The first Bentley job was at Crockham Hill Village Hall in Kent for the Edenbridge Music and Arts Trust. This had come about through Will McQuillan who had seen *Thank You, Mr Atkins* at Bateman's and *Shipmates O' Mine* at the Players' Theatre, and this programme was a mixture of those two which we called *Soldiering and the Sea*. We were grateful to Will for taking an interest in our work. The hall at Crockham Hill was brand new, and it had very good acoustics. The piano, which had been lent for the occasion by a local lady, was not so good, but the audience participation in the sea shanties was excellent.

We had known for some time that a tour planned by Joanne Rile for 1997 had been cancelled: this was mainly due to the fact that Kenneth Sandford, now in his early seventies, had finally decided to leave the group. I wasn't surprised by this as we had all noticed on the previous tour that his walking was not very good. But as he was on the Riles' publicity they thought that they might not be able to sell the tour without him. However, one of the dates was to have been at the Sheldon Concert Hall in St Louis MO where some of us had performed in 1988, and the Riles hadn't reckoned on the indefatigable Walter Gunn who ran the Sheldon. He had booked us early on, and he was determined to have us, presumably telling Joanne that she wasn't going to get out of this one very easily. And so it was agreed that we would have a long week-end in St Louis with just one concert (there had been two in 1988) for which, without Ken Sandford, we had to produce a new programme. The group was otherwise the same - Deborah Clague, Lorraine Daniels, Geoffrey Shovelton, John Ayldon and me - although Deborah and John had not been with us in 1988.

We flew out on February 14. On the way across, John Ayldon discovered that our concert was listed in TWA's in-flight magazine, but, not surprisingly, as "The D'Oyly Carte Opera Company perform The Best of Gilbert and Sullivan". We hoped that this wouldn't somehow get back to the relevant authority. Em Ware in St Louis had offered to put us up for the first night with hotel accommodation provided for the remaining nights, but in the end all of us except John Ayldon stayed with Em for the entire week-end. We rehearsed at the Sheldon on the 15th with much of the rest of the day devoted to socialising with Em and her daughter Nina. The concert took place on the 16th; as this was a Sunday it was an afternoon performance. We had a full house, and they were very responsive. Afterwards, we went to an Italian restaurant where we discovered that some of the diners had been at the concert. One lady, who had heard that we were going to be there and who wanted to see us, drove so fast that she was stopped by the police: she told them that she hadn't heard their siren as she was playing a G&S tape very loudly. We dutifully signed a book that she had brought; I hope that was some compensation for her brush with the law.

We flew home next day, but not until the evening; this allowed us time for some sightseeing. Deborah had not visited the famous Gateway Arch, and she and Geoffrey set off to see it. Lorraine went to a shopping mall; John was still at his hotel. Walter Gunn then gave me a tour of St Louis which included Scott Joplin's house, now a listed building, and the Anheuser-Busch brewery, the Busch family being one of the most prominent in St Louis. Back at Em's house we had a final meal which John Ayldon had prepared, and Geoffrey then presented Em with one of his cartoons which he had had framed. It was based on one of my quasi-clerihews:

> Do not begrudge
> The Learned Judge
> His fun. It would be quaint if
> He married the Plaintiff.

It had been a successful week-end, and we hoped that this would stand us in good stead with the Riles, even although Kenneth Sandford was no longer with the group. Back in London the regular work started again, the routine punctuated from time to time by other concerts including several under the Lorian banner. Lorraine and Brian had moved from London to rural Essex, and most of the concerts they arranged were either there or in Suffolk. One was a return visit to the Plaza Centre in Southend-on-Sea with our North American group; yet again we were billed as Stars of Gilbert & Sullivan. There were also concerts in Saffron Walden, Radwinter and Woodbridge. Some of these involved just Lorraine, Ralph Meanley and myself, and Ralph and I would often go up to Essex to rehearse and stay overnight in Lorraine and Brian's lovely old house.

This year marked the centenary of the CAA, and although I couldn't now go there on Monday evenings I was able to attend the Centenary Ball on Sunday March 23 at the London Marriott Hotel in Grosvenor Square. The president this year was Ruth Madoc of *Hi-de-Hi!*

Arthur Jacobs, whom I had met at the Sullivan sesquicentennial function at the Savoy Hotel in 1992, died in December 1996, and I attended a memorial concert for him at the Royal Academy of Music on May 4. Among the items performed, from a wide range of music, was "When a merry maiden marries" from *The Gondoliers,* sung by Della Jones and accompanied by Sir Charles Mackerras.

Manor House's production of *Princess Ida* took place in the middle of May. There were still six in the band, now called The Empyrean Ensemble, but we had another pianist Nick Pope. Philbeach's *Dick Daredevil* followed in June.

This year turned out to be the best one for Bentley Concert Productions with no less than seventeen concerts. We had started with just two programmes, *Rolling Down to Rio* and *Shipmates O' Mine,* and had added a third, *Thank You, Mr Atkins,* which was much more specialised; we now also had *Ballads, Songs and Snatches* which we did on a return visit to the Historic Dockyard at Chatham in April. (Although this wasn't a programme of sea songs we had specifically been asked for it.) We did *Rolling Down to Rio* at the delightful Georgian Theatre in Richmond, Yorkshire in June; we did it again at Bateman's in July and at the Players' Theatre in November. We also did *Shipmates O' Mine* at Hastings in May (a concert we put on in association with the Royal National Lifeboat Institution at the Hastings Museum and Art Gallery) and at Bilston Community College in June. Bilston was the birthplace of Sir Henry Newbolt (1862-1938), the author of *Drake's Drum,* set by Sir Charles Stanford, which we always included in *Shipmates O' Mine,* and this was by way of a tribute to him.

Ralph and I spent a few days in Cumbria in October, staying again with Richard and Angela Evans. This time we did two concerts: *Ballads, Songs and Snatches* in Cockermouth and *Thank You, Mr Atkins* at the Victoria Hall, Grange-over-Sands. And there was another date at the Runnymede Hotel for the Arts and Heritage Club on Christmas Day: this time they wanted a history of the British musical starting with some G&S. Originally I had only been asked to play for Lola-Maria Gibbard whom I had met at the Concert Artistes Association, but at the last minute it was thought that another singer was necessary, and so Ralph joined us: we rehearsed in the Magna Carta Suite.

Ralph, Lorraine and I now had a number of lighter programmes such as *The Fleet's In* which we did on a return visit to HMS *Warrior* in June and at Grim's Dyke in November. With these we could do most things that were asked of us, and one of these 'mixed bag' evenings came about in an unusual way. Diana, Princess of Wales had died on August 31, her funeral being held on September 6, the day on which the Ashridge Circle in Eastbourne was holding a Golden Jubilee dinner in the De Vere Grand Hotel. The guest speaker was to have been the novelist and politician Jeffrey Archer (by now Lord Archer of Weston-super-Mare), but he had been invited to Diana's funeral, and he asked to be relieved of travelling down to Eastbourne. I knew David Allen of the Ashridge Circle, and we had stepped in for them in 1996 when their guest artists had called off. He got in touch to ask if we could help again, and Ralph, Lorraine and I went down for a second time and gave them half an hour's entertainment after the meal. This was a mixture of G&S, ballads and songs from musicals.

Finally, on New Year's Eve, Ralph, Lorraine and I did another cabaret spot which Lorraine had been asked to organise. This was at the Stansted Hilton Hotel at Stansted Airport; Ralph and Lorraine were only required to sing one number each, a not unusual occurrence at such an event.

These concerts alone (including the Lorian ones) would have been very acceptable as our Bentley quota for 1997, but there were three other concerts and a radio interview involving just Ralph and me which stood apart from our regular dates in that they all took place in Indonesia. This had come about through another university friend of Ralph, John Arnold, a business man who now lived and worked in Jakarta. With many British people in the city there was a Jakarta branch of the Royal Society of St George, and it was having a dinner on October 25, close to Trafalgar Day, as part of a British Week; to provide some suitable entertainment at this John asked Ralph if we could perform *Shipmates O' Mine*. It was also planned that to make the journey worthwhile we would stay for just under two weeks, do more concerts and have some time for sightseeing.

We flew out on Trafalgar Day itself, October 21, touching down briefly at Kuala Lumpur before arriving at Jakarta on the 22nd. We were then picked up by John Arnold's driver and taken to the Shangri-La Hotel where we were joined by John and his wife Gillian. John had to go on to some function, but Gillian, Ralph and I remained at the hotel where we sat by a wonderful swimming pool and were plied with beer and cashew nuts, a pleasant start to a somewhat unusual venture. We also met some other people from London who had come out for the British Week, and we thought we saw the former Tory politician and former Chancellor of the Exchequer Norman Lamont who, we presumed, was there for the same reason. We eventually got back to the Arnolds' house (a single-storey villa that also had a swimming pool: very necessary in that climate as I was about to discover) where we had a Thai curry prepared by their own cook. We were in the wrong business.

Before leaving London we had to be inoculated for various things such as hepatitis. There were four doses altogether: one was a pill, and the other three were jabs. But I was still constantly bitten by mosquitoes: they seemed to find my blood attractive although they didn't bother Ralph quite as much. It was very hot and humid, and I don't like humidity; this was where the Arnolds' swimming pool came into its own.

The next two days were spent sightseeing. I also tried to cash some traveller's cheques, but this proved rather difficult. John Arnold's office was in the Jakarta Stock Exchange building, part of the new Western-style influence (including the Shangri-La Hotel) which was a far cry from most of what we could see of the city: much of it looked like a shanty town, with ramshackle buildings and shops with makeshift awnings. But there were some attractive buildings including a lovely old theatre. The Arnolds lived about 10 kilometres from the centre of Jakarta, and driving in was very slow with traffic crawling most of the time. Beggars would come right up to the car, pressing their faces against the windows and usually trying to sell you something. When I commented on all of this Gillian said "You think this is bad? You should see Bangkok".

The Royal Society of St George had its Trafalgar Day dinner on October 25 at the Shangri-La Hotel in a vast ballroom which seated about two hundred people. Ralph and I were at the top table as 'distinguished guests', but before that we were roped in to help welcome the other guests: it seemed odd welcoming total strangers to a function that we knew almost nothing about. The British Ambassador and his wife were among those that we greeted; I think the Australian Naval Attaché was there too. Originally we were to have been quite a considerable way from the company (who were all still seated at table when we performed), but I managed to get the piano moved nearer to the tables, and Ralph insisted that both he and the piano were miked. This helped, but by the time we started most people had had rather a lot to drink, and it was an uphill struggle to hold their attention. Ostensibly performing our *Shipmates O' Mine* programme, we had been asked to include some community singing, and this proved to be the best part of the evening as far as the audience reaction was concerned as they joined in heartily with numbers like *All the Nice Girls Love a Sailor* and *I Do Like To Be Beside the Seaside. Rule, Britannia!* also went down well, but it is very hard to perform under generally adverse conditions, and in some ways it was our least successful concert. But we had been brought out at considerable expense which included staying at the Shangri-La Hotel after the performance, and so we just battled on regardless.

Two days later we were interviewed on Radio Klasik [sic] FM by Fransiska Beding. We were told that this would be broadcast within a few days; it would also include three excerpts from the recording that we had made in 1995: *The Fishermen of England*, *Sea Fever* and *Shipmates O' Mine*. This was followed by more sightseeing which included a visit to the docks where we watched some very old-fashioned ships unloading cargoes of teak planks; we then went to see the house where we were to give our next concert. After that there was more sightseeing which included a visit to the Zoo. It seemed very down-at-heel by European standards, but it did have the famous Komodo dragons. The concert, a G&S evening, was on the 29th; it was in the modern and very luxurious home of a publisher. The house had a full-size Steinway grand, and the concert went very well. There was much audience participation, and I was surprised how well they seemed to know this repertoire, but it turned out that one lady was from Edinburgh, and another, from Clydebank!

The following day was one of the best for me as we all went to the coast where the Arnolds had a small beach hut: just some forty miles to the west was Krakatau which had erupted in 1883. We had lunch on the veranda and then swam in the Indian Ocean: it was a relief from the humidity. When we got back to Jakarta Ralph and I took the Arnolds out for a meal. This was to thank them for their hospitality; also because they had just celebrated their Silver Wedding.

Our last concert was on October 31, and this was at the British School in Jakarta. We did just forty minutes here (sea songs and some G&S) for some one hundred and fifty children who joined in enthusiastically with several chorus items. It turned out that the head of music was a Scot, and the head of the junior department had been a student with Ralph at the Birmingham School of Music: not for the first time we were finding that it is indeed a small world. In the evening we were invited with the Arnolds to a Hallowe'en party; we had to find some headgear as you had to be wearing a hat to get in. The party was in a splendid house, and we were mixing with some very high-powered people including heads of banks and major organisations. The British Ambassador and his wife, whom we had met at the Shangri-La Hotel, were also there.

The work was now over, but we had one more completely free day before we left. We drove into the hills in central Java and later visited a tea plantation. There had been talk of a visit to Bali, but that didn't happen; through some misunderstanding with the British Council we also lost an opportunity to do a concert in Surabaya. On our last day, November 2, we visited the local National Park before heading for the airport where we discovered that there was a two-hour delay which eventually became a four-hour one. While we were waiting, Ralph spotted someone he knew, a singing colleague from Scotland called Bill Mackie (no relation) who was with a group who were touring Asia. Their plane was also delayed, and this gave Ralph and Bill time to catch up on their various musical activities. We didn't finally take off until after midnight. This time we were in Club Class which was more comfortable and allowed us to get some sleep. I had had a particularly nasty mosquito bite which was still giving me trouble, and the cabin crew provided something which eased the pain. But when I got back I had to get cortisone to clear it up.

Despite not having a full US tour for the Riles (although we had enjoyed our week-end in St Louis) it had been quite a good year with Indonesia being the highlight - apart from the mosquitoes and the humidity. There had also been many other concerts including a performance of both *Trial by Jury* and a slightly abbreviated *HMS Pinafore* at Culford on August 28, organised by Michael Heyland for the Bury St Edmunds & District Cancer Research Campaign; the following day I played for a group at the Royal Overseas League in London. On September 7 there was another visit to Oak Hall Manor where Melvyn Tarran was presenting a tribute to the former D'Oyly Carte principal baritone Rutland Barrington (1853-1922): following a talk by John Cannon I had to play for Gareth Jones, Simon Butteriss and Janine Roebuck. There were two concerts for Judith Baxter on October 10 and 11 and one with Valerie Masterson on October 13. But there were also two new contacts. In May I played the organ at a Christian Science Church in Dorking. The format of the service was quite new to me, but I soon got used to it. I continued to play at Dorking from time to time until I finally left London.

If the first new contact was a sacred one, the second contact was definitely secular. This began in July when I paid my first visit to Claridge's - not as a paying guest but as a deputy playing in the foyer as part of a small group. I think Claridge's was the last hotel in London that still employed musicians in this way although it was very common at one time. The group - violin, cello, double bass and piano - was called the Hungarian Quartet. It had started at the end of the nineteenth century as a small gipsy orchestra, but the numbers had gradually been reduced. Over the years the group had acquired a large quantity of suitable music - gipsy airs (of which there were many arrangements, usually featuring the lead violin), Strauss waltzes, selections from operettas and shows, and numerous individual pieces such as Frederic Curzon's *The Boulevardier* - and the leader would simply select items as the evening went on. The regulars knew it all, but any deputy who came in had to be a good sight-reader, and thankfully I was able to cope with whatever was put in front of me. We had to wear sleeveless green jackets, a remnant of the gipsy orchestra; I was told to come in to the hotel in a dinner jacket and black trousers and simply exchange the black jacket for the green one. We played from 19.00 to 23.00 with two breaks during which we went down to the basement where there was a small band room at the end of a long corridor. There was no food, but we could get tea or coffee from a machine. I much enjoyed this work; like the organ playing at Dorking it continued (although latterly not at Claridge's) until I left London.

III – 1998

As a free-lance artist you have to take whatever work comes, and that also means *when* it comes. I had been at the Stansted Hilton Hotel on New Year's Eve with Ralph Meanley and Lorraine Daniels, and I now had a Music in Hospitals concert on New Year's Day with Caroline Dixon and Noel Drennan. This was in Harperbury Hospital at Radlett, just north of London, one of the many mental health hospitals where we performed regularly until, one by one, they were closed down. Concerts in these places could be quite difficult at times: at one of them I had a pillow thrown at me. At another I was given what purported to be an opera that a resident had written, but it was just a series of indecipherable scribbles. Could I play it, please? I put the sheets on the piano, and I made up something which seemed to satisfy him. As usual, there were plenty of these hospital concerts throughout the year; one of them was at Stoke Mandeville with which the notorious Jimmy Savile was much associated. Later in the year there were two tours of a week each: one was in the North-West in November, and the other was in East Anglia in December. Full weeks were good as you normally did at least two concerts every day, and you were paid a set fee for each one.

Just before Christmas 1997 we heard that the 1998 US tour for Joanne Rile had also been cancelled. This was disappointing. The tours had started well, with nineteen concerts in 1993, but the number of dates had gradually declined: fifteen in 1995, ten in 1996 and just one in St Louis in 1997. We wondered if the agents would be able to organise any more tours for us.

The first Bentley concert was in February, and it came about as a consequence of my being a vice-president of the

Gilbert and Sullivan Society. It was part of their programme of events 1997-98, and it was held at the CAA in Bedford Street; the Society had asked for our *Ballads, Songs and Snatches* programme. There would normally have been no more than about twenty-five people present, but this number was almost doubled by the presence of some American students from Bridgewater College VA, led by Ralph MacPhail, Jr., who were in London on one of their many visits. It was a very successful evening, and it was good to see Ralph again.

One of our former D'Oyly Carte choristers Pat Elliott, later known professionally as Patricia Rea, now taught very young children, and she asked me to play for her classes; I also played occasionally at her son's school. No one of these varied musical activities was ever going to be a full-time occupation, but collectively they were the backbone of my working week. Pat's classes were enjoyable, and it was good to keep in touch with her.

Despite the constant fear of having the flat repossessed by not being able to keep up the mortgage repayments I had built up a solid foundation of contacts, and I was almost at a point where I couldn't take on any other regular commitments as I had to find deputies for Manor House, Philbeach, the Hepburn Starey Blind Aid Society or other work if I was in the United States or on a Music in Hospitals tour (MiH celebrated its fiftieth anniversary this year), or, even if it was a one-off, in Indonesia with Ralph Meanley. Although Manor House and Philbeach rehearsed on different evenings I now felt that one society would be quite enough (particularly with all the other work), and so in May I wrote to Philbeach's current president Josie Matthews to tender my resignation after the next performances: not a show this time but two evenings in June entitled *Songs from the Shows*.

The second Bentley concert this year came about through our connection with an agency called Triple C that had been helping us with publicity. We had been asked to provide some entertainment for an RAF Veterans' Day at Hendon Aerodrome on VE Day (May 8); this consisted of a half-hour spot (more of a cabaret-style performance) which we later repeated: in preparing earlier programmes we had come up with a title *Combined Operations* which we used here. Lorraine Daniels was with us again, and we gave them well-known wartime numbers such as *We'll Meet Again* and *The White Cliffs of Dover* as well as ones more appropriate to the RAF such as *Wings Over the Navy* and *Lords of the Air*; I also played *The Dam Busters* march. The following week saw Manor House's annual production, this time of Kalman's *The Gipsy Princess*. I still had six players (the pianist was again Margaret Eaves who also did the next three shows), and this time the group was called The Orpheum Ensemble.

Terry-Anne Preston of Triple C also helped us with the next two Bentley concerts, the first being *The Fleet's In* at the Marina Theatre in Lowestoft in June. There was quite a small audience here, and even that was partly made up by one coach party. The concert went well enough, but it is hard work with small numbers in the audience. In July Terry-Anne asked us to do a workshop as part of an Arts Festival at Braintree College in Essex; while we were there we met Kinny [sic] Gardner who had been in the cast of *Dick Whittington* in 1986-87 when I first met Ralph. Later that month I went to a concert given by my friend and colleague Sylvia Clarke which she had entitled *Ballad Belles*. Ralph and I hoped that we might be able to use Sylvia in one of our future concerts.

With no Best of Gilbert and Sullivan tour this year for Joanne Rile the Bentley concerts were something of a substitute for me (Ralph spent much of his time as a supply teacher and also sang with other groups); there were eight more of these, mainly a mixture of the programmes we had already devised. The first one, at the beginning of August, was a return visit to the church in Great Witley with *Ballads, Songs and Snatches*; once again we took the opportunity to visit John and Ella Whitehead. At the end of the month we gave a shortened version of *The Fleet's In* as part of the Portsmouth International Festival of the Sea. We had Lorraine Daniels with us for this one, and once again we were in costume. We played on a stage constructed in the open area beside HMS *Victory*, and Ralph, Lorraine and I were all miked. This was a morning concert, and we spent the rest of the day at the Festival reminding ourselves of Great Britain's maritime heritage.

There was no Trafalgar Day concert on October 21, but that happened to be the day of my cousin Winifred's funeral. The next Bentley concert was in November, and that was a return visit to Edenbridge Music and Arts Trust, again arranged by Will McQuillan and with the concert again in Crockham Hill Village Hall. This time we had been asked to prepare a programme to celebrate the eightieth anniversary of the Armistice in 1918, and Ralph and I were joined by the actress Diana Walsh who read some poems. One of these was *Apologia Pro Poemate Meo* by Wilfred Owen from which Will McQuillan extracted the line "These men are worth your tears" as a title for the evening. As usual, there were several G&S-related evenings. At the end of June there was a concert *An Evening of Harmless Merriment* followed by a Midsummer Supper in the Lancaster Room at the Savoy Hotel organised by the Friends of British Youth Opera, my contact with that having come through Valerie Masterson; in July there was a G&S evening at the CAA organised by one of its members Audrey Joyce who also sang. In August I made an appearance at the Buxton G&S Festival (the brainchild of Yorkshire business man Ian Smith, a life-long devotee) when my D'Oyly Carte colleague Paul Seeley and I gave a two-piano recital in the Paxton Theatre. One of the pianos, which had been brought in from the bar, was really not up to standard, but this is a problem that pianists constantly face. Among the items we played was the first movement of *Pineapple Poll*, Sir Charles Mackerras's arrangement of tunes from the Savoy Operas for John Cranko's ballet, which Paul had previously rearranged as an overture to the earlier D'Oyly Carte in Concert programmes. In September I was in Scotland to attend the twentieth anniversary dinner of the Glasgow Gilbert and Sullivan Society of which I was now the honorary president.

The Glasgow Gilbert and Sullivan Society's twentieth
anniversary dinner: the honorary president delivering his speech.
L-r: Alison Dixon, David Mackie, Geoffrey Dixon,
Linda Wood, Russell Renwick.

Around this time Nationwide decided that their customers should become shareholders, and with a number of shares at my disposal I decided to sell some and have a proper holiday, the first one since 1989. This was a coach tour of Germany, a country that had always fascinated me, and it included a visit to Colditz Castle. When I was growing up I thought that I would never see Colditz as it was then in East Germany and much less accessible. But the Berlin Wall had come down in 1989; East and West Germany were united, and Colditz was now a major tourist attraction.

We flew to Frankfurt on October 4, and we were able to see something of the city before moving on next day to Rudesheim at which point we took a short river cruise past the Loreley rock and many wonderful old castles to Boppard where we re-joined the coach. We were now heading for Cologne, but we stopped at Remagen to see the famous bridge taken intact by the Americans at the end of the Second World War although it collapsed shortly afterwards. These tours, which try to fit in as many points of interest as possible, are often termed 'whistle-stop'; this one was no exception. We only had forty-five minutes in Cologne, but that was just enough time to get in to the cathedral which had miraculously survived the wartime bombing despite some damage.

After brief stops at Hameln (of Pied Piper fame) and the old East-West border post we then arrived at Berlin where we stayed for two nights. There was a coach tour of the city which included the famous Checkpoint Charlie and much of what had been East Berlin; we also went to Potsdam and saw Sans Souci and the room in which the Potsdam Agreement was signed. But I was amused to see that the Prince of Prussia's Library contained, of all things, *A Gentleman of Leisure* by P.G. Wodehouse, an author I had only recently begun to read.

After Berlin we drove to Dresden, and it was obvious that the infrastructure in what had been East Germany was still trying to catch up with the West, even after a decade of unification. I was fascinated to see Dresden and everything that had been achieved there since the still controversial bombing of 1945 although again we only had about forty-five minutes. One of the passengers in our group had actually taken part in the bombing raid on Dresden all those years ago, but I had to remind myself that even I was alive (if only a baby) when some of these raids took place, and that most of Frankfurt, Nuremberg (which we would also see) and Berlin, as well as Dresden, was still intact when I was born: and so to Colditz.

Driving from Dresden, road widening and construction were evident everywhere. The small town of Colditz was delightful; the castle, which dominates the town, I knew from photographs. Growing up in the 1950s with so many black and white war films, including *The Colditz Story*, it was almost strange to find that there was colour in the castle; indeed, it all seemed quite benign and not particularly intimidating although presumably it had not been pleasant for those who were imprisoned there. It had been a hospital for fifty years after the Second World War, and it had only been open to the public for two years; at the time of our visit there were even plans to turn it into a school of music. Perhaps I should have applied for a job.

Nuremberg was the next stop, and again we saw quite a bit of the city. This included the castle, the Nazi Party rally grounds (which still retained the platform where Hitler spoke) and the vast unfinished Colosseum-like building where the Party conferences were to have been held, now simply used as a car park. Next, we travelled along part of the Romantic Road and saw Rothenburg ob der Tauber, which seemed just like a film set, Dinkelsbuhl and Nordlingen before finally arriving at Munich where we looked in at the famous Hofbräuhaus - crammed to overflowing and very noisy. I had been to Munich with Geoffrey Shovelton in 1984, but much of what we saw this time, including the Nymphenburg Palace, was new to me. The tour also included visits to King Ludwig's castles of Linderhof and Neuschwanstein which I had seen in 1984, but they were well worth a second visit. After this there was a stop of an hour and a half at Lindau on Lake Constance, the Bodensee.

On the last full day we drove to Heidelberg, where we had a tour of the castle, and finally back to Frankfurt where there was some free time. As a bonus, we then drove to Wiesbaden and spent the last night there. Next morning I was able to see something of this very elegant city before we flew home from Frankfurt. It had been a welcome break from all my work, and there had been some interesting characters in the party including a man who had been in the Polish Air Force during the War. He had volunteered to work for the Germans in the hope that he might be sent to help build the Atlantic Wall from where he would try to escape to England. In the end he was sent to the Russian Front! It all made me realise just how close we still were to the Second World War.

Our Bentley concerts were becoming more varied as we often had to tailor the content of each programme to suit particular clients. There was a return visit to the Hastings Museum and Art Gallery on November 21, again in association with the RNLI, at which we performed one of our original programmes *Rolling Down to Rio*, but the remaining four were all quite different. For the first of these, on December 5, we were guest artists in a programme given by the Milton Glee Club at the Guildhall, Portsmouth, and we were again joined by Lorraine Daniels who had got this job for us. We had been asked to do two twenty-minute spots, and we gave them numbers from our *Perfect Harmony* repertoire. The Glee Club was accompanied by the Band of H.M. Royal Marines (Portsmouth), but I played for Ralph and Lorraine. This concert was repeated the following evening. On December 14 the three of us were back at the Congress Theatre, Eastbourne for the Ashridge Circle with a mixture of *The Fleet's In* and some seasonal items; the final date was our third visit to the Runnymede Hotel on Christmas Eve when we gave them a mixture of G&S, operetta and seasonal items that we called *Victorian Varieties*. It was hard to promote these concerts ourselves, and it seemed that we would have to rely more and more on what any prospective clients wanted. Graham Jenkins of the Arts and Heritage Club seemed to think that he could get us more work like the Runnymede dates, and we could only hope that this might happen.

Aside from work there were other things of interest. One of them was an appearance on a BBC Radio 4 quiz programme *Words in Music*, chaired by Denis Quilley whom I had previously met, which was recorded at the end of May. I didn't win.

I had started to read P.G. Wodehouse in the 1980s, and I was amazed to find numerous references to the Savoy Operas in most of his books; as a result of this I joined the P.G.

Wodehouse Society. In 1997 it began to issue a quarterly journal, perhaps not surprisingly called *Wooster Sauce*, and I contributed a number of articles to it. The first of these appeared earlier this year (Number 5, March 1998) and was entitled *The Influence of W.S. Gilbert (1836-1911) on P.G. Wodehouse*. The Society now instituted an annual dinner, and I attended the first of these, in the Inner Temple Hall, on October 15: a splendid evening in a splendid location which cost £30.00.

Conrad Leonard, almost certainly Britain's oldest working musician, celebrated his hundredth birthday on Saturday October 24. On Sunday there was a celebratory dinner for him at the Plaisterers' [sic] Hall where I had to play for Michael Wakeham, formerly of D'Oyly Carte; there was another celebration for Conrad at the CAA on Monday.

In November I received a letter from Stephen Turnbull of the Sir Arthur Sullivan Society offering me a vice-presidency of the Society; once again I was more than happy to accept this offer.

On December 8 I played for Valerie Masterson at the Theatre Royal, Drury Lane. Valerie had been asked to sing Noel Coward's "I'll see you again" at the unveiling of a life-size statue of Coward (1899-1973) by Angela Conner ahead of the forthcoming centenary. The unveiling was done by Her Majesty Queen Elizabeth the Queen Mother (the real Queen Mum, not Gladys Crosbie of the CAA). My name was given as Derek [sic] Mackie in the programme, but Valerie later received a letter from Graham Payne, Coward's executor and trustee, in which, as well as thanking her for her magnificent singing, he apologised for the mistake. This event was certainly one of the highlights of 1998.

I spent Christmas with Vivienne Jay and her husband Gerald Johnson at their home in Pagham, just west of Bognor Regis, along with the now hundred-year old Conrad Leonard. The house had begun life as one of a number of old railway carriages that had been left near the beach to be used as holiday homes. Over the years they had all been extended; most now looked like ordinary houses so that it wasn't obvious what they had originally been although there was one whose provenance could not have been mistaken; even Vivienne and Gerald's house still had some of the old carriage windows in the kitchen when I first visited it although these were later removed. I walked along the beach after our Christmas lunch: it was very cold (the weather, not the lunch), but invigorating nevertheless. I stayed overnight before heading back to London on Boxing Day. It had been a delightful and relaxing visit.

IV – 1999

We were now just one year away from the millennium, and it would soon be twenty years since the closure of D'Oyly Carte. There were some new contacts this year, and thankfully there would be another US tour, but there was still plenty of the usual work. The first job, on January 6, was again for Music in Hospitals, this time with Patricia Sabin who lived fairly near me. I did a number of these concerts with Pat (there was another one the following day), and I got to know her and her husband Nicholas well as I often stopped off at their house afterwards for a cup of tea. Also in January there was a hospital job with flautist Mark Underwood and another one with singer Anne Mitchell. Anne and her husband Peter became good friends, and I visited their lovely old house in the country on a number of occasions. I played for many artists, mainly singers, for Music in Hospitals, but there were some I only saw occasionally; with the passing years I can't remember all of them.

I was still playing for Pat Elliott's classes for young children, and she now asked me if I would make some tapes that she could use if I wasn't available: we had several recording sessions in January and February. This was useful for Pat as the next major event was our eleventh US tour with The Best of Gilbert and Sullivan, our fourth for Joanne Rile. We were relieved that these were still happening. This time we had yet another change of personnel as Lorraine Daniels had decided to leave the group. We had already lost Kenneth Sandford, and as Lorraine now had a young family she felt that she didn't want to be away from home for long periods. We were sorry to see her go, but we were able to secure the services of Patricia Leonard who had latterly performed the principal contralto roles with D'Oyly Carte although she was really a mezzo-soprano. The group now consisted of Deborah Clague, Patricia Leonard, Geoffrey Shovelton, John Ayldon and me - all ex-D'Oyly Carte apart from Deborah. There were seven concerts on this tour and five lecture recitals.

The tour began in Washington DC (our ninth visit) where we were to give another two concerts in the Baird Auditorium. Waiting to greet us at our hotel were Deborah's mother and stepfather and Em Ware from St Louis MO who had provided accommodation for us on our long week-end there in 1997. We had arrived during Bill Clinton's impeachment trial, and we wondered if the audiences might be down on previous visits, but both concerts, on Sunday February 15, were sold out.

The following day we had a six-hour drive, via Routes 66 and 81, to Norton VA in the south-west corner of the state where we stayed at a Holiday Inn for three nights. We had hired a seven-seater minivan (a Dodge Caravan) which had extra luggage space at the back and was ideal for the group. There were no internal flights on this tour, and we had to be reasonably comfortable if we were travelling long distances. We had previously found this particular mode of transport to be very suitable, and it was even better now that there were just five of us.

The sponsor for the next six engagements, all in the Norton area, was a lady called Daisy who was originally from Cuba. The first concert, on the day we arrived, was presented by

Pro-Art in collaboration with Clinch Valley College, Wise VA (part of the University of Virginia) and held in the John I. Burton High School Auditorium in Norton. For this one we had the added attraction of a small choir of just eight voices who sang with us in the first half of the programme which was also memorable in another way when the lights failed during the trio "Never mind the why and wherefore" from *HMS Pinafore*. Despite all my G&S experience in D'Oyly Carte and elsewhere I rarely played from memory, preferring to have music in front of me, but this was one number that I seemed to be able to play not only from memory but in total darkness. And so we all kept going until the end of the singing when I decided not to continue with the dance that follows. As the number finished there was a great cheer from the audience among whom was a man from Emory and Henry College, about thirty-five miles east of Norton, where we had performed during our first tour for Joanne Rile in 1993. Thankfully the lights came on again after about five minutes.

The remaining five concerts in Virginia were daytime ones, and they were different from our usual performances. They were all for students, the first one being listed on our itinerary as a convocation (defined as an assembly) which took place at Mountain Empire Community College. We were collected from the hotel by Daisy and driven there. This concert started at 12.15 and lasted for an hour; Geoffrey introduced the numbers as he did during our regular concerts. The students were also supposed to ask questions, but they seemed content to listen to Geoffrey (a former teacher) who was in his element giving them an illustrated lecture on the history of the operas and the D'Oyly Carte connection. Later that day we were collected again by Daisy and driven to Clinch Valley College where there was a reception at the home of the Chancellor although he wasn't present. Hospitality was a welcome and ever-present feature of these tours.

We were up early next day as we had two fifty-minute presentations at nearby Powell Middle School: these were described as lecture demonstrations, but they were more or less the same as the previous day's programme. This time we were collected by another lady, Mary. The first concert, at 09.00, was for younger children who were quite receptive, but the second one, at 10.00, was for an older group who just seemed bored by it all. The rest of the day was now free, and we decided that we would go to the local cinema. We were going to go out for a meal beforehand, but we discovered in time that the indefatigable Daisy had arranged for us to eat at the hotel at Clinch Valley College's expense; very nice too. We then went to the cinema.

Our last day in Virginia began with another early start as we had two more fifty-minute concerts (again lecture demonstrations, and again at 09.00 and 10.00), this time at Addington Middle School in Wise VA. The children here were more receptive, and these concerts, a marked change from our regular ones, were well received. We then checked out of the hotel. The last three concerts were in Florida, some six hundred miles away, and this involved a two-day journey with an overnight stop at Macon GA (we were told that it was pronounced Make'n). It was a lovely drive, taking us through Tennessee, North Carolina and into Georgia, and we passed close to the Great Smoky Mountains which reminded me of both Scotland and Wales. We got to Macon at about 21.30. Next morning we were off again on a slightly longer journey that took us to Tarpon Springs FL just north of Clearwater on the Gulf of Mexico.

On the day of our concert here, February 20, we went out for an early evening meal. As we looked at the menu we discovered that this restaurant gave reductions for 'seniors' - and the concession started at age fifty-five. It was a shock to realise that I was now a 'senior' having reached this milestone the previous November. I thought that John Ayldon was about my own age, and I knew that Geoffrey Shovelton was definitely older, but I didn't know how old Patricia Leonard was. For a while we were all very quiet, and then John Ayldon said "Well,

I think I'll have..." (an item on the 'seniors' list). This broke the ice, and we immediately chorused "Yes, yes, good idea..." and chose something each from the same list: all, that is, except Deborah Clague who had not yet reached her half century and had to pay a full rate for whatever she had chosen. Amusing, yes, but it began to bring home to us that we were not getting any younger, and of course this can be particularly apparent with performers on the stage. We often had very good responses, but these could be, as at the Baird Auditorium in Washington, from aficionados who would pardon just about any lapse of memory, vocal ability or obvious signs of ageing. How were we coming over to audiences generally?

The concert in the evening was at the Tarpon Springs Performing Arts Center which doubled as local government offices; we played to a full house of some three hundred people. Our programme included a scene from *Ruddigore* which was started by Patricia Leonard and John Ayldon who were good friends as well as colleagues and worked well together (they were particularly good at entertaining us on our many long car journeys). In this scene, Mad Margaret, now more composed, suggests to her new husband Sir Despard Murgatroyd that he use "...some word that teems with hidden meaning - like 'Basingstoke' - ..." whenever she appears to be lapsing into her 'mad' state. It has never been satisfactorily explained why Gilbert chose the name of this Hampshire town as the magic word that would recall Margaret to her saner self, but as we thought that many of our American audiences might not have heard of Basingstoke we often changed the name, asking in some venues if there was a location in the area that might elicit a laugh. Here, we were told to say Chop Soppy which Patricia duly did, pausing in expectation of a response. But it was greeted with a stony silence which sent Patricia (usually known as Trish) into a fit of the giggles and quite unable to continue with the dialogue. John was similarly affected, but they somehow managed to struggle on. Geoffrey Shovelton then came on as Robin Oakapple (really Sir Ruthven

Murgatroyd in disguise), and by now he too had caught the giggles. Sitting at the piano I couldn't keep a straight face myself, and it was a merciful release when we started the number at the end of the dialogue, the patter-trio "My eyes are fully open to my awful situation". Earlier, we had had a visit from an over-enthusiastic American who performed in local shows. He informed us that he could take on any of the G&S roles from tenor to bass. "But I'm really a tap dancer. Someone just discovered I could sing!" Altogether it was a very entertaining day. The piano here was a Knabe.

The next day was a Sunday, and we had the usual crop of religious programmes on TV. Among these, Dr Schuller, still in his Crystal Cathedral, was now offering an 'hour of power'. This was his fifteen hundred and sixteenth telecast, and I thought that he must be as old as Methuselah. American TV, always different and often unintentionally amusing, was a good way of helping to pass the many hours we spent in hotel rooms.

We left Tarpon Springs at 11.00 to drive north to New Port Richey FL where we were in an Econo Lodge which was better than the one in Washington. As it was a Sunday there were two concerts (at 15.00 and 19.00); these were in the Mariner United Methodist Church at Spring Hill FL, some miles further north again. They were presented by the Community Performing Arts Guild; the piano here was a Young Chang which was very good. The matinée audience numbered some five hundred with about seven hundred and fifty (almost a full house) in the evening; the church provided us with sandwiches and drinks between the shows. In the *Ruddigore* dialogue Patricia Leonard substituted Weekie Wachee (a local name, possibly of Native American origin) for Basingstoke, and each time there *was* laughter: a welcome change from the response to Chop Soppy.

The final concert, on February 23, was at Boynton Beach FL on the state's East Coast. This involved another long drive, but it was our last one: we eventually covered about fifteen hundred miles on this tour. It had been more leisurely than some of the previous tours, and we had been able to see more of the places that we had visited. Here, we went down to the beach which was very relaxing. Our performance in the evening was at Coral Lakes, a Florida-style condominium, for the Music Society of Coral Lakes; it was held in the Coral Ritz Theater. There was a capacity audience of about six hundred and fifty; the piano was a Hyundai. I knew that Daewoo made keyboards (Ralph Meanley and I had bought one), but I had not yet come across a Hyundai. The stage manager said "When you finish playing it you can drive it away". The concert went very well, and we were invited to a reception afterwards. We sat at a top table and had to introduce ourselves and answer a number of questions, mainly about D'Oyly Carte. The tour was now over, but we had time before we flew home later next day, and we were able to see something of Miami Beach, a separate town which has some wonderful Art Deco architecture, before dropping our hired minivan at the airport.

Back in London I was told that there had been a crit in *The Washington Post* (when an press agency sent the crit to recipients of Savoynet it was headed 'Subject: D'Olyle [sic] Carte visit Washington DC' although the *Post* had the correct spelling); while it was quite complimentary in some ways - the singers had "a twinkle in their eyes" with their voices "gloriously intact" and I was "nimble and supportive at the Steinway"- it didn't disguise the fact that we were all getting older (our average age on this tour was fifty-seven), and this was definitely a concern for the future despite the fact that we already knew that another tour was being planned for 2000. But any immediate worries were offset for me by another new contact, this one coming from the work at Claridge's. I was now asked to deputise in a trio that played in the afternoons in the Georgian Restaurant at Harrods of Knightsbridge: the repertoire here was similar. It was supposed to be a ladies' trio, but if someone dropped out for any reason they couldn't always get a female replacement, and I spent many a pleasant afternoon there. As at Claridge's you often saw well-known people in the restaurant; one was the novelist Jilly Cooper who, on leaving, smiled at us and said "Lovely, darlings, lovely".

Another regular date started when I became the musical director for the G&S performances at Gilbert's former home Grim's Dyke, now a hotel. The Grim's Dyke Opera Company had its origins in G&S Unlimited, formed after the demise of D'Oyly Carte by Andrew Whittaker with former principal tenor Meston Reid and Andrew's wife, former chorister Ann-Louise Straker. Paul Follows, the general manager at Grim's Dyke, then invited the group to be the resident company there and to give costumed and semi-staged performances of the operas during dinner on specific Sunday evenings in the large music room. Some of the regular principals such as Michael Rayner, Gareth Jones, Barry Clark, Ann-Louise Straker and Jill Pert were ex-D'Oyly Carte, but there were many others who now regularly sang G&S. Later, I managed to introduce Sylvia Clarke to the group, and she took on the contralto roles. The chorus was recruited from local amateurs: they appeared in evening dress and sat at the back of the stage, standing up when required to sing. The pianist was Hilary Morgan; I conducted from a podium placed stage right. My first opera as musical director was *The Pirates of Penzance* on February 28, shortly after our return from the American tour, but I had previously deputised for a performance of *The Mikado* in 1997. After *Pirates* came *The Mikado* in March, and thereafter it was usually one per month although eventually this number increased. At first we performed only the most popular of the operas, but we later extended the repertoire.

The first concert for Bentley Concert Productions (yet another *Victorian Varieties*) had been in February, shortly before the American tour, and it happened to be our fiftieth concert. This milestone performance, at the Quay Theatre,

Sudbury, was with Lorraine Daniels, and it was a mixed bag of items from Victorian ballads to music hall: we made a recording in March of some of these numbers for use as a demo tape. We were now doing more programmes that we had been asked to prepare for specific occasions, some of these dates coming from the Arts and Heritage Club for whom we performed at the Green Dragon Hotel in Hereford in April. This was effectively 'cabaret between courses' but with an eighteenth century flavour. At the end of the year we were back at Runnymede for the Arts and Heritage Club, again with Lorraine as they had asked for *The Fleet's In*. That was its third performance this year. Lorraine had organised the first one at Finchingfield in Essex in July, and it included a choir of school children that she had trained. She had also had some costumes made, and the hall was decked out in red, white and blue. The second one, also in July, was held on yet another ship, Brunel's famous SS *Great Britain* in Bristol. We had a captive audience here including Ralph's parents as it happened to be his father's eightieth birthday.

Earlier, in May, Ralph and I were back on the Isle of Man as Billy and Margaret Skelly had asked us to perform at their Ruby Wedding celebration in the Empress Hotel in Douglas. Billy and Margaret chose the items that they wanted to hear; I played Leroy Anderson's *Forgotten Dreams*. Among the guests were the singer Moira Anderson, whom we had met on our previous visit in 1996, and John and Janette Croft from California. Janette was an old school friend of Margaret, and I was to meet them again on yet another Best of Gilbert and Sullivan tour.

We were on the island for a long week-end, and I finally met someone I had corresponded with for some time. This was Maurice Farrar, a retired policeman from Lancashire who was another G&S aficionado. Over many years he had been compiling a list of all known D'Oyly Carte performers from 1875 to 1982 and trying to get details of where and when they were born, dates of death and the roles that they played.

He also included a separate list of musical directors, and it was because of this that I received a letter from him in 1990, introducing himself and asking if I would mind supplying him with the relevant information. I was happy to do this, and we began a regular correspondence. Maurice was a great letter writer (an art that seems to be dying out), and so when we finally met I felt that I knew him well. He turned out to be a surprisingly shy man, and he wasn't even keen to have his photograph taken although when the three of us were in a pub I managed to catch him unawares. His book finally appeared later this year, published by a former librarian Geoffrey Dixon who lived in Ayr (I had met Geoffrey and his wife Alison through the Glasgow Gilbert and Sullivan Society). Margaret Skelly kindly sent me a copy.

In September I accompanied Valerie Masterson and two young singers in a programme called *Ring up the Curtain* at the Britten Theatre in the Royal College of Music in aid of the Charing Cross Holiday Dialysis Trust. Given in the presence of HRH Princess Alexandra it was introduced by the newsreader Richard Baker with whom I would work again.

The first of the two remaining Bentley engagements was our annual Trafalgar Day concert. This year, October 21 fell on a Thursday, and as this was the day that I played for the Hepburn Starey Blind Aid Society, and Ralph had sung for them on a number of occasions, we decided, in the absence of any other work, to give them a Trafalgar Day concert in the afternoon. Most of the items were nautical, but we also tried out some numbers that we would be performing at our next concert in two weeks' time. Sadly, the Hepburn Starey Society, having existed since 1864, would soon be closing down due to falling numbers, but they still managed to have their annual outing, and at the beginning of July I went with the group to Brighton. As the century drew to a close it seemed to symbolise the end of an era as the Bentley concerts (and possibly our North American tours) also appeared to be winding down.

There were just eight this year, and only six of them had been open to the general public.

On November 7 we gave our third concert at the Players' Theatre, a new one called *Mr Bentley's Ballad Concert*. Lorraine Daniels, who no longer sang with The Best of Gilbert and Sullivan, now also elected not to take part in this one because of increasing family and teaching commitments, and Ralph and I were joined by Sylvia Clarke. For this concert we all became individual characters, listed as such in our publicity material: Sylvia, an Australian, was The Belle of Wooloomooloo, Ralph was The Singing Sergeant of the South Staffordshires and I was Formerly Music Master to the Maharajah of Bangalore; we also had some dialogue linking the numbers which even I had to take part in (shades of Brahms with Dione Livingstone). There were difficulties with the theatre this time as they had omitted to put the concert information on their mailing list, and the bar wasn't open during the performance. Barry Clark, an old friend from D'Oyly Carte, was in the audience, and as the bar had opened by the end of the concert Barry, Ralph and I settled down for a 'session'. It was a Sunday, and the concert had been a matinée, and so we spent most of the evening in the bar with some predictable results all round on the Monday morning: mixing business with pleasure can sometimes have its drawbacks.

In July I spoke at a symposium as part of this year's Buxton G&S Festival, and in November I took part in *Fairchild's Folly - Murder Mystery*, an event organised by Simon Fisher-Becker whom I had met at the CAA and who ran Just Deserts - Theatre for Any Occasion. I had already taken part in similar events: this one was held in the dining room of a school in Caterham. The story was set on a ship in 1929; I was the ship's pianist who was to be the victim. Six of us took part, and we sat at various tables with the other guests. At a pre-arranged time I had to pretend that I had been poisoned, clutch my throat and emit a strangulated sound before collapsing and being carted off, leaving the assembled company to work out 'whodunnit'. These evenings were fun, and, as so often with engagements, you got a nice meal as well as a fee.

In December I played for Sylvia Clarke at a carol concert in Bristol. This was for the Eleanor Children's Charitable Trust, founded by Eleanor Felton who was present that evening, and we were just one item on the programme. During the interval I was speaking to a lady, and I discovered that she lived in the same village as my colleague Peter Riley and his wife Joy, and so another friendship blossomed as I often saw Jane and her friend Ian when visiting Peter and Joy.

I also contributed another article to *Wooster Sauce* (Number 11, September 1999) called *Silly Village Names - Who Started It?* Wodehouse's books are full of these, but Gilbert also produced some gems such as Spiffton-extra-Sooper and Assesmilk-cum-Worter in *The Rival Curates*, one of his *Bab Ballads*.

There was plenty of G&S including the regular work at Grim's Dyke; Manor House did *The Gondoliers* in May, this time with a new producer. Shane Collins, who had produced the shows since 1994, had moved on, and his place was taken by Carole Mudie whom I had previously worked with. Carole now had a new professional name Jessica Grant. I persuaded the Society to let me have one more player, another violinist to assist the leader Donna Chapman, and Donna's husband Charles Beldom, who had played for D'Oyly Carte during our long London seasons, joined the group whose name this year was The Venetian Ensemble. Manor House Hospital had closed in March, and the Society assumed the provisional name Manor Opera.

One other G&S-related event was the preview of Mike Leigh's film *Topsy-Turvy* which tells the story of the production of *The Mikado* (1885) after the less successful *Princess Ida* (1884). This took place at the Columbia Tristar Preview Theatre in London's Golden Square on Friday October 22. A keen G&S buff himself, Mike Leigh gathered much information about D'Oyly Carte from former members; I was rung up one day by one of his researchers and asked for my memories of the Company. The credits at the end of the film list a number of people who helped in this way, but so many had been approached that there wasn't room for all our names. Mike Leigh was present at the preview, and we were able to talk to him afterwards. The film was given a general release in February 2000.

Bob Wilson, a colleague of mine and an expert on the music of Sydney Smith, the centenary of whose death we had marked in 1989, was also interested in player-pianos, and early in September I went to a party at which he demonstrated how they work. It looks easy as you apparently just put a roll into the piano and set it going, but like so many other things in life it is not so easy when you try to do it yourself: giving a good performance on one is quite an art. During my years in London I met other people who were also interested in these fascinating instruments.

On Friday September 10 a group of us put on a concert for John and Heather Andrew at their home, Umberleigh Manor, in Devon. John was a G&S aficionado who had a large collection of D'Oyly Carte memorabilia, and the event was described as The Umberleigh Manor Gilbert & Sullivan 25th Anniversary Concert and Dinner Celebration. It was held in a marquee at the rear of the house, and a video recording was made of the performance. We were all ex-D'Oyly Carte: Julia Goss, Patricia Leonard, Geoffrey Shovelton and John Ayldon, with me 'at the piano'. The following day I went down to Pencarrow in Cornwall where we had performed in 1982. On the way I managed to see Castle Drogo, near Exeter, a wonderful mock-Norman building designed by Sir Edwin Lutyens: mixing business with pleasure again. I was back in London on Monday for Manor Opera's first meeting of the season: next year's production would be another non-G&S, and they had decided to do Johann Strauss the younger's *Die Fledermaus* which I was looking forward to conducting.

With the passing years there definitely seemed to be less interest in G&S despite the revival of the D'Oyly Carte Opera Company in 1988, Jonathan Miller's *Mikado* at ENO, productions by Scottish Opera, Welsh National Opera and Opera North, numerous smaller-scale productions and the annual Buxton G&S Festival. At one time, schools and amateur societies would do almost nothing else, but there were now many more shows that had not been written when I was at school, such as the musicals of Andrew Lloyd Webber and Stephen Sondheim, and it was perhaps inevitable that G&S would lose at least some of the hold that it had previously had - and not just among performing groups: the appreciation societies also mirrored this decline. The Birmingham Gilbert and Sullivan Society had closed some years before, and in September I received a letter from Linda Wood to say that the Glasgow Society would now close owing to an insufficient number of members. It was worrying that the two largest cities outside London could no longer sustain interest in these masterpieces. And so I was no longer the honorary president although I was still a vice-president of the London and Manchester Gilbert and Sullivan Societies and of the Sir Arthur Sullivan Society.

Following my arrangement of *The Pirates of Penzance* for the Canadian Children's Opera Chorus I was asked to make a similar arrangement of *The Mikado*, and this occupied me between September 9 and December 28. There were to be some unforeseen problems with this one.

In December there was a music hall evening in Melton Mowbray for Rodgers & Payne Productions with Judith Baxter and others, and just after Christmas I was at Runnymede again with Ralph Meanley and Lorraine Daniels. But the concerts were not over yet. This year there was to be a New Year's Eve concert at Grim's Dyke to welcome in a very special year. There had been talk of some sort of melt-down of computers when the clock struck midnight, and everyone was at least mildly concerned that something might happen. But of course nothing did. What would the new century bring in the way of work?

Interlude

As there was no 'year nothing' 2000 was really the last year of the 20th century and not the first year of the 21st century, but with the change of prefix from 19- to 20- it was hard to think otherwise, and it is convenient to think of these round figures - 1700, 1800, 1900 - as starting points: most people therefore accepted 2000 as the beginning of a new century and a new millennium.

Many people I had known, including my father, had lived in just one century; others, like my mother and most of my contemporaries, would live in two: Conrad Leonard (1898-2003) and Sidonie Goossens (1899-2004) were among a handful who would live in three. I also knew a third musical centenarian Ernest Lawson who was born in 1900 and died in 2004, and so, strictly speaking, he too lived in three centuries. But by that token Arthur Sullivan (1842-1900) lived only in one century while Richard D'Oyly Carte (1844-1901) lived in two, as did Queen Victoria (1819-1901).

Chapter 8 – A new century

I – 2000

New century, new millennium, or not, the year started quietly: the first job, a Music in Hospitals concert, wasn't until January 7. But there was plenty of socialising. I had discovered that a colleague from Scotland, Muriel Levin, who had been a pupil of Lawrence Glover, my piano teacher at the RSAMD, also lived in Raynes Park, and she invited me to a gathering on New Year's Day. The following day I went back to St Leonards where Louise Denny was hosting a similar function. Tim McDonald, who had produced the 1989 Radio 2 G&S series, and his wife Jenny were also there.

A sadder event, two days later, was the funeral in Guildford of David Frame, a former fellow-student at the RSAMD who had organised some work for me with English National Ballet. David had died at the end of December. The minister who took the service was an old school friend from Greenock, John Nicol, who was now in Bridge of Allan where both David and my other college friend Sandy Oliver came from. Also present was George McVicar, the former music adviser for Stirlingshire, whom I had met through David and Sandy. Next day, I met Ralph MacPhail, Jr. from Bridgewater VA who was once again in London with his students, and I also caught up with Andrea Phillips, my old travelling companion from D'Oyly Carte. Later in the year I saw Harry Forbes from New York: like Ralph MacPhail, Harry was often in London. But the regular work - Music in Hospitals, Grim's Dyke, Claridge's, operatic society rehearsals and other things - soon began to fill up the weeks.

Our connection with Joanne Rile had not yet ceased despite most of us being 'seniors' and with the agency finding it more and more difficult to get dates for the group, and we began our twelfth tour of The Best of Gilbert and Sullivan (our fifth for the Riles) on February 10. The personnel was the same as on the previous tour - Deborah Clague, Patricia Leonard, Geoffrey Shovelton, John Ayldon and me - and we used the same programme. We were only in the North-West, and there were just nine concerts, one for students; we also gave a masterclass. We flew to Seattle WA where we were met by our sponsors and driven (in a very comfortable Cadillac stretch limousine) to Bremerton WA: we gave our first concert there the following evening at the Admiral Theatre. This building, which had an excellent Baldwin piano, looked as if it had been a cinema, but the seats had been removed, and the auditorium had been set out with tables and chairs so that the audience could eat before the concert. We were well looked after by the sponsors, and the performance was well received.

The next two concerts were in California. From Seattle we flew to Oakland CA (via Portland OR) where we hired a minivan (a Dodge Caravan, or similar, that we had previously found to be just the right size) and drove to Moraga CA. The concert here was in the LeFevre [sic] Theatre at St Mary's College of California. This was also well received, and the audience bought a number of our tapes. The piano here, a Kawai, was brand new, and I was the first to play it. Next day, we drove to Saratoga CA, just south of San Jose, where we gave the third concert. This was in collaboration with the Gilbert & Sullivan Society of San Jose, and it was held in the Carriage House Theatre at Villa Montalvo, Saratoga, a small venue of just three hundred which was ideal for us. It also had an excellent Baldwin piano. This was on a Sunday, but because of the travel arrangements we were not able to do two concerts as we had so often done on previous tours. Around this time we discovered that Mike Leigh's film *Topsy-Turvy* was already showing in the United States although not scheduled for release at home until February 18.

Although there were only nine concerts on this tour there was much travelling and very little free time. On February 14 we had to leave our hotel at 05.15 to return our transport and catch a flight at 06.50 back to Seattle from where we had yet another flight, this time to Pullman WA close to the border with Idaho. The airport here is midway between Pullman and Moscow ID, but it is in Washington and so by just a few miles I missed being in my forty-first state. The concert in Pullman was for Washington State University (WSU, commonly known as Wazoo), and it was held in the Beasley Performing Arts Coliseum. In the afternoon we gave a masterclass to some students who were about to perform Mozart's *The Marriage of Figaro*, and they sang one or two excerpts from the opera before we began. Our singers were miked, but this wasn't very successful.

We were now almost halfway through the tour, and the remaining five concerts were all in Oregon. From Pullman we first had to drive some eighty miles north to Spokane WA. It was a beautiful day, but it had snowed during the night, and the strange undulating treeless country looked even more unusual because of the patterns caused by the snow. At Spokane we hired yet another Dodge Caravan and now drove south-west through Washington, crossing the Columbia River and on to Portland OR before turning south to Corvallis OR which we finally reached at about 21.00. It had been a superb scenic journey, perhaps the most memorable of all the road journeys we had made in some sixteen years of touring.

The accommodation at Corvallis was in private homes: I was with Ivan and Roxana Bodine. On February 16 we gave a fifty-minute concert in the Austin Auditorium at Corvallis Middle School in the morning, and we were then taken out for lunch by our sponsors. After lunch we went to an outbuilding owned by Ivan's friend Dennis Oehler, an eye specialist, which contained two telescopes, one for the sun and one for the moon. The evening concert was for the Corvallis OSU (Oregon State University) Music Association held in the LaSells [sic] Stewart Center which had a splendid Bösendorfer piano - a rare treat. Ivan Bodine was the president of the Association's board of directors, one of whom was Dennis Oehler. Before leaving Corvallis, Ivan and Dennis kindly gave me a Fisher Space Pen as a memento of our visit. The hospitality here had been outstanding.

The next concert was in Medford OR, not far from the border with California. This time, although we still used the same programme, we were joined by some twenty-six members of the local Rogue Valley Chorale. In an addition to the programme they also sang the famous "Hail, Poetry, thou heaven-born maid!" from *The Pirates of Penzance* and "Eagle high in cloudland soaring -" from *Utopia Limited*. Earlier that day we had visited nearby Ashland OR where the Oregon Shakespeare Festival was held each year from June to September. It was a welcome chance to relax before the concert. We performed in the Craterian Ginger Rogers Theater, named after the dancer as she had made an early appearance there in 1926, some eighteen months after its opening. Apparently she loved Oregon. Among the audience were John and Janette Croft whom I had met at Billy and Margaret Skelly's Ruby Wedding celebration on the Isle of Man: they lived in California, but close to the border with Oregon. They had booked to stay in our hotel, the Red Lion (although it wasn't much like an English pub), and we sat talking in the bar for some time afterwards.

The penultimate concert was in Pendleton OR in the north-east of the state. It would have been more convenient to have stopped there on our way south from Pullman WA, but it isn't always possible to plan tours logically. To get there from Medford involved more flights and car hire, and as that took up most of the day we didn't actually arrive at the venue until 19.00; we barely had time to change before the concert which was in the Hermiston Community Center, a similar set-up to the Admiral Theatre at Bremerton WA with tables and chairs set out for dining.

We had another early start next day, leaving at 06.00 for our final concert at Neskowin OR, a small community near the coast. I don't how we found some of these remote corners when driving ourselves from place to place, particularly as satnavs were not yet available. Deborah Clague, as an American and more used to the conditions, did most of the driving although I shared it with her from time to time. This last concert was part of the Neskowin Chamber Music Season, and it was held in Camp Winema Chapel, a few miles north of Neskowin, which was almost on the beach. After the concert we were given a meal in a stunning open-plan house that overlooked the Pacific Ocean. In our hotel there were notices on the bedside tables that told you what to do in the event of a tsunami, a word that was new to me then: apparently we were in a tsunami hazard zone. We flew back to London overnight, February 21-22, having already heard that there was the possibility of another tour in September which was very encouraging. As the group now had a new line-up we felt that we needed another recording, and this was done at University College, Northampton on Sunday June 4. This was now a CD, and to the title The Best of Gilbert and Sullivan we added A Source of Innocent Merriment, a quotation from *The Mikado*. Once again Geoffrey Shovelton did the art work.

Having finished my arrangement of *The Mikado* for the Canadian Children's Opera Chorus at the end of December 1999 I still had to photocopy it, a job that took some time. This was finished by April and was duly sent off, but by July I still hadn't heard anything from them, and I sent a fax to ask if they had received it. I got a reply two days later to say that they had indeed received it, but the retiring music director had apparently forgotten to pass it on to the new music director, and they were in the process of trying to get it back.

There were only six Bentley concerts this year, and we didn't do either of our original programmes *Rolling Down to Rio* or *Shipmates O' Mine*. The first one was not until the end of April; it was part of an Arts and Heritage Club week-end at the Swan Hotel in Wells. We performed for just an hour, giving them half of a new programme we had prepared, *A Roving Life for Me*. We did this again as the second half of a recital at Ilford Town Hall in May (a return visit to Redbridge Music Society), and we finally gave the full programme in the baroque church at Great Witley in August, our third visit. In order to keep going we were relying more and more on organisations such as the Arts and Heritage Club for whom we did yet another cabaret-style performance at the Runnymede Hotel on Boxing Day. It was our fifth visit: we must have been doing something right. This time Ralph and I were joined by Lesley Finn, a colleague of Ralph from New Savoyards of London; as well as singing they both gave some readings.

Of the other two Bentley concerts this year one was yet another cabaret performance with ballads, music hall and G&S as part of the entertainment at a Victorian-style dinner at Kingswood House, Dulwich in May. This had come about through Tricia Court whom I knew from the CAA. The other concert was at the Community Hall, Banstead in October; Lorraine Daniels was with us for this one. We called it *Magic Moments*. The first half consisted of items from various programmes that we had done, but the second half was a condensed version of *The Fleet's In* with the surprise element of our appearance in costume after the interval. The Bentley concerts, like the tours of North America, had reached a peak and now seemed to be tailing off. We had plenty of material, and we would continue to perform 'as and when', but the outlook wasn't promising.

As well as the regular Sunday evenings at Grim's Dyke the opera group performed *The Pirates of Penzance* (with its leap year connection) at Brocket Hall on February 29 for Welwyn Hatfield Rotary's Leap Year Celebration, and in April it made a recording of excerpts from *HMS Pinafore*, *The Pirates of Penzance*, *Iolanthe* and *The Mikado*.

On March 29 I conducted a performance of *Trial by Jury* at the Savoy Hotel presented by Sargent Cancer Care for Children in association with the Gilbert and Sullivan Society. It was directed by Cynthia Morey. The principals and chorus were mainly ex-D'Oyly Carte, and I had an orchestra of nineteen led by Donna Chapman who played for me at Manor Opera. There were players from the old D'Oyly Carte orchestra and two eminent clarinettists, Tony Jennings (Cynthia's husband) and Colin Bradbury. Cynthia and Colin later appeared in Dustin Hoffman's film *Quartet*.

Having adopted the name Manor Opera for the performances of *The Gondoliers*, Manor House now called itself Manor Light Opera. Its production this year (in April, earlier than usual) was *Die Fledermaus*: the orchestra became The Strauss Ensemble. After many years at the Institute, Hampstead Garden Suburb there was a new venue, the Steiner Theatre near Regent's Park, and there was yet another new producer Vanda Morgan. We used the adapted version more suitable for amateur societies, but we had a good soprano who wanted to sing her 'homeland' number in the original key, and we had to get parts for this and some other numbers.

Geoffrey Shovelton, Deborah Clague and I gave a workshop for schools in May as part of the Mayfield Festival of Music and the Arts. With the imminent demise of the D'Oyly Carte Opera Company in 1982 a project, *D'Oyly Carte for Schools* (financed by Shell UK Ltd), had been initiated, and Geoffrey had almost single-handedly prepared a folder for it: I contributed some simplified piano arrangements. For the Mayfield Festival the children had prepared some material, and they took part in our performances. We had also given some school concerts with The Best of Gilbert and Sullivan in 1999, and I wondered if this approach might be a good way to keep these tours going.

On June 24 there was a D'Oyly Carte reunion at Oak Hall Manor, home to Melvyn Tarran's wonderful G&S collection, and the following day there was a concert at the Hawth Theatre, Crawley. Most of this was conducted by David Steadman of the revived D'Oyly Carte Opera Company, but there was also another performance of *Trial by Jury* (with a different cast) which I conducted. The proceeds from this concert (over £5,000) went to Great Ormond Street Children's Charity, and this enabled them to purchase some much-needed equipment. The week-end had been a chance to catch up with colleagues from my years in D'Oyly Carte and to meet many others from earlier times. It was also one of the last occasions on such a scale as the years were taking their inevitable toll: Jimmie Marsland, who had been the assistant producer when I joined D'Oyly Carte in 1975 (and who would have revelled in the reunion), had died in March at the age of eighty-seven.

On July 4 I played for a duo called Champagne Opera (Paul Weakley, who had been in D'Oyly Carte, and Brenda Waite), and on the 27th I did my last deputising at Claridge's. The hotel had decided that it didn't want to continue with the quartet and that was worrying, particularly for the regular players. But the management at the Ritz in Piccadilly had heard about this, and they said that they would be very happy to have the group; so when I was next called upon, on August 18, it was to the Ritz that I went: we didn't have to wear the green jackets there. We played in the middle of the long corridor that runs the full length of the building from the side entrance in Arlington Street to the dining room that overlooks Green Park. In front of us was the alcove where afternoon tea is served; we also had tea there when we had a break halfway through the evening. Later, the routine was changed, and after the tea break we played in the dining room although it was seldom full. We were entitled to have a meal in the staff canteen, and most of the group ate there before we started. The repertoire was the same, but we always finished with *A Nightingale Sang in Berkeley Square* as the hotel is mentioned in the song. I always enjoyed playing at the Ritz in such elegant surroundings. (César Ritz, who built it, had been the first manager of Richard D'Oyly Carte's Savoy Hotel.) The leader of the quartet was Paul Frowde who was married to Judi Merri, a former D'Oyly Carte principal mezzo-soprano.

Thanks to the Gilbert and Sullivan Society, who always got a quota of tickets, I was able to attend a garden party at Buckingham Palace in July; in August there was a G&S concert at the Earnley Concourse in West Sussex with Geoffrey Shovelton, Deborah Clague and Leon Berger.

Despite our misgivings about the future of The Best of Gilbert and Sullivan there was a second tour this year although it was part of the 2000-2001 season: the tour in February had been part of the 1999-2000 season. Apart from the single date in St Louis MO in 1997 this was the shortest of all the tours, including the earlier ones for Byers, Schwalbe. It ran from September 29 to October 8, and there were just five concerts - two in Texas, and three in Colorado which were all at the same venue. The team was the same as in February: Deborah Clague, Patricia Leonard, Geoffrey Shovelton, John Ayldon and me. We flew to Dallas/Ft Worth TX, hired the usual minivan, a Ford this time, and drove to Sherman TX where we gave the first concert the following day: this was at Austin College which had links to the Presbyterian Church. The concert, part of the Community Series, was held in the Wynne Chapel, Austin College Campus which had excellent acoustics; it also had a very good Steinway piano, and we had a responsive and enthusiastic audience.

The next day was Sunday. We had an early start as we had to return the minivan and catch a flight to San Antonio TX where we were met by Frank Valani who worked for the organisation that had booked us. We were then driven to our hotel which was very near the famous Alamo, 'the cradle of Texas liberty' (we were reminded of our accident in Los Angeles with the cars hired from Alamo). The concert was in the Empire Theatre which had been turned into a dining venue similar to those at Bremerton WA and Pendleton OR where we had performed in February. The piano here, a Baldwin, had a note that stuck when you used the soft pedal. After the show we were taken to a wonderful Mexican restaurant by Frank Valani who kindly paid the bill.

Monday was a free day, and we visited the Alamo complex in the morning; we then went on the Yanaguana Cruise (we were told you had to say "I wanna-go-onna Yana-guana"). Yanaguana was the old Native American name before the Spaniards named the settlement San Antonio. The river meanders through the city with a path alongside; the cruise was delightful: it was almost like being in Venice although the buildings and foliage were very different. The weather too was wonderful. Later, we saw a film *Space Cowboys* and then had a drink in one of the riverside cafés. Our free day had been a very pleasant interlude. This was the epitome of mixing business with pleasure, but we did wonder if there would be any more such opportunities for The Best of Gilbert and Sullivan.

Next, we had a travelling day. Frank Valani drove us to the airport where we got a flight to Dallas/Ft Worth followed by a second flight (with Frontier Airlines, a new one to most of us, which offered a complimentary package of toothbrush, toothpaste, shampoo, shaving cream and razor) to Denver CO. We were met by our sponsor, but our luggage had not arrived, and we had to wait until another flight came in. Thankfully most of the luggage, except Geoffrey's (it had to be Geoffrey's), was on this one, but we couldn't wait any longer. We hired another minivan and drove to our hotel where we stayed for five nights.

The following day, October 4, was another free day. The hotel was very isolated, but there was a nearby shopping mall which had over a hundred stores and almost twenty restaurants. In the evening I ate in the hotel restaurant with John and Patricia, but when their food came they said that it was cold. The manager apologised and offered them something else, but they declined and went off to find a Denny's (we ate regularly in these restaurants and found them excellent; John seemed to have a sixth sense in locating them). I had no complaints about my meal, and so I stayed on and finished it, but I then found that it was on the house because of the earlier upset. I said that I was quite happy to pay, but the manager insisted that there was no charge. It was embarrassing, but it was also a pleasant bonus. At this stage Geoffrey's case hadn't yet appeared.

Next morning Geoffrey had to go to the shopping mall to be kitted out with everything he needed for the evening performance; he then had to have the trousers altered. We all tagged along as there wasn't much else to do except watch TV (I had even seen a version of *Teletubbies* with an American voice-over: it was barely intelligible). The concerts, at Littleton CO, were all in the Town Hall Arts Center (with Geoffrey now in his new suit, shirt, tie, cufflinks, socks and shoes). The first one went well, but in the middle of "Alone, and yet alive!" (*The Mikado*) we were once again plunged into darkness. I had coped with "Never mind the why and wherefore" (*HMS Pinafore*) in a similar situation, but this time there were a few strange chords during the number. The blackout was caused by the timing in the computerised lighting board, and as we still had to do two more concerts we managed to get the sequence changed.

When we got back to the hotel we found that Geoffrey's case had finally arrived. But it had been damaged, and so next day we had to take it to the airport to have it inspected. In the end he was given a new one, and we then went in to Denver: I had last been there during the D'Oyly Carte tour in 1978. The show that evening was again well received, and there was a reception afterwards.

The next day was our last full day. Deborah had friends here who kindly provided lunch; also present was a lady we had met in Colorado Springs CO in 1986. The house, on Lookout Mountain, had a superb view. It also possessed an Ampico reproducing piano, and we heard some interesting performances: Richard Strauss playing a version of his song *Devotion*, the violinist Fritz Kreisler playing his *Caprice Viennois*, and a piece played by the composer Rudolf Friml. The last show also went very well although the audience was the quietest of the three. But they did join in with "When a felon's not engaged in his employment - " (*The Pirates of Penzance*). Next day, we split up and went our separate ways. Patricia Leonard and I flew first to Dallas/Ft Worth TX and then back to London, overnight October 8-9. It had, as always, been an enjoyable tour, but with so few concerts it presumably hadn't made much of a profit for Joanne Rile. Efforts were made to secure future engagements, but this was the last tour for John Ayldon, Patricia Leonard and me. The Riles did organise some more concerts, but these only involved Geoffrey and Deborah after they had moved to the United States permanently: other American singers and a pianist made up the group.

We had had a wonderful time travelling across the United States and Canada, giving more than one hundred and fifty concerts over a period of sixteen years (although only Geoffrey Shovelton and I had done every one of those); it had also been financially very advantageous. We all had countless memories of the tours such as Ken Sandford drinking copious amounts of cola, and Lorraine Daniels apparently able to fall asleep at the drop of a hat. Lorraine would often be asleep on a plane as soon as she had fastened her seat belt; she didn't even wake up when we took off. But once, in a hotel room in the middle of the night, she *was* woken up by an enormous bang from the room next door: this was Geoffrey's room. Next morning he appeared at breakfast with a bruised face: he had got up and had walked into the wall. With all the travelling that we did he had just forgotten where he was.

Geoffrey certainly had the lion's share of the accidents and incidents. He and I were exploring Providence RI one morning, and he was taking photographs. He tripped on a raised paving stone and fell on the pavement. Almost immediately a car pulled up, and the driver, assuming that he would sue the local authority, shouted "Wanna witness?" Geoffrey politely declined the offer.

But there was one thing that stood out for me as it might have been the end of the group, and it would have been my fault. On this occasion we had one of the minivans, and we had to return it first thing in the morning as we had to catch an early flight; it was my turn to drive. We all managed to get up in time, and everyone piled into the van, but the others immediately fell asleep again. From the hotel car park I had to turn right on to a dual carriageway. When I got to the road I looked right and left, crossed the first carriageway and turned right on to the second carriageway. It was already light, but as it was so early there was nothing else on the road. After a few minutes I then became aware of another car on the opposite carriageway – going in the same direction! The others were still asleep, and no-one had noticed this. I suddenly realised what I had done. With no traffic on the road to guide me I had simply forgotten that we were in America and that I should be driving on the right. Thankfully there was a gap in the barrier just ahead, and I managed to get on to the right-hand carriageway without any further problems. I don't think the others ever realised quite how close we all came to oblivion.

Arthur Sullivan died in 1900, and to mark this centenary there was a concert at London's Royal Albert Hall on November 1 which I conducted. It had been sponsored by WISE, a charitable organisation uniting the common interests of the Welsh, Irish, Scots and English: Andrew Whittaker, who ran Grim's Dyke Opera, was involved in the planning. We had a section of the Royal Philharmonic Orchestra, seven soloists from the original D'Oyly Carte Opera Company - Gillian Knight, Jill Washington, Ann-Louise Straker, Kenneth Sandford, John Ayldon, Michael Rayner and Geoffrey Shovelton - with Richard Suart from its successor, and a chorus of over five hundred drawn from thirty-three organisations and amateur societies from all over the country. Richard Baker was the compère. We shared a dressing room; he was very pleasant company. There were excerpts from *The Yeomen of the Guard*, *Ruddigore*, *The Mikado* and *The*

Pirates of Penzance as well as orchestral items by Sullivan: the *Imperial March*, the *Overture di ballo* and the overture from the incidental music to Henry Irving's production of *Macbeth* (1888). It was certainly one of the highlights of the year although it was quite daunting to have so many performers under one's baton. Later that month, on the actual centenary of Sullivan's death (November 22), there was a short ceremony at the Sullivan memorial in Embankment Gardens opposite the river entrance to the Savoy Hotel.

It had been a busy year, particularly with G&S, and it had been a good start to the new century. I could only hope that enough work would continue to come in, particularly if there were to be no more tours for The Best of Gilbert and Sullivan.

II – 2001

Many years earlier, when I was still living in Scotland, we used to celebrate New Year in a big way. I usually stayed at home until Big Ben heralded the start of another year at midnight before going out with friends to visit other friends and neighbours who would always have food and drink ready for whoever might drop in: doors were left open so that you literally just walked into other people's houses. How things have changed. This carousing and 'first-footing' usually went on until the small hours, and I was seldom home before daybreak. I would then go to bed and not get up until about 16.00 by which time it was dark again; for a number of years I never saw any daylight on New Year's Day. It was just as well that this nocturnal activity had now stopped because not for the first time, and not for the last, I had a job for Music in Hospitals on January 1.

Shortly after this I received a letter from the new general manager of the Canadian Children's Opera Chorus to introduce himself, to inform me that they also had a new artistic director, and finally to admit that with all this administrative upheaval the manuscript of my arrangement of *The Mikado* had somehow been misplaced; could I please send another copy as soon as possible? I was amazed that a fairly bulky package could go missing, but luckily it was a photocopy that I had sent in case anything like this ever happened. I told them that I would make another copy, but with all my commitments it might take some time. Thankfully, performances were not imminent. January also saw a Spaghetti Opera evening with Geoffrey Shovelton and Deborah Clague at a restaurant in Northampton; later, in May, we did the last of those at Terrazza-Est. Geoffrey and I also provided some entertainment for a Burns Supper at Oxford Golf Club for an old school friend of mine.

I tried to get back to Scotland every so often, and sometimes I could tie in a visit with something else. In March I sang in a performance of Verdi's *Requiem* at Glasgow University along with many old friends and fellow-students. This was to celebrate not only the centenary of Verdi's death but also the five hundred and fiftieth anniversary of the founding of the University in 1451. I was back again in October for a reunion of my Primary 1 classmates ('class of '48'), many of whom I had not seen since those early school-days.

There was still plenty of G&S. Manor Light Opera's production this year was *The Mikado*. The producer was again Vanda Morgan; the orchestra, not surprisingly, was listed as The Titipu Town Band. There was also a week-end of lectures at Dillington Hall in Somerset, a concert in Brighton with Geoffrey and Deborah to celebrate the fiftieth anniversary of the Sussex Gilbert and Sullivan Society, a concert in London with Elizabeth Menezes (a young singer who, with her brother David, had taken a great interest in the operas), a concert at Bungay, Suffolk in July with Gillian Knight, former D'Oyly Carte principal contralto, and a G&S course for NODA in August with Beryl Dixon, former D'Oyly Carte principal mezzo-soprano.

I now also had the regular Sunday work at Grim's Dyke. As yet, we just had monthly performances although this year there were two in December, one of them being designated a black tie dress code for the audience. The English Heritage Singers, for whom I had occasionally deputised, also gave regular G&S evenings at the hotel, and so there was plenty of entertainment for the fans. At this stage our repertoire was still limited to the most popular operas – *The Pirates of Penzance, Iolanthe, The Mikado* and *The Yeomen of the Guard* – which were done in rotation. But a welcome addition to the Sunday evenings was the reintroduction, after a break of eight years, of operetta productions in the garden. For these we were able to have an orchestra led by Donna Chapman who also led the orchestra for the Manor House productions. The company performed in the open air with the house as a backdrop; the chorus were on my right under a canopy, and the orchestra, on my left under a similar canopy. But with no cover for the principals or the audience we were dependent on good weather. Over a four-day period, July 30-August 2, we gave two performances each, on alternate evenings, of *The Pirates of Penzance* and *The Mikado*. During one performance of *Mikado* the heavens opened, and we had no option but to make a hurried dash for the house where the show continued, after a fashion, with keyboard accompaniment.

Most of the Music in Hospitals concerts this year were single dates in and around London, but there was one extended tour that was memorable in a number of ways. The organisation, based in Surrey, operated throughout England, Wales and the Channel Islands. (Scotland was organised separately; we were never sent to Northern Ireland.) On more than one occasion I had to turn down work in the Channel Islands because of tours of The Best of Gilbert and Sullivan, but I was now able to take up the offer of a week in Jersey and a week in Guernsey with the flautist Mark Underwood. I flew to Jersey from Gatwick on Monday August 27: Mark flew

separately. The concerts here, although under the banner of
Music in Hospitals, were part of Arts in Healthcare organised
by Jersey Arts Centre. We stayed in the Ommaroo Hotel in
St Helier which was on the sea-front but was still close to the
town centre.

With a busy schedule there wasn't much time for sightseeing
or socialising, but I managed to see an old school friend Bill
McGregor, a lawyer who was now working there: Bill came to
the hotel one day when I had a spare moment. I also managed
to see Hazel Oakley (who had now moved to Jersey after
Harold's death), her daughter Christine and family; we found
time to have a meal together. On Sunday September 2 there
were just two concerts in the afternoon, and in the morning
I was able to visit Elizabeth Castle (that *is* a castle, not a
person), almost the only sightseeing I was able to do on Jersey
apart from in St Helier itself.

The concerts in both Jersey and Guernsey were in a variety
of care homes, hospices, schools and day centres. On regular
tours on the mainland we would usually do two concerts a
day, but on eight out of sixteen working days here we did
three a day. On six of the days there were just two concerts,
and there was even one on the day we left Guernsey, but on
one of the days we had to do four concerts. This would have
been very hard, if not impossible, for one singer although in
those days Music in Hospitals would often send two or more
artists (Caroline Dixon and Noel Drennan, with whom
I worked regularly, had been on the islands on more than one
occasion), but instrumentalists are used to playing for long
periods. Nevertheless, even Mark found that four concerts a
day was just one too many, and on that day I had to play more
solos than I normally did just to let him get his breath back.

We had the use of a car on each island, but the venues were
all fairly close to each other, and there wasn't much travel
involved. As usual, most of the venues didn't have a piano,
and so we had the use of an electronic keyboard. It was a good
one, but the problem with good keyboards is that they are

invariably large and heavy, and so there was the added difficulty of getting it into the car, getting it out again, setting it up, dismantling it, putting it back in the car, and going through this procedure again at the next venue. It needed two of us to do this, and it was quite tiring and time-consuming.

On Wednesday September 5 we flew to Guernsey, a short fifteen-minute hop. The concerts here were organised by the Healing Music Trust in conjunction with Music in Hospitals, and we stayed in a hostel which was on a hill above St Peter Port from where there were wonderful views. The rooms were comfortable, but they were more basic than hotel rooms; the only TV was in a communal lounge. The tour continued as soon as we arrived: there were two concerts that day, and, three the following day. On the Saturday we were treated to dinner in the evening following the last concert. The next day, the second Sunday, was the one day that was entirely free. This time we did manage to see something of the island, and that included Castle Cornet at St Peter Port.

And then came the day of the four concerts: Tuesday September 11, 2001. A familiar date? Yes, that was the day of 9/11. Our four concerts were spread throughout the day: the first one was at 10.30, and the second one was at 12.45. The third venue, a hospice, had a reception area, and when we arrived shortly after 14.00 (09.00 in New York) the receptionist was looking at her computer in a rather puzzled way. "Oh dear", she said, "something is coming through here about a plane hitting a building in New York". Like many people, when they first heard the news, I assumed that it would have been a small plane: I had experienced travelling up the Hudson River in just such a plane on one of our previous tours. We didn't think too much about it, and we went in to do the concert. But when we came out the receptionist now had a better idea of what was going on, and she told us that the second tower had also been hit. We couldn't quite believe what was happening, but this was our busiest day yet, and we still had one more concert to do - and it was at 18.00. It wasn't until we got back to the hostel that we finally found out what had happened. (The lounge was crammed to overflowing with all the guests glued to the one TV set in the building.) When President Bush's plane Air Force One touched down at Barksdale Air Force Base in Louisiana he was met not by an official limousine but by a minivan like the ones we had so often used.

There was an immediate shut-down of airports everywhere, including the one on Guernsey, and it is just as well that we had more concerts the next day (Wednesday) as we would not have been able to get off the island. But we were due to travel back on the Thursday, and by then things had started to move again. When we were checking in, Mark was told that the case containing his instruments (he had a flute, bass flute, piccolo and recorders) would have to go in the hold as a result of what had happened in New York. He wasn't very happy with this, and he made a spirited protest; in the end, they allowed him to have the case in the cabin. By itself it would have been a very enjoyable, if hectic, tour, but with the addition of 9/11 it was one that I would certainly not forget. After 9/11 it became more difficult for artists to get work visas for the United States, and this contributed to the end of The Best of Gilbert and Sullivan for those of us who were still resident in the UK.

The Bentley concerts continued, but as in 2000 there were just six of them. The first one was in April, again for the Arts and Heritage Club. As well as our Christmas dates for them at Runnymede we now appeared to have regular Easter dates which were all in cathedral cities: we had been in Hereford in 1999 and Wells in 2000; now we were at the White Hart Hotel in Lincoln. As before, we gave them a mixture of items from our repertoire. The next concert wasn't until June. It was for the Worcestershire Women's Institute, and it was held in the splendid surroundings of the Great Hall in Hartlebury Castle, the official residence of the Bishop of Worcester. We gave them *Ballads, Songs and Snatches*.

After that we didn't have any more work until November when we did a concert at the Stag Theatre in Sevenoaks; again this was kindly sponsored by Will McQuillan. It was called *On Active Service* (songs and readings reflecting a century of service life), and it covered the Second World War whereas *These Men Are Worth Your Tears*, which was similar, was geared specifically to the First World War. Ralph and I were again joined by Diana Walsh.

The three remaining dates were a G&S concert at Grim's Dyke in November, a further appearance at Runnymede for the Arts and Heritage Club (this one on Christmas Eve) and a concert at Lucy Brown House in Southwark, London on New Year's Eve. For all of these we were joined by Pamela Baxter, a former chorister with D'Oyly Carte during my time there. Ralph and Pam had just become engaged.

As well as these concerts Ralph and I recorded all of Gerard Francis Cobb's settings of Kipling's *Barrack-Room Ballads*, effectively our concert called *Thank You, Mr Atkins*. This was done over two sessions at the Sutton home of Kay Laing who had a good Steinway piano; the recording was made by Simon Vout, formerly a horn player with D'Oyly Carte. The first session was in October, but the second one wasn't until November. The piano had been tuned between these dates, and Simon had to balance the different sounds which he did very well. We hoped that we could issue the recording in time for the centenary of Cobb's death in 2004. One or two of the settings had previously been recorded, but we could say that this CD of the complete set would be a 'world-first'.

Thanks to Anne and Peter Mitchell I played for a performance of Mozart's *Cosi fan tutte* by Belcanto Opera at East Grinstead on November 25. This was videoed, and many years later I acquired a copy; Anne and Peter also kindly invited me to spend Boxing Day with them. I had spent Christmas Day this year with Simon Vout, his wife Jan and Jan's sister Pam. They were former colleagues who had all played in the D'Oyly Carte orchestra, and they all lived near me. Jan and Pam's mother was also there. These social occasions were welcome bouts of relaxation. I was now also playing regularly with a violinist Ann Binks; Ann and I did concerts in one or two local care homes. This was similar to the work I did with Music in Hospitals. It had been a good year.

III – 2002

With my working life now on a reasonably stable footing 2002 was much the same as 2001, even to the extent of having a Music in Hospitals concert on January 1. These concerts continued throughout the year as before, again mainly in and around London. Sometimes they were in Guy's Hospital or St Thomas's Hospital, and I always had to take a keyboard with me for those as well as a bag of music. Parking was impossible in the hospitals, and I had to use the Underground. It wasn't too bad going in for an afternoon concert, but it was always tiresome travelling with equipment on the return journey as rush hour traffic increased. Sometimes there would be MiH concerts on consecutive days, but there were only three actual tours this year: a two-day one in and around Birmingham in August, a longer one in October that took in Swindon, Cheltenham, Gloucester and several other venues in Wiltshire, and another two-day one in December that covered Bicester, Bletchingdon, Birmingham and Royal Leamington Spa. One interesting venue, also in December, was the geometrically planned Whiteley Village at Hersham, Surrey whose design was much influenced by the Arts and Crafts movement. The money for this project had come from a bequest by William Whiteley, founder of the former department store, Whiteley's, in London's Bayswater. I did several concerts at Whiteley Village for Music in Hospitals.

At the end of January I gave a talk for Bernard Goss, former membership secretary of the Gilbert and Sullivan

Society who now organised events for the Selsdon Music Group in South Croydon. This was preceded by a very nice lunch with Bernard and his wife Jean. I would do more talks for Bernard.

The first Bentley concert was on February 27 which happened to be the twentieth anniversary of the closure of the original D'Oyly Carte Opera Company, an auspicious day for me. This concert, *The Fleet's In*, was in Broxbourne Civic Hall and was again for the Arts and Heritage Club. Ralph Meanley and Pam Baxter were both touring in America with another company, and so I asked Anne Mitchell and Patrick Ward (another Music in Hospitals colleague) to step in. This concert was to have been the first of a series of six, but the following day I was told that we had been 'dropped' although I was not given a reason for this. It was a bad start to the year. Was this the end of our association with the Arts and Heritage Club?

The second concert was at the Golf Hotel, Silloth in June. It was part of a Sea & Ships Week in this little Victorian town in Cumbria (one-time home of the contralto Kathleen Ferrier), and so we did *The Fleet's In*: Ralph and Pam were now back from America. With just two concerts in six months it looked as if Bentley Concert Productions was heading in the same direction as The Best of Gilbert and Sullivan: the earlier days, with seventeen concerts and a radio interview in 1997, seemed destined not to be repeated. But we had prepared the art work and sleeve notes for our recording of the *Barrack-Room Ballads*, and so we hadn't been idle.

The next concert, in September, was a private one at Somersby House, the home of Peter and Carol Chapman who had asked us to perform for an invited audience in aid of the National Children's Orchestra (the house had a music room that seated about eighty people). This was a G&S evening, but we had also been asked to reminisce about our careers which evidently delighted the audience. Following this, in October, there was a concert for the Isle of Ely branch of the Women's Institute which had come about through our concert for the Worcestershire branch at Hartlebury Castle in 2001. This one, a mixture of G&S and ballads, was at March in Cambridgeshire.

There were three further concerts this year. The first of these, in November, was another *Shipmates O' Mine*; it was at the Victoria Hall, Grange-over-Sands where we had performed in 1997. We were looked after by a local music teacher on the day, but we stayed for the week-end with Ralph's friends Paul and Gill Heels in Barrow-in-Furness. Audience numbers were down from our first concert which was always a worry. In December we were at the Café Caricature in Hastings Old Town where we did *Thank You, Mr Atkins*. This venue was run by Louise Denny who put on a variety of concerts and also served excellent food. It was a very enjoyable evening, but as numbers were limited it wasn't a financial success. The last concert, a Viennese and operetta evening, was at the Runnymede Hotel on December 27 for the Arts and Heritage Club. Having being dropped after the Broxbourne concert in February I wasn't expecting any more work from them. This brought our total to seven concerts, an increase of one from 2001 but hardly cause for optimism.

The world of G&S was still the source of much work for me despite the end of our tours of North America. The Sunday performances at Grim's Dyke had been increased to twenty, and one more opera had been added: we now had *HMS Pinafore*, *The Pirates of Penzance*, *Iolanthe*, *The Mikado* and *The Yeomen of the Guard* which were, as usual, done in rotation. A sixth opera, *The Sorcerer*, was given a single performance on November 17 as it was celebrating its one hundred and twenty-fifth anniversary on that very day; it was now planned to celebrate each opera's one hundred and twenty-fifth anniversary with a special performance: the next one would be that of *HMS Pinafore* in 2003. Following on from its re-introduction in 2001 we had more performances in the garden in August, again with orchestra. The operas this time were *Iolanthe* and *The Mikado*. These outdoor performances could be scuppered by inclement weather (as had happened in 2001), and so this year the stage was covered: perversely, the weather was fine.

There was one more occasion which involved the group although it wasn't at Grim's Dyke. This was a concert in the grounds of Ardington House at Wantage in Oxfordshire on June 2. It was to celebrate Her Majesty the Queen's Golden Jubilee, and it was in aid of Macmillan Cancer Relief; once again we were under a canopy in case of inclement weather, but it remained dry. The concert, with orchestra, consisted of excerpts from four of the operas: *Iolanthe* and *The Pirates of Penzance* in the first half; *The Yeomen of the Guard* and *The Mikado* in the second half. The artists were a mixture of ex-D'Oyly Carte - Michael Rayner, Gareth Jones, Barry Clark and Ann-Louise Straker - and other regulars at Grim's Dyke - Clive Bebee, John Coleman, Sylvia Clarke and Joy Rayner. We also had a large chorus, but not quite as large as the one we had at the Royal Albert Hall in 2000. We rehearsed in the afternoon, and we had a picnic tea before the performance.

There were also other G&S-related jobs. In March I had to deputise as pianist for a concert put on by Jeremy Peaker at the Coliseum Theatre in Aberdare; in April I was at a Gilbert and Sullivan Society Convention in Stockport. In June there was a G&S workshop with Geoffrey Shovelton at Duston in Northamptonshire. This was for Judith Baxter's pupils with Geoffrey giving coaching lessons to the participants. In September I played for the former D'Oyly Carte tenor Tom Round, then eighty-six, at a Gilbert and Sullivan Society meeting in London. I also wrote a review for *Music & Letters* of *A Most Ingenious Paradox/The Art of Gilbert and Sullivan* by Gayden Wren.

In the summer I conducted *The Pirates of Penzance* and *The Mikado* at the Buxton G&S Festival. Buxton was an ideal place for this Festival: the main performances were held in the Opera House, and related events could be held in the adjacent complex of buildings in the Pavilion Gardens which included the Paxton

Theatre. But Buxton was in the North of England, and many fans and aficionados lived in the South, and so to make it easier for them it was decided to have some performances in Eastbourne, not at the Congress Theatre where D'Oyly Carte had played but at the smaller Devonshire Park Theatre. It was very pleasant to be back in Eastbourne. I conducted six performances there between July 28 and August 4, and in Buxton there were another four performances over two days, August 10 and 11. The Grim's Dyke garden performances ran from August 5-8, and so that was a busy two weeks.

One abiding memory of Eastbourne was the Saturday matinée of *Mikado* on August 3. We had just reached the fanfare that heralds the entrance of Ko-Ko ("Behold the Lord High Executioner!") when the fire alarm went off. The show had to be terminated, and we were all sent out into the street. Luckily it was a fine day, and as soon as it was ascertained that there was no fire we all trooped back and started again at the fanfare. This reminded me of the bomb scare during a performance of *Princess Ida* at Sadler's Wells in 1977. In November I also had to conduct a week of *Iolanthe* for an amateur group, the Julian Light Operatic Society, at the Questors Theatre in Ealing.

Aside from G&S there was another Burns Supper at Oxford Golf Club in January, this time with Patrick Ward, and another *Carmen* in June, this time with Opera del Mar: it took place in a marquee at the Turnpike Showground at Motcombe in Dorset. There was a small orchestra for this, but I was at a keyboard to fill in for missing instruments, a sign of the times as it was becoming prohibitive for productions to have a full orchestra. Also in June, Ralph Meanley, Pam Baxter and I did an evening called *Opera in the Pub* at the Golden Hart near Spitalfields Market in East London.

Conrad Leonard had finally been persuaded by Vivienne Jay to make a CD of his songs and piano pieces, but he said that while he could cope with a certain amount of the work he would need someone to assist him, and so I was asked to play for several numbers. Vivienne had sung many of his songs, but she didn't perform on the recording, leaving this to her niece Claire Rutter (soprano) and Claire's husband Stephen Gadd (baritone). But she had written the words of one recent song *Whispering Dreams* in 2000. I played for several numbers including *The Clouds Are Horsemen*, a song with a difficult accompaniment that he had written as far back as 1925, and I joined Conrad in duet versions of two of his piano pieces *The Lone Fir Tree* and *Noonday Sun*. The recording, which was done by Simon Vout, was made at Claire and Stephen's home in Bournemouth in April. In July we gave a concert of Conrad's music in the Plantation Café at Squire's Garden Centre in Twickenham where he played every Thursday. In October he celebrated his one hundred and fourth birthday.

Manor Light Opera, having done *The Mikado* in 2001, should have done a non-G&S this year, but they broke the mould by choosing *The Pirates of Penzance*; yet again there was another producer, this time Pat O'Connell who was well-known on the G&S circuit. I still had seven players in the orchestra; this year they were called The Penzance Players. Nick Pope was with us again as the pianist. We could always get a good cast, but the chorus got progressively worse as the years went on. Gilbert's female choristers were generally supposed to be young (Major-General Stanley's daughters (*Pirates*), lovesick maidens (*Patience*) or "Schoolgirls we, eighteen and under," (*Mikado*)), and our ladies were well past those tender years. Some of the men could barely sing, but they had joined because they liked the idea of being on the stage. At one time this would not have happened as many hopefuls would have been politely told that they were just not suitable. But with an increasing lack of male choristers we needed bodies on the stage, and so we reluctantly accepted some non-singers.

It was becoming more and more difficult to keep up a musical standard, and the National Operatic and Dramatic Association (NODA)'s report on *Pirates* contained some damning comments on both male *and* female choristers.

Accordingly I told the Society that I would not take on the conductorship of their next production, Lehar's *The Merry Widow*. I did this with some reluctance as I had not yet conducted this operetta, but with no prospect of an improvement in the chorus situation I felt that I had no choice. However, there was a silver lining to this cloud: as well as putting on a week of *The Merry Widow* in 2003 they wanted to celebrate Her Majesty the Queen's Golden Jubilee *this* year with a concert performance of Edward German's *Merrie England* which was celebrating its centenary. Being a concert performance everyone would have a score, and hopefully the chorus would be augmented by members of other societies. And so I agreed to conduct *Merrie England* which had its single performance on November 30 in the Great Hall of the Liberal Jewish Synagogue in St John's Wood. I also told Manor Light Opera that if the chorus situation improved I would certainly consider coming back as the musical director.

My cousin June died in August, and I took Ken Barclay down to Hampshire for the funeral as he had known June and Ron from the Petersfield Musical Festival, and they had introduced me to Ken. But there were so many people attending the service that several of us had to stand outside.

I have always tried to maintain my interest in research into G&S and other aspects of both Gilbert and Sullivan individually. One result of this was that I contributed a third article to the P.G. Wodehouse Journal *Wooster Sauce* (Number 24, December 2002). This was the first part of *Precious Nonsense: More Wodehouse Borrowings from W.S. Gilbert*. The second part appeared in the following issue (Number 25, March 2003).

IV – 2003

This year saw a couple of milestones: my mother reached her ninetieth birthday in June, and I reached my sixtieth in November. I was becoming increasingly frustrated by many aspects of living in London, and I was looking forward to eventually moving out. At one time I thought of going back to Eastbourne, but as I got older I found that I missed my native land more and more, particularly the River Clyde, where I grew up, and the Cowal peninsula that I could see from my mother's living room window. Latterly, when visiting her for brief periods, I found myself saying "Do I have to go back to London?" Gradually the idea of coming back to Scotland began to take shape. My mother had had a stroke shortly before her eighty-fifth birthday, but she had recovered enough to be allowed to go home. Now at almost ninety she was showing signs of physical (but not mental) frailty, and I felt that I should be nearer to her. I had many cousins in Greenock who were very good at visiting her although I couldn't expect them to be on hand all the time, but I was still paying off a mortgage, and as I had just given up Manor Light Opera (and previously Philbeach) I couldn't afford to give up any more work. And so for the moment I had to stay in London. But there was some light at the end of the tunnel as the mortgage would be paid off in 2005: not too long now. I didn't do a Music in Hospitals concert on January 1 as I had done in the previous two years, and I was able to pay a New Year's visit to Muriel Levin who lived within walking distance.

Invigilating, to which I was introduced by other free-lance musicians, was a useful way of filling up empty spaces in the diary, and you could take it or not if it was offered: they would always come back to you. The year had started quietly, and I was happy to do three days of this in the middle of the month, but as other work came in I didn't do any more until May. There was quite a lot after that in various halls and hotels in London, one venue being Chelsea Town Hall.

At the end of January I had lunch again with Bernard and Jean Goss although this time I didn't have to give a talk afterwards to the Selsdon Music Group. But I did give one at the end of March, preceded by yet another very nice lunch.

Bernard and Jean were excellent hosts, and I also got to know friends of theirs, Charles and Jean Roberts, who invariably joined us. In February I played for a group at the Barn Theatre, Oxted. I would be back there again.

One sad event this year was the death, in April, of Conrad Leonard at the age of one hundred and four. His funeral was held on May 1 at Putney Vale Crematorium, and there was a memorial service for him on June 20 at St Paul's, Covent Garden followed by a reception at the CAA in nearby Bedford Street. It had been a privilege to know him. He was a link with the nineteenth century: Gilbert, Sullivan, Richard D'Oyly Carte and Queen Victoria were all still alive when he was born.

There were twenty Sunday evening performances at Grim's Dyke, of *HMS Pinafore*, *The Pirates of Penzance*, *Patience* (a particular favourite of mine), *The Mikado* and *The Yeomen of the Guard*. We had celebrated the one hundred and twenty-fifth anniversary of *The Sorcerer* in 2002, and we now did the same for *HMS Pinafore* on May 26, the day after the actual anniversary. This was designated a black tie dress code. Between April and October, on the Sundays when we performed an opera, the hotel offered guided tours followed by a cream tea; members of the opera group now entertained during these, something previously done by the English Heritage Singers. In the afternoon of one of the *Patience* performances (August 31) the hotel held an open day, part of the London Festival, and the opera group joined in to give an impromptu concert in the garden: I accompanied on a keyboard that we managed to set up. An interesting departure, on March 23, had been a performance of *The Mikado* (supporting PolioPlus [sic]) at The Stables, Wavendon, the home of Johnny Dankworth and Cleo Laine.

Aside from Grim's Dyke there was, as usual, plenty of other G&S work. In April I played for Cynthia Morey and John Fryatt at the Sussex Gilbert and Sullivan Society in Brighton, and I was there again in November to give a talk that I had previously given in May at the Sir Arthur Sullivan Society

Festival in Ely. I was twice at the London Society, first of all in March as accompanist to Ken Sandford and Lorraine Daniels, and again in October when I talked about reconstructing Sullivan's cello concerto. I also did two concerts for New Savoyards of London, the first of these in Exmouth in April. Taking part in this concert was former D'Oyly Carte chorister Jeffrey Cresswell whom I had first met when he came to Sadler's Wells from English National Opera to sing Hilarion in two performances of *Princess Ida* on Saturday February 19, 1977 as Meston Reid was indisposed: the matinée was the first time I conducted this opera. The second concert for New Savoyards was in South Shields. Ralph Meanley took part in this, and we drove up together. I was also asked to write another review for *Music & Letters*, this time of Michael Ainger's *Gilbert and Sullivan/A Dual Biography*.

There was just one Bentley concert this year which was in the Village Hall, Theydon Bois in April; this was an evening of G&S for yet another branch of the Women's Institute. With all the effort we had put into them it was disappointing that we could only get one concert in the course of a year, but both Ralph and I had other work (like mine, his was sometimes abroad), and we weren't always available at the same time. There was no Easter concert for the Arts and Heritage Club, and we had been told that there would not be one at Runnymede at Christmas. We were finding it increasingly difficult to persuade managements to put on concerts or indeed to get the public to come to them. Ralph did a lot of supply teaching, and he managed to organise a few concerts in his various schools, but these were not strictly Bentley concerts. Pam Baxter had now taken over from Lorraine Daniels as our female soloist when required, and some six weeks after the Theydon Bois concert Ralph and Pam were married on May 25, the one hundred and twenty-fifth anniversary of *HMS Pinafore* which we celebrated at Grim's Dyke the following day.

In April I saw Philbeach's production of *Guys and Dolls*, and in May, Manor Light Opera's production of *The Merry*

Widow: this was conducted by Paul Arman whom I had known from Philbeach. Paul had somehow managed to get a larger orchestra of eleven players, but this time, while still individually listed, the group didn't have a collective name.

At the beginning of May I played for another singer Deborah Eveleigh at St Mary's Church in Westerham, Kent and in June I played for a group of Old Harrovians at the East India Club in London of which Doug Schwalbe of Byers, Schwalbe had been a member. Later in June I went up to Scotland for my mother's ninetieth birthday, and on the way back I stopped off to play at a concert in Huntingdon for Tim Hurst-Brown, a G&S enthusiast who was also a skilled performer. Tim sang with a group called the Wandering Minstrels.

The author 'at the piano' at the Concert Artistes'
Association, London (see Chapter 3, p. 78).

I had often been the pianist for the Monday evening concerts at the CAA, but I had to give this up when I joined Manor Light Opera. Now I could do this again when asked. Members of the CAA had been in all branches of theatre. One was David Young, another Scot, who had also been in D'Oyly Carte but before my time. It transpired that I had known his brother Alec, a flautist, who had been at the RSAMD at the same time as me and who had married a former girl friend of mine. But I only discovered this connection one day in July when David and I were driving up to Buxton to attend a D'Oyly Carte reunion called Together Again. Life is full of surprises. The week after this reunion there were several Music in Hospitals concerts in and around Birmingham.

I still took part in music hall – 'at enormous expense' – often with Judith Baxter who sometimes organised these and other concerts in the village in Northamptonshire where she and her husband lived. These were invariably on a Saturday, and if there was a performance at Grim's Dyke on the Sunday I would stay overnight with Judith and Leonard and then drive directly to North London. I also continued to see Ceinwen Jones whose ninety-first birthday was in September. As a former D'Oyly Carte chorister, and the widow of Bert Newby (latterly the Company's business manager) Ceinwen had some interesting Company memorabilia, much of which she passed on to me.

Through his settings of Kipling's *Barrack-Room Ballads* I had become very interested in the life and work of Gerard Francis Cobb. I had also acquired many of his other compositions (mainly songs) and I was working on an account of his life. I discovered that he was the son of a rector of Nettlestead in Kent, but I couldn't find much more about him in any of the musical dictionaries. It so happened that I had a Music in Hospitals job in Ashford (Kent) in October, and afterwards I went to Nettlestead to see if I could get any more information from the church there. I was told to contact two ladies, Nancy Bennett and her daughter Jackie, who knew much of the history of the Cobb family, and they put me in touch with the Rev Andrew Bailey, a great-great nephew, and Anna Russell, a great-great niece, who were descendants of Cobb's siblings: they were both extremely helpful, and they supplied much information. Ralph and I had been planning a celebration of Cobb's forthcoming centenary, and we thought that whatever we might do in London we should also do a centenary concert in this church. Accordingly, I took Ralph down to Nettlestead at the end of November to let him see the church so that we could work out how we might present the concert there.

The Julian Light Operatic Society put on *Patience* in November, and they included my reconstruction of the Duke's song "Though men of rank may useless seem". In December I played again for Philbeach at a concert called *Musical Memories from Stage & Screen*; I spent Christmas Day with Jan and Simon Vout, and Boxing Day with Anne and Peter Mitchell. There was a Music in Hospitals job in Portsmouth on December 30 and a concert at Grim's Dyke (just myself and four singers) on New Year's Eve. And that was the end of another year.

Chapter 9 – Last years in London

I – 2004

O nce again there was no work on New Year's Day, and I was able to get to Muriel Levin's annual get-together. The first job was on January 3, and I had to play the organ the following day; then gradually things started up, and by the end of the month most of the regular work was in place: the Ritz, Grim's Dyke, Music in Hospitals, invigilating and so on. I had lunch again with Bernard and Jean Goss although this was a purely social occasion as was another lunch in June, but I was also with them in October, and this time I did give another talk afterwards to the Selsdon Music Group.

The Grim's Dyke Sunday performances had increased to twenty-two with six operas to choose from: *HMS Pinafore*, *The Pirates of Penzance, Patience, Iolanthe, The Mikado* and *The Yeomen of the Guard*. The first performance was *Pirates* on January 11, but two weeks later there was a Burns Night at the hotel as the poet's birthday, January 25, fell that year on a Sunday. Between April and October there were also the matinée cream teas during which the company would perform excerpts from the opera we were doing that night. John and Heather Andrew, for whom we had performed at Umberleigh Manor in 1999, came to the *Yeomen* performance in June; I would see them again in July. The garden performances continued with two each of *Pirates* and *The Gondoliers*, everyone (cast, orchestra and audience) now under cover in case of bad weather. These performances in July, earlier than in previous years, were timed to coincide with the Harrow Arts Festival. Finally, we were able to celebrate the next one hundred and twenty-fifth anniversary, that of *Pirates*, on the actual day as this opera had its première in New York on December 31, 1879, and so a special performance, again a black tie occasion with a six-course dinner and a champagne toast at midnight, was given on New Year's Eve. Michael Rayner, former principal baritone with D'Oyly Carte, was one of the regular principals at Grim's Dyke, and one of his favourite roles was the Sergeant of Police in *Pirates*. Shortly before this performance, on December 6, I played for Michael when he gave an evening at the CAA: it also happened to be his birthday.

Some years earlier I had formed a piano duet partnership with Ken Barclay. Although I was still in touch with Ken we had not given any concerts for some time, but I discovered that Hilary Morgan, the regular pianist at Grim's Dyke, was also keen on this medium, and so we decided to form a partnership; with her Welsh and my Scottish connections we called ourselves the Celtic Duo. Hilary lived in Essex with a large number of cats, and I would go there to practise our repertoire if we had a concert. This didn't exactly develop into a major earner, but it was always enjoyable. Our first appearance was at the Buxton G&S Festival in August when we gave a concert entitled *Sullivan for Four Hands*. At one time, much orchestral and other music was arranged for piano duet; this included the entire score of *The Tempest*, Sullivan's opus 1. In the vocal score of *The Mikado* the overture is arranged as a duet as is *Jerusalem*, the opening of the second part of his oratorio *The Light of the World*. There were also countless sets of lancers and quadrilles based on numbers from the Savoy Operas, and it wasn't difficult to make up a programme: we even made up duet versions of other solo pieces. By now most events at the Buxton Festival were being recorded, and these could be purchased in the Festival shop. Our programme was among them. While we were there

I presented a quiz for the Manchester Gilbert and Sullivan Society as part of an afternoon entertainment.

There were two anniversaries this year. The first was the centenary of Gerard Francis Cobb's death on March 31st. Ralph Meanley and I could not organise anything on or near that date, but we gave two concerts of his music later in the year. On April 3 I attended a dinner at the New Cavendish Club in Gt Cumberland Place to celebrate the eightieth anniversary of the Gilbert and Sullivan Society.

Since joining D'Oyly Carte in 1975 I had written a number of articles on aspects of Sullivan's music and Gilbert's words which had been published in various journals. I now contributed an account of D'Oyly Carte's 1979 tour of Australia and New Zealand to the Gilbert and Sullivan Society's magazine *Gilbert & Sullivan News*. Entitled *A Trip to Topsy-Turvy Land* it appeared in three parts in this year's Spring, Summer and Autumn/Winter editions (vol. lll, nos. 10, 11 and 12).

Percy Young, whom I had known since he had been the external examiner at Birmingham University in 1974 for my MA thesis on Arthur Sullivan's songs, died in May aged ninety-one. He had become a good friend, and I had stayed with him and his wife Renee on a number of occasions.

I was now doing some work in my own time on a project connected with Arthur Sullivan which came about somewhat unexpectedly. At one of the monthly Sunday meetings of the Royal Society of Musicians, in their elegant premises in Stratford Place, the secretary, Maggie Gibb (who knew that I had worked for D'Oyly Carte), said to me "Did you know that we have Sullivan's speech when he presided at the Society's annual dinner in 1883?" I certainly didn't know, and I was keen to find out more about this. The Society had been founded in 1738, Handel being a major benefactor; the annual dinners were held between 1802 and 1914, each one presided over by a notable personality: Charles Dickens presided at the 1860 dinner. Arthur Sullivan was one of the best-known musicians of the day, particularly through his association with W.S. Gilbert; just two months after this dinner, in May 1883, he would be knighted. He did not join the Society, but he had a long association with it. He had been approached the previous year to preside at the dinner, but he declined in consequence of the death of his mother. He now accepted the position, only the second musician to take the chair on these occasions, the first one being Sir William Sterndale Bennett in 1871.

In the years since its inception in 1977 the Sir Arthur Sullivan Society had explored many aspects of Sullivan's life and work, but, to my knowledge, it was no more aware of his connection with the RSM than I had been. At first I wondered if it might be possible to have the speech printed in the Sullivan Society's *Magazine*, but when I looked at it I discovered that it wasn't just Sullivan's speech but a report of the entire evening's proceedings which also included speeches by, amongst others, W.S. Gilbert and Charles Dickens, junior (the author's eldest son). It had all been taken down by a reporter in some form of shorthand, written up later and sent back to the RSM. This was fascinating, but I also discovered that there were twenty-seven letters relating to Sullivan and the RSM including some in his own hand and others written by his secretary Walter Smythe but signed by Sullivan; I now began to wonder if there might be enough material here for a small book. The RSM thought so too, and when I had a spare morning or afternoon I would go in to Stratford Place to prepare this material for publication. It took some time. As an interesting side-line to this, and thanks again to Maggie Gibb, I also managed to see the manuscript of Sullivan's song *The Lost Chord* (1877), now in the possession of the Worshipful Company of Musicians.

Ballet classes, which had temporarily ceased, started up again this year; these took place in various schools in Fulham, Wandsworth and Hammersmith, and in a church hall in Putney. Manor Light Opera and Philbeach were drawing ever closer together, and this year they joined forces to produce

Iolanthe in May, conducted again by Paul Arman. The orchestra was still quite large although two down on the previous year, but again the group didn't have a collective name. The following year would see the fiftieth anniversary of Manor's first production, and they asked me if I would come back as musical director for Offenbach's *Orpheus in the Underworld*; I was happy to do this, but I still had misgivings about the chorus. Rehearsals started in September. Philbeach also asked me to come back, and in December I was the musical director for a concert called *Musical Wonderland*, an evening of Rodgers and Hammerstein with supper. The director for this was Jill Haistead.

I continued to get around the country for one thing or another, much of it G&S-related. There was work for New Savoyards: a single concert in Yeovil in April and two concerts in Guernsey in June: a welcome return, and with no 9/11 this time. Between these engagements, and by way of a diversion, I went to Canterbury in May to see Ralph Meanley who was playing the Boatswain in a touring production of *HMS Pinafore*. It was directed by Timothy West who had also initially played Sir Joseph Porter, this role now being taken by a former Dr Who, Colin Baker. In July I went back to Devon where John and Heather Andrew were now celebrating thirty years of G&S at Umberleigh Manor. This time the singers were Elizabeth Menezes, Sylvia Clarke, Barry Clark and Ralph Meanley: only Barry and I were ex-D'Oyly Carte, a sign of changing times in the G&S world. We were now under the banner of the London Opera Company which was run by Sylvia and her husband Stuart MacWhirter. As on our previous visit in 1999 I then went down to Pencarrow; I also managed to see Coleton Fishacre, the lovely Arts and Crafts-style house on the South Coast near Kingswear in Devon, former home of Rupert D'Oyly Carte, Dame Bridget's father, and now a National Trust property. Later, in September, I was in Pagham again for Vivienne and Gerald Johnson's Ruby Wedding. Among other work I was back at the Barn Theatre, Oxted, to play for Puccini's *La Bohème*, something I hadn't done since the days at Il Boccalino; another new experience was a week of playing for a Scout Gang Show *Souwest 2004* in the Secombe Theatre in Sutton at the end of October. I can't remember how I got involved with this, but I must have been recommended by someone. What I do remember is that I had to be vetted for suitability to work with children, another sign of changing times. On the last day, October 30, there was a memorial service for Percy Young in Selwyn College, Cambridge, but I couldn't attend that as we had a matinée.

There were three Bentley concerts this year which would seem to be a slight upward turn. One was a return visit to Louise Denny's Café Caricature in Hastings, but the other two were both to mark the centenary of Gerard Francis Cobb's death, and we had decided to do these anyway, come what may; so we hadn't progressed very much from our single concert in 2003. We also performed at some of the schools where Ralph did supply teaching, but again these were not really Bentley concerts.

For the Café Caricature, in February, we presented a programme of songs that Peter Dawson had sung and recorded: it wasn't very different from *Rolling Down to Rio*, our very first concert in 1994. This was another enjoyable evening with excellent food although again we didn't make a profit. But there was a possibility that the building might not be available much longer, and perhaps this would be our last visit, even if we managed to keep Bentley going.

The first Cobb concert was on July 10, and we held it in the hall of St Columba's Church of Scotland in Pont Street where I had played regularly for the Hepburn Starey Blind Aid Society. Ralph had sung for the Society several times, and we had presented a Trafalgar Day concert there in 1999, and so we both knew the venue and the piano. As a member of the British Music Society (BMS) I was able to advertise both concerts, with a brief outline of Cobb's life and work, in BMS *News* (no. 102) in June. We did a number of the

Barrack-Room Ballads in the first half, and Pam Baxter joined us in the second half which was devoted to other songs by Cobb that I had managed to acquire. I was particularly pleased that Anna Russell and Andrew Bailey (Cobb's great-great niece and great-great nephew) were able to come to the concert; also present was Jean Armstrong who had been Greenock Academy's secretary during my schooldays there in the 1950s. Now living in London, Jean came with a friend. There were about forty people in the audience which wasn't too bad considering that virtually no-one knew anything about Cobb or had heard any of his music.

We gave the concert again on August 22 in the Church of St Mary the Virgin, Nettlestead where Cobb's father, brother and a nephew had all been rectors. It was virtually identical apart from one item, a piano piece by John Bartlett Cobb who was another nephew. After the London concert Andrew Bailey had very kindly sent me copies of all the Cobb songs that he possessed, and among them was this piano piece. It seemed appropriate to play it here. Nancy and Jackie Bennett, who had effectively organised everything for us, were also at the concert which was preceded by a garden party in the beautiful grounds of Nettlestead Place adjacent to the church: an invitation to see the grounds and to bring your own picnic. I had been trying to think of people who might be interested in coming to the concert, and I rang Joy Puritz, an old friend from my days at Birmingham University. Joy was the granddaughter of the singer Elisabeth Schumann. To my surprise, it turned out that her cousin was the wife of the present owner of Nettlestead Place, and so Joy was happy to come down from London. With my new interest in Cobb, and partly thanks to the help I had had from Anna Russell and Andrew Bailey, I wrote an article about him which was published in the next issue of BMS *News* (no. 103) in September. I also compiled a list of his works, but this wasn't published.

The CAA had an ex-servicemen's association which always held a commemoration service and dinner around Armistice

Day. This year it was on November 12, and I took part in the entertainment along with other members of the Club including Tricia Court, Terry Seabrooke and Glen Hayes. I went up to Scotland for several days over the Christmas period. My mother was becoming increasingly frail, and she now had a carer coming in regularly. I still felt that I ought to be nearer to her, but I wouldn't be able to leave London until next year at the earliest when my mortgage would be paid off. I was back in London for the special one hundred and twenty-fifth anniversary performance of *The Pirates of Penzance* at Grim's Dyke on New Year's Eve.

II – 2005

There were two milestones this year: my mortgage was finally paid off in June, and my book *Arthur Sullivan and The Royal Society of Musicians of Great Britain* was published in November. It was, however, another slow start, the first work being two concerts for Music in Hospitals on January 6 in Southampton and Romsey: further out of London than usual in just one day, but new venues always added interest to what was essentially the same job. Gradually, work started up again.

At Grim's Dyke the Sunday evening performances with dinner had become very popular, and this year there were twenty-seven of them. The operas performed were the same six as in 2004: *Pinafore, Pirates, Patience, Iolanthe, Mikado* and *Yeomen*, the first of these being *The Mikado* on January 9. But on January 8 several of the principals and I took part in a function at the famous Alexandra Palace in North London where we performed some G&S during two twenty-minute spots.

There was no special performance this year although it was the one hundred and twenty-fifth anniversary of the London opening of *Pirates* on April 3: the New York performance in

1879 had been for copyright reasons. Also, there were no outdoor performances as these were very costly to stage, but following the success of the *Pirates* anniversary performance on New Year's Eve it had been decided to have a similar evening this year, and we gave a complete costumed performance of *HMS Pinafore*, one of the shortest of the Savoy Operas, followed by a selection of Viennese numbers as midnight approached. Apart from the regular work at Grim's Dyke I also attended a Gilbert and Sullivan Society Convention there at the beginning of April. There were many of these over the years in London, Manchester or Stockport, and as I usually had to perform at them there was always a fee which was an added attraction.

There had been a Burns Night at Grim's Dyke on Sunday January 23 which didn't involve the opera group, but on the Tuesday I took part in one for Mattie Tindley, one of the ladies who ran the Hepburn Starey Blind Aid Society. Mattie lived in a block of flats that had a communal room for functions, and she asked me if I would give the toast The Immortal Memory at the residents' Burns Supper. As the room had a piano she also asked me if I could bring a singer, and Anne Mitchell, with whom I did many concerts for Music in Hospitals and who had also sung for the Blind Aid Society, kindly agreed to come. Anne and I also did a St Andrew's Night for the residents on November 30.

I now went up to Oxford regularly to get copies of songs and other music by Gerard Francis Cobb at the Bodleian Library, and on one visit in January I had the pleasure of dining at Keble College with Robin Wilson, son of the former Prime Minister Harold Wilson, later Lord Wilson of Rievaulx. I knew Robin, a professor of mathematics, as he was a great lover of G&S as his father had been. I had met him in Colorado Springs CO at the end of our third Byers, Schwalbe tour in April 1986.

There were just two Bentley concerts this year, the first one at Nettlestead in August. The first half of this was a VJ Day

(Victory over Japan) concert, this year being the sixtieth anniversary of the end of the Second World War, and we were in our naval uniforms for the first half but in dinner jackets for the second half. In September there was a third visit to Redbridge Music Society, again in Ilford Town Hall and this time with *Shipmates O' Mine*. It was now obvious that there were not going to be many more of these concerts. We had hoped to do another one at Chatham on Trafalgar Day, but that didn't happen. Ralph was still able to organise visits to his various schools, and we also did an evening for the Gilbert and Sullivan Society in London with G&S and some Cobb. Our CD of the *Barrack-Room Ballads* was issued in February, and I was able to advertise it in BMS *News* (no. 105) in March. We felt that we had at least achieved something with this.

Kenneth Sandford, who had been on the first ten tours with The Best of Gilbert and Sullivan, had died in September 2004, and there was a memorial service for him on May 6 at St Paul's, Covent Garden at which I had to play. I then went up to Northamptonshire for a VE Day (Victory in Europe) concert with Judith Baxter on May 7. Major anniversaries were useful as you could build concerts round them to generate more work.

Apart from numerous single concerts there were five tours for Music in Hospitals this year, two of them in Wales: the first of these, with a final concert in Cheltenham, was in June; the second one was in September. There were also two in July: one was in the South-West, and the other one started in Blackpool and finished in Chester. Finally, in August, we were in Norfolk where we got as far north as Cromer on the coast. As well as fees we were paid travel expenses for these tours, but such a lot of driving was definitely wear and tear on the car. And you often encountered the unexpected. On one of our tours to Blackpool we found that the digs we had booked were right in the centre of the town; there were double yellow lines everywhere so that parking was almost impossible. The landlady would come round constantly while we were having breakfast, saying to each of us "You all right? You all right, luv? You all right now?" We found this very amusing, and for a long time afterwards we would greet each other with a "You all right, luv?" (in the appropriate accent) when we met again for more work. You also needed a lot of stamina for these tours.

There was much invigilating in London, but that just involved travel on the Underground, and I didn't have to take a keyboard with me. I was always happy to do it although three-hour sessions could drag somewhat. It was only nearer the end when candidates started to ask for more paper (or handed in their papers) that it really became interesting. I was surprised that candidates could now use calculators; we also had occasional instances of cheating.

Throughout the year I had a number of meetings at the Royal Society of Musicians' premises in Stratford Place as publication of the book on Sullivan drew near. The RSM published the book, but it was printed by the well-known firm of Arrowsmith in Bristol who had published *Three Men in a Boat* by Jerome K. Jerome and *The Diary of a Nobody* by George and Weedon Grossmith. I got to know the firm's representative Gordon Young quite well; for some reason one of our meetings was held in the Fox and Grapes pub on Wimbledon Common: mixing business with a pint this time.

In May I conducted *Orpheus in the Underworld* for Manor Light Opera. There were one or two members of Philbeach in the cast, but it was still essentially a Manor production; there was another new director, the actor Simon Rawlings. Although they had increased the orchestra for their last two productions we were back to just seven players for this one, but they reintroduced the collective title: the group was now called The Olympian Strings although that included a pianist, Nick Pope this time. With such a small band you needed a pianist to fill out the texture and play any missing parts. (I remembered this from the production of *Carmen* in 2002 when I had been the pianist; also from an amateur orchestra in Greenock that my father played in: the pianist was an essential element in many such groups.) Again we were in the Steiner Theatre.

There was plenty of other work. Louise Denny's Café Caricature in Hastings was still operating, and I was there in March to play for my former D'Oyly Carte colleague Jane Metcalfe. In May there was some cabaret with Judith Baxter at a dinner dance to celebrate the sixtieth anniversary of VE Day at Nether Heyford in Northamptonshire; in June I played for Tim Hurst-Brown's group the Wandering Minstrels at the Park House Hotel in Sandringham. In October there was another talk for Bernard Goss's Selsdon Music Group, and in November there was a concert for Vivienne Jay in Pagham.

I went to two reunions this year. The first one was in the music department at Birmingham University in March; the second one was in Scotland in September. This was the one hundred and fiftieth anniversary of my old school Greenock Academy which was founded in 1855; the school's former secretary Jean Armstrong, who had come to our Cobb centenary concert in London, came with me. It was always good to catch up with friends and colleagues at these functions. There was a Grim's Dyke Sunday performance that week-end, and I had to get a substitute to conduct.

My mother was now in a unit at Ayrshire Central Hospital, and it was clear that she would have to go into a care home fairly soon although she was very reluctant to do so. It was becoming increasingly obvious that I should leave London, but this would mean giving up all the work that I had built up over twenty years. Although I had paid off the mortgage on my flat I still had to earn some money, and how could I find a suitable place in or near Greenock without numerous, and costly, visits to Scotland? It was difficult to see a clear way ahead, but this would soon be taken out of my hands.

I had recently acquired a book *Sunset on the Clyde* by a former Assistant Director of Education for Renfrewshire

Duncan Graham which told of his days as a student purser on Loch Lomond and the Clyde, something I had done on the Clyde when I worked on the paddle steamer *Waverley*. I was so taken by his reminiscences that I wrote to him care of his publisher. In July he kindly replied, suggesting that as I often travelled up to Scotland I should visit him and his wife Wendy at their home near the town of Appleby in Cumbria. I saw them several times. On my first visit in October he gave me a signed copy of the first, hardback, edition of his book. On another occasion, as I was on my way to Skelmorlie, my car broke down and had to be left at their local garage. They were good enough to lend me a car, and I was able to continue my journey, collecting my own on the way back.

Over the years I had a lot of trouble with cars, mainly because I could never afford to buy a new one. I was once travelling down from Scotland directly to a concert (luckily a fairly informal one) in a pub, and again the car broke down. I didn't have a mobile phone, and I had to wait until the breakdown service arrived before I could inform the singers that I would not be there. By that time the concert had already been cancelled. That didn't go down very well.

An old school friend, Joe Gatherer, had recently become my mother's solicitor, and he managed to find a place for her in a care home, Alt-na-Craig, in Greenock: it was a large villa where I had once delivered groceries when I had a summer job as a student. When my book on Sullivan finally appeared I sent my mother a copy with a covering letter, hoping that she was settling in. I went up to Scotland again for Christmas and saw her several times at Alt-na-Craig; as I suspected, like many older people who are physically frail but still mentally alert, she was not settling in which was worrying. I also saw Joe Gatherer again to discuss my mother's situation, and I caught up with other old friends. But I had to be back in London for our *Pinafore* and Viennese evening on December 31. I had been given Power of Attorney over my mother's affairs, but a later communication from one of the utilities referred to my Power of Eternity [sic]. So much for our vaunted Scottish education.

III – 2006

The first work of the year came on January 2 (a day job for Music in Hospitals and an evening at the Ritz), but there was nothing after that until the first Sunday performance at Grim's Dyke on the 8th with *The Mikado*. On Saturday January 14 the group was back at Alexandra Palace, but there was no Sunday performance on the 15th. In its place there was a party for our amateur chorus to thank them for turning up regularly to sing for us. Most of them, however, were great G&S fans, and they were happy to be part of the set-up at Grim's Dyke, particularly with its historic connection as Gilbert's last home. Ballet classes started on the 16th, and I was at the Ritz again on the 19th, but we were nearly three weeks into the year and I still hadn't earned very much. I was thankful that the mortgage had finally been paid off.

Grim's Dyke now offered a variety of themed evenings such as Mother's Day, Father's Day and a Burns Night. None of these evenings involved the opera group, but I did attend another Burns Supper organised by Mattie Tindley, and once again Anne Mitchell kindly came to sing to the residents. By a strange coincidence Mattie's block of flats was called Rothesay Court, the same name as my mother's block of flats in Skelmorlie which looked across the Clyde to the town of Rothesay on the island of Bute.

It had been a slow start to the year, but it gradually picked up. Grim's Dyke had decided to perform the complete G&S canon (minus *Thespis* (1871)) from *Trial by Jury* (1875) to *The Grand Duke* (1896), and there were now no less than thirty Sunday performances including the New Year's Eve concert of G&S and Viennese items. This extra work was also useful financially as other work, like the BBC job at Elstree, had ceased or, like the Bentley concerts, had fallen away. Each of the thirteen operas was given a special performance; these were done in chronological order, spaced throughout the year between other performances of the more popular ones: *Pinafore*, *Pirates*, *Iolanthe* and *Mikado*. This year also saw the one hundred and twenty-fifth anniversary of *Patience* on April 23; as this was a Sunday we were able to give the performance on the actual day.

Two of the less regularly performed operas, *Princess Ida* and *Ruddigore*, had not yet been done at Grim's Dyke, and they needed some work beforehand although most of our regular principals and chorus knew them well; we had also done *The Gondoliers* in the garden in 2004. But we did have some problems with the last two operas, *Utopia Limited* and *The Grand Duke*. Of our regular cast, only three – Michael Rayner, Gareth Jones and Barry Clark - had been in D'Oyly Carte during the centenary season in 1975 when the Company had mounted a production of the former and had given a single concert performance of the latter. These operas had not held the stage after their initial runs, and much of their music, particularly that of *The Grand Duke*, was not well-known, even to our cast or to G&S aficionados. But we somehow managed to stage them, and it was an achievement to have done the entire canon in the course of one year.

Somewhat surprisingly the Bentley concerts still seemed to have some life in them, and there were three this year: *Ballads, Songs and Snatches* in Bletchingley in March, *The Fleet's In* in North Shields, also in March, and a general concert for the Women's Institute in March (Cambridgeshire) in June (confusingly, it might have been March in March). We had performed for them in 2002. There were also several school concerts (at least we were keeping our hand in), but there were no new programmes: the existing ones were just dusted down and presented as and when required.

I went up to Scotland for a few days in April and saw a number of old friends. My mother had still not settled in the care home, and I was no closer to solving the problem of moving out of London. But I was soon in the South again for more work which included a G&S concert *All at Sea* (scenes from *Pirates* and *Pinafore*) in Margate with Cameo Opera. Judith Buckle, one of the founders of this group, took part as did Leon Berger who also directed the scenes. Soon after this I was with Cameo Opera again to present *Opera a Tavola* at a restaurant, Carluccio's, in Bicester. Hilary Morgan and I played some duets for the Gilbert and Sullivan Society in London, and there was a concert with Ralph Meanley in Brighton for the Sussex Gilbert and Sullivan Society: this was a repeat of a concert (not surprisingly of G&S and Cobb) that we had done for the Society in London in 2005.

After the Brighton concert I had a week's holiday in Prague, a city I had always wanted to see. This came about through a friend of mine Gordon Truefitt who was the grandson of Donald Miller, former school music teacher at Greenock Academy, who had effectively introduced me to G&S. As an actor, Gordon found that he could get a lot of work in Prague, and he was now living there permanently. I stayed with him; it was a most enjoyable week. I was back in London for the next performance at Grim's Dyke on May 7 which was followed by more of the usual work.

Early in the morning of Saturday May 27 (more accurately, in the middle of the night) I was woken by the phone ringing: it was Alt-na-Craig to tell me that my mother had died suddenly of a heart attack. It was perhaps a merciful release for her as she would never have settled in the home although, ironically, one of her oldest friends became a resident there shortly afterwards. I now had to cancel all work for the next few days and go back to Scotland to make the necessary arrangements, but I had to come down at the end of the week for the Women's Institute concert in Cambridgeshire on June 2. I went up again the following week for the funeral which took place on June 8.

I inherited my mother's flat, and I was now the man of property with homes in London and Skelmorlie. For a brief period I wondered if it might be possible to maintain both: this would mean that I could continue to work in London and go back to Scotland from time to time to relax. But I soon realised that as Skelmorlie was some four hundred miles away the cost of getting there, to say nothing of the time involved, meant that this simply wasn't practical. One of them would have to go, and as I had already felt the urge to get out of London and get back to my roots, whatever the cost in loss of work, it wasn't too difficult to make a final decision; in September I asked an estate agent in Wimbledon to value the flat and put it on the market. I didn't know how long it would take to sell, but I was in the happy situation of not having to look for a property myself: in fact, I had a buyer at the beginning of October, but as there was no chain involved (at least on my side) I wasn't committed to moving on the day that the new owners moved in: I could leave at any time before that. I then had to find a lawyer who would deal with the conveyancing.

Over the years I had acquired a great deal of music and a great many books, and I had stored much of this in the attic of our family home in Greenock. I moved from Islington to Raynes Park in 1988, but within a year my mother moved from Greenock to Skelmorlie, and as there was no attic there she had to send all my things (including a bicycle) down to London. My flat in Raynes Park was bigger than the one in Islington, but I hadn't felt the benefit of this for very long, and it was now full to overflowing. I knew that I would never get everything into the flat in Skelmorlie as it was already furnished, and this included a large grand piano. Most of my own stuff would have to go into storage, and I would eventually have to find a larger property. But that could wait.

A move wasn't going to happen immediately, and there were still things to do in London. I wanted to finish off the first full G&S canon at Grim's Dyke, and I particularly wanted to conduct the last two, *Utopia Limited* and *The Grand Duke*.

I had done two concert performances of the latter with Manor House in 1996, but I had never conducted a performance of the former. As we were doing the operas chronologically we had not yet come to either, and I didn't want to miss them: *Utopia* was done on October 22 and *Grand Duke* on November 19. There was also a welcome return to the garden performances from July 18-23 as they were now being sponsored by Landsbanki Commercial Finance; we did *The Pirates of Penzance* twice and *The Mikado* three times.

The year continued in the usual way, but I now had another holiday: in August I was in Poland for a week with a group from Manor Light Opera who went there regularly (these trips had come about as one of the Society's members Jadwiga Lewis was Polish). We stayed in Zakopane, in the southern region of the country, where the composer Szymanowski had lived: his house, the Villa Atma, was now a museum. We did some hill walking, but there were also trips to places of interest including a wonderful old castle by a lake, a boat trip down a river that flowed through a gorge, and a brief visit to Krakow where there was just time to sit in the vast square (the largest in Europe) and have a very expensive coffee. I decided that I must come back and see it properly.

In September, Hilary Morgan and I took part in the Sullivan Society Festival, held this year in Portsmouth, where again we did some piano duets. Later in the month there was another visit to Bernard Goss's Selsdon Music Group; this time Ralph Meanley came along, and so they had a concert rather than yet another of my rambling recollections of D'Oyly Carte. Two days later Ralph and I did another concert, this time in his church; at the beginning of November we were again in one of his schools. I couldn't complain about not being busy. Few of these engagements brought in much money, but each one was very welcome.

On October 12 there was an official launch of my book *Arthur Sullivan and The Royal Society of Musicians of Great Britain* at Stratford Place. Earlier, a revue of the book by

Raymond Walker of the Manchester Gilbert and Sullivan Society had been published in the Sullivan Society's *Magazine* no. 62, Summer 2006. Shortly after the book's launch I was in Wales again for a week's tour for Music in Hospitals. We travelled on the Monday, and there were two concerts on each of the next four days. I was never happier than when I was on the road, possibly as a result of having toured for seven years with D'Oyly Carte, but I think this is something that appeals to some people and not to others: in my case it's definitely a touch of the wanderlust. It helps to be single of course, with no family ties or commitments, but I have always enjoyed seeing new places, and even more so if someone else is paying me to be there. Later in the year I even managed a short break in Valencia: three holidays in a year - unheard of.

In November there was another concert at Oak Hall Manor with Cynthia Morey, and another St Andrew's Night for Mattie Tindley at Rothesay Court: I told her that this would almost certainly be the last one. On December 1 there was another job with Ralph Meanley and Pam Baxter, this time in Greenwich: again, this was not one of our original Bentley programmes. There were a number of individual concerts for Music in Hospitals in December, but as the year drew to a close there was, as always, a demand for concerts with a Christmas flavour, and I was in Wales again with no less than fifteen concerts: three a day from December 19-23. But as well as all this work I was beginning to inform my sources of income of my impending departure.

Having finally decided to leave London I began to think about the financial cost of giving up so much work. It had been suggested to me that I could remain as musical director at Grim's Dyke by coming down for each performance and staying at the hotel, free of charge, before going back to Scotland. The opera group always had the use of two rooms in the older part of the building, and occasionally principals did stay overnight as the rooms could not be used again for guests until they had been cleared of the costumes. Attractive as this proposition sounded I decided that it wasn't really practical. It would be too tiring to drive down and back on so many occasions (there would be another thirty indoor performances and more sponsored opera in the garden in 2007), and so it would have to be by train or plane. But no matter how many or how few times I came down the travel would eat into my fees, and so I decided, reluctantly, that Grim's Dyke would have to go.

That applied to just about everything: ballet classes, the Ritz, masonic engagements and any other work that I had been able to find. And so there would effectively be no income. But I would be sixty-five at the end of 2008, and so by the time I got back to Scotland there would be less than two years before I reached that milestone. I had taken out a pension when I was in D'Oyly Carte, but with the closure of the Company in 1982 I had found it difficult to increase payments annually, and I knew that there would only be a small sum to supplement the state pension; so I really did have to find other work. Apart from the financial side I enjoyed what I did, and I had no intention of giving it up unless illness forced me to do so.

There was one possible source of income, and that was Music in Hospitals. I knew that they operated in Scotland, and I had worked for them on one or two occasions when I had been visiting my mother. With some twenty years' experience of this work I hoped that they might take me on permanently: it was, after all, the same organisation. But that would have to wait until I was back in Scotland. I would also try to find some work as an organist.

After the Welsh tour I spent Christmas Day in London, but I went up to Scotland again on Boxing Day. I had already organised storage space in Greenock, but I had to supply a lock for this. I was then back in London for my last New Year's Eve at Grim's Dyke.

IV – 2007

I now knew that I would soon be leaving Raynes Park, and I had already contacted Pickfords who had moved my furniture from Eastbourne in 1985. They sent a representative round on January 3 to assess access, and a date was fixed for February 1. There were parking bays outside my door, and I had to ask Merton Borough Council if three of them could be suspended on the day.

My last month in London was much like any other. There was work in many of the usual areas: the Ritz, Music in Hospitals, two ballet classes (the last one on January 22), an organ job and a Burns Night at Mattie Tindley's block of flats where I told her that I was now going from one Rothesay Court to another. There was also a final evening at Grim's Dyke on January 21 when the opera was *The Yeomen of the Guard*, the most serious of all the Savoy Operas. I would have preferred to end my association with the group on a cheerier note, but that was the way it worked out. There had been another party for the chorus on the previous Sunday, but this one was also partly for me on my retirement as musical director. I was presented with a photograph album filled with some splendid shots taken at our many productions, most of them at the garden performances. It was beautifully put together, and it is a treasured reminder of those days. Andrew Whittaker also treated me to lunch at the Savile Club on January 31.

Pickfords duly turned up on February 1 and cleared the house. They had previously given me a number of cardboard boxes for books, music, crockery and other items which had all been packed away. I was greatly helped through the day by two close family friends as there was still much to be done after Pickfords had left: the flat had to be cleaned, and there were items that I had to take with me in the car. I stayed with these friends overnight before driving up to Scotland the following day. It was a fairly tense journey, and I was relieved when I got to Skelmorlie. On February 3 Pickfords arrived in Greenock, and my goods and chattels were deposited in storage. I had now come home. What would the future hold?

Chapter 10 – First years back in Scotland

I – 2007

It was a strange feeling to be home again after so many years in London although Skelmorlie too was a new home as I had been brought up in Greenock where many of my school friends still lived. I had kept in touch with some of them, but there were others I hadn't seen for many years, and it was a pleasure catching up with them again from time to time (one of my 'class of '48' schoolmates was now also living in Skelmorlie). Coming up regularly from London I had already met my mother's carer and some of the residents of Rothesay Court. I had also been introduced to other friends that she had made, and so I didn't arrive as a complete stranger.

Skelmorlie is some eight miles from Greenock. This is roughly the distance from Raynes Park to Trafalgar Square, but here, with countryside between (and far less traffic), the journey didn't take nearly as long; if I went via Gourock (a slightly longer journey) I could also see the River Clyde which I had always missed. The view from Gourock to Dunoon and the Cowal hills is magnificent, but the view from Rothesay Court was also good, the flats being right by the pier at Wemyss Bay in neighbouring Inverclyde (Skelmorlie is at the extreme northern tip of North Ayrshire).

I didn't have much to unpack as most of my possessions were now in storage, and at first it was almost like a holiday.

But it wasn't a holiday: I needed to find some work. I got in touch with Music in Hospitals Scotland whose office was in Edinburgh, and I was relieved that they were happy to take me on although that didn't happen immediately. The first work came somewhat unexpectedly through another Greenock friend Kareth Paterson who had also lived in England and who had recently come back to Scotland. Kareth was living some miles further down the Clyde Coast, and she now sang with the Stevenston Musical Society. They were looking for a temporary accompanist as their regular one was currently indisposed, and I was happy to stand in: the first rehearsal was on February 21. I also played for another choir that Kareth was involved with, the New Irvine Community Choir: this was for a coffee morning fund-raiser in a church hall.

But I now had a new toy to help fill in the time. The Royal Society of Musicians had given me a computer to thank me for my work on the Sullivan book, and this was an opportunity to drag myself into the twenty-first century. I am not good with technology, and I had quite forgotten the little that I had learned about computers when I was working with David Winnard at Methodist Central Hall, Westminster some years previously, but the RSM had also said that their resident computer expert Joe Easley would be happy to 'talk me through the basics'. Joe was on a telephone contract that allowed him to make a certain number of free calls, and he rang me once a week for about an hour at a time. I had the computer in front of me, and he attempted to tell me how it worked: I didn't find it very easy. In May I went to an Adult Learners' Week in Greenock, but I found that courses for 'beginners' seem to assume that you already know a certain amount. I also attended a course in Gourock, but again I found that it was assumed that you knew the basics. It took me literally years to become even moderately computer-literate.

If I thought that I wouldn't see England again for a while I was very much mistaken: I was there no less than nine times this year, twice in February despite having just come back to

Scotland. First of all, I saw Duncan and Wendy Graham in
Cumbria, and shortly after that my cousin Ron died and I had
to go down to Hampshire for the funeral. Next, I was away
for several days at the beginning of April as Ralph Meanley
had managed to secure two dates for the Arts and Heritage
Club: a return visit to Wells and one in Torquay. Again, these
were simply after-dinner entertainments. The long journeys
were tiring, and to break them up I usually tried to see friends
or relatives on the way down or on the way back. The cost of
driving to London and further afield rose every year, but on at
least some occasions I was being paid for concerts which
helped to defray the expense.

I was on the road again just days after I got back from
Torquay, this time to Stockport for another Gilbert and
Sullivan Society Convention. Beti Lloyd-Jones came with me,
and on the way back we visited John Reed, former D'Oyly
Carte comedy baritone, now ninety-one. Beti had acted as
John's 'stage mother' for many years, wishing him good luck
before each performance; they hadn't seen each other for some
time. I now saw Beti regularly, and we invariably reminisced
about D'Oyly Carte which had been a way of life for many of
us and not simply a job. One day she asked me if I would like
to do some invigilating for the Scottish Qualifications
Authority (SQA) exams in Greenock, something she had
already done. I was happy to take this on, and there was quite
a lot of it in April and May, but soon after this the man who
was running it retired; when he was replaced, both Beti and
I were told that our services were no longer required. I was
used to this in the free-lance music world, but I had not yet
come across it in invigilating. But the little that I did was
useful financially.

At the end of April I was in London again, and I stayed
with the Huggins family of Manor Light Opera. This was a
convenient halfway house as I was travelling down to Hastings
to see my former D'Oyly Carte colleague Jane Metcalfe who
was having a birthday party. Jane had asked me to bring Pat

Elliott from London, and it was good to catch up with her too. On the way back I also managed to see Anne and Peter Mitchell.

Next, there were two concerts with Ralph Meanley and Pam Baxter. The first one, at the end of June, was again for the Women's Institute; it was held in the Moot Hall, a large function room in Colchester Town Hall. The second one, at the beginning of July, was in another of the schools in London where Ralph did supply teaching: these were always less formal and more relaxing. Later in July I was back in London, staying again with the Huggins family, but this time I went by train.

The first work for Music in Hospitals Scotland was an evening concert on May 4 at Ayrshire Central Hospital in Irvine (my mother had been a patient there). From then on I found myself working regularly with several singers although at first I was mainly with Mark Hathaway. We were asked to provide a name for ourselves, and so we became Two in Tandem. After we had done several concerts Mark said "I think we've worked together before". Neither of us could recall where or when this was, but he showed me a transposed copy of Captain Corcoran's song "Fair moon, to thee I sing" (*HMS Pinafore*) which was in my handwriting, and so we had clearly been in touch at some time. We eventually worked out that we had both taken part in Cynthia Morey's 1996 concert at Oak Hall Manor commemorating the life of Isabel Jay.

The work for Music in Hospitals began to pick up in July. As well as working with Mark I eventually started working with his wife Daniela and with Katie Morrell whom I remembered from Andrew Meadmore's G&S productions in London. In my early days with MiH we were often in hospital wards, but these were becoming more 'high tech' and less suitable; the majority of the concerts were now in care homes or nursing homes where there was always a communal lounge which was more convenient – for the artists as well as the residents.

Two of the homes were in Greenock (my mother's younger sister was now in one of them and one of my school teachers was in the other), but I was soon in towns that I had never previously visited such as Alloa, Beith and Cumnock, and I also got to know much of the East End of Glasgow: hitherto I had only known the centre of the city and the West End. But as with the concerts in England there were tours as well as individual dates. The first of these was in August, and we had four concerts in two days, one in Kingussie (another town I had not yet been to) and then three in Inverness which would become a regular date over the next few years as would Aberdeen: these two places would often serve as centres for concerts further afield. The first two-day visit to Aberdeen was at the beginning of December, and this was followed by a tour to Cumbria where Mark and I had six concerts spread over two days: this was unusual as these would normally have been done by artists from England. While we were there we had a meal with Ralph Meanley's friends Richard and Angela Evans who lived near Cockermouth: Ralph and I had stayed with them on several occasions.

During the summer I began to attend Sunday afternoon concerts in the Cathedral of The Isles (Britain's smallest cathedral) in Millport on the island of Greater Cumbrae just off the Ayrshire coast at Largs: these were organised by the cathedral's director of music Alastair Chisholm. My friends Jane Guy and Philip Button often took part in these, and I discovered that another regular was a young pianist Andrew Johnston whose parents also lived in Skelmorlie. They remembered my school performances in G&S, and I soon got to know them too.

In August I was once again at the Buxton G&S Festival where I took part in a concert to celebrate the life of Helen Beechinor who had sung for us at Grim's Dyke and who had now died. Several of the regular Grim's Dyke principals took part, and it was good to see them again. Hilary Morgan and I provided the accompaniments as well as playing a duet.

In September, just before I moved (or 'flitted' as we say here), my Australian cousins Wilma and Arthur, whom I had last seen during the D'Oyly Carte Opera Company's Australasian tour in 1979, arrived in the area as part of a European holiday. I had a spare room at Rothesay Court but they opted to stay in a local hotel as they thought this would be easier. One day, we went to the iconic Falkirk Wheel, a new experience for all of us.

The sale of my London flat had been completed in March, and I was now in a position to look for a bigger place that would accommodate not only the contents of Rothesay Court (including the seven-foot Broadwood grand piano) but all my possessions which were in storage in Greenock. If I hadn't acquired so much stuff over the years and could live 'minimally', as some people can, I would probably have stayed in Rothesay Court: as a purpose-built flat it was bigger and far better than the London one (which was a conversion) although its market value was much less. But it was still too small for me, and so in July I had it valued and put up for sale. I had a buyer by the end of August, and I then started to look for another property, hopefully one with an equally good view of the river.

I had considered moving back to Greenock, but I had now got used to living in Skelmorlie, and it was there that I found what I was looking for. When I came back in February I often went out for walks, and I discovered that most of the village was on much higher ground and not visible from Rothesay Court which was at sea level. The area had developed mainly as a result of the rail link to Glasgow which had opened in 1865 with its terminus at Wemyss Bay; as had happened elsewhere on the Clyde, wealthy business men from Glasgow and further afield now began to build villas, some of them very large. Most of these still existed although usually divided into two, three, or sometimes even more, apartments. As I walked round the village I found myself admiring these substantial properties and wondering if I might ever live in one of them. In due course one such conversion did come up for sale. When I went to view it I realised immediately that it was just what I wanted. It was the top half of a large villa comprising the first floor and an attic which may have been the servants' quarters. There was enough room here for all my belongings, and the lounge would comfortably accommodate the grand piano, but apart from the extra space it was the view over the river, essentially the same as that at Rothesay Court but even better as the property was on higher ground, that was the selling point. And so I moved to 16a Eglinton Gardens in Upper Skelmorlie.

The house dates from 1869-70 (curiously, around the time that Gilbert and Sullivan first met, and yet another coincidence in my life connected with G&S), and it was named Tigh Geal which translates as White House although like most of the properties here it is built of red sandstone. It had latterly been owned by the composer and arranger Brian Fahey, an Englishman who had been appointed principal conductor of the BBC Scottish Radio Orchestra in 1972. He later converted it into two homes (a third home was created out of what had been the stable block); he and his wife retained the ground floor. After her death in 2006 he moved back to England, but he died in April of this year just after I had arrived in Skelmorlie. I knew his name although I never met him. Perhaps his best known composition was *At the Sign of the Swingin' Cymbal* (1960) which was used as the signature tune for Alan Freeman's Radio 1 programme *Pick of the Pops*.

Once again there was no chain involved in the move which went very smoothly: the previous occupants had already moved out. I acquired the keys one Friday at the end of September, and I spent a leisurely week-end transferring carloads of items such as books, pictures, glassware and crockery. One of my many Greenock cousins helped me with this. Pickfords came on Monday October 1 after picking up what was in storage, but the piano had to be moved separately by a firm that specialised in this delicate operation. I then had to get it all sorted out; this took some time.

After the Music in Hospitals tour in Cumbria there was a further concert on December 23 and one on December 28.

Andrew Johnston's parents kindly invited me to spend Christmas Day with them, and I went to a New Year party in Greenock at the home of an old school friend Stewart McMillan and his wife Kate. In our youth, Stewart had often accompanied me on our wanderings round the town in the early hours of each New Year's Day, but we were older and wiser now, and we were happy to remain indoors. There were people there I hadn't seen for many years, and I met others who would become good friends. These social interactions also led to other contacts, other work and even holidays. And so my first year back in Scotland came to an end.

II – 2008

It was a sobering thought that by the end of this year I would be a pensioner, but I would then have a regular weekly income over and above what else I might earn. The first job wasn't until January 8, and it was for Music in Hospitals. It was in Dalmoak Castle, a Victorian mansion near Dumbarton that had become a care home, and it was a ninety-fifth birthday party for the mother of Daphne Neville with whom I had done my first pantomime *Cinderella* in 1983. At the end of the month there was the first of many tours to Oban and Argyll; one of the care homes was in the village of Benderloch where we had had family holidays in the 1950s. The next tour, to Inverness, wasn't until March, and the only other one was in August when we were in Aberdeen for three days, but there was still plenty of work for MiH, often just one concert per day, but sometimes two.

In February I received a letter from Billy Strachan, a former D'Oyly Carte chorister whom I had not seen for almost thirty years. Billy had latterly been with Scottish Opera, but they had disbanded their permanent chorus and he was now auditioning for Music in Hospitals. Our D'Oyly Carte colleagues Patricia Leonard and Michael Buchan had worked for MiH in England

and knew that I also for worked for them; they suggested to Billy that he contact me to ask if I would play for his audition which was in May. He was accepted although we didn't do our first concert until July, but from then on I did more concerts with him than with anyone else. For Music in Hospitals we called ourselves For You Alone, the title of an old ballad that Billy often sang. Apart from MiH I occasionally did other concerts with him. On the day of his audition I played for another singer Helen Lothian who was also taken on; as well as MiH concerts I did other work with Helen and Katie Morrell. Once again this shows that one contact can often lead to something else, and that is how work builds up.

Although I had given up Grim's Dyke I thought that there might be some G&S work here, but I found that interest was waning, certainly in Glasgow and the West of Scotland. But I still had many contacts in England, and I was asked to give another talk to the Manchester Gilbert and Sullivan Society in April; I combined this with a visit to cousins in Tyne and Wear. I was in London again in May for the funeral of Eileen Huggins of Manor Light Opera, and I also had to rehearse with Ralph Meanley as yet another job had materialised. We were to have given this programme *Songs from the Shows* in Cheltenham at the end of June, but unfortunately the job was cancelled. However, as work was beginning to build up in Scotland I wasn't too concerned: concerts in the South were not really very practicable now, and I did have another concert much nearer home the following week.

I had been asked to do one of the Sunday afternoon concerts in Millport's Cathedral of The Isles, and I devised a programme devoted entirely to the music of Gerard Francis Cobb which few, if any, of the audience would ever have heard before. Jane Guy and Philip Button agreed to take part: Jane sang, and Philip played some of Cobb's violin pieces. But I felt that we also needed a male singer, and so we were joined on this occasion by James Boyd, a friend of Jane and Philip.

The year continued with an ever-growing number of Music in Hospitals concerts and various other jobs. Some of the singers that I worked with for MiH also taught singing, and I sometimes played for their pupils' lessons, concerts or exams. In November I played at a graduation ceremony in Paisley Abbey for another former D'Oyly Carte colleague Bob Crowe who had organised some singers to provide entertainment as parents and friends assembled. The singers left when the ceremony began, but I had to stay on to play the organ as people filed out after the graduations. I seldom got the opportunity to play such a wonderful instrument.

The minister who conducted my mother's funeral in 2006 had asked me if I had a regular organ job. I said that I didn't want a full-time commitment as this often involved a choir practise one night during the week, but I would be happy to deputise at any time if required. There was a regular organist at the church in Skelmorlie, but I was only asked once when she took a week-end off to celebrate a wedding anniversary. However, I soon found myself sharing a job with another organist as I had done briefly in London. One of my neighbours discovered that I had played for Christian Science services, and she gave my name to the church in Glasgow that she sometimes attended. (There had been a Christian Science Church in Greenock, but dwindling numbers had brought about its closure.) I then received a phone call to ask if I would be interested in playing at this church. I said that I would be happy to share the job with someone, and this is what happened. At first I did all four Sundays in September, and then I did just two in November: alternating Sundays would be roughly the pattern in the years to come.

I now had two main sources of income: Music in Hospitals and a more or less regular, if intermittent, organ job, and I could always deputise elsewhere if I wasn't playing in Glasgow. This happened from time to time; on one occasion I had to play at a funeral service in Lochwinnoch. But a third source of income now presented itself. A church group in Gourock,

Old Gourock and Ashton Parish Players, had presented pantomimes for a number of years. Their musical director was the church's organist, but he was about to have an operation, and he wouldn't be able to do this year's show which was *Humpty Dumpty*. The group was therefore looking for a musical director, and Stewart McMillan gave them my name. I started rehearsing with them at the beginning of November; the performances were in the first week of December. I had assumed that this would just be a temporary appointment, but the organist eventually had to retire from his duties, and while the church appointed another organist I stayed on as musical director for the pantomimes and other shows that they put on. I was grateful to Stewart for the introduction.

In the week before the show I reached my sixty-fifth birthday and became a pensioner although, like Conrad Leonard, I had no intention of retiring. But this new source of income was very welcome. I could now afford regular holidays, and I began to consider the possibilities. It also allowed me to go back to London regularly for purely social events. One of these was a dinner to celebrate the fiftieth anniversary of the Philbeach Society: it was held at the Little Ship Club in Bell Wharf Lane, EC4 in November. I also had to play for some cabaret entertainment there.

Immediately after the run of the pantomime I was again asked to deputise, this time as accompanist for a local choir who were giving carol concerts over three nights in Ardgowan House, home of the Shaw Stewart family who were the local landowners (I was born in Ardgowan Street in Greenock). Then came the run-up to Christmas. This was always the busiest time for Music in Hospitals as everyone seemed to want a concert, but the week after Christmas was invariably quiet. This year was no exception although there was a concert on New Year's Eve; it was in Greenock, and so there wasn't much travel involved. My gamble in moving back to Scotland in 2007 seemed to have paid off, and I now had a pension as well as a certain amount of work. What else might I expect?

III – 2009

I missed the various jobs that occurred from time to time in London, but I was now more available for Music in Hospitals which provided the first work of the year: coincidentally, as in 2008, this was on January 8. We had to give MiH prior notice of our availability, and so we knew well in advance when we would be working. As January was invariably quiet I then had a short holiday in Spain, staying with Sandy Leiper who, now retired, spent the winter months in Malaga. I was surprised how mild it was in January. Thanks to a recently opened motorway we were able get to Granada where we saw the wonderful Alhambra.

Also in January we began rehearsals for Old Gourock and Ashton Parish Players' spring show which took place at the beginning of March. These evenings, which later had titles such as *Hooray for Hollywood*, *Way Out West* or *The Golden Years*, consisted of a mixture of songs from shows and musicals or perhaps songs from the 1920s, 1930s and 1940s; there were also sketches, and sometimes there would be a short play. As in the Charles Haley pantomimes the band consisted of just me and a drummer, Douglas 'Dougie' Warnock.

As well as individual concerts for Music in Hospitals there were several tours that covered much of the country: Inverness, the East Coast (from Dundee to Aberdeen) and two in Argyll, each of which included Oban. When I did MiH tours in England and Wales I had to find deputies for other day-time work such as the ballet classes, and I couldn't do casual evening work such as masonic dates or playing at the Ritz, but so far there was none of that here.

The tours went on throughout the year, and this often meant coping with bad weather. On one occasion we were travelling north on the A 90 when we encountered a blizzard, and it got so bad that we could hardly see anything although it would have been even more dangerous to stop. Billy Strachan was driving, and I had to open my window, look out (with the snow in my face), and yell at him to move to the right if he was getting too close to the edge of the road. We were heading for Edzell, near Brechin, which we eventually reached safely. One of the concerts had to be cancelled, and we spent extra time in our digs. By the following day it had stopped snowing, and I walked to Edzell Castle, a property of Historic Scotland, on the edge of the town. It wasn't open at that time of year, but the countryside looked lovely in the snow although it was extremely cold.

On another occasion Billy and I had been in Inverness for a few days; this time I was driving. We had just set out on the return journey when again it started to snow, and as the A9 south from Inverness climbs steeply after leaving the town (a city now) it just got worse and worse. It was so cold that my wipers could hardly clear the snow which was freezing on the windscreen as we climbed higher and higher. It was now dark, and you couldn't see the road. I was following the car immediately ahead of me, and the car behind was following me: it was almost impossible to stop. Luckily we then reached the highest point and began to descend; I noticed a change almost immediately as the wipers at last began to work properly. We saw deer that had come right down to the roadside to avoid the snow; the journey home that night took much longer than usual.

These situations were inevitable when driving in winter. But it wasn't just snow that was a hazard. On one of the Argyll tours our first job was in Lochgilphead. We were within two or three miles of the town when we found that the road was blocked by an overturned lorry. There are few roads in Argyll, most of them coastal roads, and we had to turn back to Inveraray, some twenty-five miles away, before we could find another road that brought us in to the other side of Lochgilphead. The concert had to be cancelled, but we were able to re-schedule it at the end of the tour on our return from Campbeltown at the foot of the Kintyre peninsula.

Work was now building up: I had the shows in Gourock, and I was working again for Music in Hospitals; I was also playing regularly at the Christian Science Church, roughly twice each month. Luckily there was no choir, and so there was no extra rehearsal during the week. The Sunday service always included a solo. When I started, the soloist was a member of the congregation, but she eventually gave it up, and other singers were brought in. Later, Mark Hathaway, and occasionally his wife Daniela, took it on.

Early in the year I also started to rehearse with a local group in Greenock who were putting on *Tarantara! Tarantara!*, a show that told the story of the Gilbert and Sullivan partnership using words and music from the Savoy Operas, but this was cancelled when one of the lead singers had to withdraw due to illness. I seemed destined not to be involved with any more G&S in Scotland, but I was back at Grim's Dyke in April for another Gilbert and Sullivan Society Convention celebrating the Society's eighty-fifth anniversary. It was graced by the presence of HRH the Duke of Gloucester, now the Society's patron following the death of his mother HRH Princess Alice, Duchess of Gloucester, who had been the Society's president for forty-eight years.

In August I played for Jane Guy again at one of the summer concerts at the cathedral in Millport. This time we celebrated the two-hundredth anniversary of the birth of Mendelssohn and commemorated the fiftieth anniversaries of the deaths of Haydn Wood and Billy Mayerl: the latter had once been resident pianist with the Savoy Havana Band at the Savoy Hotel. I played his famous piece *Marigold*.

The two operatic societies that I had conducted in London, Manor Light Opera and Philbeach, had finally decided to combine their resources, and they sent out a newsletter headed "Together – at last!!" Their first joint productions would be John Rutter's *Wind in the Willows*, Gilbert and Sullivan's *Trial by Jury*, and *Captain Noah and His Floating Zoo* by Michael

Flanders (of the famous Flanders and Swann duo) and Joseph Horovitz. I wished them luck in their new venture.

I had long been a member of the Incorporated Society of Musicians (ISM), a professional body that offers legal and other advice, but so far I had not been much involved with it. When I came back to Scotland I was persuaded to join the committee of the South-West Scotland branch. This was unpaid work, but I did get to know other committee members, and as some of them were teachers I found myself playing for yet another set of pupils' lessons, concerts and exams. Some of the concerts were held in the Glasgow Unitarian Church which was opposite the Christian Science Church in Berkeley Street; others were at Adelaide's in central Glasgow, formerly a church. This *was* paid work which was useful. Also on the ISM committee was the composer Martin Dalby who had been one of my lecturers at Glasgow University. In October I gave a talk on D'Oyly Carte to an ISM group.

In July and August I was in Canada for three weeks. Another Greenock friend Nina McKechnie also had property there, spending the summer in Canada and the winter in Greenock; Stewart and Kate McMillan, close friends of Nina, went out every year for a holiday. The property was in rural Ontario, an area that had been settled by Scots; this was still obvious in many family names such as MacLeod, MacDonald and MacMillan, and in the names of towns and settlements: Nina lived in Dalkeith, and the nearest large town was Alexandria. The local church was St Columba Presbyterian in Laggan Glenelg Road; it also had an annual ceremony called the Kirkin' o' the Tartan whose origin dated back to the time when tartan was banned after the Jacobite rising of 1745-46. This ceremony would take place again during Stewart and Kate's annual visit, and I was invited to join them this year and to take part in the service by playing the organ; I was also asked to write descants for two of the hymns. John Cook, another mutual Greenock friend (then living in

Musselburgh) who was a minister in the Church of Scotland, was also invited, and he was asked to deliver the sermon and give the blessing of the tartans. There was a further attraction in that the Glengarry Highland Games, one of the largest events of its kind outside Scotland (and held at nearby Maxville), would also be happening at the same time, and so John and I were both delighted to accept our invitations.

Initial planning had started in 2008, and I duly wrote the descants for the hymns and made arrangements of other songs that I was to accompany. The holiday lasted from July 24 until August 14; knowing that I would be there for three weeks another plan began to take shape. Geoffrey Shovelton and Deborah Clague now lived in Maine, and this seemed an ideal opportunity to see them if it could be arranged; perhaps, too, I might see Vivian Tierney who with her Canadian husband Alan Woodrow (also a singer) was now living in Ontario. But I particularly wanted to try to see Ferne Stonham and Clarence 'Clare' Townson. As young Canadian service personnel they had been stationed in Greenock during the Second World War, and they had met and befriended my parents. They were now in their late eighties, and this might be my last chance to see them. I had met Ferne in 1978 when I was in Ottawa with D'Oyly Carte, but I had not met Clare although I knew that Ferne was in touch with him. Ferne was now in the northern part of New Brunswick, and Clare was in Wiarton, a three-hour drive to the north-west of Toronto. In the end, it proved impossible for the three of us to get together, but I did manage to see each of them separately.

The holiday got off to a bad start. The flight to Montreal was from London, and I had to get a connecting flight from Glasgow. John Cook had a similar connection from Edinburgh, but he took an earlier flight, and he got to London without any problems. When we got to London we couldn't land because of bad weather, and we were redirected to Birmingham to refuel. More delays followed before we finally landed at Heathrow, and I missed the flight to Montreal and had to spend the night in a hotel before catching another flight the following day. But after that it all went very smoothly.

There was much hospitality and entertaining during the first week. On the Monday we had a day in Ottawa; this was followed by a day in Montreal where we were looked after by a judge, His Honour Fraser Martin, who had been in the same class as Stewart at Greenock Academy. (Who coined the phrase "It's a small world"?) There was a Tartan Ball on the Thursday, and the Glengarry Games were held on the Friday (July 31) and Saturday (August 1). On the Friday evening there was a Tattoo with singers, sky divers, massed pipe bands and country dancing: the bands included a group from George Watson's College in Edinburgh. The Games also celebrated the centenary of the Ontario Provincial Police, and there were souvenirs of that. The Kirkin' o' the Tartan service was on Sunday August 2. Earlier, I had rehearsed the descants with the choir, but they proved to be too difficult, and so we didn't use them. As the service had a Scottish flavour I wore my kilt, but I then discovered that I couldn't see the organ pedals, something I hadn't thought about earlier.

I did wonder if my plans to see various people might be too ambitious, but they fitted in well with what Nina, Stewart and Kate wanted to do. They had decided to explore the coast of Maine, and they said that they would be happy to take me to River's Reach Farm, Geoffrey and Deborah's home at North New Portland ME, where I would stay for a few days. John Cook flew home on August 3 for family reasons, but just before he left we visited Le Château Montebello, a hotel that is the world's largest log-built structure.

Deborah Clague, Geoffrey Shovelton and David Mackie
in a 1916 Stanley Steamer.

We set off very early next day (to avoid traffic) and crossed into
the United States. It was good to see Geoffrey and Deborah
again, and I had a very pleasant time with them. One place that
we visited was the Stanley Museum at nearby Kingfield ME,
devoted to the life and work of twin brothers F.E. and F.O.
Stanley who had produced the famous Stanley Steamers, early
steam-powered automobiles which were popular up to the
1920s by which time the advancement of the petrol engine had
heralded their demise. I was picked up again on August 7, and
we headed north back into Canada: we stayed one night in
Moncton NB. The following day we took Ferne Stonham out to
lunch. It was good to see her again, but we couldn't stay too long
as we had to drive south, this time to a town called St Andrews
NB where we stayed for another night. Incredibly, the town had
a Greenock Church (we were constantly being reminded of
Scotland) whose steeple carried a large green oak tree as part
of the design, the one thing that is *not* supposed to be the origin
of Greenock's name. We then moved back to the United States.

The last part of this holiday within a holiday took us first of all to Mt Washington, the highest point in New Hampshire, where you can drive to the summit: this was first done by a Stanley Steamer in 1899. We had intended doing so ourselves, but the weather wasn't too good, and we abandoned the idea. Finally, we crossed the state border into Vermont and stopped at the delightful town of Stowe. Stewart and Kate had been here with Nina on a previous holiday, but this was my first visit. After we had looked round the town Nina said that we were going to a local view point, but they had actually planned a surprise for me, a visit to the home of the von Trapp family, now a hotel and tourist attraction. The scenery here is similar to the Austrian scenery that they had left behind.

We were back in Dalkeith on August 11, my last day there. Next day I took a train to Toronto where I was met by Clare Townson, who had driven down from Wiarton, and his granddaughter Kathy. Not having seen Clare since I was a baby it was effectively a first meeting. We then drove to Kathy's home at Ancaster, near Hamilton, where I met her husband Chris and their two daughters. I was glad that I had managed to engineer these meetings with Clare Townson and Ferne Stonham. Clare died a few years later, but Ferne celebrated her one hundredth birthday as this book was in preparation. I spent one night in Ancaster, and I flew back from Toronto the following day. But before that I also caught up with Vivian Tierney and Alan Woodrow. They were both free, and they kindly agreed to pick me up at Ancaster and drive me to the airport. Before we left they were shown some old photographs: one of them was of Clare holding me as a baby in 1945. On the way to the airport we stopped at an English-style pub that had old photographs on the walls; amazingly, one of them was of Millport. I hadn't seen Vivian and Alan for some time, and we caught up with each other's careers.

I finally got back to Skelmorlie after more delays on the shuttle from London. It had been the longest holiday I had ever had, and it was one that I could not have afforded earlier.

On the flight to Montreal, my case, a hard one with wheels at one end, had been damaged, and one wheel had unaccountably vanished; this had become a talking point throughout the holiday, and it prompted a response from Stewart McMillan. Stewart had certificates in Scottish country dancing, and when we were at school I had played for a demonstration class that he ran. In 1962 he had devised a dance *The Jubilee Jig* for the Golden Jubilee of the Scottish Schoolboys' Club of which we were both members, and I had composed the music. He now devised some dances in honour of our holiday: a reel, strathspey and jig. The jig was called *The One-wheeled Case*, and when I wrote a tune for it I gave it that name. But these dances usually have alternative tunes, and I wrote another one called *Mrs McKechnie of Auldhouse Farm* after Nina and her property. The strathspey was called *Sauntering round at the Games*, and the reel, *The Fields of Dalkeith*; I also wrote tunes for these. This occupied me during October and November although later I added other alternative tunes for all three dances. I gave them names associated with people I had met, and with places and events that had been part of the holiday. I spent Christmas Day with Nina, Stewart and Kate.

IV – 2010

On January 1 I was invited to the home of Ann and John MacLeod, friends of Nina, Stewart and Kate who were all there too. Ann and John became good friends, and I would spend each subsequent Christmas Day, Boxing Day and New Year's Day with at least some members of this group at one or other of their homes, sometimes with others present too. Neighbours in Skelmorlie also gave annual New Year parties, and so a good social life was never far away.

Work started on January 3 when I had to play the organ in Glasgow. This would remain a regular job although I also played elsewhere from time to time, occasionally deputising for Alastair Chisholm at the cathedral in Millport. The service here was Scottish Episcopal, and I found it quite difficult to follow despite having played for Anglican services in England. I also played for a further three graduation ceremonies in Paisley Abbey in November. As before, I had been asked to do this by Bob Crowe. Earlier in the year I had played for Bob and Katie Morrell at a masonic function in Perth. It was my first (and, at time of writing, only) masonic date in Scotland. Luckily I still had some contacts in England, and in April I did another concert with Judith Baxter.

The first work for Music in Hospitals was on January 18 although they held a social gathering in Edinburgh on the previous day: it was useful to meet other artists who worked for the organisation. This work continued as usual throughout the year, but as with most free-lance work it wasn't regular, and some weeks were much busier than others. But there were eight tours which again covered much of the country, taking me to places I had not yet visited. On one tour we had to drive from Aviemore to Elgin, and the road took us through Aberlour and past signposts to Knockando and Cardhu, places whose names were familiar from brands of malt whisky; on another tour we had to take the road from Cock Bridge to Tomintoul in the Grampian region, notorious as invariably the first road to be closed when bad weather sets in. Luckily, this particular tour wasn't in winter.

As well as dealing with inclement weather there were numerous other incidents on these tours. Billy Strachan and I once arrived at our digs to find that the boiler had broken down, and the lady had booked us in at another B&B. Unfortunately this wasn't suitable, and we had to look for something else. We stopped at a pub, only to discover that it was being renovated and wasn't quite ready. But they took pity on us and let us have two rooms.

There were lighter moments too. On another tour I was with Billy in Aberdeen. We had done an afternoon concert, and we were trying to find a care home where we were to have a meal before the evening concert. We were held up in rush-hour traffic on the old ring road (Anderson Drive), and we were late in arriving at the home (itself a rather strange building that looked for all the world like a child's toy fort or an outpost of the Foreign Legion) where we were presented with our meal which they had kept warm for us. But having been in the oven for some time the meal was now quite literally stuck to the plates: you could hold them upside down with the food still attached. We got the giggles over this; Billy likened it to 'wall art'. At another home, in Strathpeffer, there was an electronic keyboard. I moved it away from the wall so that I wouldn't have my back to the audience, and there, behind it, was a set of false teeth. Expect the unexpected.

The concerts for Music in Hospitals were designed to be interactive and were not 'concerts' in the traditional sense; audiences were encouraged to join in with items. In hospitals and care homes we were dealing with a cross-section of the public, and the music performed had to reflect this; in care homes there was the added problem of an older population. Many residents would have dementia, and so the programme had to consist (at least partly) of items that most people would know and, more importantly, remember. Musicals were popular, and many older films had musical items sung by performers such as Judy Garland and Mario Lanza. And so most of the material had to come from a period when our audiences were younger. Sometimes a resident in a home could be seen singing the words of a particular song when he or she might not have spoken for literally weeks. This was always gratifying to the performers and also to the staff. Here in Scotland we were told by MiH to include Scottish songs to which people always reacted well. (We had also performed traditional Welsh music in Wales although we did very little traditional English music in England.)

This year saw two further additions to the work portfolio. The first of these was the Inverclyde Music Festival, one of many similar competitive festivals held throughout the country.

Originally the Renfrewshire Musical Festival it was held each year at the end of January in Greenock Town Hall. When I was at school I was always entered for the appropriate piano class here; sometimes I was in the piano duet class with other pupils of my formidable teacher Mrs Scrymgeour. I now became one of the accompanists for the various vocal classes. The music would be sent in advance, usually before the end of the previous year, so that I knew what I would be playing. Despite having spent much time on this, some entrants might withdraw at the last minute; also, an entrant might turn up on the day with his or her own accompanist without letting the Festival organisers know beforehand. There were classes for both children and adults; sometimes the test piece was an 'own choice', and some of these might have very awkward accompaniments: they were often excerpts from operas or oratorios where the piano part is a reduction of a full orchestral score. But I had to be able to play everything that was sent to me, and I was being paid for a set number of sessions, no matter how much or how little I had to play. It was good to be working at new repertoire as so much of what I had done so far, such as G&S or the concerts for Music in Hospitals, was familiar material.

The second new contact was with an amateur operatic society, the Glasgow Light Opera Club (GLOC). They had decided to do some fund-raising concerts, but their musical director didn't want to take on this extra work. One of their members lived in Gourock and also sang with Old Gourock and Ashton Parish Players: she kindly suggested me, and this became another source of work for several years. My first rehearsal with the group was on November 2, and I discovered that their president was someone I had known many years before, again through the Scottish Schoolboys' Club: he in the Glasgow branch and I in the Greenock branch. We would meet every year at SSC camps at Easter and in the summer: yes, a small world.

I was at Grim's Dyke again in February. This time I had to give a talk, conduct *Iolanthe* and play some duets with Hilary

Morgan: that was all the G&S for 2010, and all crammed into one week-end. But this year also saw the deaths of a disproportionate number of people who had either been in D'Oyly Carte or who were much involved in the world of G&S. Three of them - John Reed, Patricia Leonard and Gareth Jones - had been in the Company during my time there, 1975-82; the list also included former principals Mary Sansom and Helen Roberts (at the age of ninety-eight) and choristers Eileen Bruckshaw, Fred Sinden and Neville Griffiths. Another former chorister was Ceinwen Jones (at the age of ninety-seven) who had been married to former business manager Bert Newby and who had introduced me to Manor House Hospital Operatic Society. I had to remind myself that it was almost thirty years since the old D'Oyly Carte Opera Company had closed, but so many deaths in one year was a great shock. Others who contributed much to the G&S world were Maurice Farrar on the Isle of Man, Ric Wilson in the United States and Sir Charles Mackerras who had arranged the music for the ballet *Pineapple Poll* and with whom I had collaborated in the reconstruction of Sullivan's cello concerto. This truly was an *annus horribilis*, but on a happier note I went to the Buxton G&S Festival in August where I met Scott Hayes, a great-great nephew of Arthur Sullivan, who was descended from Sullivan's brother Frederic. Scott had done much to increase our knowledge of the private and family side of the composer's life.

Once again I had three short holidays in one year, a luxury undreamt of until recently. The first was a visit to Mull in June with Sandy Leiper: neither of us had been there before. Thanks to good weather we were able to get to the island of Staffa and the magical Fingal's Cave (immortalised in Mendelssohn's famous concert overture *The Hebrides*): in bad weather this is not always possible, and tourists are often disappointed. The second holiday, in August, was with Interesting Times, run by Yorkshireman Mike Higginbottom. This was a guided tour of country houses in Leicestershire; we were based in one magnificent house, Harlaxton Hall, which I had known from photographs. It was now an American educational establishment, and it could be hired in the summer months when the students had gone. Finally, in November, I went to Krakow for four days: having had a day trip there on a previous holiday I had promised myself that I would go back again one day. The itinerary included visits to Auschwitz and the historic salt mine at Wieliczka.

I had now begun to play golf. Neither of my parents had been interested in sport, and with poor eyesight I was never good at ball games; while still at school and taking part in rugby as part of our physical education my parents were always concerned that as a pianist I had to be careful not to damage my hands. But a cousin had recently given me a set of clubs as he was no longer able to play, and golf is a game that you can play later in life (the journalist and broadcaster Alistair Cooke famously it took up in his fifties). Golf is an expensive pastime, but it was half the battle to have a set of clubs, and so I joined Skelmorlie Golf Club. I befriended one of the members John Murphy who kindly agreed to give me some lessons. John was now eighty, but he still enjoyed playing, and so we would go out on a quiet day so that he could give me advice and also play some holes himself. He had had an interesting life, and we talked of many things as we made our slow way round the course; we also enjoyed the views over the Clyde. But John and his wife then moved to the Outer Hebrides, and bereft of a tutor I found that I wasn't making any further progress. I persevered for some time, going out on quiet days to practise, but I finally had to admit defeat. I never got to the point where I could play with anyone (I would only have held them up), and it was too expensive to keep up a subscription without getting much benefit from it. It had been a brave but futile attempt to broaden my canvas and have a sporting interest.

I was also attending more concerts, such as those in Millport, and other events. In March I went to a talk by the singer Donald Maxwell whom I had known for some time (he sang in *The Pirates of Penzance* and *The Mikado* that I conducted at the Buxton Festival in 2002). This was held in Knock Castle, a mansion that lies between Skelmorlie and Largs, which regularly hosted concerts. It was the first time I had been there, and I mistakenly drove into another property only to get my car stuck in the mud. Another friend was also at Donald's talk, and he was able to tow me out later. That escapade wasn't exactly the crowning achievement of 2010.

Chapter 11 – Theme with variations

The final part of this story can be told briefly, partly to spare the reader further details but also because most of my new contacts were now in place, and each successive year was pretty much like the previous one. Also, there were no more tours of North America, and there was no more cruise work. There were plenty of tours for Music in Hospitals, but having at first been for three or even four days these were latterly reduced to just two days. On my return to Scotland I had acquired a light portable keyboard for MiH and other concerts.

I wasn't working as much I had been in London, but I was more financially secure now that I had a pension, and everything that I earned on top of that was a bonus. I could now have one or two proper holidays each year as well as some long-weekend breaks, but if I had free days I would sometimes visit places of interest that I hadn't yet seen or revisit places that I hadn't seen for many years. I often ventured quite far afield, sometimes to the remoter parts of Argyll or to Perthshire and Fife and even down to Carlisle.

The paddle steamer *Waverley*, now the last sea-going paddle steamer in the world, was still sailing, and it was wonderful to be on her again regularly. I also joined the Clyde River Steamer Club where, to my surprise, I discovered that the man who had bought my flat in Rothesay Court was also a member. As well as attending CRSC meetings in Glasgow I went on day excursions that the club organised, seeing parts of Scotland's West Coast (such as the islands of Islay, Jura,

Colonsay and Gigha) for the first time and sailing again through the wonderful Kyles of Bute, one of the most scenic journeys anywhere in the world. This was more or less on my doorstep although you might think yourself a thousand miles away from the hustle and bustle of modern life. Most of this activity happened during the summer months, but it was always by way of an extra to the work-load which continued as usual throughout each year.

I – 2011

January 1 was, as always, a purely social occasion. I didn't play the organ every week, and so not always on the first Sunday of each month. But this year January 2 was a Sunday, and that was my first job although there was no more work until I played again on January 16: the first Music in Hospitals job was not until January 19. Despite the slow start I wasn't too concerned about the lack of work (as I would have been a few years earlier) as I did now have the pension. The 2011 Inverclyde Music Festival started on January 24 and ran until February 5. I wasn't employed for all of this time as not every class required an accompanist (and there were several of us), but I did four sessions over the two weeks. Not working there every day meant that I could also do other work if it came along. There were rehearsals for Glasgow Light Opera Club's *Showstoppers Past and Present* which had three performances at Adelaide's in Glasgow at the end of February; there were also rehearsals for the Parish Players' spring show in Gourock at the end of March.

In May I went to Amsterdam to see Sandy Oliver who was now living there permanently, but I chose the week-end of a volcanic eruption in Iceland; on the day that I was due to fly home all flights were grounded, and I had to spend an extra night at Schiphol Airport. I was lucky to get away the following morning, but I still had to cancel a Music in Hospitals job: it is at such times that even I appreciate the convenience of mobile phones. A few days later I was travelling again, this time to see Ross and Ginny Jenkins with whom I had lived for over a year in London when I moved up from Eastbourne in 1984. They were now living permanently in France, and they were celebrating their Ruby Wedding.

The Music in Hospitals work gradually built up throughout the year; this included nine tours which covered much of the country from Ullapool and Tain in the North to Dumfries & Galloway and the Borders in the South. I did several individual MiH concerts with Jane Guy, and I usually did the driving. On one occasion my car broke down again, and while we managed to get to the venue we had to use a breakdown service to get back which was very embarrassing. I also played for Jane again at one of the Sunday concerts in Millport; this time we marked the centenary of the death of W.S. Gilbert. Rehearsals for the Parish Players' pantomime *Goody Two Shoes* began in August with the show in the last week of November, and there was another concert given by ISM teachers' pupils at Adelaide's.

There were several G&S-related events this year. Following John Reed's death in 2010 there was a tribute to him at Conway Hall in London on March 12. Maureen Melvin, a former D'Oyly Carte principal soprano, had written a poem called *Fifty Years On*, and I had to arrange suitable music which I played as she read it. A number of former Company members were present, and we had to give our own reminiscences of John. In April I was in Crosby where I gave a talk on G&S, and shortly after that I began work on *Tower Green*, a piece for organ based on "Night has spread her pall once more" from *The Yeomen of the Guard*. This was a commission from Tony Gower of the Gilbert and Sullivan Society. There was no deadline, and it took me several years to finish it.

In July I was at a family wedding in Stratford-upon-Avon, and I extended this trip to catch up with my D'Oyly Carte colleagues Peter Riley, who lived just north of Bristol, and Margaret Bowden who now lived in Exmouth. In August

I saw the rarely performed *Utopia Limited* at Buxton. In September I went to the Sir Arthur Sullivan Society's annual Festival (mainly Sullivan without Gilbert), held this year in Cirencester; finally, on November 25, I played at a G&S concert in Greenock's Arts Guild Theatre where we had given a London Airs concert in 1984. This one was called *Here's a How-de-do!* after a line in *The Mikado*; Bob Crowe and Katie Morrell also took part.

II – 2012

The first work this year was for Music in Hospitals: five concerts between January 6th and 12th; I played the organ again on the 15th. Both of these sources, which accounted for the bulk of my earnings, then continued much as before. There were eight tours for MiH this year, two of them over four days, and again these covered much of the country. Single concerts tended to be in and around Glasgow although there were also many in Ayrshire; I was now doing well over one hundred concerts in a year. Another MiH singer was Helenna [sic] Fraser with whom I did some touring. In one concert I played for Helenna and the flautist and piper George McIlwham whose name had been known to me for many years. In November there was a fund-raising concert for MiH at Buchanan Castle Golf Club; this was a Viennese evening with Billy Strachan and Katie Morrell.

The Inverclyde Music Festival took place at the end of January, and in March I had another short holiday in Krakow which I had found so fascinating. Shortly after this came another spring show for Old Gourock and Ashton Parish Players. They rehearsed on a Monday evening, and I tried to attend all of the rehearsals although this wasn't always possible, particularly if a Music in Hospitals tour was offered: the free-lance world can often involve a balancing act where work is concerned.

Stewart McMillan ran a Scottish country dancing class on Tuesday evenings in the church hall where we put on the Parish Players' pantomimes and spring shows, and he persuaded me to come along if I was free. Despite having played much Scottish country dance music and having written several tunes for Stewart I often caused mayhem in the set as I didn't know the steps of any of the dances. But it was good exercise and good fun. As so often, it was a predominantly female group, some of whom I had known from my schooldays.

As well as playing the organ in Glasgow I played at St Columba's Episcopal Church in Largs on a number of occasions, again deputising while they looked for a permanent organist: I still found the Scottish Episcopal service hard to follow. I didn't play at any more of Alastair Chisholm's concerts in Millport, but I continued to support them when I was free. Many of the artists that he used were Scottish or based in Scotland, but others came from further afield. One was the London-based Jonathan Cohen who had portrayed Liszt in one of Dione Livingstone's plays about the women in composers' lives (when I was Brahms to Dione's Clara Schumann). In addition to one grand piano the cathedral had acquired a second one, a splendid Bösendorfer that had belonged to the Scottish pianist Wight Henderson who had been head of piano studies at the RSAMD when I was a student there; Jonathan and Alastair now gave an annual two-piano recital during the summer concert season. Like me, they were both great fans of the paddle steamer *Waverley*.

I was sorry that there seemed to be so little G&S in Scotland, but there were still plenty of G&S-related events in England. I went to a D'Oyly Carte reunion in Stockport in February, staying with Brian and Valerie Bailey whom I had met through G&S and who lived in Manchester; in April there was yet another Gilbert and Sullivan Society Convention, and this too was at Stockport. I went to Buxton again in August, this time to see a rare production of *The Grand Duke*: these visits were always a good opportunity to catch up with former colleagues and aficionados.

There was another performance of the Glasgow Light Opera Group's concert *Showstoppers Past and Present*, this time at Old Gourock and Ashton Church. These concerts were compèred in a very entertaining way by Walter Paul whom I had met on my first visit to Glasgow with D'Oyly Carte in 1975: his parents, who were avid G&S fans, had given a party for the Company; it was good to be working with him now. Walter had been much involved in G&S as performer and producer, and he too was aware of a lessening of interest as societies turned increasingly to more modern repertoire.

There were no more Bentley concerts, but Ralph Meanley and Pam Baxter were in Scotland in July, and they stayed with me for a few days. In September I spent a few days in County Durham with Alan and Hazel Lamb: I had worked with Alan some years before. Judith and Leonard Baxter were also there. And there was yet another reunion in October, this one at Birmingham University to coincide with the opening of a new building for the music department. I went down by train, and I stayed in Wolverhampton with Renee Young. The Parish Players' pantomime at the end of November was *Puss in Boots*, and December, as always, was one of the busiest months for Music in Hospitals. And so another year came to an end.

III – 2013

This year followed much the same path, but it was memorable in several ways. There were ten tours for Music in Hospitals including one on the Isle of Skye in August which I did with Billy Strachan. But it almost didn't happen. The first concert was in Fort William at 14.00, and the second one was to be in Portree at 18.30. We had just left Fort William at about 15.30 when yet again my car broke down. We were able to leave it at a garage, to be collected on our return, but I had to hire a car to get us to Skye. Luckily, although we were late in arriving, there was still time to do the concert. The opening of the Skye Bridge in 1995 had facilitated access to the island, but with an increase in tourism it could be difficult to find accommodation. This was always arranged by the office in Edinburgh (unlike my days with MiH in England) who informed us that we would be staying in Elgol, a tiny village in the south-west of the island. Although only sixteen miles from Broadford (itself some twenty-five miles from Portree) it was a full hour's drive on a very narrow road, and you had to slow down even more when cattle appeared. On one occasion a cow with very large horns seemed to be coming straight towards us, and I was fearful of damage to the hired car. Thankfully it moved out of the way. The following day we had to drive to Uig, some fifteen miles north of Portree; much of our time on this tour was spent getting to the venues and getting back to Elgol. I was able to collect my own car in Fort William on the return journey; we then had a concert in Ballachulish on the edge of Glen Coe.

Sometime later I had an even worse problem with another car when working for MiH; once again I was with Billy Strachan. We were driving to the North-East for a tour, and we got as far as Aberdeen when the car broke down. This time it had to be brought back to Skelmorlie, and the tour was cancelled. These concerts could sometimes be re-scheduled, but when something like this happened I was more concerned that the other artist would also lose money. Luckily, Billy and I had plenty of work with Music in Hospitals, and we soon made up the financial loss.

Inevitably there were more deaths among the G&S community, among them John Ayldon who had been on our tours of North America for Joanne Rile; also Andrew Whittaker who had run the opera group at Grim's Dyke. I went down to London in May to attend a memorial service for Andrew which was followed by a reception at the Savile Club where he had kindly treated me to lunch after my last performance at the hotel in 2007.

In June I went to the Common Riding in Selkirk. I had been invited to attend this by Renee Young, and we stayed in a lovely old house a few miles out of the town which was owned by a friend of Percy and Renee who was the son of the musicologist and Handel expert Winton Dean, himself the son of the film and theatre producer Basil Dean who, with Leslie Henson, had set up ENSA (Entertainments National Service Association) in 1939 to provide entertainment for the armed forces. (ENSA was soon corrupted into supposedly standing for Every Night Something Awful.) The Common Riding was part of a long-established Borders tradition, taking over the town for a day (in some communities this can last for several days). It was a fascinating experience. A few days later Renee introduced me to the composer and pianist Ronald Stevenson and his wife who lived near Edinburgh. I was surprised to see that on his piano he had a large photograph of Lawrence Glover who had been my piano teacher at the RSAMD. Apparently they had been good friends.

Shortly after this I had another holiday which was again a combination of business and pleasure. A small group of enthusiasts in Germany had founded an Arthur Sullivan Society (Deutsche Sullivan Gesellschaft) in 2009, and although I am a poor linguist I became a member. They held each AGM in a different city, and I decided to attend this year's which was in Regensburg. I was there for several days. I couldn't follow all of the business which was in German, but most of the members spoke English, and the social side of the week-end was very pleasant; there was plenty of time for sight-seeing in this wonderfully preserved UNESCO World Heritage City. Two of the people who ran the Deutsche Sullivan Gesellschaft were Meinhard Saremba and Beate Koltzenburg; as they were coming to Scotland in October I offered to show them something of the country. I met them in Pitlochry, and we drove to Rannoch Station on the edge of Rannoch Moor, one of the most desolate areas in the Central Highlands. Meinhard and Beate became good friends. In August I also went to

Bruges for a few days, travelling from London by Eurostar: yet another new experience.

I had found it hard to believe that I had become a pensioner in 2008, but it was even more sobering to realise that I had reached my seventieth birthday in November. But I still had as much work as I wanted - Music in Hospitals, organ playing, pantomimes, spring shows and the Inverclyde Music Festival - and I had every intention of continuing with all of this for as long as I could.

IV – 2014

Once again the theme was much the same while the variations were different. The first job wasn't until January 17 when I played for another old college friend who was teaching in a local Primary school. Thereafter it was the mixture as before. There were five sessions at the Inverclyde Music Festival and nine tours for Music in Hospitals, one of which took us to Wick and Thurso. Most of these tours were later in the year. There were also more Glasgow Light Opera Club concerts, three in Glasgow at the end of March and another one at Old Gourock and Ashton Church in August; these were now given the name *A Little Light Music*. A second member of the Parish Players had joined GLOC, and the three of us now took it in turn to drive to rehearsals in Glasgow. These were on Tuesday evenings, and this put paid to my attempts to master the intricacies of Scottish country dancing. But the group always had a dinner in April to mark the end of the year's work, and I was able to attend this. There was usually also a social evening just before Christmas.

The death toll of friends and colleagues continued to rise. Beti Lloyd-Jones died in March and I played at her funeral. With the gradual passing of so many of the old D'Oyly Carte Opera Company I thought that those of us who had worked for it should have formed a tontine, as in the novel *The Wrong*

Box by Robert Louis Stevenson and Lloyd Osbourne (the story even involves a Broadwood grand piano), although the eventual survivor might be too old to enjoy the fruits of such a scheme. At the end of the month Manor and Philbeach Light Opera (now MAPLO) held a sixtieth anniversary dinner in London which I attended.

In May there was another Gilbert and Sullivan Society Convention at Grim's Dyke, this one celebrating the Society's ninetieth year; once again we were graced by the presence of HRH the Duke of Gloucester. I had to play at several of the week-end's events. There was always a short service on the Sunday morning at which Sullivan's hymn tunes were used: sadly, most of these no longer appear in modern hymnals. Back in Scotland there was finally some G&S when I became the musical director for *HMS Pinafore* in a new production by Walter Paul who also played Sir Joseph Porter. This was in June as part of Glasgow's West End Festival, and it had the added attraction of being held on Glasgow's Tall Ship, the barque *Glenlee*, a particularly suitable venue for this nautical opera. There were three performances which were given in the ship's hold with the audience in the round; with no room for an orchestra I was the substitute with my electronic keyboard.

Following my account of the 1979 D'Oyly Carte tour of Australia and New Zealand which was published in *Gilbert & Sullivan News* in 2004 I wrote a similar three-part account of the 1978 tour of the United States and Canada which I called *Five Months in North America*. The first part was published, again in the *News*, in the Autumn/Winter edition (vol. v, no. 6) with the second and third parts in the Spring and Summer 2015 editions (vol. v, nos. 7 and 8).

In 2012 the Deutsche Sullivan Gesellschaft had published a volume of essays on various aspects of Sullivan's work called *SullivanPerspektiven* [sic]: some of these essays were in German, but the majority were in English. This year they published a second volume to which I contributed *The Songs* of *Arthur Sullivan* which had been my research subject at Birmingham University in the 1970s. A third volume was published in 2017.

I was also on the editorial board of a critical edition of the G&S operas being published by the American firm of Broude Brothers Limited: I had first met Ron Broude in New York during D'Oyly Carte's 1978 tour of North America. I knew several other members of the board including Ric Wilson of the Pierpont Morgan Library, John Wolfson who had allowed me access to the manuscript full scores of *The Sorcerer* and *The Grand Duke* for the BBC Radio 2 series in 1989, Percy Young who had edited *HMS Pinafore* (one of the few editions that appeared before Percy's death in 2004) and Gerald Hendrie who was editing *Iolanthe* which appeared in 2017. I had known Gerald since my time in D'Oyly Carte when the edition was already under way.

In September I drove down to Pagham for Vivienne and Gerald Johnson's Golden Wedding celebration at which I had to play for Stephen Gadd with whom I had recorded some of Conrad Leonard's songs: Stephen's wife, Claire Rutter (Vivienne's niece), was singing elsewhere and was not able to be present. Driving had always been part of my work, particularly with D'Oyly Carte and Music in Hospitals, but the further south I got the more crowded the roads became; with endless hold-ups I was glad to be back in Scotland where the weather was usually more of a problem than the traffic. My main holiday this year had been a long-awaited trip to Venice and Murano. This year's pantomime was *Sleeping Beauty*.

V – 2015

Once again, work followed the same pattern although it was a particularly busy year with fifteen tours for Music in Hospitals: as always, despite the name, most of these concerts were in care homes. Apart from the tours there were also many individual MiH concerts, and with other work there were few days when I wasn't fully occupied. As usual, the Parish Players produced a spring show and a pantomime and there were four GLOC concerts. The first of these was in Glasgow in February, and on this occasion the group was joined by the Club's honorary president Jamie MacDougall who sang two numbers. Of the remaining concerts, two, in Largs and Kilbarchan, were both in March; the third was in Glasgow in September.

In May I attended my second Deutsche Sullivan Gesellschaft AGM, this time in Bamberg, another lovely UNESCO World Heritage City. The AGM had been timed to coincide with a series of concerts of British music, *Britannia in Bamberg*, masterminded by Meinhard Saremba and others. These had been running since March, and we were able to attend two of them, one devoted to the music of Purcell and Sullivan: I wrote an account of *Britannia in Bamberg* for the Sullivan Society's *Magazine* no. 88, Summer 2015. As in Regensburg there was plenty of time for sightseeing. Shortly after this I was in London to attend the launch of a book called *Charles Mackerras*. It was a collection of essays on aspects of Sir Charles's life edited by Nigel Simeone and John Tyrrell, and I had been asked to write about the reconstruction of Sullivan's cello concerto in which we had collaborated.

Michael Rayner, former D'Oyly Carte principal baritone and a stalwart of the Grim's Dyke Opera productions, died in July; as had happened when John Ayldon died in 2013 I was asked to write an obituary for *Gilbert & Sullivan News*: this was a less pleasant part of the writing that I was now doing. Tom Round, former principal tenor with D'Oyly Carte, reached his hundredth birthday in October.

I had another holiday in October with Interesting Times. Based in Scarborough it was called Yorkshire's Seaside Heritage, and it covered much of the coastline from

Saltburn-by-the-Sea and Whitby to Filey and Bridlington. Apart from Scarborough itself it was one part of England that I had never visited, and I had always wanted to see it. We were blessed with well-nigh perfect weather that week. In Scarborough we were shown round the famous Grand Hotel and I also walked up to the castle, but I was particularly interested in a visit to the famous Spa where some of our regular D'Oyly Carte orchestral players found employment with Max Jaffa when we were on foreign tours.

On October 21 (Trafalgar Day) I gave a talk about my life in the world of music to a WEA (Workers' Educational Association) group in Skelmorlie. This was in the morning; I then had to drive to Kilmarnock to give the talk in the afternoon to another WEA group. I would do this again.

My cousins from Australia were here once more, but I had discovered a hitherto unknown cousin Ian Mackie who also lived in Australia. He had done much genealogical research into the family history, and it was through yet another cousin, now living in Toronto, that I became aware of him. He too was in Scotland although not at the same time. We met at the Falkirk Wheel.

Greenock had now become a port of call for many cruise liners. One of them did a two-night cruise to Dublin, and so I decided to do this as well. D'Oyly Carte had once played there regularly, but because of the political situation during my time with the Company both Dublin and Belfast were off-limits. This was in December, a brief relaxation between the pantomime (*Ali Baba* this year) and two further tours for MiH. Some of the hospitals and care homes asked for us on a regular basis, and we got to know them, and their staffs, very well. Two of these were in Glasgow, but another one was the Riverside Centre in Newton Stewart which was a victim of this year's December floods. Our planned visit during the second tour was cancelled although the Centre was eventually restored.

VI – 2016

The year began in much the same way with organ duties, Music in Hospitals (there were six tours this year), the Inverclyde Music Festival, the first GLOC concert in March and a spring show for the Parish Players in April. GLOC had now acquired a new name *GLOC 'n' Spiel* for its concerts, and there were five of these including a return to both Gourock and Largs and a *Christmas Special* at Adelaide's. During the year there was a change of compère for the shows as Walter Paul had relinquished this position. Also in March I finished my organ piece *Tower Green* for Tony Gower.

Royston Nash, D'Oyly Carte's musical director from 1971-79, died in April. I learned much about conducting the operas from Royston after almost literally being thrown in at the deep end to conduct my first opera *The Mikado* for D'Oyly Carte in Brighton in 1976. But we also became good friends, sharing the same sense of humour, and I kept in touch with him when he moved to the United States. I saw him briefly in Boston at the beginning of our third Byers, Schwalbe tour in 1986, and I saw him just twice after that at Gilbert and Sullivan Society Conventions in Stockport. He had been president of the Manchester Gilbert and Sullivan Society, and I was delighted when I received a letter at the beginning of October inviting me to be his successor.

Deborah Clague, Geoffrey Shovelton's wife and our soprano for the series of North American tours organised by Joanne Rile, had been ill for a year with cancer, and she died in June. Geoffrey had kept everyone informed of the progress of her illness, and her death was not unexpected, but soon afterwards Geoffrey was diagnosed with a brain tumour, and he died in July. Seemingly always the hale and hearty type his sudden death was a profound shock to those who knew him, particularly coming so soon after Deborah's death. Again, I wrote obituaries of Royston, Deborah and Geoffrey for

Gilbert & Sullivan News. A further death was that of centenarian Tom Round in October. His funeral was held on what would have been his one hundred and first birthday.

With Michael Rayner's death in 2015 Geoffrey Shovelton was left as the sole survivor of the six male principals in D'Oyly Carte when I joined in 1975, and his death, and that of Royston Nash, galvanised me into starting work on a project that had been simmering for a long time, namely to write an account of my time in the Company (its last seven years) before it was too late: Beti Lloyd-Jones had thought about writing *her* memoirs, and she had even planned to use a line from *The Gondoliers* "List and learn" as a title, but she never got around to it. I had made numerous jottings over the years with the intention of getting down to this one day, and I made a more definite start in 2012 when I compiled a chronological list of all the places we had visited along with various other notes. I now began to write in earnest, and the first draft of Chapter 1 was finished by the middle of July.

A more light-hearted G&S-related event this year was the publication of the lavishly illustrated *Cookery à la Carte*, a collection of recipes from D'Oyly Carte performers past and present compiled by David Steadman and Melvyn Tarran. I contributed a pasta dish which I called Spaghetti Palmieri after the two brothers Marco and Giuseppe Palmieri in *The Gondoliers*.

I had two holidays this year. In May I paid a return visit to Berlin, Dresden (where I saw the rebuilt Frauenkirche, still a ruin when I was there in 1998, and had a sail on the Elbe on a paddle steamer much older than *Waverley*) and Colditz. In October I spent a few days in Fort William visiting places that I was not able to see when we were working in the West Highlands for Music in Hospitals: these included Glenfinnan and Mallaig. Also in October I attended a memorial service for Geoffrey Shovelton in his home town of Atherton. In November I was in Paisley Abbey again for a concert with Mark and Daniela Hathaway, but I didn't have to play the organ. This year's pantomime for the Parish Players was *Hansel and Gretel*. Throughout the year I continued to write in whatever spare time I had, often sitting up late after a hard day's work.

VII – 2017

There was little that was new in the way of work, but I was getting on with the book at every available opportunity. The first draft was finished by the middle of May, but there were many drafts before it was finally completed.

I had enjoyed the *GLOC 'n' Spiel* concerts, but like Walter Paul I had decided not to do any more: I now had quite enough work with organ playing and Music in Hospitals as my main sources of income. But I still kept in touch with GLOC, and I continued to attend their recently inaugurated annual Burns Suppers held in conjunction with the Glasgow Indoor Bowling Club at whose premises we had latterly rehearsed. I could also now continue with Scottish country dancing on Tuesdays.

Although there were plenty of individual concerts for MiH there were just five tours this year. With the bulk of these now in care homes the title of the organisation was changed to Music in Hospitals and Care (MiHC). In February I played for a workshop with Patricia MacMahon, my fellow-student at the RSAMD in the 1960s, who was now a well-known singing teacher. I also continued to give talks on my musical life. In March I spoke to a group of IBM retirees in Greenock (IBM had been one of the town's major employers after the closure of the shipyards and the end of the remaining sugar industry); in October I gave another talk to the WEA in Skelmorlie.

There was a further Gilbert and Sullivan Society Convention in Stockport in April; not for the first time I had to propose the toast The Immortal Memory of Gilbert and Sullivan. In May I went to my third Deutsche Sullivan Gesellschaft AGM which was in Leipzig. On this occasion we visited the Mendelssohn-Haus, the last remaining private residence of the composer, and I encountered an ingenious piece of technology that lets you conduct a recording by adjusting its tempo to your beat. I 'conducted' Mendelssohn's overture *A Midsummer Night's Dream*, but it was a bit unnerving. After Leipzig I spent a few days in Mannheim with Meinhard Saremba and Beate Koltzenburg, and we did some more sightseeing. This included a trip to Heidelberg which I had previously visited. Finally, in Frankfurt, and before catching a train to the airport, I sat in the famous Romerberg and had a glass of beer: mixing business with pleasure as always.

I had a holiday in Northern Ireland in August: this was a coach tour based in Belfast that included the Titanic Experience and a visit to the Giant's Causeway. I was also enjoying catching up with people I hadn't seen for many years: old school friends, and colleagues from the RSAMD and Glasgow University. Sometimes we would meet in Glasgow, but meetings were often further afield. I was used to driving long distances for work and I rarely found this irksome.

At the end of August there was a reunion of members of the Glasgow Arts Centre, an organisation founded by Iain Turpie who had been the principal music teacher in Glenwood School where I taught in the 1960s: Sandy Leiper had also been involved in this. There was no active G&S, but in October I went to *A Gilbert and Sullivan Gala* put on by Walter Paul. The pantomime in November (*Treasure Island*) was followed by a busy December with two MiHC tours, and another year came to an end.

VIII – 2018

In February I gave a talk to a WEA group in Renfrew; for MiHC there were a number of concerts but only four tours, one of them being our third visit to Skye.

The year was dominated by the completion of my book. After several drafts it was finally ready in May. Most of the Savoy Operas have a subtitle, and so I decided to call it *Nothing Like Work or Right in the D'Oyly Carte*. The first part, a quotation from *The Gondoliers*, was out of copyright, but the alternative title is from *The Dreaded Batter Pudding Hurler (of Bexhill-on-Sea)*, one of Spike Milligan's scripts for the famous radio series *The Goon Show*; as this was still in copyright I had to get permission to use it although this was granted readily enough by Norma Farnes, Milligan's long-standing, and long-suffering, agent and manager. I then had to find a publisher; after several rejections I turned to self-publishing. I had to send the text via the internet which I managed to do: sending the photographs that way was more difficult, but John MacLeod kindly helped me with this. The book was published later in the year.

In July I had another continental holiday. At first we stayed in Florence, with visits to Siena, Lucca (birthplace of Puccini and home to the Puccini Museum which I managed to visit) and Pisa (whose Leaning Tower I saw but didn't have time to climb). We then moved to a delightful walled hill town Colle di Val d'Elsa for the last few days; from there we visited Volterra (famous for its production of alabaster) and San Gimignano with its fascinating towers. There was also a visit to a vineyard. I was certainly making up for all the years when I couldn't afford to have holidays.

I saw a production of *Haddon Hall*, by Sullivan and Sydney Grundy, at the G&S Festival (now held in Harrogate) in August, and I went to another Sullivan Society Festival in Cirencester in September where I managed to persuade a few people to buy my book. Another pantomime (*Dick Whittington*) in November; another MiHC tour in December, and yet another year was over.

Finale

I – 2019

Work followed much the same pattern although there were just three tours for MiHC: these were based as usual in Aberdeen, Inverness and Newton Stewart. Organ playing continued too, but with one addition. I was one of four organists who took it in turn to play at a new crematorium near Largs. We each chose a specific day although this was interchangeable: my first service was on January 29. But there was not as much work as we had expected as there were now many changes in funeral services: some were humanist, and hymns were not always sung. The new building had a built-in system which enabled CDs to be played, and items sung or played by particular artists could now be requested: formerly, the organist had to play whatever was required.

The Parish Players could not do a spring show at the usual time, but they gave a single performance in May. Also in May there was another Gilbert and Sullivan Society Convention at Grim's Dyke, this one celebrating the Society's ninety-fifth anniversary; once again HRH the Duke of Gloucester was present. An effort had been made to assemble as many vice-presidents as possible, and there were nine of us, including Valerie Masterson, along with the Society's president Cynthia Morey.

I had two holidays this year. One in Staffordshire, again with Interesting Times, was called Pugin and the Gothic Revival (the Victorian architect Augustus Welby Northmore

Pugin is perhaps best known for his work in the Houses of Parliament). We saw a number of churches and the ruins of Alton Towers, once claimed to be the largest private house in England, to which Pugin contributed some interior decoration; it was also interesting to see the Theme Park. The second holiday was a river cruise on the Danube taking in Budapest, Bratislava, Durnstein, Melk (which Geoffrey Shovelton and I had passed on our hotels tour in 1984), and Salzburg and Vienna (both of which we had seen briefly): again, something of a whistle-stop tour although the cruising itself was very relaxing.

In September and October I gave talks to two further groups, both all-female, in Greenock; this was followed by the Parish Players' pantomime, *Cinderella* again, in December.

But another project was underway - the present volume. Part of my idea in writing *Nothing Like Work or Right in the D'Oyly Carte* was to give a strictly chronological account of the Company's last seven years from its centenary year in 1975 as no-one had yet done that. I hadn't intended writing anything else, but several people suggested that I should continue where I left off, and so I began writing this one in January. The first book's title and alternative title suggested the present ones although here neither is a borrowed quotation.

At the end of the year news began to reach the West of a strange new virus which had caused a number of deaths in a city in China that most of us had never heard of - Wuhan. Little did we know that it would change all of our lives, possibly for ever.

II – 2020

The first MiHC job was on January 3. I played the organ on the 5th, and I gave yet another talk on the 6th. I played for Billy Strachan at a function on the 10th, and I played at the crematorium on the 14th; I also did several sessions at the

Inverclyde Music Festival at the end of January. So far, this had been like most previous years although the continuing spread of the new virus was alarming: it had not been confined to China and was now in Europe, most noticeably in Italy and Spain.

As the honorary president of the Manchester Gilbert and Sullivan Society I gave a talk there at the beginning of February, and there was work for MiHC and organ playing throughout the month. But Covid-19 had now become a pandemic, and by the beginning of March Italy was in lockdown, closely followed by Spain. How long would it be before this happened in the UK? On March 13 (not inappropriately a Friday) Billy Strachan and I drove to Dumfries for MiHC to entertain a group of war-blinded veterans. They said that this would be their last meeting for some time as more and more cases of Covid-19 were being reported, and a lockdown in the UK seemed imminent. This was also our last job for MiHC. We had several dates in the diary for later in the month and further ahead, including a tour based in Aberdeen in June, but these were now cancelled.

On the following Sunday I played at the church in Glasgow, but I had been told that I didn't have to come if I was worried about the situation: like the crematorium they too had a system that could play CDs. We were not yet in lockdown, and so I decided to go, but there was very little traffic on the road, and the congregation was very small. That was my last service. Next, the Parish Players' spring show was cancelled; shortly after this the lockdown began, and any remaining work, including organ playing at the crematorium, also ceased. I had booked a cruise to Orkney, Shetland and the Faroe Islands in May, but, not surprisingly, this too was cancelled.

Covid-19 was tragic for many people, and the lockdown was also very frustrating for many more, but despite the loss of income the enforced idleness turned out to be useful for me as I was able to finish the book sooner than I had anticipated.

In retrospect I seem to have been something of a Tail-end Charlie. The conductor Isidore Godfrey was with D'Oyly Carte for over forty years, but I only managed the last seven. And even in the succeeding years there seemed to be a gradual lessening of interest in G&S itself. After D'Oyly Carte I had worked in variety and music hall, but these too were in their last throes; our Bentley concerts, which admittedly were trying to resurrect a moribund art form, also had a fairly brief existence. I think I should have lived in a previous era.

Whether there will be any more work, even if I survive to take it on, remains to be seen. With these thoughts in mind, the refrain of Clifton Bingham's *Such is Fame*, set to music by Gerard Francis Cobb in 1892, is perhaps an appropriate valediction:

> Heigh-ho, high and low,
> Sooner or later the shadows fall,
> The story is done,
> And the glory won,
> And the green earth covers us, one and all!

THE END

Index

G&S refers to 'Gilbert and Sullivan'. Page numbers in *italics* relate to photographs.

CPSIA information can be obtained
at www.ICGtesting.com
Printed in the USA
BVHW082343301121
622869BV00009B/335

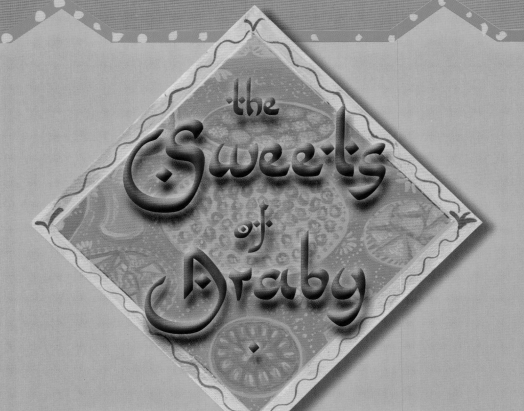

the Sweets of Araby

Leila Salloum Elias and Muna Salloum

illustrated by Linda Dalal Sawaya

The Countryman Press
Woodstock, VT

Illustrations © Linda Dalal Sawaya
Book design and composition by Sherry Melinda Charles

Library of Congress Cataloging-in-Publication Data have been applied for

The Sweets of Araby
978-0-88160-929-8

Published by The Countryman Press,
P.O. Box 748
Woodstock, VT 05091

Distributed by W. W. Norton & Company, Inc.,
500 Fifth Avenue, New York, NY 10110
Printed in China

10 9 8 7 6 5 4 3 2 1

For Mom,

who taught us that love is the most important ingredient of life.
The aromas from the kitchen—syrups being cooked, nuts being pounded,
phyllo dough being baked—these can never be replaced.
Yet the love that came with every piece of dough and every confection
that you prepared for us and for your grandchildren
will forever remain as memories of you, wife, mother, and "Sitty."
Mom continued the traditions of old Damascus, passed down from mother to
daughter for generations. She taught us too so they would never be forgotten.
And when she had her first granddaughter, Mom told her that the most
important commitments she would make would be to continue the
same cultural traditions and to take pride in who she was and where
she came from. Mom passed the torch to Jinaan; to her brothers,
Laith, Mazin, and Shaadi; and to her great-grandson, Bilal. Mom's love
was for her family and our heritage and it is because of her family's
profound love for their Sitty Freda that the torch will be carried on.

And also for our wonderful father, Habeeb,

who instilled in us the same strong sense of tradition as Mom and
encouraged us to move forward with our dreams. He, the scholar and writer,
is our inspiration; he embodies that in which every son or daughter takes pride.
He has been a great husband, father, grandfather, and now great-grandfather.
Dad has taught all of us how to be proud of and appreciate
our heritage as well as the country in which we live.

Contents

Introduction

Who would have thought that more than four thousand years ago, etched on clay tablets in the cuneiform alphabet, recipes were recorded for us by Baghdad's ancestors! Recipes for us! The tradition of good and healthy eating continued through the centuries and reached its golden age in medieval Baghdad. The culinary history carved into clay tablets became cookbook manuscripts in medieval times, and little did these culinary writers of Arab history know that one day two sisters in Toronto, Canada, would decide to re-create the delicacies of one of the world's most magnificent civilizations.

It hit us first as we roamed the streets of Damascus, the oldest continuously inhabited city in the world; then again as we walked the streets of Fez, the centuries-old colorful Moroccan intellectual center; and finally as we wandered through Córdoba, the historic capital of the glory that was Arab-Islamic Spain: these hidden treasures of Araby had been lost to the gastronomical world for centuries. We had a mission.

It was in these three cities that we delighted in the sweets of the *Arabian Nights*. Honey-succulent pastries, almond-filled fritters, phyllo dough oozing with rosewater or orange-blossom syrup, fried sesame treats, and pastries filled with sweetened cheese all had their roots with the Arabs, we learned. The Arab-Islamic conquests spread over more and more territories, and their foods arrived with them, with changes made here and there based on what ingredients were available. As the conquerors encountered new cultures, they absorbed new ingredients and added them to their traditional preparations, creating a kitchen of the proverbial thousand and one sweet delights.

When Dad and Mom returned from their first visit to Baghdad, in the 1960s, and spoke of the sweets they had feasted on, we tiny tots were in awe and jealous that they had partaken of, as they described it, "the sweets of Paradise." A decade later, our parents took us to the famous cities of the Arab world, and we finally tasted those delights ourselves. We ate, we savored, we enjoyed, we tried everything.

As our interests were piqued, we began to ask questions. How were these delicacies made? The women from the old country would smile and say, "It's a family secret." Even if we were lucky enough to find a cook willing to reveal a recipe, she gave measurements in units of palm-sizes or finger-lengths or even the occasional "just a little bit here and a little bit there." Unfortunately, Umm ʿAdnan's hand-size in Damascus was a great deal larger than Umm ʿUmar's in Fez, and Umm Ghassan, who explained to us what she considered to be a tiny tidbit of saffron, had arm wrestled with Dad and beat him soundly, so obtaining exact measurements was problematic for two sisters attempting to replicate, in a step-by-step manner, traditional recipes.

What were we to do? We were obsessed with the idea of telling the world about these delicious pastries; virtually nothing had been written about them in modern times.

Then we discovered a vast repertoire of medieval Arabic culinary texts, originating mainly in Baghdad, that taught one how to cleanse the hands, prepare utensils, set a table, decorate platters, chop and shape ingredients, and adorn with perfumes and spices the final dish. These books gave us the necessary rough measurements as well as poetry lauding the taste and beauty of each dish. Deeply enamored of certain desserts, people composed verses of praise and desire that, if you didn't know any better, you would swear were dedicated to a lover.

We grew up in Canada, a multicultural nation in which traditions and heritage play a great role. This was evident in our home life; our commitment to study and work was rooted in the pride of belonging to two cultures: the one into which we were born and the other from which we had come. Our grandparents were emigrants from Syria who had left their homeland to further their dreams of a better future. With them came their memories, traditions, culture, and food, and with them remained their pride in their origins.

So off to school we went and learned the history of the world. But something was missing. The great historical contributions and advancements of Arab civilization were mentioned only in passing in our schoolbooks. At home, however, the books we read and the conversations we heard reflected a world with a rich past. It was at home that we learned that many words in the daily English language, simple words related to the food we ate, derived from the Arabic: *rice, sherbet, sugar, saffron, syrup, coffee, julep,* and *marzipan.*

Our father was a human encyclopedia. For every question, he had an answer, especially for questions concerning Arab history and culture. He grew up on a farm in western Canada, and he knew that no matter what was planted, his mother would use it to present the family with the healthiest and most delectable of Arab foods. Sweets were a treat for him and his seven siblings. His father and mother often spoke of the multitude of delicious pastries in Syria that were enjoyed on festive occasions. Saskatchewan lacked many of the needed ingredients used to create these gems, so our grandmother devised new ways to reproduce the recipes.

Dad always spoke so highly of his mother's talent for creating feasts out of any food available that one day we rallied our courage and asked him, "If that was true, Dad, then how come you ran away to join the Royal Canadian Air Force?" He looked at us, obviously surprised. "Well," he said, "why do you think I came back home?"

And our mother cooked and cooked. From bread dough to the thinnest of thinnest phyllo dough, she kneaded and kneaded to satisfy a growing family. The holiday activity we remember best is watching her in the kitchen weeks before Christmas or Easter as she ground nuts and prepared syrups, clarified butter and pitted dates, in order to produce the most mouthwatering of desserts. Like her mother and others of her generation, she made everything from scratch. We remember well how we enjoyed the aroma of fresh-baked *sambūsak,* the shine of the syrup-laden *baqlāwah,* the crunch of the crispy *kunāfah,* and the taste of the rich, buttery, date-filled cookies called *maᶜmūl* that graced the kitchen counters over the years.

The neighbors enjoyed them as well. They would suddenly "drop by" when they smelled the fresh pastries, and they'd stay and revel in sweets whose recipes were centuries old. Once sated, they would comment on their sophistication and elaborate presentation, especially when compared with the standard brownies and chocolate chip cookies. In this way, Mom did the same thing as Dad: she used her culinary knowledge to make her audience better understand her heritage.

So why *The Sweets of Araby*? We'll give the credit to a discussion-turned-argument among good friends who hailed from Baghdad, Damascus, Fez, and Arab Spain, respectively. They were all sitting at our dining table, close friends who suddenly became antagonists as each satirized the others' desserts and lauded his own.

On this evening, after a feast of a meal, my mom's *baqlāwah* and *kunāfah* were placed on the table. Our Iraqi guest, Nabil, raved over the exquisite taste of the hot *kunāfah,* but insisted that Baghdad's desserts were the epitome of succulent sweets. Jamil, our friend from Damascus, wouldn't hear of it. "How can you say that? Can you beat the taste of *zunūd al-sitt?*" To which Mahdi, from Morocco, proclaimed, "Look, guys! If you really knew your sweets, you wouldn't even be discussing anything but Moroccan *zalābiyah!*" Our friend Fernando, of Arab Spanish ancestry, just shook his head and announced that he could not believe these guests of Arab origin didn't know their own culinary history. "*Amigos,* it's best that you read before you claim to know what's right!

Have you forgotten *qananīṭ*, those delicious tubular fritters that even traveled to Sicily and there became what we know today as cannoli?"

Watching them argue that their own homelands were the source of the best sweets, we decided then and there that there would be no more procrastination. We had to write a book of sweets to settle the debate.

It was Nabil, however, who gave the coup de grâce. "Look, it's very simple. There can be no argument. The best sweets are from Baghdad, my city, in which almost all of your sweets began, the city where the recipes were recorded in Arabic—just look at the stories in the *Arabian Nights*, stories that have traveled the world and carried with them the names of Baghdad's sweets! And he reached for a piece of Damascene *baqlāwah!*

We began our quest, delving into those medieval Arabic culinary manuscripts, with their detailed recipes, procedures, and instructions. *Unbelievable,* we thought as we turned the pages of a tenth-century cookbook written in Baghdad. Here before us lay the sweets that medieval Baghdadi society partook of, sweets we would bring to twenty-first-century tables.

We chose from six medieval Arabic manuscripts sweet delights that Scheherazade described in her tales for King Shahryar, stories she told to keep his interest and curtail his wrath against the unfaithfulness of all women. Our cookbook of sweets would be for people to use today to please their mates and families, just as Scheherazade did for her husband. It was an adventure for us. Our biggest problem was choosing recipes from the great index of desserts in the thousand-year-old manuscripts. Our next biggest problem, of course, was losing the pounds we gained after trying all of them!

We adapted each recipe to suit the modern kitchen. History that was once hidden now comes back to life.

As Scheherazade dazzled Shahryar with her stories, so we will attempt to dazzle, please, and seduce our readers with these sweets of Araby.

O king of time! O king of this palace and of my existence! Amidst the scents of ambergris and musk, of camphor and desire, tonight I present to you visions and tastes of what our forefathers took pleasure in and a promise that you, too, will enjoy . . .

Muna Salloum

Leila Salloum Elias

9

Qaṭr
(Sugar Syrup)

2 cups sugar

1 cup water

2 teaspoons lemon juice

1 tablespoon orange-blossom water
   or rosewater

❧ In a saucepan, stir together sugar and water then bring to boil over medium heat.

❧ Continue simmering for 10 minutes, then stir in lemon juice and allow to simmer for 1 more minute.

❧ Stir in orange-blossom water or rosewater.

❧ Reduce heat and keep warm.

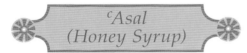

ʿAsal
(Honey Syrup)

2 cups honey

¼ cup butter

❧ In saucepan, pour in honey, then add butter.

❧ Bring to a boil over medium heat, stirring constantly.

❧ Reduce heat and keep warm.

Qashṭah
(Cheeselike Milk)

6 cups milk

1½ cups heavy whipping cream

4 tablespoons sugar

4 tablespoons rosewater

4 tablespoons orange-blossom water

1½ cups cornstarch

❧ In a deep saucepan, stir together 4½ cups of the milk and all the cream. Add sugar and mix well.

❧ Stir in rosewater and orange-blossom water; blend well.

❧ Over medium-low heat, continue to stir until liquid is heated through, almost hot to the touch.

❧ In a separate bowl, mix cornstarch and remaining 1½ cups of milk together. Stir until smooth, making sure there are no lumps in mixture. Add this mixture to the heated milk and continue stirring over medium-low heat until thick and bubbly.

❧ Remove from heat, pour into bowl, and let sit until cool. Refrigerate until ready to use, usually about 2 hours. This mixture will thicken as it cools.

❧ Excess qashṭah can remain refrigerated, covered with plastic wrap, for up to a week.

11

Scheherazade, Shahryar, and the 1001 Nights

The fragrance of musk and camphor mixed with the scent emanating from the candles of ambergris that were placed seductively around the bedroom chamber. The only light came from the moon, and it crept in through the layers of chiffon covering the windows. Scheherazade had taken time to prepare for her husband, King Shahryar, an ambience of romance, this being the one thousand and first night of their marriage. This anniversary was special, and dear, tenderhearted Shahryar deserved the best.

The soft, plush cushions, the reams of Damascus brocade and velvet, the soft silk from Mosul, the gold satin sheets upon the divans and couches, and the Baghdadi baldachin brocade of the bed's canopy would receive him well. Near where he would eventually lie amid the down pillows stood a table inlaid with mosaic and pearl; on it, she had placed two jewel-encrusted goblets filled with rosewater sherbet cooled to his liking.

She loved him dearly despite the anxiety of the past—the dreaded dawn of each day that could be her last. Deep within her heart, she had known that the stories she told would extend her life by a thousand and one nights. Had it been the first story or the last that had stirred Shahryar's heart to the passion of love? Had it been the tale of Aladdin or the one of the porter that had ignited the spark of the profound love he felt for her? She had become the very breath he inhaled, his morning and his night, the quenching of his thirst, the fulfillment of his desires.

Scheherazade did not want anything to change. Shahryar had asked her to begin to retell all the tales as a token of memory on this, their special anniversary, but she had devised a twist to how she would do so. She must ensure that his love for her became even more powerful. Starting tonight, she would serve with each tale a sweet from Araby that would please him even more.

Had not these confections been on the tables of caliphs and nobility? Had not the desserts of Araby, whether cakes stuffed with nut meats or dates, puddings, tarts, fritters, pies, or candies, retained their sumptuous and sophisticated texture, taste, and flavor for centuries?

In this way, Scheherazade would give him another set of nights to remember, presenting him with the bliss of *kunāfah, luqum al-qāḍī, kul wa ushkur, barad*, and so many others.

She rearranged the cushions, fluffing up each one and caressing it to smooth out the silken covers that Shahryar would soon lie upon. She loosened her veil slightly, so that when it was lowered it would allow her king to see a little of what lay covered. The atmosphere was seductive already, and the tray of sweets lying beside her added even more to the ambience. Sweet and succulent, dipped in a honey syrup, the cinnamon, the rosewater, and the pistachios of the *aṣābiᶜ Zaynab* could do nothing but lure him to her. She was ready to tell a story, and as Shahryar entered, Scheherazade lowered her veil and removed the cover from the tray of sweets.

"Come hither, my love! Here is what you asked. Here I am to obey your every command. Sit near me and recall the memories of the past as I feed you, from this tray, the sweets of Araby."

And so Scheherazade began. "Know, O king of mine, that when Sinbad the Porter sat with Sinbad the Sailor, he was seated at a feast of feasts. Oh, auspicious king, lay your head upon my lap and let me relate to you the story of one confection that Sinbad the Porter was offered . . ."

Aṣābiʿ Zaynab
and Sinbad the Sailor

There once was a poor porter in Baghdad known as Sinbad the Porter. One very hot day while he was carrying a heavy load, he entered a neighborhood where the pavement was sprinkled with rosewater. The fresh scent and the cool breeze enticed him to lay down his load. He sat his weary body on a bench near a large mansion to relax.

While resting, he heard singing and the sounds of musical instruments coming from within the estate. Looking through the gate, he saw a garden filled with flowers and trays of luxurious foods being set on tables. He saw that a grand feast was about to be served.

Assuming that some great prince lived there, the porter asked one of the servants passing by his bench to whom the house belonged. He was told it was Sinbad the Sailor's. He couldn't believe that two people with the same name could be so different. While Sinbad the Sailor lived in luxury like a king, Sinbad the Porter lived poor and miserably.

Feeling even more dejected, he got up, picked up his load, and whimpered about how life was unfair. At that moment, a servant approached and informed him that Sinbad the Sailor wanted to speak to him.

The porter was embarrassed. He tried to say no, but on the insistence of the servant, he accepted the invitation.

He went through the spacious gardens, into the dazzling mansion, and then he entered a grand sitting room to join the other guests. Lords and nobles sat at magnificent dining tables being entertained by beautiful maidens singing songs of love and pleasure. It was a sight that was fit for only a king and his royal entourage. Sinbad the Porter was in awe and at a loss for words.

The host, Sinbad the Sailor, asked the porter to repeat what he had complained about at the gate of his mansion. At first, the porter was embarrassed, but finally he was convinced that no harm would come if he repeated what he had said.

Sinbad the Sailor listened. He was moved by the porter's anguish, and in response told him how he had gained his fortune through his adventures and travels.

Before the tale began, however, Sinbad the Porter, having had his fill of an elegant meal, was served the most succulent of sweets, *aṣābiᶜ Zaynab*, which made him feel as royal as any prince or king.

So the porter listened to Sinbad the Sailor's tale, no longer filled with envy but relaxed and content. No matter how much fortune he had or did not have, as long as he could eat *aṣābiᶜ Zaynab*, he felt as rich as the other Sinbad. Really, food does make the man.

Christmas in our household was always celebrated with *aṣābiᶜ Zaynab*, translated as "the fingers of Zaynab," which we simply called *aṣābiᶜ*. When we were children, whenever we saw Mom's wedding rings sitting on the counter and cornstarch all over the kitchen table, we knew that she was stretching out her homemade phyllo dough to make this, one of her many exquisite sweets.

Although the source recipe calls for a specific dough for the fingers, we have opted for phyllo. In these fast-paced times, tradition continues but is now aided by ready-made ingredients that eliminate several time-consuming cooking tasks. Though Mom's homemade phyllo dough took a full day to prepare, she never complained because she knew the end result would be greatly appreciated by family and friends. She was the one who devised the renovation of this traditional sweet by using phyllo dough instead of the crispy-hard shell of centuries ago.

Although phyllo dough makes it a delicate pastry, the *aṣābiᶜ Zaynab* filling is quite rich, a mixture of almonds and pistachios. This type of stuffing has been around for centuries. In fact, in one thirteenth-century culinary treatise, pistachios, either shelled, toasted, or ground, were commonly used in a number of savory and sweet dishes.

Aṣābiᶜ Zaynab has not changed from the time it first appeared in history, centuries ago. These tubular, crispy, nut-filled sweet rolls look like what they are named for, the fingers of Zaynab, whoever she may have been. Because of their delicate formation, the appellation *fingers* serves well in this dessert's name.

Take pure white flour
and knead with a thin syrup. Put a little yeast
in it (or natron), an amount enough to make it rise.
Take cane tubes, the thinnest you can find, in the length of
your fingers. Grease them with sesame oil and coat them
completely with the dough. Fry them lightly in sesame oil.
Remove the pan from the heat. Remove the cane tubes and discard.
Take shelled pistachios and almonds in equal portions and
pound them and then mix pounded white sugar with them. Sprinkle
musk-scented rosewater over them. Knead and stuff the tubes.
Color them before frying, if desired. Fry until they are browned.
Toss in syrup or honey. Remove and use.

SOURCE: *Kanz al-Fawā'id*

Aṣābiᶜ Zaynab

About 35 pastries

INGREDIENTS

1 cup water

1 cup honey

2 tablespoons rosewater

1 cup coarsely ground pistachios

1 cup coarsely ground
   blanched almonds

1½ cups sugar

¼ teaspoon cinnamon

1 pound phyllo dough

1 cup melted butter

6 six-inch cannoli tubes

1 egg, beaten

Light sesame oil for deep-frying

❧ To make the syrup: In a small saucepan, mix together ¼ cup of the water and the 1 cup of honey. Bring to a boil over medium heat, stirring occasionally. Add 1 tablespoon of the rosewater, then reduce the heat to very low and simmer for 1 minute. Stir, then remove from heat and cover to keep the honey syrup warm.

❧ To make the filling: Stir together in a mixing bowl the pistachios, the almonds, the sugar, the cinnamon, and the remaining tablespoon of rosewater. Set aside.

❧ Cut the phyllo dough into 4-by-4-inch squares and cover with a slightly dampened towel to keep the sheets from drying out.

❧ Place two sheets on top of each other and brush the top sheet with the butter. Place a cannoli tube at an angle on the bottom corner of the phyllo square, then roll the dough over the tube. Seal to close by brushing with the egg, making sure the egg does not touch the tube.

❧ In a large saucepan over medium-low heat, pour in the sesame oil, enough to deep-fry the tubes. Once the phyllo tubes have turned a light golden color, carefully remove them with a slotted spoon and place them gently on paper towels, allowing them to cool slightly. Carefully remove the cannoli tubes from the fried phyllo and gently set the phyllo tubes aside.

❧ Once all the phyllo tubes have been fried, carefully and gently fill each from both ends with the filling. Gently dip each *aṣābiᶜ* in the honey syrup and place on a serving platter. The *aṣābiᶜ* should be laid side by side.

Luqum al-Qāḍī and the Porter

During the reign of Hārūn al-Rashīd there was a young man, a porter, who waited daily for his next opportunity to work. Despite his apparent bad luck, he was patient and of good humor.

One day, as he stood idly milling around, he heard a woman's kind voice asking for his help.

She was the essence of beauty, the perfection of femininity, and she caused him to breathe deeply as he took in her beauty. When she removed her veil, he saw that her hair was in plaits and that she had jet-black eyes and soft lashes. Here stood a woman of grace and beauty. He was struck by her. "Oh, what a happy day; oh, what glorious fortune for me!" he said to himself, taken by the woman who walked before him.

He picked up his crate and catered to her every whim and desire. First, they

stopped to purchase wine, which she placed in the porter's basket. "Lift this and follow," she said. He listened and obeyed. After all, God was kind in presenting him with both work and infatuation.

Next, at the fruit seller's shop, she purchased a variety of luscious fruits imported from every city of the Arab world, and these all were placed in the porter's basket. She ordered, "Hoist, O porter!" which he willingly did. He delightedly did everything he was told. Never in his life had he been offered such a blessed day as this.

And so it continued. From the butcher, the finest of cuts of mutton were placed in the basket; from the grocer, dried fruits and pistachios; and from the perfume seller, ambergris and musk and scented waters of rose, orange, and water lily.

Finally, they reached the bazaar of sweets, and from it rose the intoxicating aroma of fritters, tarts, and every type of honeyed and sugared patty there was to offer. Yet what he looked at most, even more often than he gazed at the picture of beauty before him, were the sweet balls of a delicacy that she had the confectioner place on an earthenware platter. These were the *luqum al-Qāḍī*, their golden color a reminder of the golden adornments of his beautiful employer.

Never in his life had the porter seen so many edibles at one time. As he carried the baskets laden with the tasty foodstuffs, the aroma of the *luqum* almost drove him mad with desire. He didn't know which he wanted more: the sweet or this woman of his dreams.

They reached his employer's home and entered the kitchen so the porter could put down the load. He removed the items from the basket and handed her the tray of *luqum*.

"You have carried out my wishes to a T. Your pleasure is now my pleasure. You may now enjoy that which you so desire. This is your payment for all that you have done."

She slowly removed her veil, revealing once again the darkest of sultry eyes, and while removing her cloak she exposed the perfect body that any man would crave. She reached out her hand to the shaking porter, and he reached out toward her. Each searched the other's eyes, their passion nearly at a point of no return. She sighed and he cried, "No! Not you but the *luqum* will be my reward!"

It was probably the name of the sweet that drew our attention. It translates to "tidbits of the judge," and evoked visions of a sweet catered to judiciary tastes, or so we thought. In fact, these sweets cater to the taste of anyone who enjoys eating morsels of syrup-dipped deep-fried dough.

What fascinated us is that this centuries-old dessert continues to be known throughout the Arab world. They are called simply *luqum* or, popularly, *ᶜawaymāt. ᶜAwaymāt* means "floaters" and the name comes from the fact that

as the tidbits are fried, they turn golden and then float to the surface of the oil.

We discovered that we didn't need a judge to declare a verdict on their quality, taste, and easy preparation.

In almost every one of the twenty-two Arab countries, these sweet balls are served for all occasions. Easy to make and delicious to eat, they are one of the most popular desserts in the Arab world.

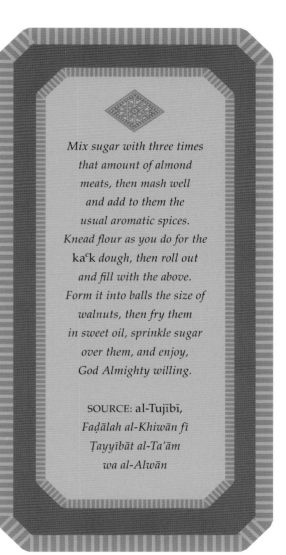

Mix sugar with three times that amount of almond meats, then mash well and add to them the usual aromatic spices. Knead flour as you do for the kaᶜk dough, then roll out and fill with the above. Form it into balls the size of walnuts, then fry them in sweet oil, sprinkle sugar over them, and enjoy, God Almighty willing.

SOURCE: al-Tujībī, *Faḍālah al-Khiwān fī Ṭayyibāt al-Ta'ām wa al-Alwān*

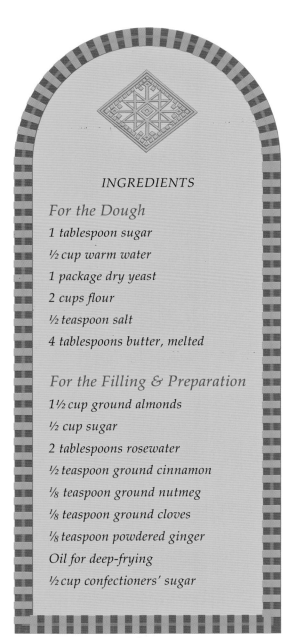

INGREDIENTS

For the Dough

1 tablespoon sugar

½ cup warm water

1 package dry yeast

2 cups flour

½ teaspoon salt

4 tablespoons butter, melted

For the Filling & Preparation

1½ cup ground almonds

½ cup sugar

2 tablespoons rosewater

½ teaspoon ground cinnamon

⅛ teaspoon ground nutmeg

⅛ teaspoon ground cloves

⅛ teaspoon powdered ginger

Oil for deep-frying

½ cup confectioners' sugar

Luqum al-Qāḍī

Makes about 3 dozen balls

❧ Dissolve the sugar in ¼ cup of the water, then sprinkle in the yeast and stir. Allow to sit in a warm place until the yeast begins to froth.

❧ Meanwhile, combine the flour and the salt in a mixing bowl. Make a well in the center, then add the remainder of the water and the yeast mixture. Knead well, adding more warm water or flour if necessary. Do not allow the dough to become sticky.

❧ Shape into a ball, then brush the entire outside of the ball with some butter, and place in a floured pan. Cover with a dampened cloth, then place in a warm spot and allow to rise until doubled in size.

❧ Make the filling by mixing all the listed ingredients except the oil and the confectioners' sugar, then set aside.

❧ Roll the dough to ⅛ inch thick, then cut into 3-inch diameter circles, cover, and set aside.

❧ Place 1 tablespoon of the filling in the center of each circle. Pull up the sides of the circle and close with dampened fingers to form a walnut-size ball.

❧ Heat 2 inches of oil over medium heat in a saucepan, then fry the balls until they turn golden. Remove with a slotted spoon and allow to drain on paper towels. When cool, dip each in the confectioners' sugar and place on a serving platter.

Luqum are best when served the same day.

Zalābiyah and Aladdin

Now Aladdin, who hailed from Arabia, was known for the indolence of his youth, the idleness of his adolescence, and his loitering with wayward friends. It was only with the appearance of the magician that his character changed. He had spent his life miserably poor, living with his mother on meager means. Then the young Aladdin took possession of the genie and the brass lamp.

It happened like this: One day, Aladdin was hanging out with his group of thieves when a stranger approached and introduced himself as Aladdin's long-lost uncle. Aladdin, stupefied by this news, took the stranger home to his mother. Unbeknownst to the boy and his mother, the stranger was actually a sorcerer who had an ulterior motive in mind.

After the magician promised Aladdin's mother that he would set the boy on the right track in life by opening a shop for him, he led Aladdin to a remote place and directed him to a cave. In it, he explained to the young lad, was Aladdin's successful future. There, if he avoided the traps and ignored the multitude of precious items, he would find an oil lamp.

Aladdin did as he was commanded, but he collected more than just the brass lamp; he also filled his pockets with the precious stones lying all over the cave.

23

Aladdin ascended with difficulty to the entrance of the cave, and the sorcerer attempted to seize the lamp without assisting Aladdin. It was then that Aladdin realized the evilness of the magician and thereupon escaped his clutches and got out of the cave, all the while hanging on tightly to the lamp and the jewels he had found.

At home he explained the trickery to his mother, and both bemoaned the vicissitudes of luck and fate that had befallen them. With no food or drink at home and, thanks to the false promises of the sorcerer, no established future for the lad, both mother and son retired, not knowing what the morrow would bring.

Aladdin may have been a lazy fellow but he was also a quick thinker. The next day, he grabbed the jewels, went down to the souk, and sold them. With this money in hand, he purchased enough food to last a week or more and went happily on his way home. En route, he passed by the women's bathhouse, and his old ways surged as he saw a latticed window on the wall. He peeked in and, lo and behold, he saw a vision of extraordinary beauty preparing for her bath. He was in love.

Food on the table was not enough for Aladdin. He had to have this girl, no matter who she was or from whence she had come.

By the time he reached his house, he'd become so forlorn and uncommunicative that even after his mother had set the dinner table with all the food, he had no appetite. She begged him to tell her what was wrong. No response. When he did eat, it seemed as if he was doing so out of habit and not out of the love of food. Even when his mother placed before him his favorite sweet, *zalābiyah*, Aladdin showed no interest.

Finally, he broke down and told her of his passionate love for the young girl he had seen at the bathhouse. Knowing that the girl must be of royal blood because of the entourage assisting her, Aladdin's mother promised to go to the king, as her son begged her to do, and ask for the girl's hand in marriage. Aladdin's mother kept her promise to her only son even though she knew the exercise would be futile.

Anticipating his mother's return with good news, Aladdin ate the *zalābiyah* as its lattice shape reminded him of seeing the girl through the lattice window of the bathhouse.

In the meantime, his mother received an audience with the king, contrary to the wishes of his vizier, who felt that allowing a woman of such peasant stock inside the palace would taint the entourage of the royal household.

The king, however, felt that his subjects all deserved the right of an audience if they so desired. He let her present her request.

Needless to say, the king was quite taken aback when Aladdin's mother asked for Princess Badralbudur's hand in marriage. It was the vizier who came up with the idea of handling the situation in a diplomatic way, but he did this for his own ulterior motives. Unbeknownst to the king, the vizier had long planned for the princess to marry his own son. The vizier had to play this right. He advised the king to ask for an exceedingly large dowry that included jewels, dinars, brocade and silken dresses for the bride and her ladies-in-waiting, and a palatial residence. The vizier smiled, knowing full well that this would be impossible for Aladdin to obtain.

The mother returned home, forlorn, with the bad news. She found her son excitedly waiting for her. She told him what had happened, and they both retired to their rooms, he never so depressed in his life.

For days he did not eat or sleep. No matter how much his mother urged him to forget his royal love, he continued to refuse food or sleep. Even the *zalābiyah* could not lure him out of his bed. He could not touch it because of the memory it brought back.

Early one morning Aladdin's mother came running into his room exclaiming passionately, "I've found a way to solve the situation! From the cave, you brought jewels that we sold. We still have this brass lamp. It looks old and could well be worth many dinars. I will shine it up and go to the souk to sell it. With the money, we will at least be able to present a small dowry."

Now Aladdin was alert. He watched as his mother began to bring the luster back to the old lamp. She rubbed and rubbed the antique piece, and suddenly a mist of smoke came out and, lo and behold, before them stood a giant genie.

With businesslike flair, the genie introduced himself to the shocked pair and explained that he was at their service and command to grant them whatever they so wished.

And thus was the beginning of Aladdin's tale, and the rest is history. It was thanks to the lamp that Aladdin was able to present himself to the king with the dowry requested and more, thereby allowing him to marry Princess Badralbudur and become the most beloved ruler of his people.

As for his love of *zalābiyah,* it increased more and more. Unbeknownst to anyone around him, he kept the genie at hand for those midnight snacks that a prince often calls for—his wife and the *zalābiyah.*

Take as much spiced flour as you want and knead it well. Then add water, bit by bit, until the water is absorbed into the flour. Let there be a sufficiency of leavening in it. After kneading it in this way, take enough sesame oil and put it in the tajine; *boil the dough until it is done, and then take it up.*

If you want it lattice shaped, take the dough that you have kneaded, put it in a pierced coconut, and make mushabbak *with it.*

If you want it yellow, color the flour with saffron; if you want it red, color the dough with wine lees, then fry and put it in musk.

It comes out excellently.

SOURCE:
The Description of Familiar Foods

On our first trip to Syria, when we were young children, we were introduced to this delectable lattice-style sweet at the home of an old family friend. It not only looked intriguing but was also absolutely scrumptious. Commonly known throughout the Arab East as *mushabbak*, its name in Morocco is *zalābiyah*, or "latticed sweet." It is a delicious, golden, deep-fried twisted fritter that allows the cook to demonstrate his or her artistic talents. The trick to making these fritters is being quick with the hands; the objective is to make each one a little different from the others.

Probably one of the most striking sights we ever witnessed was the trays of *zalābiyah* piled high in pyramid shapes in the ancient souks of many Arab cities. But the sweets are not only there—even in the most modern patisseries of the most up-scale neighborhoods in the biggest cities of the Arab world, these fritters continue their legendary status as a must on every dessert table. From the tenth century to today, these lattice-shaped crisps continue to be popular.

Zulābiyah

Makes about 30 pieces

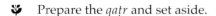

❦ Prepare the *qaṭr* and set aside.

❦ Mix the sugar in ¼ cup of the warm water and add the yeast. Cover and keep in a warm spot, allowing the yeast to rise for about 10 minutes.

❦ In a large mixing bowl, add the flour, the cornstarch, and the salt, and mix well. Form a well and add the yeast mixture, the remaining water, and the egg white. If using food coloring, add the drops. Beat with an electric mixer for 1 minute to make a smooth batter.

❦ Cover the bowl and let sit for 1 hour to allow the batter to rise. After it has risen, stir the batter. If the batter has thickened too much, stir in a little more warm water to maintain a crépe-like consistency.

❦ In a large saucepan, heat the oil over medium heat.

❦ Take a funnel, cover the opening with your finger, and spoon 3 tablespoons of the batter into the top of the funnel. Place the funnel over the saucepan, remove your finger from the hole, and allow the batter to drop into the oil as you quickly move the funnel in a circular motion and back and forth, creating a latticed-shaped form. Fry on both sides until golden brown.

❦ Remove from the oil and immerse in the *qaṭr*, making sure to cover both sides of the *zulābiyah*. Place on a serving platter.

INGREDIENTS
Basic qaṭr (sugar syrup
    recipe (see page 11)
1 tablespoon sugar
1¼ cups warm water
1 package yeast
1 cup flour
¾ cup cornstarch
⅛ teaspoon salt
1 egg white, beaten until stiff
Few drops food coloring,
    yellow or red (optional)
Oil for deep-frying

Kunāfah
and the Browbeaten Husband

In the great city of Cairo, there was a cobbler by the name of Maʿrūf who had a worthless wife named Fāṭimah. She did not treat him well. Whatever money he earned, he spent on her, fearing her wrath and vindictiveness. She gave him no choice but to cater to her every whim. If he did not, she would subject him to her cruelty. So it was that whatever little profit he made from patching his customers' worn shoes, his wife was rewarded. Life was miserable for poor Maʿrūf.

One day the humble cobbler's wife told him, "I want you to bring me this very night a vermicelli cake dressed with bees' honey." Poor Maʿrūf tried to explain that he did not have the money to purchase the *kunāfah*. His wife would hear of no such nonsense. He was to return only once he'd gotten the bee-honeyed vermicelli, otherwise she would make his night as "black as the fortune that befell you when you met me." Knowing God to be bountiful, the cobbler sadly got himself together, prayed the dawn prayer, and opened his shop.

However, this was not a good day for Maʿrūf. He had no customers. Anticipating that his evening would be worse than his day if he didn't do what he'd been told to, he once again pulled himself together and then went to the *kunāfah* seller's shop. Taking pity on Maʿrūf, the baker weighed five pounds of sugar-syrup-drenched *kunāfah* and allowed him to take it on credit as long as it was paid for in one or two days. The baker told him that the sugar-syrup *kunāfah* was even tastier than the kind made with bees' honey. Maʿrūf humbly took it, too ashamed to admit that it was not what he had been asked to get.

28

"Blessed be the baker who has compassion," Maʿrūf prayed as he fearfully but triumphantly approached his home. He would appease his wife with this *kunāfah* despite it not being prepared with bees' honey.

But his luck went as quickly as it had come. When Fāṭimah saw the *kunāfah* and realized that it was not what she'd wanted, she threw it in his face and then hit him so hard that his tooth fell out. He'd had enough, so he hit her on the head, and she clutched his beard and would not let go. The neighbors came when they heard his shouts for help and tore her off him.

"How disgraceful! What wife would not be pleased with her husband bringing home *kunāfah* even if it was made with sugar syrup?" they admonished her, and eventually they calmed her down, and peace was made between husband and wife.

But once the neighbors left, she refused to eat it. Poor Maʿrūf . He was so hungry that he dug into it. When she saw this she prayed that the sweet he so enjoyed would poison his body. But Maʿrūf could not stop eating. Poor, tenderhearted Maʿrūf then felt guilty and promised that the next day he would bring her the *kunāfah* made with honey that she preferred.

The next morning, after almost being beaten again by his wife and promising her again that he'd get her the sweet she wanted, he stopped at the mosque to pray. Then he went to his shop, and no sooner had he arrived than a couple of men from the judicial office showed up and informed him that the judge had ordered his presence in front of the court. Apparently, Fāṭimah had filed a complaint against her husband. To make matters worse, upon the cobbler's arrival at the courthouse, he saw a crying Fāṭimah standing before the judge, seeking compassion as she wiped away crocodile tears. She was bandaged and looked as if she had been beaten. The judge reprimanded Maʿrūf , who explained what had really happened. The judge reconciled the two. Taking pity on the man, the judge gave him a quarter dinar and sent him off to buy Fāṭimah the *kunāfah* made with bees' honey. She went one way, and he the other.

But today was not a good day for poor Maʿrūf either. The messengers who had commanded his presence before the judge arrived demanding payment for their services. They dragged him through the market until he sold his tools and gave them the proceeds as well as the quarter dinar the judge had given him, a total of half a dinar. They went on their way, and Maʿrūf sat, forlorn, now without money to buy the *kunāfah*.

And just when he thought things could not get any worse, two other men approached and demanded he appear before the judge because his wife had filed another complaint against him. Again, poor Maʿrūf found himself in front of a judge reporting the incident of the previous day. When the judge reprimanded Fāṭimah for having come to him with a settled matter, she lied and told the court that her husband had beaten her again, after the first judge's ruling. The second judge then made peace between the two and ordered Maʿrūf to give the message runners their payment. This Maʿrūf did and paid the messengers with his last half dinar. He returned to his shop more forlorn than ever.

As the cobbler was reflecting on the vicissitudes of fate, he was suddenly approached by a man who warned him to hide because, yes, once again Fāṭimah had complained, only this time to the high court. They were after him. Filled with fear and terror, Maʿrūf ran for his life, stopping only to buy some bread and cheese to take with him. It began to rain. His clothes were drenched, and he sought refuge in a mosque at the eastern gate of the city. There he found a deserted cell, and he entered to seek safety from the rain and from the wrath of his unbearable wife. Maʿrūf lamented. He cried, and tears streamed down his face. How could he get away from his demon of a wife? He implored God to help him reach some far-off country where she would never find him.

Lo and behold, a being tall in stature appeared before him and put fear into the soul of the cobbler. He identified himself as the Haunter, a spirit who had lived for two hundred years in the cell and in that time had never seen anyone enter. Maʿrūf's tears, his cry for help, and his weeping moved the Haunter. He asked the cobbler what was wrong.

Maʿrūf once again repeated his story and implored the Haunter to transport him to some faraway land to escape his wife's wickedness and the misery of his life.

"Then mount my back," the Haunter told him, and he flew with him from suppertime to daybreak and then set him down on top of a high mountain. Below was a city that was far, far away from the growling and the demands of a wife who was never satisfied.

Better yet, Maʿrūf realized, he would be able to enjoy *kunāfah* for the rest of his life, regardless of what sweetener it was made with. He learned that a wife scorned is a husband warned to run away to the farthest corners of the earth, where he will find, if not *kunāfah,* then surely a life of sweetness!

Kunāfah is a medieval Arabic term for very, very thin, almost paper-like sheets of dough. According to a thirteenth-century Syrian cookbook, it was prepared by pouring a thin batter of dough over heated Indian mirrors. This *kunāfah* dough evolved into the contemporary phyllo dough. However, the original *kunāfah,* though prepared in a sheet form, was cut into very thin strands resembling noodles or *rishtā*.

On one of our visits to Syria a few years ago, in a village south of Damascus, we saw women preparing *kunāfah* dough on mirrors over hot coals and then dripping it through a utensil with perforations at its bottom. The long and complicated process seemed unchanged from medieval times. It drew us in awe. Moreover, they made it look easy.

Kunāfah dough is used in many sweets in the Arab East. One popular dessert is made by shredding the dough into threads, rubbing them with melted butter, then placing a stuffing of cheese, *qashṭah* (see page 11), or walnuts or pistachios between two layers of the shredded dough. The original recipe calls for the *kunāfah* to be prepared on a stove; the contemporary version of *kunāfah* is baked in the oven. Whatever the choice, we guarantee it will be one of the most enjoyable, elegant, and royal sweets ever. *Elegant and royal?* one wonders. Well, it is said that on the advice of his physician, the first caliph of the Umayyad Dynasty ate *kunāfah* in the evening during Ramadan to satisfy his hunger after each day of fasting.

Take for each raṭl *of* kunāfah *a half* raṭl *of sesame oil. Put the oil in a pot. Light a fire beneath it until it boils. Take a* raṭl *of* kunāfah *and cut it up in pieces like noodles and throw it over the sesame oil and fry. Sprinkle over that a half* raṭl *of crushed white sugar and leave it until it is well absorbed. Then sprinkle over it a* raṭl *of honey and stir until its oil is separated and takes on a fragrance.*
In the meantime, crush almond and pistachio meats and color them with saffron. Add it to the kunāfah *and stir well. Add musk and rosewater while it is over the fire. Remove. It can be kept for a year without spoiling.*

SOURCE: *Kanz al-Fawā'id*

Kunāfah

Serves 8 to 12

❧ In a large saucepan, combine together the almonds, the pistachios, and the diluted saffron. Set aside.

❧ Pull apart the shredded dough and then cut into approximately 3-inch pieces and set aside.

❧ Heat the oil in a large saucepan until it boils, then add the *kataifi* and mix into the oil until all the dough is moistened. Stir-fry over low heat for a minute. Stir in the sugar, making sure to coat all the shredded dough. Then stir in the honey and cook over low heat, stirring constantly, for 5 minutes or until the honey is heated through.

❧ Pour the cooked *kataifi* into the nut mixture then stir in the cinnamon and rosewater. Cook over low heat for about 5 minutes, stirring occasionally, making sure that the nut mixture is distributed evenly. Remove from the heat and spread onto a large serving platter.

INGREDIENTS
½ cup coarsely ground almonds
½ cup coarsely ground pistachio nuts
⅛ teaspoon saffron dissolved
in ¼ cup of water
1 pound of **kataifi** *shredded dough*
(if frozen, thaw to room temperature)
1 cup sesame oil
1 cup sugar
2 cups honey
¼ teaspoon cinnamon
3 tablespoons rosewater

Kul wa Ushkur!
(Eat and Give Thanks!)

Caliph Hārūn al-Rashīd grew exceedingly restless one night and called for his vizier, Jaᶜfar, seeking advice on how to cope with the situation.

Jaᶜfar and the caliph discussed one idea after another; a servant boy named Masrūr was standing close by, and he began to laugh.

The caliph turned to Masrūr and admonished him. "Who are you laughing at? Are you making fun of me or have you gone mad?"

"O Commander of the Faithful! By God! I am in no way laughing at you."

The caliph was intrigued as to what was causing the boy to laugh.

Masrūr explained. "I just couldn't help it. You see, yesterday I was out for a walk and came to the banks of the Tigris. There I saw a group of people standing around a man. They were all roaring with laughter. I stopped and found that it was Ibn al-Karībī who was making them laugh. It just so happened that he came across my mind at the moment your highness was talking to the vizier. I beg that you not be angry with me."

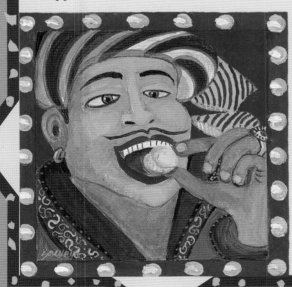

At once, the caliph ordered that Ibn al-Karībī be brought before him.

Masrūr ran to find the comedian and informed him that he was summoned to appear before the Commander of the Faithful. Ibn al-Karībī responded, "I hear and obey."

"Not so fast!" a quick-thinking Masrūr replied. "I want you to promise that whatever the caliph gives you, you will receive a quarter of it and I the rest."

Ibn al-Karībī did not agree. "No, you and I will each share half."

33

Masrūr disagreed. "No, I will take three-quarters."

Finally, Ibn al-Karībī declared, "You will have two-thirds and I the other third." Masrūr agreed and they set off to the palace.

When Ibn al-Karībī was brought forth into the presence of the caliph, he greeted him in the respectful manner of a subject to his ruler, wishing long life and happiness for the caliph and his household. He saw the elegance of his surroundings, the cushions of brocade and silk, the gold and silver adornments, the dining table filled with embellished platters of sweets and puddings. The caliph was in the midst of eating one of Baghdad's favorite desserts, *kul wa ushkur*, which would have put a smile on anyone's face; anyone's, that is, except, on this restless night, that of the caliph. Ibn al-Karībī realized he had a mission to accomplish.

Hārūn al-Rashīd warned him. "If you don't make me laugh, I will give you three blows with this bag."

Ibn al-Karībī looked at the bag and said to himself, *This is really no big deal. That bag wouldn't hurt a fly. Lucky for me he did not threaten me with a whip!*

The comedian began his monologue of jokes and funny stories. Anyone in the world would have found him funny, anyone else would have been bent over in laughter, but this evening, the caliph did not. There was no laugh and not even a smile. All the ruler did was continue to eat the *kul wa ushkur*.

Ibn al-Karībī was surprised, then annoyed, and finally frightened.

The caliph stood and announced, "You have earned the beating." Whereupon he hit the comedian with the bag, which turned out not to be empty at all. Instead, two pounds of stones came down on his neck, and it hurt so much that Ibn al-Karībī cried out. At the same time, he remembered his pact with Masrūr.

"Wait, O Commander of the Faithful! Let me say something before you continue. Masrūr made an agreement with me that whatever payment you give me for my performance, I take but one-third and he takes the rest. I have had my share and now it is his turn. Here he is, ready to receive his payment!"

At this, Caliph Hārūn al-Rashīd fell over in laughter and dropped the plate of *kul wa ushkur*, and then he ordered that each man be paid one thousand dinars.

Ibn al-Karībī picked up the sweet and looked at it. Never in his entire life had he wanted to eat and give thanks as much as he did just then.

Ibn al-ʿAdīm, a member of the sultan's royal family, included this delicacy in the haute cuisine of his time. However, when we first saw the name of this sweet in a thirteenth-century cookbook from Aleppo, we skipped over it, thinking only that it was very interesting that this same dessert was popular throughout Syria and Lebanon today. So we flipped through more pages, seeking something more unique, whether in name or preparation.

Then we thought that, out of respect for our mom and our grandmother, the latter of whom hailed from Damascus, we should pay tribute to this flaky and crispy dessert that came from Sitty's land of origin.

We called in Mom and asked her if she wanted to join us in preparing this sweet. She said sure but made it clear that there was no need to refer to the medieval recipe since she knew her recipe by heart. "No problem," we responded, and she proceeded to make her *kul wa ushkur*, which, of course, turned out absolutely scrumptious. Using Mom's measurements and methods, we referred to the original recipe so we could translate and adapt it.

Well, what a surprise! Mom's *kul wa ushkur*, which she learned how to make from her mother, was completely different than the one described in the thirteenth century. Mom's version is a rolled phyllo dough that is stuffed with mixed nuts, sugar, and rosewater, baked, and then drenched in syrup. The medieval recipe involves a dough that is wrapped, cut, and fried, then covered with syrup and pistachios.

What we learned from this culinary exercise was that everything changes. Time, place, and circumstances lead to innovations and alterations. What was there at the beginning, however, remains a part of the contemporary version, and the good news is that both versions are absolutely delicious!

Make a dough by mixing flour with butter and kneading with water. Roll out as in the manner mentioned previously (with a rolling pin) with butter. Roll the dough over the rolling pin, then remove the dough from it and stand it upright. Cut into rounds. Fry in sesame oil. Put on it sugar and syrup.

SOURCE: Ibn al-ʿAdīm, *Kitāb al-Waṣlah ilà al-Ḥabīb fī Waṣf al-Ṭayyībāt wa al-Ṭīb*

Kul wa Ushkur

Serves 8 to 10

INGREDIENTS

Basic qaṭr (sugar syrup)
recipe (see page 11)
1 package phyllo dough
(1 pound)
1 cup clarified butter, melted
Oil for deep-frying
¼ cup sugar

❧ Prepare the *qaṭr* recipe using rosewater and allow to cool.

❧ Remove the phyllo dough from its package. Divide the dough in half. Put aside one half of the dough and cover with a slightly dampened cloth.

❧ Take the other half of the phyllo dough, remove one sheet, and place horizontally on a flat surface. Brush it lightly with the butter. Take another sheet and place it over the buttered sheet and butter that one lightly. Continue the process until all the sheets are done. Do not butter the final sheet.

❧ Put a rolling pin dusted with flour on the left side of the horizontal phyllo layers and roll the phyllo over it, turning it carefully until the phyllo reaches the right side, making sure that the rolled phyllo sheets are not too tightly wound around the rolling pin.

❧ Gently pull the rolling pin from the phyllo. Carefully, slice the roll into 3-inch rounds and place on a tray until ready to fry.

❧ Take the other half of the phyllo dough and repeat the same process.

❧ In a large saucepan, add the oil and heat it over medium-low heat. Carefully place the rounds, two or three at a time, in the oil and deep-fry until the dough begins to turn golden. The rounds will separate in the oil as it is frying, creating a series of rounds.

❧ Remove with a slotted spoon and place on paper towels to soak up any excess oil. Transfer to a serving platter. Continue with the remaining rounds until all the rounds are fried.

❧ Pour the cooled syrup evenly over the rounds, then sprinkle with the sugar.

Al-Sanbūsak al-Mukallal and Shakashik

There was once a young man by the name of Shakashik, otherwise known as the barber's sixth brother. After suddenly finding himself without money, he began to wander the streets of Baghdad, begging for alms to stay alive.

One day, he came upon a mansion of exquisite beauty and extreme size. He was told that the owner was of the well-known Barmaki family. Shakashik was hungry. He wanted to eat and thus got up his nerve and knocked at the door. He asked for help and was kindly invited to enter. There, in the entry hall, he met Barmecide, the owner of the house.

Barmecide was in shock, in total disbelief that in this day and age in Baghdad, a city of affluence and grandeur, a peson would suffer hunger. "Such a disgrace!" the concerned man exclaimed. He invited Shakashik to dine with him.

The host called for the servant to bring the basin and ewer so that his guest could wash up before the meal. The servant appeared, but the water and cleansing utensils did not. The host began to wash his hands and face with what seemed to Shakashik to be invisible items. Despite Shakashik's bewilderment, he played along, anticipating that this was a ruse before the elegance of a feast.

Yet it continued. Shakashik, whose hunger was pounding away at his stomach, pretended to enjoy each invisible entrée as his host called for the tender and moist meat dishes, the fattened chicken stuffed with pistachios, the bread, the *harīsah*—that famous dish of succulent meat pudding—the marinated stew of *sikbāj*, and then the dried fruits, all invisible but apparently being enjoyed one by one by Barmecide. Shakashik's hunger was not a deterrent to his pretending to savor the invisible cuisine, explaining after being told to eat more, "O my lord, one who hath eaten of all these dishes cannot be hungry!"

Then, the ultimate food was announced. "Bring in the sweets!" the host cried to his servant. The barber's sixth brother was invited to eat the luscious but invisible *al-sanbūsak al-mukallal*. Shakashik's mouth watered for these sweets.

It was almost too much to bear, especially when Shakashik's host declared that he had asked that *al-sanbūsak al-mukallal* be prepared in the manner that he liked best—a dinar's weight of musk in every honey fritter and half that quantity of ambergris.

So it was that poor Shakashik had to suffer more, pretending to enjoy that for which he longed. That is, until he decided to turn the tables on his host. When presented with the invisible wine, Shakashik drank a great deal; the cuff he gave his host he blamed on drunkenness and intoxication.

Barmecide reacted with laughter, exclaiming that never before had he met anyone with such patience, humor, and wit. Then he ordered Shakashik a real feast, and the starving young man was able to satisfy his hunger and bask in the delight of *al-sanbūsak al-mukallal*.

As the host and his guest lay back on their cushions, sated with the night's feast, Shakashik pondered life's mysteries: one may see a jackass standing before him, but in the end, the jackass that apes the bigger jackass turns out to be king of the jungle.

Al-sanbūsak, also known as al-sanbūsaj, was popular in early-ninth-century Baghdad, described then as a stuffed pastry. Another reference to it appears in a tenth-century work, where it appears to be fried dough stuffed with meat, onions, and spices. In the original source recipes, both versions appear: al-sanbūsaj with a meat stuffing and al-sanbūsak al-mukallal with a sweet nut stuffing.

One evening, after we'd served a five-course meal, we removed the plates from the table and announced that it was time for dessert and that everyone should get into the mode of medieval Baghdad. Excitement among our guests reached a fever pitch. Which sweet would they be tasting this time? We brought in the dessert dishes and proclaimed, "The sanbūsak al-mukallal is on its way!" Our guests turned and looked at one another, perplexed by the announcement. "But we just ate our fill of dinner! Why would you bring out another main course?" That's when we realized that the al-sanbūsak al-mukallal had evolved to mean meat-filled turnovers.

In medieval times, the most popular shape of al-sanbūsak al-mukallal was triangular, but over the centuries, creativity in the kitchen led to innovation. Today, we find them in either triangular or half-moon shapes. In medieval Andalusian recipes, the dough was shaped into the forms of oranges, apples, or pears.

The Arabic term mukallal means "crowned," so royalty comes to mind with this dessert. And maybe that's why our dinner guests cleaned the plate of al-sanbūsak al-mukallal and announced that the meal they had just eaten had been topped off with a dessert fit for a king.

As for al-sanbūsak al-mukallal, *that is the bread stuffed with sugar and tempered with ground almonds instead of meat. Fold it and fry it in sesame oil; take it out when done and place it in syrup. Then take it out of the syrup, dry it, sprinkle it with finely milled sugar, and eat. The thin flatbread of this variety should be made without salt.*

SOURCE:
The Description of
Familiar Foods

Al-Sanbūsak al-Mukallal

Makes about 25 pieces

INGREDIENTS

Basic qaṭr (sugar syrup) recipe
(see page 11)

2 cups flour

1 tablespoon sugar

2 tablespoons unsalted butter,
softened

½ cup warm water

1½ cups ground almonds

1 cup sugar

1 tablespoon rosewater or
orange-blossom water

Oil for frying (either light sesame
or vegetable oil)

Confectioners' sugar (optional)

❧ Prepare the basic qaṭr recipe and set aside.

❧ In a mixing bowl, place the flour and the sugar and mix well. Add the butter and the water, and knead into a soft dough. Cover and let rest for a half hour.

❧ While the dough is resting, in another bowl stir together the almonds, the sugar, and the rosewater or orange-blossom water to make the filling.

❧ Roll the dough to a ⅛-inch thickness, then use a pastry cutter to make rounds about 3 inches in diameter. Roll out each circle with a rolling pin, then place 1 level tablespoon of the filling in the center of each circle. Fold to form either a triangle or a half-moon shape:

Triangle Shape: Pull up the two opposing sides of the circle over the filling and pinch together, starting from the middle and going to the ends. Lift the bottom edge up and pinch it to the middle, forming a triangle. Pinch again along the three seams to ensure they are sealed well.

Half-Moon Shape: Pull up one side of the round and pull over the filling, forming a half-moon, then pinch the edges together to ensure the edges are sealed well.

❧ Fry the *sanbūsak al-mukallal* in the oil over medium heat until both sides are golden. Dip immediately in the syrup for about 30 seconds, then place on a tray to cool.

❧ Once the *sanbūsak al-mukallal* has cooled, you can dip each into confectioners' sugar, then arrange on a platter for serving.

Ka^ck
and Shattered Dreams

There was once a simple and devoutly pious man who lived in a simple house and lived a simple life. He was supported by one of the town's nobles. Each and every day, he would receive from the nobleman three *ka^ck* and a little clarified butter and honey. This was his daily sustenance and it satisfied his hunger.

But alas, every man—no matter how devout—dreams of more.

The *ka^ck* he ate daily, relishing it for his breakfast, lunch, and dinner. As for the butter, he realized how expensive it was. He decided to collect each drop that he was given and put it into a jar. He hung the jar from the ceiling for safety, so that no one and nothing would touch it. Every day he placed the clarified butter in the jar and then devoured the *ka^ck* and honey.

One day, sitting on his bed, his staff in his hand, his mind began to wander. He looked at the jar and recognized its value. Although this was a man of goodness and devotion, he, like any human being, dreamed of better things.

Thus began his flight of the imagination. He closed his eyes and pondered. "Thank goodness for the *ka^ck* for, as a result of these biscuits, I have accumulated enough butter to sell for the price of a ewe and then take into partnership a farmer who has a ram! In the first year the ewe will bring forth a male and a female lamb; then, in the second year, a female and a male. These female lambs will eventually bear other males and females, until there is a great number. Subsequently, I will be able to take my share."

He smiled and said to himself, "With the males, I will be able to buy cows and bulls. These will increase and swell in number and become many. Upon selling these, I will buy a piece of land and build a luxurious palace on it with a beautiful garden. Additionally, I will don extravagant robes and clothing. I will purchase servants and slave girls and then find a woman to marry and put on a wedding the likes which no one has ever witnessed. I will slaughter cattle and make the finest of feasts with rich meats, elaborate dishes, and sweets beyond belief, including *ka^ck*. After all, I must give credit where credit is due, for without them I would have been given no butter!"

He continued to muse, his thoughts turning now to the musicians, singers, and entertainment he would provide. "I will decorate the halls with flowers and perfumes. I will adorn this feast with the most lavish of décor. I will then invite everyone, from the wealthy to the destitute, the religious men and the religious scholars, captains and lords, the important and the petty. Anyone who so desires will be my guest!

"Finally, I will go to my bride and unveil her and revel in her beauty. It is then that I will sit back and say that the time for devotion has passed; I will rejoice in the birth of my new son. I will make banquets in his honor and teach him the disciplines of life: philosophy, mathematics, science, and culture. I will rear him to be polite and well mannered, of good repute, so that he will become famous among the learned and will be well respected. He will learn piety and righteousness, and I will bestow on him the gifts of affluence and status. Yet if I find him to be disobedient, I will punish him with this staff!"

As he said this, he raised his hand as if to punish his son, and the staff hit the jar of butter that hung from the ceiling above his head. It broke, and the pieces of pottery came crashing down, as did all the dreams before him. The butter that had made his future ran down his head and onto his beard and his ragged clothing.

Perhaps counting chickens before they hatched would have been a lot safer than adding up drops of butter.

What could be more exciting than re-creating what food historians who specialize in Arab cooking consider one of the most ancient baked products? *Ka^ck*: the name itself, whether it's Aramaic or Egyptian, indicates the ancient nature of this biscuit.

In the medieval sources we find *ka^ck* shaped in various forms: rings, rounded cookies, even fruits and birds. Their texture is crispy on the outside and flaky inside. In some cases, the dough contains an interesting combination of spices, forming a not-too-sweet bread. Although the biscuit was popular in the Arab world, the Western kitchen also felt its effects. Because of the Arab-Muslim conquest of Spain, the Crusades, and the developing spice trade, the cooking techniques and ingredients of the Arabs spread into northern Europe. The introduction of new spices to the West came about because of the Arabs, so here's something to consider: *cookie* and *ka^ck* have the same consonants —could there be a connection?

Although the ancient recipe is for a stuffed *ka^ck* with a filling of *sawīq* (which was a barley-based product for the poor and a wheat-based mixture with sugar, almonds, or even pomegranates for the affluent), we have chosen to make the plain *ka^ck*. The plain *ka^ck* recipe is similar to a western Arabic recipe found in the 13th century *Anonymous Andalusian Cookbook*, in which it is explained that oil is preferred over butter, as it keeps longer when people are traveling. Since we had no travel plans in mind, we stuck with the butter, which we also felt would be tastier.

We include this recipe partly out of nostalgia. Whenever we walked into Sitty's house, we smelled the aroma of fresh-baked *ka^ck* coming out of the oven. Sitty was the perfect grandmother. She always seemed to know when we would be there; no matter what time we arrived, let alone what day, there were dozens of freshly baked sweet *ka^ck* waiting for us. She made sure that we got to put on the last touches, dipping them into the sugar-based syrup.

Although the original recipe calls for the *ka^ck* to be fried, we found it impossible to do so, as the dough for these cookies is similar to pie dough and very flaky; the dough pieces completely disintegrated while frying in the sesame oil. We then decided to bake them, and—lo and behold—success: a flaky and melt-in-the-mouth cookie! However, according to Leila's husband, we shouldn't have made them at all; our *ka^ck* had ruined his entire diet. Nonetheless, in his opinion, these were the tastiest of all the medieval sweets.

We replaced the musk in the original recipe with ground anise seed, for the sake of easier availability.

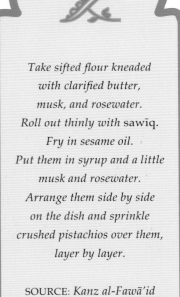

Take sifted flour kneaded with clarified butter, musk, and rosewater. Roll out thinly with sawīq. *Fry in sesame oil. Put them in syrup and a little musk and rosewater. Arrange them side by side on the dish and sprinkle crushed pistachios over them, layer by layer.*

SOURCE: *Kanz al-Fawā'id*

43

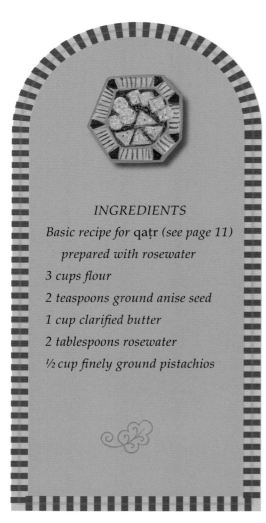

INGREDIENTS

Basic recipe for qaṭr (see page 11)
prepared with rosewater

3 cups flour

2 teaspoons ground anise seed

1 cup clarified butter

2 tablespoons rosewater

½ cup finely ground pistachios

❧ Prepare the *qaṭr* and set aside to cool in a shallow bowl. Place the flour and anise seed in a bowl and mix well. Add the butter and rosewater and work them into the flour mixture by hand to form a soft and pliable dough.

❧ Preheat the oven to 375 degrees.

❧ On a floured surface, roll out the dough to ¼-inch thickness, flouring the rolling pin every so often.

❧ Cut into rounds, triangles, squares, or rectangles. Excess pieces of the dough can be gathered up and rolled again. Carefully and gently transfer the dough cutouts to an ungreased baking tray.

❧ Bake the *ka^{c}k* for 14 minutes or until the bottoms turn golden. Place under broiler for about 2 minutes or until tops are golden. Remove the tray from the oven and allow to sit for about 2 minutes. Carefully and gently remove the *ka^{c}k* from the tray with a flat metal spatula, and then place the *ka^{c}k* in the syrup, gently pressing them down to ensure the *ka^{c}k* is immersed in the *kaṭr*. Remove the *ka^{c}k* from the syrup with a slotted spoon, allowing the excess syrup to drain off. Place the *ka^{c}k* in a serving dish.

❧ Once all the pieces have been arranged on the platter, sprinkle with the ground pistachios.

Barad –
the Hail of Love

Sayf al-Mulūk set out on his quest to find the love of his every breath and desire, Badīᶜah al-Jamāl. It was the *barad*, the hail of a torrential rainstorm, that had caused the onset of Sayf's torment, which wouldn't end until he found the one he sought.

When Sayf al-Mulūk was named crown prince, his father gave him a special present: a tunic made of the fabric worn by genies, those spirits that can be either good or bad. As Sayf spread it out he saw, on the lining of the cloth, a portrait of a girl, delicately embroidered in gold. Oh, how wonderful her loveliness, how boundless her beauty! The moment Sayf set eyes on the image of the girl, his mind left him and he became almost mad with love for her.

So it was that the days and weeks passed while he wept and lamented, beat his face and breast, and fell to kissing her likeness upon the tunic. From these wailing utterances of a lovesick man, his vizier and boon brother, Saᶜīd, finally learned from what malady he suffered. Sayf bemoaned:

> Had I known the assault that love takes on
> I would have, by God, made my armor strong.
> Unprepared was I for this thief of soul
> I knew not to guard from love's hold.

45

They discovered that the girl in the portrait was Badīʿah al-Jamāl and that she was of this world and lived in Babel City in the Garden of Iram. The lovesick prince and faithful Saʿīd brought forth the merchants, fakirs, travelers, pilgrims, and paupers to ask them the whereabouts of this city and the garden. But alas, to no avail.

Sayf's father was distraught. What was wrong with his son? All the physicians he summoned could not restore the health of the young prince. Finally, one of them announced, "O King of the Age, your son is in love." There was no cure for this malady if he could not have his love with him. Nothing would divert his mind without his beloved.

A suggestion was made that the prince travel to China to ask of the garden. Sayf and Saʿīd set sail on the vast ocean with a number of their men. The waves were high, the winds strong. A storm arrived. The hail hit the sails hard; both the rain and the hail came down in a vicious way. For twenty days, the sea bubbled from the cruelty of the wind. All were drowned except for Sayf al-Mulūk and some of his servants, who saved themselves in a small boat. Sayf was nearly inconsolable when he discovered his brother Saʿīd was among those missing.

The boat landed, and then the drama of the unknown unfolded. Going from place to place, Sayf and his men met up with strange beings who tried to slaughter them or imprison them. Years went by, and Sayf came near the point of accepting what God and fate had decreed for him. Sometimes Sayf and his men escaped, but every day Sayf lost more of his men. Finally, Sayf was the only survivor.

Then one day, Sayf reached an island. Apes bigger than he-mules surrounded him and directed him to a castle made of gold and silver bricks; within it were rare jewels and precious stones such that the tongue could not describe. There he met a prince who wined and dined him for thirty days, pressuring him to remain and one day become king of the island. But Sayf was set on accomplishing that which he had set out to do—finding the love of his life, the hint of breath that made him breathe and continue to live.

Sayf left and continued to climb over hill and dale. He had just decided to turn around and retrace his steps back when he spied before him a tall palace. He went inside, and in the great hall with its silken carpets there was a throne of gold upon which sat a damsel whose face shone like the moon. Royally dressed, she sat as a bride on the night of her presentation. Before her lay forty trays spread with gold and silver and dishes full of dainty types of delicious food. The crown prince greeted her. She asked of him,

"Are you human or a genie?" Sayf answered, "I am a man of the best of mankind, for I am a king, son of a king."

The princess told him her story. She was the daughter of the king of India and had been kidnapped by the blue king of the genies, who had seen her and been taken with her beauty. Every Tuesday he came there simply to look at her and have her in his presence. She did not even try to escape, as he had told her that her homeland lay 120 years away.

Sayf then revealed his story and the mission he had set out to accomplish. Upon hearing the name Badīʿah al-Jamāl, the beautiful princess began to cry, the tears flowing from the memories brought up by her milk sister's name. Sayf realized that something had to be done, and so it was that the princess informed him that the blue king's soul must be destroyed for them to escape imprisonment. They sought it out, destroyed it, and from the doors of the palace, they made a raft upon which to sail. They drifted and landed at a port, and lo and behold, it was in the city of her uncle.

It was there that the crown prince found the long-lost Saʿīd. It was also there that Sayf met the eye of his desire, Badīʿah al-Jamāl. They were married, and their wedding feast, as he had instructed, included a huge tray of *barad*, which ultimately became their special sweet.

If it was the *barad* of the torrential storm that began Sayf al-Mulūk's adventure, then it was the *barad* of culinary sweetness that ended their quest for love.

Throughout the new kingdom banners were hung and the new proclamation issued: *Rain, rain go away, barad's barad are here to stay.*

Its preparation is to take the best of fine white flour and to make it into a batter. Leave it until it rises. Then place a large brass pot on the fire and put sesame oil in it. When it boils, spoon the batter out with a perforated ladle and stir quickly so that whenever a drop of batter is dripped in the sesame oil, it hardens. As each piece is cooked, scoop it out with another perforated ladle and drain it of the sesame oil. Take the required amount of honey and dilute it in rosewater and place it over the fire until it boils and has reached the right consistency. Remove it from the fire. Beat it while it is in the pot until it turns white. Then throw the barad *in it. Place the mixture on a thin greased tile, collecting it together into the shape of the mold. Cut into pieces and eat.*

SOURCE: al-Baghdādī,
Kitāb al-Ṭabīkh

Barad are little beads of crispy fried dough immersed in honey and baked together to form a hail of delight!

It takes some time to prepare the *barad*, but the time and effort are well worth the end result. It is a dessert that is very sweet but extremely light to the palate. One wonderful way to enjoy it is to serve it with mint tea.

Barad is similar to the popular cereal squares made nowadays with marshmallows.

INGREDIENTS
1 package dry yeast
*   (¼ ounce)*
1 tablespoon sugar
2¾ cups warm water
2 cups flour
Sesame oil or olive oil
*   for frying*
2 cups honey
3 teaspoons rosewater

Barad

Yield: Fills a 10″ x 14″ baking pan;
cut to desired number of pieces.

❦ Dissolve the yeast and the sugar in ¼ cup of the water and cover. Let stand until the yeast begins to froth (about 10 minutes).

❦ In a bowl, mix together the flour and the remaining water until smooth. Add the yeast mixture and stir until well blended. Cover the bowl with a towel and allow to sit for 1½ hours.

❦ In a medium frying pan, add oil to about 2 inches deep and place over medium heat. Pour the batter through a large perforated spoon or a large cooking spoon with holes in it so that the batter drips through, forming small balls in the oil. Fry until golden and drain on paper towels. Continue until all the batter has been fried. Allow to cool completely.

❦ In a deep, medium saucepan, over medium heat, mix the honey and the rosewater and cook, stirring constantly, until bubbles form. When the honey begins to foam, lower the heat, stir, and simmer for 5 more minutes. Remove from the heat and immediately beat the honey by hand until its consistency is similar to whipped butter and it turns a golden yellow.

❦ Fold the fried balls into the honey, coating them carefully, then immediately spoon into a buttered 10 x 14-inch baking pan. Press down evenly with fingers, waxed paper, or buttered spatula. Chill for at least 1 hour, then cut into serving pieces.

Aqrāṣ Mukarrarah and Justice

This is the story of Kisrá Anúshirwán, the Just King. One day while hunting, he was overcome with thirst and he stopped at a small village to ask for water.

The young woman who answered the door complied. She prepared his drink by pressing the juice from a sugarcane into a bowl and then mixing the juice with water. On top of that, she sprinkled a type of aromatic and something that looked like dust. She presented it to the king. He sipped it slowly and then told her that the drink was sweet and perfect, except for the dust in it. Was there a reason?

The young woman explained that the dust in the drink stopped the king from drinking the sugared water in one gulp; instead, he would take the time to enjoy it. The king observed that her reasoning was sensible and then asked her how many sugarcanes she had used to sweeten the water. When she told him that she had used only one, he quickly called on the village tax collector and told him to raise the village's taxes. They had been assessed as far too low given what a single one of its sugarcanes could produce. A village that gets that much juice

out of one sugarcane, he thought, should have its tax increased.

He returned to the hunt but again found himself extremely thirsty. He returned to the the same door of the village and asked for a drink of water. The same girl appeared and then disappeared.

The king waited and anticipated the refreshing bowl of water. It took a long time, though, much longer than it had before.

Finally, the maiden appeared with the water. He asked her why she had taken so long, and she replied that one single sugarcane was not enough to sweeten the water. She had pressed three of them, and even three had not produced as much juice as the single one had before.

The king was surprised. He asked her how this was possible. After all, sugarcane was sugarcane, especially when they all came from the same batch. With the twinkle of an eye, she explained that when a king makes a decision that is unjust against his subjects, their prosperity and fruitfulness end. The situation of the sugarcane reflected this. Mother Nature could no longer produce the sweetness in all sugarcane equally. It could no longer produce the sweetness it should.

King Kisrá Anúshirwán laughed and laughed and took the maiden to be his wife. Together they lived happily in his glorious castle, the king having learned that Mother Nature could very well be controlled by a woman.

It was of great benefit for the king to have married a woman who knew not only how to use sugarcane to her advantage but also how to create magnificent sweets, such as *aqrāṣ mukarrarah*, that kept her king in check.

Reading over this thirteenth-century recipe, we hesitated to re-create it. It seemed awfully time-consuming with all the tedious frying, dipping, re-frying, re-dipping, and so forth. So we set aside three hours to prepare and make this *mukarrarah* or repeated sweet and, in order to break the monotony, we invited a group of girlfriends over to watch and, hopefully, assist us.

We worked out the measurements from the original recipe, then placed on the counter the cooking utensils needed to make our sweet. We mixed the batter, formed the patties, then announced that we were ready for our friends to help. No such luck! With their manicured fingernails, lotioned hands, and outfits purchased from the finest boutiques in Toronto, our friends did not volunteer their services for anything other than indulging in the final product.

The outcome of this afternoon of baking was that our group agreed that thirteenth-century Aleppo had had an absolutely magnificent dessert. A recipe involving so much time and effort to prepare reflects the height of culture from which these buns emerged. No wonder *repeated* is part of its name. When one eats *aqrāṣ mukarrarah*, the natural response is to ask for another one—over and over again.

Take fine white flour and knead it into a medium-soft dough. Allow to rise. Take a raṭl *of sugar and one-third* raṭl *of pistachios or almonds. Pound them and knead them with rosewater and syrup to make a firm paste. Make into patties. Cover them with the dough, fry them, and remove them. Dip them in syrup, then dust them with sugar. Then re-cover them with the dough and fry. Remove them, dip them into the syrup, and dust them with sugar, repeating the process three times. Then sprinkle sugar over them and serve.*

SOURCE: Ibn al-ᶜAdīm, *Kitāb al-Waṣlah ilà al-Ḥabīb fī Waṣf al-Ṭayyībāt wa al-Ṭīb*

INGREDIENTS

4 eggs, beaten

⅔ cup shortening or butter

2 cups plus 2 tablespoons flour

1 cup plus 2 tablespoons water

1¾ cups confectioners' sugar

1 cup ground almonds

2 tablespoons rosewater

2 tablespoons honey

Basic qaṭr *(sugar syrup) recipe
   using rosewater (see page 11)*

Light sesame oil for frying

*¼ cup confectioners' sugar for
   garnish (optional)*

*1 teaspoon cinnamon for garnish
   (optional)*

Aqrāṣ Mukarrarah

Makes about 36 pieces

☙ In a mixing bowl, add the eggs, the shortening or the butter, 2 cups of the flour, and 1 cup of the water. Beat with an electric beater until a smooth batter is formed. Cover and let rest for half an hour.

☙ While the batter is resting, prepare the filling. In a separate bowl, mix together 1 cup of the confectioners' sugar, the almonds, the rosewater, the honey, the remaining 2 tablespoons of the water, and the remaining 2 tablespoons of the flour. Form this mixture into patties about 1½ to 2 inches in diameter.

☙ Prepare the basic *qaṭr* recipe and allow to cool.

☙ Dip the patties into the batter and fry until golden in color on each side. Remove with a slotted spoon and dip first into the cooled syrup and then into the remaining ½ cup of confectioners' sugar. Re-dip into the batter then fry again. Remove with the slotted spoon, then repeat the process, dipping the refried patties into the syrup and the confectioners' sugar and then once again into the batter. Fry again, then remove with the slotted spoon, place the patties on a tray, and allow them to cool.

☙ While the patties are cooling, if desired, mix together in a bowl the ¼ cup of confectioners' sugar and the cinnamon. Sprinkle the cooled patties with this mixture and place them on a serving platter.

Khudūd al-Aghānī and the Singing Girl

There was once a slave girl who was more beautiful than can be described. She was known not only for her beauty, but for her grace, her elegance, her charm, and her manners. Whoever saw her expressed amazement at the brightness of her dark eyes, the smoothness of her skin, and the perfection of her body. She could also play the lute, and when she sang as she played the instrument, her cheeks bloomed like flowers reaching out to the morning rain. No one could compare to her.

So it was that al-Amīn, the son of the caliph, heard of her. He approached the noble Jaʿfar, who was her master, and asked that he sell her to him.

But her master graciously declined, as his dignified position did not allow him to sell slave girls. Had he been anyone else, he might well have presented her as a gift to the caliph's young son.

A few days later, Jaʿfar invited al-Amīn to join him in an evening of merriment and song. A feast was presented that included meat and rice dishes, all types of vegetables and fruits, and, finally, the finest and most delectable sweets. From among them al-Amīn saw his favorite, *khudūd al-aghānī*, the dessert whose name means "the cheeks of the beautiful singing girl." He reached for the first bite but suddenly stopped. A melodious voice had begun singing a ravishing piece of music. He looked up, and there before him stood the beautiful slave girl. The melody of love emanating from her lips made his ecstatic heart beat faster.

As the musical verses issued forth, he saw her cheeks blooming like a bouquet of baby roses. Fate plays strange games, for he held the *khudūd al-aghānī* in his hand and before him stood another type of *khudūd al-aghānī,* causing his heart to be in the hands of the beautiful singer.

Al-Amīn and his host were drinking, but the caliph's son could well have become drunk without the alcohol. He was intoxicated by the girl and her voice.

He had an idea, and he put his plan into action.

The men's spirits that evening were joyful and merry, and al-Amīn bade the cupbearers fill his host's cup with so much wine as to make him beyond intoxicated. This done, al-Amīn took the girl and carried her to his house. But he did not touch her.

The next evening he invited Jaᶜfar to his home. He had the wine served and then bade the girl to sing for his guest from behind a curtain. The nobleman recognized her voice and was angry, but being a gentleman, he said nothing.

The evening ended and al-Amīn ordered servants to fill the boat the nobleman had arrived in with dirhams and dinars and all kinds of jewels and hyacinths, expensive clothing, and an assortment of goods. The caliph's son also had placed in the boat a thousand types of money and a thousand fine pearls, each worth twenty thousand dirhams. He continued to have his servants fill the boat until the boatmen cried out, saying that the boat could hold no more. Only then did al-Amīn command that all this be sent on to Jaᶜfar's palace.

Magnanimous Jaᶜfar thanked al-Amīn but wished that he could see the most beautiful *khudūd al-aghānī* once more. Al-Amīn obliged his grand friend and ordered his servant to bring forth that for which his guest had asked. Jaᶜfar was elated. He would see her one more time.

Or so he thought.

What al-Amīn sent to him were the *khudūd al-aghānī*—the ones served on a tray of sweets.

We chose this sweet simply because we loved the name! "Cheeks of the naturally beautiful singing girls"—an unusual name for a dessert, but sure to attract with both its name and its taste.

We were not sure why this fritter was so named until we actually made it. The dough puffs up when fried and turns golden as it cooks. The analogy also seemed apt when we witnessed our guests filling their cheeks with the sweet. Our *khudūd* filled their cheeks, and their *oohs* and *aahs* became the voice of the beautiful singer who entertained al-Amīn.

INGREDIENTS

2 cups flour

2 tablespoons cornstarch

3 tablespoons light sesame oil

3 tablespoons butter

2 tablespoons lukewarm water

2 tablespoons any type of sweet syrup

Half of basic ᶜAsal (honey syrup) recipe (see page 11)

Oil for frying

½ cup sugar

Khudūd al-Aghānī

Makes 30

🌿 In a bowl, combine the flour and the cornstarch together, then make a well and add the sesame oil, the butter, and the water. While mixing, add the syrup, then knead to form a slightly sticky dough, adding more flour or water if necessary. Cover the bowl and let sit for 2 hours.

🌿 Prepare half of the basic ᶜAsal recipe and keep warm.

🌿 Roll out the dough to a ¼-inch thickness and cut with a cookie cutter into rounds about 2¼ inches in diameter, making a hole in the center of each circle (like a doughnut).

🌿 Heat the oil over medium-low heat and fry the *khudūd* until golden brown on each side. Remove from the oil and place in the warm honey for about 30 seconds, turning them over to cover both sides of the *khudūd.* Place on a serving dish and allow to cool.

🌿 Sprinkle with the sugar.

Note: These pastries should be eaten within a day or so, otherwise they become stale.

Baqsamāṭ bi Sukkar and the Dirham-Pincher

There was once a miserly merchant who spent nearly nothing on food and drink.

One day, on a journey far from home, he went to the local market in the town to look for his daily meal. There he saw an old woman with *baqsamāṭ bi sukkar* that looked very tempting. He was hungry.

"Are these for sale?" he asked her. She answered that they were. The miser, however, could not imagine paying full price for any type of food, even in a moment of extreme hunger. He began to bargain.

Every time she gave a price, he countered it with a lower one. She said four dirhams, and he offered three; to her three he offered two. Finally, he beat her down to almost nothing, and he took them with him to eat at the place where he was staying. They were delicious, still warm and soaked in butter.

The next morning, he returned to the same market and again found the woman with two more scones of *baqsamāṭ bi sukkar.* He bought them, again bargaining their price down to almost nothing. He returned to his place of lodging to enjoy their flavorful taste.

For twenty-five days he performed the same ritual: going to the market, finding the old woman, purchasing the scones at the lowest price, returning home, and then taking pleasure in their savory taste. He simply could not understand how she could sell him the *baqsamāṭ bi sukkar* for such a small sum of money.

On the twenty-sixth day, following his daily routine, he returned to the market, but he discovered the woman was not there. He searched and searched. It was as if she had disappeared. He could find her nowhere.

He asked around but no one knew a thing about her or her whereabouts. He continued to go to the market, day after day, up and down the streets, in search of the woman, and one day he unexpectedly found her. He excitedly approached her with his usual greeting, "*al-salāmu ʿalaykum,*" wishing her a long life of fortune and prosperity. He missed her delicious *baqsamāṭ bi sukkar* and thus made sure he was gracious and on his best behavior.

He asked her where she had gone, she and her daily two scones. At first, she avoided the question, but when he persisted in asking it and explained how much he had missed her *baqsamāṭ bi sukkar*, she began her tale.

"Please hear me well, my lord. I was caring for a man who had a type of ulcer on his spine. His doctor had advised me to knead flour with butter into a poultice and then lay it on the painful ulcer. I was told to leave it on that spot all night. The following morning, I would take that poultice, and so as not to waste it, I would turn it into a dough and form it into two *baqsamāṭ bi sukkar*. I then baked them and would come to the market and sell these two same scones to you."

At this the merchant went near mad. "This is appalling, terrible, horrifying! How could this happen?" He felt ill, unable to move.

The woman looked up at him with solemn eyes. "My son, you feel sick. I understand. I know this is probably the most dreadful event of your life, as it is for me. I know why you are unhappy: the old man has died and now, unfortunately, I have no more flour to continue making and selling to you the *baqsamāṭ bi sukkar*."

At this point, our miserly merchant passed out.

So much for the expression a penny saved is a penny earned!

Sometimes, after a rich and filling meal, we serve tea to, as the Arabs say, *haḍam*, or facilitate digestion. This does the body good after a heavy meal, and at this time, dessert would involve a not-too-sweet cookie, such as *baqsamāṭ bi sukkar*.

The dough is simple to make—a yellow dough that becomes a smooth and slightly sweet white cookie. They are twice-baked cookies in varying shapes; the longer the cookies are baked, the drier they are.

Baqsamāṭ bi sukkar are a sweet variety of the *baqsamāṭ* dry biscuit of the Arab medieval period; they're described as a dry version of *kaᶜk* (see page 41).

Take flour and sugar, moisten, and knead with butter. If it is not sweet enough, add finely pounded sugar to it. Make for it a liquid mixture of yeast with a little water. Make baqsamāṭ *in any variety that you wish. Bake on a tray in the oven a second time after having baked it once.*

SOURCE: Ibn al-ᶜAdīm, *Kitāb al-Waṣlah ilà al-Ḥabīb fī Waṣf al-Ṭayyibāt wa al-Ṭīb*

Baqsamāṭ bi Sukkar

Makes 24

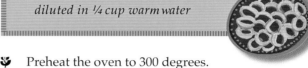

INGREDIENTS

2 cups flour

1 cup confectioners' sugar

1 cup unsalted butter at room temperature

1 package yeast (¼ ounce) diluted in ¼ cup warm water

☙ Preheat the oven to 300 degrees.

☙ Mix the flour and sugar together. Work the butter into the dry ingredients by rubbing them together by hand. Make a well and add the yeast mixture. Mix together by hand to form a dough.

☙ Break off a piece of the dough and roll it into the shape of a ball, the size of a golf ball. On a flat surface, roll out the ball by hand to form a 6-inch-long rope. Place on an ungreased baking tray and loop together both ends of the rope to form a ring. Continue the process until all the dough is used.

☙ Bake for 20 minutes. Remove from the oven and allow to cool on the baking tray for 15 minutes.

☙ Return the *baqsamāṭ* to the oven and bake an additional 20 minutes. Remove from the oven and allow to cool. Transfer to a serving platter.

Fālūdhaj
and Hospitality

One day, while riding in a state procession, Caliph al-Ḥākim bi-'Amr-Allāh passed near a garden. Flowers and shrubbery, palm trees laden with their fresh dates, and running waters in fountains and streams attracted his eye.

Looking closely, he saw a man surrounded by servants and slaves. The day was hot, the sun pounding down its rays of heat. The caliph yearned for a dose of cool and refreshing water. Here was the ideal place to ask for something to drink, here in this vision of earthly paradise.

Approaching the man, he asked him for the water. The man complied and, realizing that this was the caliph, he invited him in the most gracious Arab fashion to honor him by relaxing in his garden and asked that the caliph and his entourage stay and enjoy a meal with him as his guests.

The caliph agreed to do so, and he dismounted and entered the garden, along with the palace procession. The host appeared with a hundred rugs, a hundred leather mats, and even

a hundred cushions. After this, he set before them a hundred dishes of meat, a hundred dishes of marinades, a hundred platters of fruits, a hundred bowls of *fālūdhaj*, and a hundred jars of sugared sherbets.

Everyone was more than surprised. The caliph was speechless and in awe that their unexpected arrival could be met by such preparations and a feast. In amazement he looked at his host and said, "Truly, this presentation is wondrous. Did you know of our coming and prepare all this for us?"

The man replied, "By God, O Commander of the Faithful! I knew not of your arrival. I am but a merchant and one of your subjects who is more than honored to entertain you and to glorify God that you are my guest this day."

"But how could this have come about without your being aware that my procession would stop here? These must be all of the foodstuffs you depend on for at least a month or more."

His host explained, "I have a hundred concubines. Thus, when the Commander of the Faithful honored me by entering my garden to sit with me, I sent instructions to each concubine telling her to prepare my noonday meal and send it to me in my garden. Each one sent me a rug, a leather mat, and a cushion. Then each one sent me a dish of meat, a dish of marinades, a platter of fruits, a bowl of *falūdhaj*, and a jar of sherbet. This, sir, is my noonday meal. I have not added anything to it. I have not embellished more than what I have daily."

The caliph thanked God for his host's fortune and bounty and praised God for his generosity to such a hospitable and deserving human. He then sent for all the dirhams in the treasury that had been struck that year. The caliph did not leave until all the money came and was given to the merchant. Before parting, al-Ḥākim told his host to use the money for whatever he needed, his generosity deserving even more. The caliph then got on his mount and rode away.

The merchant smiled, realizing that doing something good only makes things better. He turned to go into his garden, preparing to explain to his one hundred loving concubines the beauty of generosity. Surprisingly, they were already waiting for him there.

With tender words of thanks and gratitude the merchant began to talk. But he was cut off curtly by one of the hundred angry maidens.

"So, our generous and kindly master, who is going to wash the dishes?"

Throughout our readings we found a number of historical anecdotes that mention *fālūdhaj* as being the crème de la crème of desserts, a dish of honor and delicacy presented to caliphs and royalty. The recipe we decided to make is from al-Warrāq's tenth-century cookbook, a *fālūdhaj* that was prepared for the cousin of the eighth-century caliph Hārūn al-Rashīd, the Prince ʿĪsà ibn Jaʿfar. In the stories of the *One Thousand and One Arabian Nights*, *fālūdhaj* is the paragon of sweetmeats: regal, smooth, sweet, and its taste exquisitely divine.

There is a famous story of a Bedouin Arab who, upon being served *fālūdhaj*, cried out that he wished that death and *fālūdhaj* were wrestling on his heart, as death itself would be distracted in its presence. Another tells of a man in the early ninth century who was asked before his execution what he wanted for his last meal; the man announced simply, "*Fālūdhaj*."

Even better yet is a tale from the early seventh century. Talks were in progress between the Persians and the Arabs before their famous battle. The Persian commander presented the Arab leader with *fālūdhaj*. The Arab turned to his wife and asked her if she knew what this sweet was, since he'd never seen or tasted it before. She replied—more than likely in a huff—that it looked like the Persian commander's wife had attempted to make some type of dessert that just didn't work out. So much for compliments, we say. Yet we also say that envy evokes no praise, especially from a jealous wife.

We decided to add ground almonds to this pudding to enhance its texture and also to mirror other *fālūdhaj* preparations that were popular in the tenth century and earlier and that appeared on the tables of the affluent.

Take as much as you wish of a good-quality white honey and pour it into a copper pot with a rounded bottom, skim its froth, then pour into it starch diluted in water. For every raṭl *of honey, use one* uskurrujah *of the diluted starch that has been colored with saffron or with the liquid of a houseleek. The starch solution should be thick. Light a gentle fire beneath it and allow it to cook over low heat while beating it very well with an iron rod. Once it begins to thicken, gradually add good-quality fresh butter or fresh sesame oil. Continue adding the butter or oil after having added enough sweet starch to it. Allow it to thicken until it's done. When it separates from its oil, remove it, God willing.*

SOURCE: al-Warrāq,
Kitāb al-Ṭabīkh

61

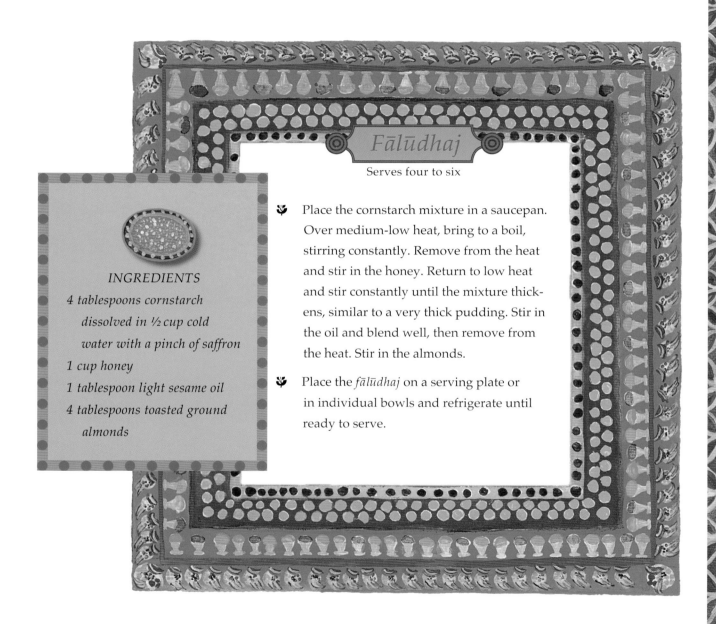

Fālūdhaj

Serves four to six

INGREDIENTS

4 tablespoons cornstarch
dissolved in ½ cup cold
water with a pinch of saffron

1 cup honey

1 tablespoon light sesame oil

4 tablespoons toasted ground
almonds

❧ Place the cornstarch mixture in a saucepan. Over medium-low heat, bring to a boil, stirring constantly. Remove from the heat and stir in the honey. Return to low heat and stir constantly until the mixture thickens, similar to a very thick pudding. Stir in the oil and blend well, then remove from the heat. Stir in the almonds.

❧ Place the *fālūdhaj* on a serving plate or in individual bowls and refrigerate until ready to serve.

Al-Danaf
and a Woman's Advice

King Chosroe of Persia loved to eat fish. One day he and his wife, Shirin, were sitting in their palatial garden. The outdoors and the vigor of the fresh air with the fragrance of the sea around him made him think of his favorite meal—a big fish grilled on hot coals. However, his wife could not bear the thought of having fish near her, let alone eating it. To please him, however, she had a dinner of lamb and rice prepared for him, as well as his favorite dessert, *al-danaf*, the light and crispy sweet her husband so enjoyed. Afterward, he was full, so sated he could not move.

Yet if someone had placed a grilled fish before the king, nothing would have stopped him from eating again. How kind his wife had been to prepare his favorite *al-danaf*. Each crispy bite reminded him of a nice crispy grilled fish.

Suddenly, as if in answer to his prayers, a fisherman approached with a gigantic fish, which he placed before the king. *Tomorrow's dinner*, the king thought. *A perfect dinner, and then the perfect sweet of al-danaf would make for a completely heavenly meal.* King Chosroe ordered that the fisherman be given four thousand dirhams for the fish.

Shirin was stunned and said to her husband, "Kind sir, you have erred greatly." Chosroe was surprised and asked her why she had come to this conclusion.

His wife explained that from that moment on, if the king gave one of his courtiers the same sum of money, that courtier could turn up his nose in scorn, as he would never accept the same amount that had been given to a fisherman. In other words, the king had now set a precedent for payment: four thousand and one dirhams was the least amount that could be given.

The king pondered his wife's take on the situation and agreed. However, he could not ask the fisherman to return the money. It had been a gift, and to ask the fisherman to return it would be dishonorable and a disgrace for a king.

Shirin was quick to reply. "I've got a plan. I know how to get the money back. All you have to do is request that the fisherman return here and then ask him if the fish is male or female. If it is male, you inform him that you wanted a female fish, and if he says that it is female, then you tell him that it was a male fish that you wanted."

The king followed the plan. He sent for the fisherman, a wise and sharp man. When King Chosroe asked him if the fish was male or female, the fisherman bowed his head to his highness and replied, "This fish is a hermaphrodite. It is both male and female."

At this, Chosroe roared with laughter and commanded that the fisherman be paid another four thousand dirhams.

With the eight thousand dirhams in his sack, the fisherman set out to leave. As he threw the sack over his shoulder, a dirham dropped. He stopped and bent down to pick it up.

Shirin was still upset, and now was the opportunity to vent her displeasure about what had taken place. She pointed out to her husband how miserly the fisherman was to pick up the dirham; if he were a kind and generous soul, he would have left it for one of the king's servants.

The king agreed and grew exceedingly angry with the fisherman, telling him that he should be ashamed of himself and that only a low-minded, selfish miser would have picked up the fallen dirham and not left it for someone else.

"How could you worry about one dirham when your sack is filled with a multitude of others? Only a greedy boor would have done this. You are not a man!"

Then the fisherman kissed the earth in front of the king and replied, "May God prolong King Chosroe's life! I picked up the dirham not because it was a piece of money but because on one side is the image of the king and on the other his name. Had I left it on the ground, someone might have come along and unknowingly stepped on it, thereby humiliating and disgracing the name and presence of the king. Would I not be blamed for this insult?"

King Chosroe thought for a bit and then applauded the fisherman's shrewd response. He commanded that yet another four thousand dirhams be given to him. But, more important, King Chosroe made a proclamation to his kingdom:

"It is important that no one be guided by a woman's advice.
For whosoever does will lose for the sake of one dirham, twelve thousand."

This recipe has a texture similar to marshmallow fluff but with an extra punch, crunchy almonds and the taste of orange blossoms. It caught our attention because we were intrigued by the fact that it was beaten with sugar syrup rather than with sugar alone. The catch was that we weren't sure if we could replicate it, since the process was not that well described in the original text. As it turned out, we ended up producing what we feel is a unique and unusual sweet.

Just like the other sweets we'd made, we needed our tasters. So we made our calls, and within half an hour eight friends "dropped by" to check out what we were up to.

When we placed the dessert on the dining table, the expressions of our guests told us what was going to happen next. They dug in and couldn't stop. They were lured by not only the taste but also the appearance of this mass of white fluff; it seemed to hide something within. The sweet was quite the topic of discussion: Which caliph preferred it, which noble commanded its appearance on his dining table, which royal household held it as its favorite? By the time everyone's opinion was given, the plate was empty.

What bothers us the most is that this recipe seems to have disappeared into the annals of history; we feel that it is our task to restore it to its former glory.

We had a dilemma: the source recipe instructed the reader to roll out the *danaf* and then sprinkle it with sesame seeds, but the mixture that we'd made was not solid enough to be rolled. This might have been the result of a misinterpretation of the instructions or of the original author's ambiguous directions for its preparation. Nonetheless, we feel that we have re-created *al-danaf* as closely as possible.

This dish is best served in a communal way: place the platter in the middle of the table and offer all the guests their own spoons, allowing them to scoop according to their wishes.

Al-Danaf

Serves 8 to 10

Take syrup and heat it
until it thins. Then remove
it from the fire and throw
an egg white in it and
beat it until it whitens.
Take for every raṭl of it
one ūqīyah of prepared
pistachios or almonds and
one-quarter ūqīyah of
finely pounded starch.
Mix together and then roll
out with a rolling pin and
add sesame seeds to it.

SOURCE: Ibn al-ʿAdīm,
*Kitāb al-Waṣlah ilà al-Ḥabīb fī
Waṣf al-Ṭayyibāt wa al-Ṭīb*

INGREDIENTS

2 cups of the basic **qaṭr** recipe made with orange-blossom water
  (see page 11)

2 egg whites

1 tablespoon cornstarch

3 tablespoons blanched almonds or pistachios

2 tablespoons sesame seeds

🌼 Place the *qaṭr* in a small saucepan, bring to a boil, and remove from the heat. Pour the *qaṭr* into a mixing bowl, then whisk in the egg whites until completely absorbed into the syrup. Using an electric mixer, beat the mixing bowl contents on high speed for 1 minute, then gradually beat in the cornstarch. Continue beating for about 10 to 15 minutes, or until the mixture forms stiff white peaks.

🌼 Fold in the almonds or the pistachios. Spread mixing bowl contents onto a serving platter. Sprinkle evenly over the top with the sesame seeds.

🌼 Refrigerate until ready to serve.

66

Tamr Mulawwaz
and the Woman of Wit

There was once a woman whose beauty surpassed that of all others. She was a good woman, a chaste woman, a woman who never did wrong and who was utterly loyal to her husband.

There was also a young man who was rude, vulgar, and uncouth and who admired her; he harassed her not once, not twice, but on a daily basis. Her beauty maddened him with love for her, so he continued to pursue her, despite the fact that she ignored his approaches.

It so happened that one day her husband left on a journey for another city. The rude young man began to send her messages, to which she did not respond. So crazed was he with love for her that he searched out an old woman and beseeched her to help him. He complained to her of his suffering for love and told her how he longed to be with the object of his desire. The old woman promised to see what she could do. He gave her a dinar and left with his hopes somewhat higher than before.

The next day the old woman met the good wife and began to visit her daily, spending the entire day with her and even eating meals with her. So regular were the visits that they began to joke and tell stories and became so close that the wife could not bear to spend a day without her newfound friend.

Now, this was a crafty and sly old woman. Every day the wife would give her leftover food to take home to her children, and the old woman would take a cake of bread and feed it to a stray dog in the quarter. Some might think this was a kind act, but actually the old woman had an ulterior motive. The dog became used to her, so one day when the old woman left the wife's house with the cake of bread, she added a lot of hot pepper to it. When she fed it to the dog, the dog's eyes completely teared up. The poor dog that could barely see began to follow the old woman, tears streaming from its eyes because of the very hot pepper.

When the wife saw the dog crying, she was shocked and asked the old woman why this was happening. The cunning old woman told the wife that this dog had once been a close friend of hers, an attractive woman of perfect grace. A young man, one of her neighbors, fell in love with the friend and begged her to return his love. She would not, and he fell near death from loving her so greatly. This young man told of his suffering to one of his friends, who, by chance, was a magician. Feeling sympathy for his lovesick friend, he cast a spell on the woman and turned her into this dog.

The old woman explained in her deceitful fashion, "She began to follow me until I learned who she really was. I was upset with her because I had warned her not to anger a man in love. She did not heed my advice and brought all this on herself. Nevertheless, I felt sorry for her, and I keep her near me now and give her food whenever I can."

The wife was nearly beside herself. Seeing her fraught with worry, the old woman cunningly asked her why her story had such an effect on her. The chaste woman told her the story of the young man who had fallen in love with her and how she refused to give him the time of day, since she, a married woman, would never consider responding to something so lewd as a stranger's words of love. However, she fearfully complained, "I have repelled him and now I am scared by what you have just told me."

In her conniving way, the old woman warned that the circumstances appeared similar. She worried aloud that the virtuous wife would share the same fate as her friend if she angered the man who loved her. The old woman pledged to help her and asked the wife to describe the young man so that she might bring him to her. The old woman promised the wife that she would find the young man for her.

Of course the old woman knew where to find the young man, and she left and went straight to him.

She informed him of the trick she played on the wife and told him that the next day, at noon, she would meet him at the head of the street and take him to the wife. At this, the young man gave her two dinars and promised another ten gold pieces once she'd delivered him to his lady love.

The old woman returned to the righteous wife and told her that, luckily, she had found the young man at just the right time, as his anger had been leading him to do harm to his beloved. Instead, the old woman said, she had calmed him down and would bring him to the wife on the morrow.

The lady was elated and told her that if her suitor indeed came, she would give the old woman ten dinars.

The next day arrived, and the old woman advised the wife to dress in her best clothing and prepare a sumptuous meal that included the most tempting of sweets, such as *tamr mulawwaz*, the ultimate concoction of dates and almonds. This the wife did, and the old woman left to get the young man.

Up and down the streets the old woman searched but could not find him. Under no condition would she lose the gold pieces that she had been offered. What could she do? Her scheme had worked up until the young man disappeared. Fearing to lose the promised gold, she decided to find another man and take him to the wife.

Again, up and down the streets she searched until she came across a handsome and distinguished-looking fellow. She approached him and asked him if he would accept an invitation of a good meal and a beautiful lady for his company. He was interested and followed her to the good lady's house. There, she knocked at the door, and then the wicked old woman walked in, followed by the noble gentleman.

As the deceitful woman was congratulating herself on what she had accomplished, the virtuous wife walked in and came face to face with none other than her husband, the master of the house.

Virtue makes for quick thinking. Realizing the circumstances facing her, the wife took off her shoe and cried out to her husband, "Is this how you uphold our marriage vows? Is this how you betray me? When I heard that you were returning from your journey, I sent for this old woman to test you, and now I know you have broken my trust! How could you do this to me? I thought you were a faithful husband, but now I see your immoral intentions."

She began to beat him and beat him with her shoe, all the while crying out for him to divorce her. The innocent husband swore to her that he was faithful and that, by God, all his life he had never done anything that should make her distrust him.

The virtuous wife, unabashed in her deceitful torment, continued to weep and attack him, calling for the neighbors to witness an unfaithful husband. He tried to stop her screams, and she bit his hand so that he humbled himself to her and kissed her hands and feet.

Still she did not stop until she gave a wily wink to the old woman, indicating she should come and hold her back. The old woman had husband and wife sit together, upon which the husband thanked the old woman for saving him from the wrath of his wife.

As the meal was placed before them and as the old woman bit into the soft-textured *tamr mulawwaz*, she marveled at the wife, whose cunning was even craftier than her own.

She smiled and smugly swallowed the *tamr mulawwaz*, reminding herself that a virtuous woman can be just as calculating as a wicked one.

 This sweet's name is translated simply as "dates of almonds," two ingredients that the Arabs love. The date is considered the quintessential fruit, and the almond one of the most favored of nuts. In this dessert, the two are presented in a sauce flavored with rosewater.

Tamr mulawwaz is a very sweet side dessert—a little goes a long way. We found the best way to eat it is with *kaʿk* (see page 41) or with a piece of toast. One of our guests revolutionized this medieval Arab sweet in a unique way, taking a couple of scoops of *tamr mulawwaz* and spooning them over a dish of vanilla ice cream. According to him, nothing could compare with the taste of the dates and vanilla ice cream with the tinge of rosewater. It must have been good because when we asked to taste his creation, he refused us, saying, "Go make your own!"

We did, and we enjoyed it.

Tamr Mulawwaz

Makes 40 to 45 pieces

🌺 Place dates in a bowl, cover with hot water, and allow to sit for 10 minutes. Strain in a sieve.

🌺 Remove the pits from the dates and replace the pits with the blanched almonds, then set aside.

🌺 Place the honey, the vinegar, and the water in a medium saucepan and bring to a boil, removing any white  scum that appears on the edges. Carefully add the dates, then cook over medium-low heat until the liquid boils, about 15 minutes. Gently stir in the remaining ingredients and cook for 10 more minutes. Transfer to a serving bowl and allow to cool before serving.

INGREDIENTS

½ pound dry dates (about 20)

Hot water

20 large blanched almonds

½ cup honey

2 tablespoons vinegar

1½ cups water

⅛ teaspoon saffron, dissolved in 2 tablespoons water

¼ teaspoon ground cloves

1½ tablespoons rosewater

Maʿmūl min al-Tamr and the Woman Wise

There was once a woman, a merchant's wife, whose husband traveled constantly. So it was that one day came along when he left for a long journey to a far-off land.

He was gone for a very long time, and, as it happened, she fell in love with a handsome young man, and he with her.

An incident took place in which the young man argued with another man and then was charged by the chief of police and thrown in jail.

Upon hearing the news, the woman became near mad. In order to help her beloved, she put on her very best clothing and went to the chief of police. She presented him with a petition of support for the young man, explaining that he was, in fact, her brother and that the charges against him were false. Furthermore, she informed him that her "brother" was her sole provider. She pleaded that he be released from his wrongful imprisonment.

The chief read the petition, looked at her, and immediately fell in love. He told her he would release the young man only if she joined him in his house alone. The woman objected, reminding him that it was improper for a woman to go to a man's house. She suggested, for the sake of privacy, that he meet her in her house on such-and-such a day and at such-and-such a time.

She left and set off to find the grand judge of the city to seek his help. When she found him, she repeated her story and asked that he release her "brother." The judge, like the chief of police, looked at her and immediately fell in love. He promised her assistance but only if she would come to his house to spend time with him. Again, she repeated that it was improper for a woman to enter a man's house, especially a house that was constantly filled with people, as his was. Instead, she invited him to her own home at the same designated day and time as she had the chief of police.

Next, she decided that the vizier could help her more, so she went to him to plead her case.

After presenting the vizier with her petition and the request for release, the merchant's wife was faced with the same dilemma as she had been twice before. "Come to my home so that I may enjoy your company, and once you do, I will release your brother," he told her amorously. "Oh no!" she told him. "My house is not far, so for the sake of privacy, you should meet me there." To the vizier she gave the same date and time that she'd given to the others.

Her last hope was with the king. When she informed him of the false accusations against her "brother," the king asked her who had thrown him into prison. She explained that it was the chief of police, and the king, upon hearing her words, was profoundly taken with her. He invited her to enter his palace so that they could enjoy a private evening together, and afterward, he told her, he would have the young man released. However, instead she invited the king to come to her house at the same time as she had told the others.

On her way home, in anticipation of the suitors, she stopped by the carpenter and had him build for her a cabinet with four compartments, one above the other, each of the compartment's doors made with a lock. The carpenter was no different than the chief of police, the judge, the vizier, and the king. He told her that the price of four dinars would be waived if she would spend time with him. "Yes," she said, "I will do so, but only if you make this same cabinet with five doors and locks, instead of the four." She told her where she lived and when he should come—the same day and time as the others.

The day of the rendezvous arrived. She prepared four men's lounging robes of different colors. Then she made herself ready, wearing the most extravagant of dresses. A lavish dinner was spread with a multitude of dishes and desserts, the most tempting being the *maᶜmūl min al-tamr*. She made sure to place the sweet in the center of the table, alongside the wines and fruits. Then she spread out the rich carpets, the flowers, and the perfumes, and awaited her first visitor.

The chief of police arrived first, and after kissing the ground before him, the merchant's wife led him to the couch, where she began to flirt with him, tempting him here and there with the *maᶜmūl min al-tamr*. She urged him to get comfortable and presented him with a yellow garment to wear as she readied more *maᶜmūl min al-tamr*. She also took away his clothes.

Suddenly, there was a knock at the door. "Quick!" she warned him. "My husband is here!" The frightened police chief asked what he should do. She guided him to the cabinet and told him to hide in it. She pushed him into the cabinet's lowest compartment and locked it.

The merchant's wife answered the door. The chief judge entered and she kissed the ground before him and then led him into the sitting area. "My great lord! This house is yours and we will spend time together after eating a splendid meal and the most delectable of sweets, this delicious *maᶜmūl min al-tamr*. But first, I want you to relax so we can enjoy ourselves. Remove your fancy dress and don for me this red garment and place this old piece of cloth on your head so that you are comfortable." The judge did as he was told.

She sat with him and began to flirt with him, and when he reached his hand toward her she asked that he first write an order for her brother's release. This he did, and again she began to flirt; then they heard someone rapping at the door. "Quick! You must hide. My husband has come home!" She led him to the cabinet, had him go into the second compartment from the bottom, and locked it.

Now, the chief of police had heard all of this but could say nothing. Instead, he listened as the merchant's wife opened the door to the vizier.

The woman kissed the ground before the vizier and invited him to relax and take comfort in his surroundings. She had him remove his official dress and gave him the blue robe and a tall red hat. She fed him the *maᶜmūl min al-tamr*, and she flirted with him and he with her until they heard a knock at the door.

She quickly led the frightened vizier to the cabinet, had him get in the third compartment from the bottom, and locked it.

The merchant's wife opened the door and came face to face with the king. She kissed the ground before him while praising him for his honored presence and then led him into the cushioned room. "Take your leisure, my goodly king! Remove your royal clothes and relax in this garment of lounging." She gave him a patched garment to wear and began to talk and flirt with him.

Needless to say, the three other men were listening but dared not utter a word.

As the merchant's wife fed the king the crispy *maʿmūl min al-tamr*, a sudden knocking came at the door.

When the king asked who would be arriving at this time, she told him that her husband must have returned home, and for safety's sake, it would be wise for him to hide himself in the cabinet. She led him to the fourth compartment from the bottom and locked him in.

She opened the house door and found the carpenter, who saluted her. As quickly as he entered she admonished him, saying, "What type of cabinet have you made me?"

"What is wrong, my lady?"

"There is something wrong with the top compartment. It is too narrow."

The carpenter, somewhat perplexed, responded, "Impossible, my dear woman. It is wide enough for four."

"Check for yourself, my good man," the merchant's wife said. "See if you can fit in it."

The carpenter entered the top and fifth compartment and immediately she locked him in it.

Without any time to waste, she took the judge's order to the proper authorities, and her lover was released. The woman told the young man all that had happened, and the two decided to leave the city once and for all.

As for the five men who were in the cabinet, three days passed. They had nothing to eat or drink and finally they could take no more. One by one they began to complain, save for the king, who was too embarrassed to say anything. As they got louder they recognized the others' voices and realized the trick that had been played on them.

Amazed at their gullibility, the vizier finally admitted that they had been conned by a cunning woman. "Look at us. We are the masters of the state, the learned and the intellectual, and look how we have been duped by a shrewd female. You realize, don't you, that had she attempted to deceive the king, he would never have fallen for her treachery."

Remove the pits from the dates and put in pistachios that have been kneaded with sugar, rosewater, and musk. Stuff them in the dates. Take qaṭā'if dough, add to it cornstarch, and cover the dates with the dough. Fry in sesame oil and throw them into the syrup that has reached a thin consistency. Then cover them another time in the dough. Fry them a second time and toss them into the syrup. Arrange them on a plate and sprinkle with sugar, pistachio meats, rosewater, and musk.

SOURCE: Ibn al-ᶜAdīm, *Kitāb al-Waṣlah ilà al-Ḥabīb fī Waṣf al-Ṭayyībāt wa al-Ṭīb*

At this the king spoke up and admitted that he too had been taken. But it was the carpenter who said he was doubly swindled, as not only had he been locked up like the others but he was out four gold pieces.

As they discussed their misfortune and tried to relieve the king's embarrassment, the sound of the neighbors' voices was heard, and they fell back into silence.

In good-neighborly fashion, they had arrived to determine why the house seemed abandoned and to see if anything was wrong. As citizens of a country where brother helps brother and stranger helps stranger, they must show their concern for one of their own. The neighbors decided to break down the doors. For what type of true neighbor would not worry about another human being? Would they not be shamed if the chief of police or the chief judge or the vizier or even the king found out that something was amiss among one of their own and that they hadn't tried to help?

Dates serve us well in our household. If we feel like something sweet, we eat dates. If we feel like something healthy, we eat dates. If we feel like eating something unique and tasty, we eat *maᶜmūl min al-tamr*.

These are dates double-dipped in a batter. This dessert is sweet, and the pleasure comes from biting into a deep-fried piece of syrupy bread with a pistachio-stuffed date inside. Granted, dates alone are a delicious fruit, but when pistachios and rosewater are added, the sweet becomes scrumptious.

As a side note, after you've prepared the *maᶜmūl min al-tamr*, make sure to put them away until ready to serve. People tend to devour them as soon as they see them, so if you don't put them out of sight, half the dish will be gone when you're ready to serve it. With this dessert, there is no such thing as trying *one*; at least two or three seem to be needed just to get a taste.

We have replaced the musk with ground cloves since cloves are more readily available.

Maʿmūl min al-Tamr

Makes about 45 to 48

- ❧ Prepare *qaṭr* and set aside to cool.

- ❧ To make the filling for the dates, combine in a small mixing bowl the pistachios, the sugar, the rosewater, and the cloves.

- ❧ Take one date at a time and stuff with about half a teaspoon of the filling, depending on the size of the date. Slightly squeeze to close. Reserve the extra filling.

- ❧ Prepare the *qaṭāʾif* batter, then mix the cornstarch into the batter. Set aside.

- ❧ Place the oil to about 2 inches deep in a medium saucepan and heat over medium-high.

- ❧ By hand, coat the dates well with the *qaṭāʾif* batter then deep-fry until golden brown, turning over a few times. Remove with a slotted spoon and shake off any excess oil. Dip into the *qaṭr* for a few moments and set on paper towels. Continue until all the dates are finished.

- ❧ Repeat the frying process again—coat with the *qaṭāʾif* batter the second time; deep-fry; then dip into the qaṭr. Remove with a slotted spoon and place on a tray until cooled.

- ❧ Arrange on a serving tray, then sprinkle with the reserved filling and serve. These are best eaten the same day they are made.

INGREDIENTS
One basic qaṭr *recipe (see page 11)*
1 cup ground pistachios
4 tablespoons sugar
2 teaspoons rosewater
¼ teaspoon ground cloves
1 pound dates, pitted
   (about 45 to 48 dates)
1 recipe qaṭāʾif *batter (see page 119)*
1 tablespoon cornstarch
Vegetable oil for deep-frying

Ḥays
and the Bedouin and the Mule

One day the emir Maʿan and a company of friends went out hunting. When a herd of gazelles surprised them and the pursuit began, Maʿan became separated from the group and ended up chasing one of the gazelles on his own. He was lucky that day, and after capturing it he intended to boast about it to his friends when he caught up with them.

Now, it so happened that as he was busy preparing to pack up the gazelle, he saw someone approaching from the desert on a mule. He mounted his horse and moved toward the Bedouin man.

Maʿan asked the stranger from where he had come. "I come from Kuzaʿah, where for two years straight a drought hit us hard. However, this year has been fruitful, and our date trees have produced more dates than ever before. Our Ḥays has never been better, made of the choicest of dates and butter. This Ḥays has been made from the first picking of the young and tender blooming date palms. It is the ultimate of sweets when made with these first fruits. For this reason I have set out to see Emir Maʿan; because of his reputed kindness and well-known generosity, I thought he might buy the sweet from me."

Maʿan smiled to himself. "And how much do you expect to get from him for the Ḥays?"

Almost at once the Bedouin answered, "One thousand dinars."

Ma^can just as quickly responded, "What if he says that the price is too high; what then?"

The Bedouin said he would lower the price to five hundred, to which Ma^can again asked, "What if the emir says that price is too high as well?"

"I will then tell him three hundred dinars, and if this be too high for him, then two hundred, then one hundred, then fifty, and finally thirty!"

"But," said Ma^can, "what if the thirty is still too high?"

The Bedouin answered, "I will make my mule put his four feet in the prince's home, and I will know that even though I will be disappointed and return empty-handed, I will have dishonored him."

Ma^can laughed at him and remounted his horse and returned to his place of abode. There he told his chamberlain that if a man with *Ḥays* appeared at his door, he should let the man enter and bring him forth.

The Bedouin arrived and was shown into the emir's home. Now Ma^can was dressed in his emir's clothing and sat in a majestic atmosphere on his chair of state, looking stern and serious, attended by his servants and courtiers. The Bedouin approached him with the *Ḥays* and did not recognize him as the same man he had spoken to in the desert; he gave him his salaam.

Ma^can asked the reason for his presence. The Bedouin explained, "I am hoping that the emir would like to buy the freshest and sweetest *Ḥays* from my land made with the first dates of the season."

"My good man, this looks delicious. What is the price you are asking?"

Said the Bedouin, "One thousand dinars."

"Far too much!" announced Ma^can, to which the Bedouin replied, "Then five hundred dinars."

Back and forth the emir and the Bedouin haggled, until the seller of the *Ḥays* reached thirty dinars and Ma^can retorted, "Too much!"

Finally, the Bedouin cried out, "By God! The man I met in the desert today brought me bad luck! This is it! It is thirty dinars for the *Ḥays*, love it or leave it!"

When Ma^can roared with laughter, the Bedouin realized that this was the same man whom he had met earlier and said, "My lord, if those thirty dinars are not brought forth to me for the *Ḥays*, as you can see, my mule is parked at the door, ready to enter."

Ma'an laughed so hard he fell off his chair, and then he commanded that a thousand dinars be given to the Bedouin, and five hundred, and three hundred, and two hundred, and one hundred, and fifty, and thirty—and, more important, that the mule be left tied up where he was standing.

The Bedouin, amazed, left a much richer man than than he had arrived, thanks to the generosity of the emir and thanks to his fear of a mule.

Ḥays is one of the oldest sweets recorded in Arab history. It originated with the Arab desert people. For this reason, we chose to include this recipe, since it became a stepping-stone for subsequent sweets, even ones we eat today. As the Arab empire and its cities expanded, tastes became more cultivated, and advances were made in the culinary arts. Almonds, pistachios, and sesame oil, once expensive commodities, became part of the medieval middle class's repertoire. *Ḥays* was a part of this development.

Given our keen interest in re-creating Arabic culinary history and teaching it to the world through friends, colleagues, neighbors, and family, we invited some friends over and announced that we had redacted a recipe for a medieval Arab sweet that was first created in the Bedouin society. Our city-folk friends hemmed and hawed at the prospect of delving into such a poor man's food.

Obviously, we, the recipe adapters and cooks of these balls of dates, were offended, but being good hostesses, we smiled and thought, *Who cares? More for us then!* So we and all our friends sat around and talked about world events, and we, the authors, stuffed our mouths with this delicious sweet. We couldn't stop.

In the same way that Tom Sawyer got his friends to help whitewash the fence, we ate, and our guests, one by one, took a *Ḥays* and popped it into his or her mouth. Well, as we figured, modern man connected with his Bedouin past! Diana spoke for everyone when she said, "I've got to have this recipe!"

By the way, she had to say it three times before we understood her, since her mouth was so stuffed with *Ḥays*!

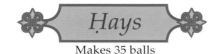

Ḥays

Makes 35 balls

INGREDIENTS

¾ pound fresh, pitted dates, chopped

2 cups finely ground bread crumbs

4 ounces ground almonds

4 ounces chopped pistachios

½ cup plus 1 tablespoon light sesame oil

Confectioners' sugar or superfine sugar

❧ Place the dates, the bread crumbs, the almonds, and the pistachios in a food processor and process for 2 minutes. Pour the sesame oil evenly over the mixture and process for a further 5 minutes. Press a small amount of the mixture in the palm of the hand to make sure it sticks together. If it doesn't, process the mixture a little longer until it begins to bind.

❧ Form the mixture into balls that are each about the size of a walnut.

❧ Roll the balls in the confectioners' or superfine sugar and place on a serving plate.

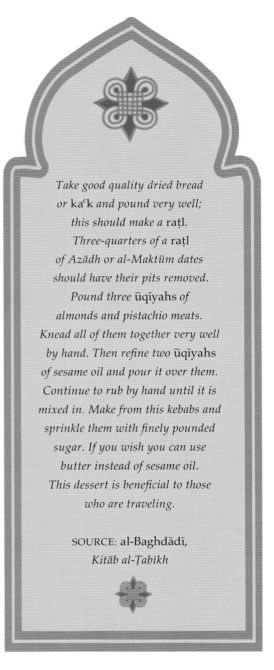

Take good quality dried bread or kaᶜk and pound very well; this should make a raṭl. Three-quarters of a raṭl of Azādh or al-Maktūm dates should have their pits removed. Pound three ūqīyahs of almonds and pistachio meats. Knead all of them together very well by hand. Then refine two ūqīyahs of sesame oil and pour it over them. Continue to rub by hand until it is mixed in. Make from this kebabs and sprinkle them with finely pounded sugar. If you wish you can use butter instead of sesame oil. This dessert is beneficial to those who are traveling.

SOURCE: al-Baghdādī, *Kitāb al-Ṭabīkh*

81

Mukhannaqah
and Suffocated Verses of Love

Caliph Hārūn al-Rashīd, unable to sleep one night, began to pace the palace from room to room, hoping that the excessive walking would tire him out. It was useless. As he watched the sun rise, he realized how quickly the night had passed. Restless and not knowing how to relax, he called for al-Aṣmaʿī, his poet friend, to keep him company. The poet arrived and the caliph asked him to provide some poetry or tales about women and love.

Keen to keep the caliph's friendship, al-Aṣmaʿī told the story of three sisters whom he had encountered by chance one sunny and hot day in the city of Basra. Seeking a place to rest, he had found a wooden bench in a shaded porch area. He sat his weary body on the bench and soon discovered that the bench was located beneath an open latticed window of a magnificent home; out of it emanated the aroma of musk.

As sweet as the scent were the voices he heard: voices of three young ladies who turned out to be sisters. They were discussing ways in which to keep themselves busy on such a hot day. One of them decided that they should hold a poetry competition among themselves to see who could compose the most amorous couplet. Each sister would put one hundred dinars on the table, and whoever won would take the total three hundred.

The girls agreed, and the eldest began:

> If while I sleep my lover arrives, what a delight!
> But better I be awake when to me he alights.

The second sister then spoke:

> Oh beautiful night! Come to me so that I may see
> My lover in dream approaching me.

And finally, the youngest sister declared:

> From my heart and my soul, from his body to his head
> I smell his musk aroma from the sheets of my bed.

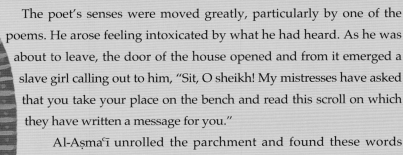

The poet's senses were moved greatly, particularly by one of the poems. He arose feeling intoxicated by what he had heard. As he was about to leave, the door of the house opened and from it emerged a slave girl calling out to him, "Sit, O sheikh! My mistresses have asked that you take your place on the bench and read this scroll on which they have written a message for you."

Al-Aṣmaᶜī unrolled the parchment and found these words elegantly written in the most beautiful of Arabic calligraphy:

Know, O sheikh (God lengthen your days!), that we are three maiden sisters who have agreed on a friendly contest and who have each laid down a hundred dinars. The condition is that whosoever recites the best and most amorous couplet shall have the whole three hundred dinars. We have appointed you judge among us. You are to decide which is the best of verse. We end our message with our wishes for peace upon you!

The poet responded by asking the slave girl to provide him with an ink case and paper so that he could record his vote. She obeyed and returned with the items.

The slave girl waited for him to write up his decision; al-Aṣmaᶜī thought a moment, then took up his pen, dipped it in the ink, and laid out the scroll, composing lines of poetry in response to the three sisters' poetic creations. He smiled at what he wrote, then rolled up the scroll and returned it to the slave girl, who promptly went upstairs to present it to her mistresses.

Al-Aṣmaᶜī rose from the bench with the intention of leaving but heard one of the damsels call out to him by name and ask him to sit. The poet turned toward the window, calling out, "How did you know my name? How do you know who I am?" One of the sisters responded, "We knew not your name only until we read what you had written on your scroll. We could not put a name to your face, but we could put a name to your rhapsodizing words of rhyme."

He sat down, amazed at their knowledge of his poetry and style of writing. As he contemplated what had just passed, the door of the house opened and out walked the eldest sister carrying a dish of fruits and another dish replete with *mukhannaqah*, freshly prepared and still warm, its aroma of musk almost suffocating him with delight. He ate from both dishes until he was sated.

Al-Aṣmaʿī arose from the bench again ready to depart but heard a sweet voice call out to him, "Sit down!" The voice mesmerized him and he turned to see the most exquisitely beautiful woman that he could ever have imagined. "That was my poem that you chose as your favorite," she said, and with this she laid three hundred dinars down in front of him. "Because of your judgment, I now pay you for your choice of my words."

Having told this story, al-Aṣmaʿī turned to the caliph and asked his opinion about the events of the day that he encountered the three sisters. Hārūn al-Rashīd, wide awake at this point, asked his poet friend why he had chosen the youngest sister's couplet as the best. The poet responded that the eldest sister's verse referred to a visit by her lover as only as a possibility. The second sister's poem related a lover's visit as only a dream. But the youngest sister's rhyming words had caught the poet's soul, for neither possibility nor fantasy could grip the heart as tightly as the reality of the one who had actually enjoyed her lover and who still smelled the scent of his lingering musk.

The caliph was satisfied and congratulated al-Aṣmaʿī on making the difficult choice. He awarded him another three hundred dinars, to which the poet responded, "Never mind, my honorable Caliph, for does not the expression 'practice makes perfect' allow for the third sister's cognizance of what be true love?"

"Well, yes," said the caliph, "but also remember that it is better to practice what you preach in order to get to that point of perfection!"

The unusual name of this luscious dessert, *mukhannaqah*, derives from the process involved in soaking, or suffocating, the dough with syrup. When we tried this recipe for the first time, it turned out much too sweet. It worked out much better when we cut the sugar content down somewhat.

The trick is to work quickly with the dough. It is sticky but worth the effort.

As was our usual pattern, once we redacted the recipe for a medieval sweet, we picked up the phone and invited over a group of friends and family to be our taste testers. In this case, the RSVPs took a turn toward the absurd. "Why would you want us to be suffocated when we eat your new sweet?" And "What kind of an invitation is this; why would you invite your guests to suffocate?" Easiest response: "Simply because this is 'sweet suffocation!'"

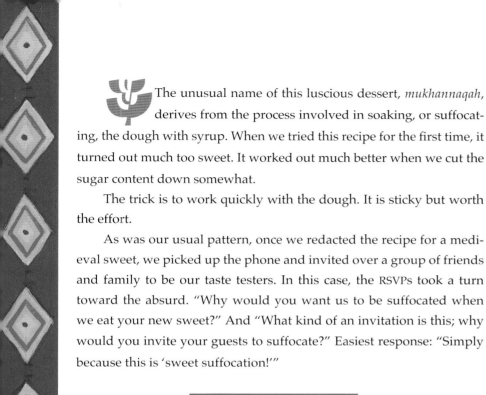

INGREDIENTS
Half basic **qaṭr** *(sugar syrup) recipe (see page 11)*
1 pound **kunāfah** *dough (also known as* **kataifi** *or shredded phyllo dough), thawed*
1 cup honey
2 tablespoons light sesame oil
¼ cup fruit sugar
½ cup coarsely chopped pistachios

⟨ Mukhannaqah ⟩

Number of pieces depends on size of serving pieces

- Prepare the *qaṭr* recipe and keep warm.

- Remove the *kunāfah* dough from the package and, over a large tray, carefully separate the strands of dough with your fingers, allowing them to drop onto the tray. Loosen them by fluffing them up. Then loosely cover with a cloth until ready for use.

- In a large saucepan, add the *qaṭr*, then stir in the honey. Bring the *qaṭr*-honey mixture to a boil over medium heat for 1 minute. Lower the heat to medium-low, then stir in the sesame oil.

- Stir in the *kunāfah*, mixing it quickly with the saucepan contents, ensuring that the dough is well coated with the *qaṭr*-honey mixture. Remove from the heat and stir in the fruit sugar and half of the pistachios.

- Spread the *mukhannaqah* evenly on a flat serving platter, then sprinkle with the remaining pistachios. Allow to cool, then cut into serving pieces.

Al-Mukaffan
and the Accusation

It was early on a Friday morning when a man brought home to his wife a live fish and told her to cook it for their dinner. He returned to work and ate nothing all day, anticipating the meal his wife was preparing for him.

While the woman's husband was at work, her neighbor came to visit and invited her to a wedding at his house. At first, the woman declined, knowing that she had much to do that day and no time for wedding festivities. However, when the neighbor told her of the feast being prepared and that *al-mukaffan* was to be the main sweet served, she quickly changed her mind. She remembered the fish, took it, and laid it in a jar of water. She left and spent the entire week celebrating in the wedding merriment.

During that week, her husband went from door to door looking for his wife, asking one neighbor after another if anyone had seen her. No one had seen her; no one knew where she was.

On the following Friday, the wife returned home, and her husband hit the roof. How dare she leave for a week and not inform him of her whereabouts! How dare she leave her home without guilt or shame!

But the wife ignored the accusations and brought out the breathing fish, which he had not known had stayed alive because she'd put it in the jar of water. She brought all the neighbors to the house to hear her story and to bear witness that she had done nothing wrong.

The husband then spoke, but no one believed him. Even when he explained that his wife would run to all the corners of the earth if she knew that *al-mukaffan* would be there, they told him over and over that it was impossible that his wife had left him for the week. After all, they reminded him, the fish was alive and kicking.

They proved that he was mad, and as they took him away he called out to the unbelievers:

> *How ironic when one tells the truth,*
> *To believe the lies from one uncouth*
> *For proof you took that living fish*
> *For a wife to enjoy the mukaffan dish.*

What is tastier than deep-fried dough? Simple: deep-fried dough filled with almonds, sugar, and rosewater. Apparently, Ibn al-ʿAdīm felt the same way, because he chose to include *al-mukaffan*, or "that which is covered" in his thirteenth-century culinary work.

Al-mukaffan are sweet and crunch-filled fritters that go well with a hot cup of unsweetened tea or coffee; after being dipped in the sugar syrup, these fritters are sweet enough on their own.

The process of preparation involves folding dough over an almond filling. The trick to keeping the stuffing intact is to pinch the edges of the folded dough.

Al-Mukaffan

Makes 25

*Take one ra*ṭ*l sugar and
one-half ra*ṭ*l crushed almonds,
and stiffen it up with a little
white flour. Then make a
dough with some other white
flour: for each ra*ṭ*l, three
ūqīyahs of sesame oil and
whatever is needed of rosewater. Cut into pieces and
fill them. Fry over a gentle
fire. Place them in syrup and
sprinkle sugar on them.*

SOURCE: Ibn al-ᶜAdīm,
*Kitāb al-Wa*ṣ*lah ilà al-*Ḥ*abīb fī
Wa*ṣ*f al-*Ṭ*ayyībāt wa al-*Ṭ*ib*

INGREDIENTS

One basic qa*ṭ*r *recipe (see page 11)*
2 pounds frozen bread dough, thawed according to package directions
3 tablespoons rosewater
2 cups sugar
1 cup ground almonds
2 tablespoons flour
4 tablespoons light sesame oil
Vegetable oil for deep-frying
4 tablespoons sugar

❧ Prepare the *qa*ṭ*r* and set aside to cool.

❧ Knead the dough with 2 tablespoons of the rosewater. Form the dough into 28 to 30 balls and place on a tray, leaving space between the balls. Cover with a towel and allow to stand for 1 hour.

❧ In the meantime, make the filling by combining in a mixing bowl the sugar, the almonds, the flour, the sesame oil, and the remaining 1 tablespoon of rosewater and mixing well. Then divide into portions, the same number as you have dough balls. Set aside.

❧ Roll the balls out into 4-inch rounds. Place one portion of the filling on the center of each round, then turn the dough over to cover the filling. Pinch closed in a half-moon shape and place on a tray until ready to fry. Continue until all the rounds are finished.

❧ Place cooking oil to about 2 inches deep in a medium saucepan, then set over medium heat. Deep-fry the *mukaffans* a few at a time, turning them over until golden on both sides. Place on paper towels for about a minute. Dip the *mukaffans* into the *qa*ṭ*r* for a few moments. Place on a serving platter and allow to cool. Sprinkle with the sugar just before serving.

Ḥalwà Wardīyah
and the Rosy Reward

In years long ago, during the rule of Caliph Hārūn al-Rashīd, there lived in the city of Damascus a well-known wealthy merchant who had a handsome and kind son named Ghānim bin Ayyūb and a daughter, Fitnah, who was the epitome of beauty and charm.

When the father died, he left his two children abundant wealth, including hundreds of yards of silks and brocades, musk pods, and mother-of-pearl handiwork, all packed in crates. On each crate was inscribed *This package is intended for Baghdad*, meaning that Ghānim was to take these goods to that city to sell.

So Ghānim set forth to the famous capital with a company of merchants, putting his trust in God that he and his group would arrive safely. When he got to the city, he rented a modest home; he furnished it with carpets and cushions and curtains and tapestries, and he stored his crates and stabled his mules and camels. The night he arrived, the merchants and notables of Baghdad came to give him their salutations.

The next morning Ghānim woke early to begin his day at the merchants' souk. He took with him one of the crates, and by sunset he had sold all its contents and made a profit of double the value. And so this continued day after day, week after week, until one year had passed and Ghānim had become very wealthy.

Almost a year after his first sale in Baghdad, Ghānim went to the souk to begin his day but found that the gate to the area was locked shut. He inquired as to why and was told that one of the merchants had died and that his fellow merchants had gone to the funeral. Ghānim felt it his duty to attend the sad ceremony. He reached the mosque where the prayers were being read.

Now, Ghānim, who was a kindhearted man, was also a very shy soul. He admired his fellow businessmen. However, they were colleagues, not family. Ghānim worried that he, as an extremely wealthy stranger in the great bustling city, might become a victim of thievery if he didn't return to his home by early evening. The funeral was taking too long and he really did not know these people well. He wanted to go but was too embarrassed to be the first to depart. He waited for the first man to leave, but after many hours, no one had gone.

Ghānim, fearing for his property, just couldn't wait any longer and finally left. He reached the city walls but found the entrance gate had been locked, as was customary at sunset. He panicked, terrified by the howls of dogs and wolves, and frantically searched for a safe place to sleep. He found a mausoleum and climbed to the top of it, figuring that he could lie there until the morning.

But sleep did not come to Ghānim. He began to pace, and suddenly he heard voices from below. In the moonlight he saw three figures; one was carrying a lantern and the other two were carrying a large chest. He watched as they dug a deep hole in the ground, buried the chest, then covered it. And then they left.

Curiosity overtook the merchant, and since he couldn't sleep, he decided to investigate. As the sun rose, Ghānim descended to the spot and scooped away the earth with his hands until the chest appeared. He took a large stone and hammered at the lock until it broke off. He opened the lid and he beheld a maiden, a model of beauty and loveliness, clad in the richest of garments and jewels.

She was still breathing, and he realized that she had been drugged. He was enraged that someone had done this to her. He lifted her out and laid her on the ground so that the fresh air would revive her.

She awoke confused, calling out the names of her friends and asking where the Damascene curtains and latticed windows of the harem were. Ghānim, realizing that she was a member of the caliph's court, assured her that she would be safe with him and quickly told her the story of what he had seen that had caused her to be in this circumstance.

Surprisingly, she asked that he place her back in the chest and take her to his home and that he disregard who she was. Ghānim obeyed her because he had fallen in love with her, and a lover will move heaven and earth for his beloved.

At his house he opened the chest, and the lady of his dreams emerged, looking about her. She saw that his place was handsomely spread with carpets, that it was delightful and cheerful with color, and that it was richly decorated with other adornments. She also noted the large piles of crates and the packed bales, indicating that he was a merchant of great wealth. At this moment the maiden removed her veil; she saw in Ghānim a man of youth and beauty, and she too fell in love.

She was hungry and asked him for something to eat. Ghānim went out and in a wink returned with a roasted lamb and all its trimmings, dried fruits, and candied nuts, and he also brought with him a plate of ḥalwà wardīyah, Baghdad's choicest sweetmeat. When it came time to serve the dessert, Ghānim proclaimed, "I present to you ḥalwà wardīyah, 'sweet rose,' because you are my sweet rose."

For two days they wined and dined, enjoying each other, the wine causing them to issue words of hidden love. "Quench my heart as the wine quenches my thirst," he requested. She told him that she could do so only if she was fully intoxicated. Ghānim was devastated.

"You cannot possess me because of who I am," she said; she removed her belt and asked the young merchant to read what was written on it.

Ghānim read the words out loud: "'I am yours and you are mine, O descendant of the Prophet!'" He said to her, "Tell me who you are!"

She answered, "Know that I am one of the concubines of Caliph Hārūn al-Rashīd, and my name is Qūt al-Qulūb. I was brought up in his palace, and when I reached puberty our ruler discovered that God had given me excessive beauty and poetic talent. I became the favorite in the caliph's harem. However, his wife Lady Zubaydah grew jealous of me and arranged to have me drugged and removed from the palace in a chest in order to make me disappear."

The merchant, who held great respect for the caliph, could not bring himself to touch Qūt al-Qulūb, and they both stood together, hand in hand, weeping, for they knew that their love was a great passion but that neither one could be disloyal to the caliph.

Meanwhile, back at the palace, Zubaydah was drowning in guilt for what she had done to Qūt al-Qulūb. She sought the advice of an elder, who told her that she should tell the caliph that his mistress had died and that Zubaydah had ordered that she be buried in the palace. Also, in case the caliph wanted to see the shrouded body, Zubaydah should have a body made out of wood and then covered with a shroud. Zubaydah did just that.

Hārūn al-Rashīd returned to his palace and when he entered his wife's quarters he found her and her handmaidens dressed in black. They gave him the sad news, and Hārūn wept from his heart, for he truly loved his concubine. He went to the tomb and prayed and wailed over his lost love. He fell asleep after thanking Zubaydah for all she had done.

But the caliph was not in deep sleep. He overheard the handmaidens discussing how his wife had duped him. He also learned Qūt al-Qulūb was living in Baghdad in the home of the wealthy merchant Ghānim bin Ayyūb. He went wild and immediately ordered that his vizier, Jaᶜfar, and an army of men bring his mistress to him and destroy to rubble the home of Ghānim.

At the home of Ghānim, the merchant had just set the table with the *ḥalwà wardīyah* when Qūt cried out to him, "Hurry! Take off your clothes and put on this beggar's garb and escape! The caliph's men have surrounded the house and I fear for your life!"

In this way, he escaped the clutches of the caliph's men, walking through them as a man of poor destiny. When Jaᶜfar approached Qūt, she knelt and kissed the ground in front of him and told him that Ghānim had left for Damascus. She then turned and pointed to a chest filled with gold, jewelry, precious stones, and rarities and asked that it be taken with them. As Jaᶜfar and Qūt rode away, the army of men plundered Ghānim's house, bringing it down to rubble.

Upon Qūt's return to Baghdad, the caliph ordered that she be imprisoned in a dark chamber and had an old woman take charge of her. The caliph wanted nothing more to do with Qūt, for he believed that she had been

Boil roses in water until the water takes on their color. Then make it into a syrup, taking on its consistency. Gradually add rosewater to it. Once it is almost thickened, dissolve starch in rosewater. Mix it into the syrup. Swirl over it two ūqīyahs of sesame oil and two ūqīyahs of musk and remove it.

SOURCE: *Kanz al-Fawā'id*

dishonored by Ghānim. He then wrote a letter to his viceroy in Damascus commanding him to find Ghānim and send him back to the caliph.

By the time Ghānim reached Damascus, his health had deteriorated. He was weak with hunger. He entered a mosque, where he rested. Those who saw him recognized him as a former man of wealth, but all they could do was to cover him from the cold and bring some honey and *ḥalwà wardīyah* to revive him. But he had no appetite.

The viceroy's men, in the meantime, had located Ghānim's house in Damascus and demolished it. Ghānim's mother and his sister, Fitnah, were questioned and then released. They had nowhere to go for refuge except the mosque. There they saw a pitiful sight: a sick man who looked to be on death's door. This destitute being was Ghānim, but they did not recognize him. Though suffering and forlorn and too sick to lift his head, he felt pity for these two women and gave them the food the do-gooders had given him.

The next day the neighborhood men brought a camel and instructed the cameleer to take the sick man to Baghdad to recuperate in a hospital there.

They reached the city, and the cameleer left Ghānim on the ground at the entrance of a hospital. He lay like this until the market inspector found him at dawn and, feeling compassion for him, took him to his house, knowing that God favors those who assist the meek. The inspector's wife tended to him, but every time Ghānim began to feel a little better, he thought of his love, Qūt al-Qulūb, and relapsed.

On the eightieth day of Qūt's confinement, the ruler passed by her door and heard her reciting a poem praising Ghānim for keeping her chaste, not touching her, and treating her with dignity. The caliph suddenly realized that he had wronged her, and he sent for her.

Hārūn al-Rashīd asked for her forgiveness and asked how he could reverse what he had done. She declared her undying love for Ghānim, and as recompense for having lost him, she asked that thousands of dinars be distributed to the poor, helping others as Ghānim had helped her.

To the souk she ventured, after having distributed a thousand dinars to the elders of the various faiths of the city and another thousand to charities. When she met up with the market inspector, she asked him to give a thousand dinars to a stranger in need. The inspector told her of a destitute fellow whom he had taken in and invited her to meet him so that she give the alms herself.

At the inspector's house she saw the stranger, sat with him, and furnished him with wine and medicines. He looked oddly familiar to her, seeming like a prince lost in his own land. She returned to the palace, all the while wondering about the beggar.

One day, the good-hearted market inspector arrived at the palace with two shabbily dressed women, asking for an audience with Qūt al-Qulūb. He told her that the women seemed of good breeding and dignity and it broke his heart to see them begging. Then he returned to his home. When Qūt saw the women, she wept, for she too felt their pain. She asked for their story, which they recounted, ending with the loss of their son and brother, Ghānim bin Ayyūb.

When Qūt al-Qulūb heard this she wept harder and felt faint, but she gathered her strength and said to them, "Today is the first day of good fortune, and this is the last day of misfortune!"

She ordered that the women be bathed and given the best of clothing, and then all three left for the home of the inspector to thank him and his wife for bringing them together. And it was there at the inspector's house that mother and sister recognized Ghānim, and it was also there that Ghānim heard the name Qūt al-Qulūb, which revived his weary soul, and he cried out for her. Qūt and Ghānim were reunited.

Qūt asked for an audience with the caliph and brought with her Ghānim, his mother, and his sister. At this meeting she told the entire story, and the caliph was intrigued. He asked to speak to Ghānim separately and was so impressed with his dignified manner of speech and stature, and especially with the protection that he gave Qūt, that he invested him with a dress of honor, a monthly allowance, rations, donations, and a part of the palace in which to reside. Ghānim became a wealthy man again.

The family moved in and it was at that time that the caliph heard of the beauty of Ghānim's sister, Fitnah, and asked for her hand in marriage. And it was on the same day that the chief judge of the city was called in to perform two marriages.

As for the lesson learned: destiny is a thing to be marveled at, for those who are good will be rewarded.

Yield depends upon size of pieces

This is an interesting dessert, similar to thick Jell-O but not as sweet. It can be made with various types of nuts, such as hazelnuts or pistachios; with sesame seeds or poppy seeds; or with dates. It can be colored with saffron for a different look. In some recipes, honey is used instead of sugar.

It can be cut into various shapes: squares, diamonds, or triangles. We tried this recipe out on friends, some of whom found it delightful and some of whom thought that it should be a little sweeter.

Ḥalwà remains the most popular sweetmeat in the Arabian Gulf, especially in Oman, where one can purchase it in the same manner that Americans buy doughnuts.

❧ In a medium saucepan, mix the sugar with the water and cook over medium-high heat and stir continuously, until it comes to a gentle boil. Lower the heat to medium and continue cooking for 10 more minutes, stirring occasionally.

❧ Stir in the rosewater, the cornstarch solution, and the oil. Continue cooking over medium heat, stirring constantly, until the mixture thickens and pulls from the sides of the saucepan (about 10 minutes). Remove from the heat and quickly stir in the chopped pistachios. Spread evenly on a serving platter and decorate immediately with the whole pistachios, pressing them down slightly.

❧ Once the *ḥalwà* has cooled, cut into serving pieces.

❧ *Ḥalwà* should be refrigerated. It keeps well for up to 3 days.

INGREDIENTS

¾ cup sugar

1½ cups water

1 tablespoon rosewater

½ cup cornstarch mixed
    with ½ cup water (stir until
    smooth with no lumps)

2 tablespoons light sesame oil

½ cup chopped pistachios

1 tablespoon whole pistachios

95

Murakkabah
and the Layer of Peace

Yaḥyà, son of Khālid, and ʿAbd Allāh, son of Mālik, had not spoken for years. Their quarrel had been a long one but its cause was a secret between the two men. Yaḥyà was jealous that Caliph Hārūn al-Rashīd's favor lay with ʿAbd Allāh, so much so that the caliph had made ʿAbd Allāh governor of Armenia and sent him to rule the region. This had led to the enmity between the two men.

There came one day to ʿAbd Allāh from among the people of Iraq a man who was esteemed and well-bred, cultured but crafty. He had lost his entire estate and all his wealth, but he was clever and had devised a plan to gain all back. Ingeniously, he wrote a letter to the governor, signed it with Yaḥyà's name, and then appeared with it before the governor's gate.

To the chamberlain, he gave the letter, who then carried it to his master. ʿAbd Allāh was enjoying a platter full of *murakkabah* when he was informed of the stranger's presence. In his wise manner, after reading the letter, ʿAbd Allāh knew it to be forged, and he sent for the stranger.

The stranger saluted him and his court with salaams of exaltation. ʿAbd Allāh asked his question: "What possessed you to bring forth this letter of forgery? Be honest with me and nothing bad will happen."

He responded, "May God prolong your life! If I have bothered you with my presence, then expel me. It is truly a letter I bring you from Yaḥyà, son of Khālid. It is not a forgery."

96

"Then I will write a letter to someone I know in Baghdad and order him to ask about this letter. If it in fact be true, then you will be given the choice of receiving the rulership of one of my cities or two hundred thousand dirhams—this with distinguished horses and camels and a robe of honor. However, if I find that this letter be a forgery, I will order that you be punished with a beating of two hundred blows and that your beard be shaven."

ʿAbd Allāh sent a letter to Baghdad and waited for the truth to reveal itself; meanwhile, he confined the man in a room with whatever he needed until the answer was brought to him.

To his agent in Baghdad he had sent a dispatch informing him that a man had appeared bearing a letter allegedly written by Yaḥyà, son of Khālid. He explained his suspicions and asked the agent to check immediately to see if the story was true. Upon receipt of the order, the agent set out at once.

At the house of Yaḥyà, son of Khālid, the agent found Yaḥyà sitting with his entourage of officers and friends. He found the son of Khālid quietly munching on a platter of *murakkabah* in the same manner ʿAbd Allāh had. Greeting him, the agent then produced the dispatch from the governor. Yaḥyà read it and asked the agent to return the following day so that he prepare a written response.

Yaḥyà just did not understand. What purpose was served for this man to forge a letter from Yaḥyà and then take it to Yaḥyà's rival? His entourage began guessing this and that, contemplating the situation but coming up with no solution or reasonable explanation. They began to propose various types of punishment for the stranger from Iraq, at which point Yaḥyà declared, "You are all mistaken. You are choosing a pessimistic point of view over an optimistic one. Do you not believe that there is a reason that God made this man forge a letter in my name? Do you not believe this is a higher sign that it is time for reconciliation between ʿAbd Allāh and myself, that God has used this gentleman as the means of putting out the fire of anger in our hearts after two decades? It is therefore in the interests of peace that I verify this letter as mine and that ʿAbd Allāh, son of Mālik, increase the honor of this man and reward him."

This is what made Yaḥyà a man of all men, and when those around him heard his words of understanding, they called for God's blessings for his generosity and fairness.

Yaḥyà, son of Khālid, called for paper and ink and wrote ʿAbd Allāh in his own hand with the following words:

May God grant you long life! I am pleased to hear that you are well and
that life is prosperous for you. You inquired as to the validity of a
certain letter written in my name—I herewith declare the letter to be
legitimate and not a forgery. Please honor the bearer of the letter
generously, for what you bestow on him in kindness you grant to me
in honor and munificence. I thank you profoundly.

Upon receipt of the letter, ʿAbd Allāh was fascinated and charmed. He sent for the Iraqi man and asked which of the promised gifts he would choose. He disbursed to him the two hundred thousand dirhams and ten Arabian horses with silk and saddles, twenty chests of clothes, slaves, and expensive jewels. As well, he bestowed on him a robe of honor and sent him to Baghdad in great majesty.

The man from Iraq went straightaway to Yaḥyà's house, where he entered and kissed the ground before him. Yaḥyà did not know him. All he saw was a man dressed in splendid and magnificent garb.

"Who are you?" Yaḥyà asked.

"Hear me, my lord. I was once a man near dead in misfortune, but because of you destiny has given me wealth and fortune, for I am the man who forged a letter in your name and presented it to ʿAbd Allāh, son of Mālik. Because of your generosity and kindness, your compassion and bounty, Governor ʿAbd Allāh bestowed on me gifts and great favors, which I bring to you today as yours and not mine."

"No, no, my noble man! It is not you who should give me thanks but I who should give them to you. You have brought together two ends of a rope and changed hate to love between two men who now respect and honor each other. It is I who owe the gratitude. I therefore declare that what the great governor granted you, I bestow the same. Now sit with me and enjoy what the good and dignified people savor—*murakkabah*. You have given the meaning of its name—'layers of peace'—honor, for you have taken ʿAbd Allāh's and my enmity and fitted the two of us together in a friendship that, God willing, will last our lifetime!"

The simplest description of this sweet is that it's a multilayered *(murakkabah)* pancake made with honey and semolina; it has a lightweight texture, like a sweet, layered crèpe cake.

One of the first sweets introduced to us on a visit to Morocco was *murakkabah*. It came as a surprise when we sat down to it at the home of our friends the Kittānīs in the capital city of Rabat. Our hostess, Aunt Amīnah, a lady whose family descends from Andalusia, explained to us that this dish was the Moroccan version of the North American pancake. In true Arab hospitable fashion, rather than placing one or two pancakes on the dish, she served them in the Moroccan style, piling them up and offering them in quantity.

Fascinated with its name, we were stirred even more by its description, a pancake-like cake that sounded like crepes in layers, a heaven-sent treat. We were ready to partake of the taste of an Andalusian paradise. We learned that the sweet was a medieval one and had been brought to North Africa when the Moors were expelled from Spain.

*Knead good semolina
into a firm dough with hot water
after having moistened it
with water, salt and a little yeast.
Continue adding water and kneading until it
becomes a light dough. Then knead it again
with egg whites: for every* raṭl *of semolina,
add four whites of eggs, until the eggs are
blended in with the dough. Then place
a wide clay unglazed pan over the fire.
When it is heated, wipe it with a piece of cloth
in which salt has been tied up and that has
been dipped in oil or melted clarified butter.
Spread the dough out in the pan.
Once it becomes white, add more dough and
turn it. Continue doing this until the dough
finishes and so that all the loaves look the
same. Then layer it, one piece over another.
When it is done, place it in a wide vessel
and pour enough honey and butter over it
to soak it, and sprinkle cinnamon over it.
Eat and enjoy, God Almighty willing.*

SOURCE: al-Tujībī, *Faḍālah al-Khiwān fī Ṭayyībāt al-Ṭaʿām wa al-Alwān*

99

Murakkabah

Preparing the Syrup:

1 cup honey

¼ cup butter

❦ Mix the honey and the butter in a small saucepan and bring to a boil.
Keep the syrup warm over very low heat.

Preparing the Batter:

1 tablespoon sugar

1¼ cups warm water

1 package yeast

2 cups extra-fine semolina flour

2 egg whites, beaten to soft peaks

Olive oil

❦ Mix the sugar in a ¼ cup of the water and add the yeast. Cover and keep in a warm place, allowing the yeast to rise for about 10 minutes.

❦ In a deep mixing bowl, add the semolina and make a well. Add the yeast mixture, the remaining water, and the egg whites and mix well. Cover the bowl with a towel and leave the batter to rise for 2 hours.

❦ After the batter has risen, stir well. The batter should be similar to crepe batter. (Add a little more warm water if the batter is too thick.)

Preparing the Murakkabah:

❦ Brush oil on the bottom of an 8- or 9-inch frying pan. Using a ladle, spoon the batter into the frying pan, spreading it out into an approximately 7-inch circle. Over medium-low heat, fry for about 2 minutes or until browned. Lift the crépe and brush the frying pan with oil again, then turn the crépe over and cook the second side. On the top part (the already-cooked side), spoon another ladleful of batter, then spread it out evenly over the entire top, smoothing it with a spatula. Once the bottom is cooked, lift the layered crépe, brush the pan with oil again, and return the layered crépe, uncooked-side down, to pan. Continue the process until all the batter is finished. Once the last side of the *murakkabah* is cooked, turn the loaf on its side and roll it around the frying pan to make sure its edges are cooked.

❦ Place the *murakkabah* on a serving platter. Using a skewer or the handle of a tablespoon, punch many holes into the top of the *murakkabah*, being careful not to punch into the bottom layer. Pour the syrup several times evenly over the top to allow the *murakkabah* to absorb the syrup.

❦ Slice into wedges and serve warm.

Nātif and the Wily Woman

In Baghdad one day, the police took away a man for disturbing the peace during a solemn procession. As people walked in silent meditation, he was heard to shout, "I beg you, let her once more be angry with her husband so that I may see her again!"

He was taken to the emir. When questioned, he begged to tell his story before any judgment be made so that his circumstances be understood and punishment waived. The emir granted the request.

"Know, O great prince, that I am but a worker in a slaughterhouse and daily it is my routine to clean and take the rubbish outside the gates. One day I was about to unload my heap of rubbish when, suddenly, I saw people running away.

"One of them stopped to warn me to enter an alley lest I be seen. Hurriedly, he explained to me that the wife of a notable was passing by and her servants had been ordered to drive any person they saw out of her way and beat them. I quickly took the advice and ran with my donkey, then hid further along the route to see what was happening.

"I waited and waited and was able to see the noblewoman's servants with sticks in their hands walking ahead of a group of her handmaidens who encircled the lady. My eyes had never been so consumed with passion as when I saw her—a woman of grace, stature, beauty, and exquisiteness. I was awestruck.

"When she came near to where I was, I saw her lean toward one of her menservants and whisper in his ear. In a moment he appeared before me and laid hold of me. Everyone ran away, and I was left to fend for myself, knowing his stick would be raised at me. Instead, I was bound and tied and dragged after him, all the while the crowds yelling in my defense that I had done nothing wrong, pleading out of pity to let me go.

All I could think was that I had been taken because my shabby appearance and smelliness had offended that vision of beauty.

"I was taken to a great house and then into a huge hall furnished with the most magnificent of furniture. Then servants came in and took me into the bathhouse, where they bathed me, threw away my tattered clothing, replaced them with new clothes, and ordered me to put them on. Unfortunately, I had no idea how to don this type of expensive clothing and had to be assisted. After they sprinkled me with rosewater they took me to another hall, where I saw, sitting upon a lush couch with her ivory feet raised, this noblewoman of grace.

"She called me to sit beside her and had the servant girls bring in all manner of food and sweets, the like of which I had never seen. She fed me with her own hands a sweet she called *nāṭif*, which was as sweet as her voice singing songs of love.

"The wine was then brought out, of which we drank our fill, and when its effect had taken a toll on us both, I imagined it all a dream as she put her arms around me and we both relaxed. Each time I held her closer I smelled the scent of musk and other perfumes from her body. I thought, *If Paradise be this, then let me be here forever.*

"The next day before I departed she handed me a kerchief with something tied in it. I hoped that in it would be at least a few coppers so that I could buy my breakfast and perhaps even find some *nāṭif* in the souk. I returned to my battered shack of an abode and opened the kerchief to discover fifty dinars of gold!

"I buried them in the ground and sat at my front door, thinking of what had happened to me and pondering if it had been a dream or if I had actually entered Paradise.

"It was then that the servant girl appeared and commanded me to attend once again to her mistress. I arrived at her home and kissed the ground before her and again she called for the meat, *ādhān*, and wine, and we spent the night together as we had done before. The next morning was the same as the previous— she sent me off with a tied kerchief with fifty dinars in it, and I buried these dinars with the others.

"For eight joyful days this continued: I'd go to her home and come back with a kerchief full of fifty dinars, which I buried. But on the eighth night, as we lay in each other's arms, one of her servants came running in and told me to quickly hide in the closet. This I did, even more quickly than she told me.

"Then I heard the sounds of the tramping of a horse; I looked out of the window and saw a handsome young man dismount with a number of servants and attendants around him. He entered the hall and found my lady on the couch. He approached her and kissed the ground before her and then kissed her hands. Although she did not speak to him, he continued to speak words of humbleness and compassion to her. He remained with her that night.

"Early the next morning the handsome young man left with his soldiers. She came to me and told me that the man who had spent the night had been her husband. With this, she began her story.

"She had been sitting in the garden with her husband, the two sipping tea and snacking on *ādhān*, when he excused himself for a moment. The moment turned into a matter of a long while, so she decided to find out where he had gone. She found him, not alone but with one of the kitchen maids.

"She was angry and swore that she would get back at him with the filthiest and most foul man in Baghdad. That is when she found me; apparently, I fit the description to a T. She now informed me that her retaliation was complete and she no longer needed me, but if she ever found her husband again with the kitchen maid she would restore me to the position again. I cried and cried, knowing that this was the end of our rendezvous; my heart was pierced with the knowledge that the affair was over.

"And so it is today that I cried out for my lady and begged God that her husband would return to the kitchen maid and that she would be angry with him so that I might be united with her again."

The emir looked with sympathy at the young man, considered his story, and then set him free with a few words of advice:

> *Hell hath no fury like a woman scorned*
> *This you now learned, you have been warned*
> *On her man this woman's revenge she has taken*
> *As you ate her nāṭif, your love she's forsaken.*
> *There is woe, there is pity for your filth and your grime*
> *From the story you tell you have committed no crime.*
> *You've been had, you've been duped, her revenge was sweet*
> *Her charms, her nāṭif, which you considered your treat.*

Nāṭif can be compared to today's peanut brittle. The method of preparing the sugar continues in the homes of many Arab emigrants whose families left the old country at the turn of the nineteenth century. Our grandmother taught our mother how to make candy this way, and she told us that the procedure had been around since her grandmother's time and before.

Here we have a hard and enjoyable brittle candy, the recipe for which has passed through the centuries virtually unchanged other than variations of the nuts that are added, based on what's available.

What makes this source recipe unique is the suggestion that chickpeas, a standard staple of Arab cooking in appetizers, soups, or entrees, can be used as part of this sweet. If you decide to use chickpeas, as we do on some occasions, we recommend purchasing roasted chickpeas from a Middle Eastern grocery.

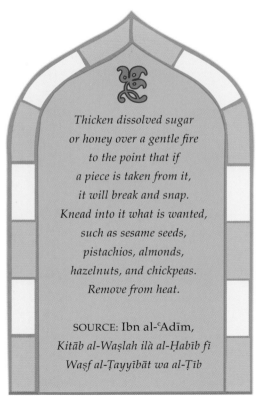

*Thicken dissolved sugar
or honey over a gentle fire
to the point that if
a piece is taken from it,
it will break and snap.
Knead into it what is wanted,
such as sesame seeds,
pistachios, almonds,
hazelnuts, and chickpeas.
Remove from heat.*

SOURCE: Ibn al-ᶜAdīm,
*Kitāb al-Waṣlah ilà al-Ḥabīb fī
Waṣf al-Ṭayyibāt wa al-Ṭīb*

Nāṭif

Makes about 36 pieces

INGREDIENTS

2 cups sugar

4 tablespoons unsalted shelled pistachios

4 tablespoons slivered almonds

4 tablespoons walnuts, halved

❧ Place the sugar in a heavy-bottomed frying pan and, using a wooden spoon, constantly stir the sugar over medium-low heat for about 20 minutes. As you stir, the sugar will slowly harden, then liquefy. The sugar is ready when you drop a small amount of liquefied sugar into a cup of cold water and it hardens into a ball. As soon as the sugar is ready, quickly stir in the nuts, then pour the mixture onto a well-greased baking tray; using a wooden spoon, spread out evenly but quickly to about a ¼-inch thickness.

❧ Allow to cool completely, then break into pieces and serve.

Lawzīnaj
and the Deception

There was once a nobleman who brought home for his wife a young man to serve as her page.

One day the man suggested to his wife that on the morrow she should go into their garden and relax and enjoy the solace and beauty of it. She loved the idea. However, unbeknownst to the two, the page was listening.

The page was a crafty fellow. He prepared some meat dishes, drinks, fruits, and *lawzīnaj*, and secretly went into the garden that same night. He hid the meat under one tree, dried fruits under another, *lawzīnaj* under one, and, under the last tree, the wine. These were all placed in the path that he knew the nobleman's wife would take.

The following morning the master of the house ordered the page to accompany his wife into the garden and to take with him whatever was needed for the day.

The page and the nobleman's wife entered the garden and, after walking a bit, they heard the cawing of a crow. The wife asked, "Do you know what the crow is saying?"

"Of course, my lady! The crow is saying that under that tree, there is meat, and you should go and eat it."

She was surprised, but upon finding the meat dish under the tree, she marveled and was positive that the young man spoke the truth—the young man did indeed understand the language of the birds. Together they enjoyed the plate of food.

The crow crowed again. "What does it say?" asked the wife, turning to the page.

"Under that tree are dried fruits and conserves." In wonderment she found the fruits, and the two enjoyed them.

Again they walked, enjoying the trees and flowers, and then for a third time they heard the crow. The nobleman's wife turned to the page and asked him what the bird was saying.

"My lady, the crow is saying that there is *lawzīnaj* for dessert beneath that tree!"

She went to the tree, found her favorite of all sweets, and sat and enjoyed every almond-filled mouthful.

Again, they began to stroll the magnificent gardens, and again, the crow began to caw.

"Pray tell, my good page, what does the crow say now?"

The page said, "Under that tree is a pitcher of wine."

She was amazed. He was right! So together they sat and drank the wine, she becoming more and more enthralled with her young man. He was surely an extraordinary fellow. He grew in wonder in her eyes.

They sauntered through the gardens again. Once more they heard the crow. "What is he saying now?" she asked in awe.

This time, however, the page did not translate the bird's tongue. Instead, he picked up a stone and threw it at him.

"Why? Why? What has he said that made you throw that stone at him?"

"My noble lady! I cannot tell you."

"Please, my good page, do not be embarrassed just because I am standing here. There is nothing that should be hidden between you and me."

But he refused to talk. She continued to urge him to speak and translate what the crow had said. He remained steadfast, but she pressed and pressed him and he finally explained, "The crow has said to me: Treat this lady as if you were her husband!"

This caused her to laugh and laugh so that tears of laughter issued from her eyes. She told him to lie beside her upon the carpet she spread beneath the tree. They began to embrace, his arms wrapped around her and his lips on hers.

And then who should appear but her husband! Without their knowing, he had followed them throughout their stroll in the garden. "What is this?" he called out to the page. "Why is it that I see my wife lying there weeping?"

"Oh, my great lord! She fell from the tree and lay down to recover from the fall. I believed her to be near dead and I was checking to see if she was breathing."

At this the lady looked at her husband, winced in pretended pain, then attempted to lift herself.

"Oh, my poor back, my poor sides! I do not know if I will get over this!" she complained weakly as she called for help.

The nobleman ordered the page to fetch his lady's horse and to help her mount it. He had the young man hold her on one side and he held her on the other so that her pain could be alleviated somewhat until she reached the house.

"I promise you," said the husband, "when we reach home I will have this page prepare for you the choicest of meat dishes, dried fruits, and wine, and most of all, your favorite sweet, *lawzīnaj!*"

> *How great the foods she will receive*
> *A page the noble did deceive*
> *A woman's passion often lingers*
> *With the passion of almond fingers.*

Take a raṭl of sugar and
finely grind it. Take a third
of a raṭl of almonds
that have been skinned and
also finely grind them.
Mix them with the sugar
and knead with rosewater.
Then take very thin bread
similar to the bread used for
al-sanbūsaj, *the thinner the better.*
Spread out a sheet of that bread
and place the paste made
of almonds and sugar on it.
Then roll it up in the form of a
rope and cut it into small pieces.
Arrange them. Refine fresh sesame
oil in the amount needed and
pour it over them. Then soak them
in syrup into which rosewater
has already been added.
Sprinkle finely pounded
pistachios over them.

SOURCE: al-Baghdādī,
Kitāb al-Ṭabīkh

Reading through *One Thousand and One Arabian Nights,* we discovered that one of the most popular sweets mentioned in the tales is *lawzīnaj.* This makes sense, since the dessert dates back at least as far as the eighth century, when it was so loved that poetry extolling its virtues was written. What makes this dessert so intriguing is that it was the subject of a contest between Caliph Hārūn al-Rashīd (d. A.D. 809) and his wife, Zubaydah. The chief judge of the city of Baghdad, Abū Yūsuf, was called upon to make the ultimate decision of which was tastier, the sweet *fālūdhaj,* Zubaydah's favorite, or *lawzīnaj,* the caliph's choice. In the end, the poor man could not pass judgment. In his quest to make a decision, he was compelled to constantly taste and re-taste each of the two dishes. Perhaps Abū Yūsuf was more wise than he was judicial, as he has left it to us in the twenty-first century to come up with our own verdict.

After tasting both sweets, we understood Abū Yūsuf's predicament. As for the vote—well, let this recipe collection help you make the judgment.

Although the source recipe does not call for frying or baking the sweet, we have adapted the recipe using phyllo dough, and thus it does need to be cooked.

Lawzīnaj

Makes about 54 to 66 pieces, depending
on number of sheets in package

❧ Prepare the basic *qaṭr* recipe using either rosewater or orange-
blossom water and set aside to cool.

❧ To make the stuffing, place the almonds, the sugar, and the rosewater in a bowl. Mix well and then set aside.

❧ Place the phyllo dough sheets horizontally, and cut the sheets
into three equal columns. Keep the dough covered with a slightly
dampened towel.

❧ Take one sheet of the phyllo, and with a pastry brush, lightly
brush butter on all edges. Place a heaping teaspoon of the stuffing near the bottom edge of the phyllo sheet and spread it out
slightly, not touching edges of the phyllo. Fold up the sides of the
phyllo, approximately a quarter inch. Roll upward, tucking in the
sides, creating a log shape. Brush egg on the seam of the *lawzīnaj*
to seal it well. Place the roll, seam side up, on a floured surface
and let stand until all the rolls are completed.

❧ Heat the oil over medium heat and deep-fry the *lawzīnaj* for a few minutes, turning them over until a light golden color on all sides. Remove with a slotted spoon
and place on paper towels for a few minutes to absorb excess oil, and then place
on a tray until cooled.

❧ Dip the *lawzīnaj* into the syrup and place on a serving tray. Sprinkle the
pistachios over the *lawzīnaj* immediately, while the syrup is still warm.

INGREDIENTS

Basic qaṭr *(sugar syrup) recipe
(see page 11)*

2 cups finely ground almonds

1¼ cups superfine sugar

3 teaspoons rosewater

*1 package phyllo dough
(1 pound)*

1 pound unsalted butter, melted

1 egg, beaten

Oil for frying

1 cup ground pistachios

Al-Kāhīn
and the Purse

There once were four merchants who together owned one thousand gold coins that they kept in a purse along with some other personal items. One day they set out together to purchase some merchandise. On their way to the souk, they chanced upon a beautiful garden with winding pathways surrounded by flowers,

shrubs, and trees of all heights. They decided to take a stroll through it and asked the woman garden keeper to keep the purse with her until they returned. She was instructed not to give it back to them unless all four of them together agreed. She accepted their request, and the men took off to delight in the wonders of nature.

They walked and talked, then found a seller of *kāhīn*, that delicious sweet puff pastry, and sat enjoying these tidbits until they had stuffed themselves to the point of delightful discomfort and ended up with sticky hands and mouths. It so happened that one of the merchants had in his pocket some powdered soap, and he said to his colleagues, "Let us wash our heads and hands with this soap in that fountain ahead of us."

They agreed but realized that they needed a comb to use on their hair after washing it. "No problem," said one of the merchants. "I will ask the garden keeper to give us the comb from our purse." At this, he left to seek her out.

"Give me the purse!" instructed the merchant to the garden keeper.

"Absolutely not!" she responded. "All four of you must be present, or you must all agree in unison when you make that demand."

The merchant called to his companions, who could see him but not hear him clearly as he cried out, "She will not give it to me." The three others called out to her, "Give it to him!," thinking that their merchant friend meant she would not give him the comb.

She gave him back the purse, and instead of returning to his friends, he ran off as fast as his legs could carry him.

Some time passed, and the other three began to worry about the merchant's absence. They went to the keeper of the gardens and asked her, "Did you not give him the comb?" She explained immediately that their missing colleague had not asked for a comb but rather had demanded the purse from her, and she, according to the agreement, had given it to him since the other three had agreed that she should.

Now, these three merchants were stupefied by what she had said. They grew angry. After hitting themselves on the heads with disgust for assuming they'd had a strong and trusting relationship with the runaway merchant, they grabbed the woman garden keeper and shouted, "We authorized you to give him the comb, not the purse." In her defense, she responded that he never asked for the comb.

The three merchants, angry at their loss, dragged the woman to the district judge. They explained to him their case against her, and then she once again defended herself by saying that the missing merchant had demanded the purse and not the comb. The judge ruled in favor of the three merchants and demanded that the poor garden keeper pay back the sum that had been taken in the purse. She was given a certain time period in which to return the money.

She left the court distraught, not knowing how she would be able to comply with the judgment imposed by the judge. She slowly wandered along the city streets, and a young lad watched her, knowing that this was a troubled woman. He felt compassion for her.

"What is it that distresses you, O troubled lady?" She did not respond, for her mind was in turmoil, causing her to shut out the world around her. He persisted as he walked alongside her, worried that she might cause harm to herself.

Finally, she turned to him and told him what was causing her sadness and anguish.

He felt for this woman, who seemed to have a kind soul and who reminded him of his mother, who had passed from the world a long time ago. He thought about how he could help, and he suddenly came up with a plan. Unbeknownst to the woman, however, though he did want to help her, he also wanted to help his own appetite, which had been whetted when she mentioned in her story the sweet delight *kāhīn*.

"If you give me a dirham to buy some *kāhīn*, I will tell you how you can get yourself out of the financial mess into which you have been thrown." She perked up when she heard his words, for she was ready and willing to take any advice to alleviate her situation.

"Now, return to the judge and say to him, 'It was agreed between myself and the four merchants that I should not give them their purse only unless all four of them were present. I therefore ask that you call for all four of them to come and I will give them the money that was in the purse.'"

So she went back to the judge and said to him all that the young lad had advised her to say. The judge called again for the three merchants and asked them if this was what the agreement had been. They acknowledged that this was true. The judge then ordered them to bring the fourth merchant to the court; only when he was present would the woman return the purse with the one thousand gold coins.

The three merchants went off in search of the missing fourth merchant, and the good woman returned home, knowing that he might never be found, for indeed Aleppo was a large city, and it might just take forever to find him.

Let it be known that whosoever takes on the protection of something from anyone else must learn to protect him— or herself first.

> They enjoyed their kāhīn *till their bellies were sate*
> Then returned for their purse after they ate
> Instead they were tricked by one of their own
> Placing the guilt on another to bemoan.
> But judgment is sweet when the game is played well
> For what goes around comes around, as in this story we tell.

Take egg whites, and for every egg white, take a weight of two dirhams of starch. Pound the starch finely and beat with the egg whites, mixing well. Throw it in a round-bottomed earthenware pot and fry them as patties. Dip them in syrup. They come out most extraordinary.

SOURCE: *Kanz al-Fawā'id*

These cookies are unique not only in taste but also texture. They are simply fried meringues. We are not sure what the term *kāhīn* means, but it could have been derived from the name of its creator or from the place where it was first developed.

The trick to making it is buttering the serving platter well, because these little delights are very sticky. We realize now why the four merchants had to wash their hands and hair after eating it.

One other piece of advice: eat them immediately. They taste better warm. You can imagine what our kitchen looked like when our taste testers gathered around the stove, with mouths wide open, ready to pop them in.

Upon the recommendation of our source author, we did fry them in butter after we'd first attempted it with oil. He was right. They tasted much better.

Kāhīn

Makes 15 to 20 pieces

INGREDIENTS

Half of basic qaṭr *(sugar syrup) recipe*
  (see page 11)
3 egg whites
1½ teaspoons cornstarch
¼ teaspoon rosewater
1 cup oil or 1 to 1½ cups butter, melted

❧ Prepare the *qaṭr*. Allow the syrup to cool before preparing the egg white mixture.

❧ In a bowl, mix together the egg whites, the cornstarch, and the rosewater. Stir well until there are no lumps. Beat the mixture with an electric beater until stiff peaks form.

❧ In a medium saucepan, heat the oil or butter over medium-low heat. Drop a teaspoonful of the egg white mixture into the oil or butter and fry the *kāhīn* until they begin to turn a slightly golden color, turning over once. Remove with a slotted spoon and immediately dip the *kāhīn* into the *qaṭr* and place on a well-greased serving platter. Continue the process until all the *kāhīn* have been made, then serve immediately.

Qaṭā'if
and the Gallantry of Man

There was once a governor in Basra by the name of Khālid ibn ʿAbdallāh al-Kasrī. One day a group of men appeared before him dragging behind them a handsome young man, seemingly of good breeding and dressed in lofty attire. He did not appear to be of the criminal type, thus evoking surprise from Khālid when he was told that the young man was a thief.

"We caught him stealing from our house last night," they announced.

Khālid looked at him again and felt that something was just not right. This person before him was too elegant and too dignified to be a thief. "Unbind him!" ordered the governor as he approached the young man. "What do you have to say for yourself? Are these accusations true?"

"Yes, what these people say is true," the young man responded.

"Well, then," said Khālid, appearing somewhat shocked, "what prompted you to do this? You don't look like you need to steal."

The young man said simply, "It was the sin of the lust of worldly goods that made me do it."

Khālid could not accept the logic of this reasoning and again asked how someone so apparently well bred and reasonable could not restrain himself from thievery. But the young man said only that he was ready to receive the punishment for theft—the loss of both his hands.

But Khālid wanted to give the young man another chance. He whispered in his ear, "Your confession confounds me. I cannot bring myself to believe that you are a thief. I know there is something else going on, a story, perhaps, that will explain all this. I am giving you the chance to tell me."

The youth replied, "Oh, kind sir! It is as I have said. There is no story to tell except that I entered the home of these people and took whatever I laid my hands on. They caught me and took back that which I had taken and then brought me here."

The governor ordered that he be shackled again and sent to prison and that a crier go out through Basra to announce that those who wished to witness the punishment of a thief should attend court on the morrow.

In the prison cell, the young man looked at his shackles of iron and began to sigh deeply and to cry, tears flowing. He began to lament in verse:

My confession I made for the sake of her honor
I would never disgrace my beloved and lover
Rather lose my hands with a confession that's wrong
Rather than shame her as my love remains strong.

The guards heard him and went to Khālid to tell him what they had heard. It was late at night when the governor sent for him. Over food and sweets, they conversed. Khālid encouraged the youth to eat what appeared to be the prisoner's favorite, *qaṭā'if*. For more than an hour, the two talked, the young man relishing all the while the stuffed pancakes and their filling of nuts. Khālid felt as if he were watching the young lad eat his last meal; he ate one *qaṭā'if* after another. The governor was now even more disbelieving of the confession the youth had made, especially after having found him to be intelligent and lively, a pleasant companion. He wanted to give him another chance.

"I know you are not a thief. Therefore, when the judge comes tomorrow and interrogates you about the robbery, I want you to deny the charges of theft, since there has to be a story behind all this."

The young man was sent back to prison for the night. In the morning he was brought before the tribunal and the judges while the city folk assembled to await the young man's punishment. It was difficult for him to walk, his legs in shackles, and all who saw him wept out of pity for him. It was as if the mourning had already begun.

The chief judge stood and asked for silence. He pointed at the prisoner and read the charges. "These witnesses say that you entered their house and stole from them less than a quarter dinar. What do you say to these charges?"

"Your Honor, no, it is not true. I did not steal less than a quarter dinar. I stole that and much more."

The judge questioned him more. "Did any of what you took belong to you?"

"No," replied the young man, "none was mine. It was all theirs."

The judge slapped the prisoner on the face and called for the punishment to be meted out. When the young man's hands were placed and ready to be struck off, behold, a maiden in tattered clothing rushed from a crowd of women and cried out. She ran to the young man and threw herself on him. She removed her veil, and from the silence of the crowd arose gasps of wonder and awe: her face was like the beauty of the moon at night. She cried above the gasps of the crowd, "I beg you, O great governor, do not strike off this man's hands until you have read what is written in this scroll!" Khālid unrolled the scroll and found these written words:

The one who carries this letter to you
Is the cause of what this man has gone through.
Her eyes are bowed from the shame of his grief

Take ripe fresh green walnuts that are easy to shell, peel them of their thin skin, and cut with a knife in the same way one chops herbs. Then take the same amount of Ṭabrazad sugar, pound it, and mix it with the walnuts. Sprinkle al-Jūrī rosewater on them and mix with almond oil. Put this in the qaṭāʾif— each stuffed qaṭāʾif should be bite size. Then arrange them in layers in a vessel and drench with fresh almond oil. Spread pounded white sugar between and over them. Serve in a big wide bowl filled with ice, God willing.

SOURCE: al-Warrāq,
Kitāb al-Ṭabīkh

116

Causing him to love her, calling himself a thief.
He swore to a crime he did not commit
To protect our love, he chose to admit
That he robbed, that he stole, that he committed a sin
To not disgrace me from his love within.
His noble nature made him confess a crime
The fault is not his; the fault is mine.

The lines read, Khālid summoned the girl and questioned her. She told them that the two were lovers and that one night the young man had thought to visit her at her home. To let her know he was there, he threw a stone into the house. However, her father and brothers heard the noise and ran to him. The young man began to gather up all he could in household goods so that it would look like he was a thief. He did this, she explained, to protect his mistress's honor.

"That is when they seized him and brought him as a thief before you, O honorable judge. Understand that he pretended to be a robber to spare me any shame. He refused to change his confession even when it meant that he would lose his hands," she lamented through her tears.

Khālid walked over to the young man and kissed him between the eyes. He bestowed on the lad ten thousand dirhams for being ready to give up his hands to spare his lover shame, and he granted the young lady ten thousand dirhams for confessing to the truth. The governor then asked the girl's father for permission for the two to marry, to which the father consented. For the wedding gift, the governor gave them another ten thousand dirhams.

Throughout Basra the people rejoiced in the marriage of the bridegroom and his bride. The story of the young man and his lady love was recounted over and over. Each household celebrated by making *qaṭā'if*, as if to remind themselves of the honorable youth who had been ready to sacrifice himself through false confession for the one he loved. They praised him, they saluted him, and they recited the Arab proverb:

Write the bad things that are done to you in sand, but write the good things that happen to you on marble.

We have to admit that this was one of the easiest recipes to make. This was one of the reasons we chose al-Warrāq's tenth-century cookbook recipe, but another reason was its original title: *Qaṭā'if That Were Made for Hārūn al-Rashīd*. Why not savor the same sweet that the eighth-century caliph savored?

Qaṭā'if has remained for many centuries one of the most common sweets served in the Arab world. Our grandmother learned it from her mother, and she taught our mother how to make these when she was first learning how to cook.

The source recipe calls for a walnut filling. Other source recipes call for other types of nuts, and in some cases for mixtures of them. As for the size of the *qaṭā'if*, recipes vary: some, like this source recipe, call for bite-size morsels, while others call for larger sizes.

Nowadays one of the most popular fillings for *qaṭā'if* is a creamy type of cheese filling. Just as in the ancient souks of Baghdad, where *qaṭā'if* could be found prepared and sold by a *qaṭā'if* seller, modern patisseries, from Baghdad to Damascus, stock many varieties of this sweet.

In the Middle East, there is no need to make the batter at home. The hostess need only purchase the cooked pancakes, then either make or buy whatever filling she prefers. All that is really required in this day and age is stuffing them and putting them in the oven until they turn golden brown. The trick to good *qaṭā'if* is to stuff them well and to make sure that they have been sealed tightly.

Now here's a good story about East meeting West. On our most recent trip to Damascus, we visited some close friends and brought with us as a gift Canadian maple syrup and a waffle iron. These two items were great souvenirs from Canada. Our friends dipped their fingers in the maple syrup and loved it. We announced that this syrup reached its peak when it was served with good old Canadian waffles, and we volunteered to teach the group how to make waffles. However, the group had disappeared. Where were they? In the kitchen dunking Arab *qaṭā'if* in Canadian maple syrup! That is a true example of East meeting West.

Qaṭā'if

Makes 22 to 24 pieces

🌸 Preheat the oven to 375 degrees.

🌸 Sift together the dry ingredients of the batter in a large mixing bowl. Gradually beat in the milk and the eggs until smooth. Add 2 tablespoons of the melted butter and beat again, then cover and allow to rest for two hours.

🌸 While the batter is resting, prepare the *qaṭr* and allow to cool.

🌸 To make the filling, mix in a medium-size bowl the walnuts, the sugar, the almond oil, and the rosewater, then set aside.

🌸 To make the *qaṭā'if*, heat a griddle, then grease it with shortening or butter. Pour about 2 tablespoons of the batter onto the griddle to make about 3-inch-wide patties (on a griddle, you can make about 4 pancakes at a time). Cook on one side only until the side being cooked is slightly golden and bubbles appear on the uncooked surface. Remove and place on a flat tray, cooked-side down. Place about 2 teaspoons of the filling on the uncooked side of each pancake, then fold over to make a half-moon shape and press firmly along the edges. Transfer to a buttered baking sheet or tray; repeat the procedure until all the batter is finished.

🌸 Pour some of the remaining melted butter over each *qaṭā'if*, then bake for 12 minutes. Remove from the oven and dip immediately into the *qaṭr*, then place in a sieve for about 10 seconds to allow the excess syrup to drain off. Place on a serving platter and allow to cool. Sprinkle generously with confectioners' sugar before serving.

INGREDIENTS

Qaṭā'if Batter
2 cups flour
1½ teaspoons baking powder
½ teaspoon salt
2 cups milk
2 eggs
1 cup butter, melted
One basic qaṭr (sugar syrup)
   (see page 11)

Filling
2 cups finely chopped walnuts
1 cup sugar
1 tablespoon almond oil
3 teaspoons rosewater

Confectioners' sugar

Nuhūd al-Ṣābūnīyha and the Chest

There once was a certain merchant in Baghdad who was an extremely jealous husband. He had a wife who was the model of beauty, excessive beyond all words and imagination.

For this reason, he built her a mansion outside the city walls, to keep prying eyes away from her. This abode was built high and its doors were double-locked. It lay far away from other homes. To ensure that no one else could enter the house, the merchant kept the key for the lock tied around his neck.

It so happened that one day, when the merchant was away in a far-off land on business, the king's son decided to take a ride in the country to relax and enjoy the scenery. He was tired of the hustle and bustle of the city. As he meandered through the open countryside, he spotted a solitary mansion and stopped, admiring its architecture. As his eyes beheld the splendor of it, they fell on a beautiful woman looking and leaning out of one of the windows. He was love-struck.

He had to reach her. He looked around for something to help him get to her but found nothing. He asked one of his pages for ink and paper and wrote a note to her expressing his profound love. He attached the note to an arrow and shot it toward the mansion, where it fell in the garden. The merchant's wife was taking a walk there, and upon seeing a paper with writing asked one of her servants to retrieve it. She read his words of love and passion, his words of yearning and desire, and quickly went up to her room and wrote him a reply.

Yes, she too felt the same, perhaps more. Her longing was more passionate, she wrote, and with that she threw the letter down to him from the window of her abode.

Her response led the king's son to venture beneath the window where she stood. He asked her to send down a rope to him so that he could attach a key to it. Once that was done, he left.

At his palace, the prince complained to one of his father's viziers of his crazed obsession for the lady, telling him that he could not live without her. When the vizier asked him what he could do to help, the king's son replied, "I want you to put me in a chest and send the chest to the merchant, saying that it belongs to you. Ask him to store it for you in his mansion for a few days. In this way I can be with her. After this, you can then ask that the chest be returned to you." The vizier agreed.

The prince put a padlock on the chest, the key to which he'd given to the merchant's wife. He entered the chest and had the vizier lock him in. The vizier left with the chest for the merchant's mansion.

The merchant met him at the door, kissed his hands as a sign of respect, and then asked the vizier to what he owed this honor. If it was a matter of business, the merchant was ready and at his service.

"I would like you to keep this chest for me in the safest place in your house until I ask for it."

He agreed to fulfill the vizier's request, and the merchant had his porters carry the chest inside his residence and place it in the back part where his storehouse of merchandise was located. After this, the merchant set out on business.

No sooner had he left than the merchant's wife unlocked the chest with the key the prince had given her. They fell into each other's arms and moved slowly, caressing each other, until they reached her chambers. There, they enjoyed each other for seven days, all the while eating the best of foods and savoring the best of wines. During that time, whenever her husband returned home, his wife locked her lover back into the chest until her husband left again.

The young prince recited poetry about his new love. He compared her to a virgin maiden, for this was her first time with him and his with her. In celebration of experiencing true love for the first time, the merchant's wife commemorated the event by serving him each day *nuhūd al-ṣābūnīyah*, a cookie for him to remember her by. She fed them to him and he fed them to her. For seven days and nights the two enjoyed each other and the *nuhūd al-ṣābūnīyah*.

Toast flour with clarified butter until it takes its limit. Remove it from the fire. Mix it with sugar and knead. Form the dough into the shape of breasts. Put them on a tray and return to the oven until evenly baked. If it is not baked in a tray, it will melt. The flour and clarified butter are in equal parts.

SOURCE: Ibn ʿAdīm, *Kitāb al-Waslah ilà al-Habīb fi Wasf al-Tayyibāt wa al-Tīb*

Back in the palace, the king realized that he had not seen his son for a week. He asked for him, and the vizier immediately rushed off to the merchant's place of business and asked him for the chest. Quickly, the merchant set off for his mansion; discovering that he had forgotten the key to his house at his place of business, he knocked at the door.

His wife realized that this was her husband at the door, and she hastily ran to her prince and told him to get into the chest immediately. In her hurry, she forgot to lock it.

Not wanting to keep the vizier waiting, the merchant ordered his porters to pick it up promptly and carry it to the minister. They grabbed it from the top and, lo and behold, the lid opened and there was the prince.

The merchant realized that the man hiding in the chest was the king's son. He went back to the vizier and said, "The king's son is in your chest and has been hiding in my house. Since he is of royal blood, I cannot punish him. Take him!"

The prince returned to the palace with the vizier, but his pockets were filled with the *nuhūd al-ṣābūnīyah* to remind him of the short moment of his life when he experienced virgin love; he knew he would never have that opportunity again.

As for the merchant, he locked his wife away. However, his friends were insistent that he let her out. They explained that something good came out of this bad affair, as now was the opportunity to punish his wife by taking on a new and young virgin wife. But our merchant was adamant. "Never will I touch a virgin's breast!" He moved the dish of sweets aside.

Without question, this recipe caught the eyes of all our friends, both female and male. The translation of this shortbread-type cookie's name—breasts—evoked much speculation when we first found it in *The Description of Familiar Foods*, called *nuhūd al-cadhrā* (virgin's breasts). But we found the same recipe in Ibn al-ᶜAdīm and decided to make them, as his breasts were not perfection! We had the choice of making them young or old.

As our guests waited, the women giggled. The men adjusted their ties, patted down their hair, sat upright, and cleared their throats when we announced that the *nuhūd al-ṣābūnīyah* were about to make their entrance.

Shaping the dough into breasts became the subject of much humor in our household. When the dough was ready, our father decided that he wanted to get involved in the process. "Let me do it! I know how these are supposed to look." At this point, our mother walked into the kitchen and said, "How would you remember?"

The source recipe instructs that the flour should be toasted with butter before it is made it into a dough. We tried that, but later we experimented with regular white flour minus the toasting process. These turned out much better in texture and taste.

The form of these shortbread-type cookies is a matter of personal artistry and fantasy.

Nuhūd al-Ṣābūnīyah

Makes 24 pieces

INGREDIENTS

2¼ cups flour
¾ cup clarified butter
1 cup icing sugar

- Preheat the oven to 300 degrees.

- In a bowl, mix all the ingredients together to form a dough. Divide the dough into 24 balls.

- Shape each ball into the form of a breast and place it on an ungreased tray.

- Bake for 30 minutes or until the breasts begin to brown underneath. Remove the tray from the oven and allow to cool. Remove the *nuhūd al-ṣābūnīyah* carefully and place on a serving platter.

Index